The South and America
since World War II

The South and America since World War II

James C. Cobb

OXFORD
UNIVERSITY PRESS

2011

OXFORD
UNIVERSITY PRESS

Oxford University Press, Inc., publishes works that further
Oxford University's objective of excellence
in research, scholarship, and education.

Oxford   New York
Auckland   Cape Town   Dar es Salaam   Hong Kong   Karachi
Kuala Lumpur   Madrid   Melbourne   Mexico City   Nairobi
New Delhi   Shanghai   Taipei   Toronto

With offices in
Argentina   Austria   Brazil   Chile   Czech Republic   France   Greece
Guatemala   Hungary   Italy   Japan   Poland   Portugal   Singapore
South Korea   Switzerland   Thailand   Turkey   Ukraine   Vietnam

Published by Oxford University Press, Inc.
198 Madison Avenue, New York, New York 10016

www.oup.com

Oxford is a registered trademark of Oxford University Press

Library of Congress Cataloging-in-Publication Data
Cobb, James C. (James Charles), 1947–
The South and America since World War II / James C. Cobb.
p.   cm.
Includes bibliographical references and index.
ISBN 978-0-19-516650-7; 978-0-19-516651-4 (pbk.)
1. Southern States—History—Textbooks.
I. Title.
F216.2.C57 2010
975—dc22   2010030682

PREFACE AND ACKNOWLEDGMENTS

It might seem that writing about what happened essentially during his lifetime in the region where he has spent most of that lifetime would not represent such a difficult assignment for a historian, especially one who has been down at least some stretches of that road a time or two already. Yet in a great many ways this has been one of the most challenging books I have undertaken. Historical perspective never seems more important than when you don't have it but are trying to write something that will pass muster with future readers who will. Books like this one are sometimes by and large a reflection of the author's synthesis of what others have written, but in this case many critical events and trends of the past quarter-century or so have yet to attract significant attention from historians or other scholars. Hence, for better or worse, much of what you'll find in the pages that follow is based on my own research and represents my best effort to make sense of what I found. It's always exciting to attempt to plow new ground, but given the number of stumps, rocks, and roots one inevitably encounters, it can also be pretty rough on the old plowman. I can only hope that readers will not conclude that I have bruised my shanks in vain as I tried to come to terms with what I think are some pretty important issues that have confronted the South and the nation in the years since World War II.

I'm grateful to the folks at Oxford University Press for the chance to speak my piece and especially for the support and guidance of Brian Wheel, Danniel Schoonebeek, Woody Gilmartin, and Christine Dahlin. I'm also indebted to those who commented on both the prospectus and the manuscript. Among these, I must single out for special thanks and praise my friend Carl V. Harris of the University of California, Santa Barbara. I never before had the benefit of anything approaching the thoughtful and thorough critique that Carl provided. However this book is received, I know it is far stronger than it would have been without Carl's help.

The thrill of finally having a book with a budget for illustrations quickly became a challenge, one I would not have met nearly so well without the kind assistance of Peter J. Roberts, Steven Engerrand, Lee Shearer, Anne Webster, Tamara Livingston, Traci Thomas, Tom Rankin, Andrew Roberts, Cara Rousseau, Glenn Weber, Lyn Frazer, Jill Severn, Sheryl Vogt, and the entire staff at the Richard B. Russell Library for Political Research and Studies at the University of Georgia.

Closer to home, I am sorely indebted to a number of those who supported (or at least tolerated) me during the effort to get this book done. This group includes a sizable flock of graduate students who sometimes came to me looking for sympathy and encouragement, only to be confronted with a crusty and distracted old fart who spent too much of the session bellyaching about his own work instead. Although they were seldom either sympathetic or encouraging, I must at least mention the members of EFD, my early morning running group, or I will never hear the end of it. So, guys, all I can say is without you I would probably have gotten along just about as well.

On the other hand, I don't exaggerate in the least when I say forthrightly that this book would never have seen the light of day without Lyra Cobb, who has once more given of herself tirelessly and unselfishly, just as she has done again and again over the course of our more than forty years together. She and I need no better reminder of how rapidly this span has passed than our still fresh memories of a certain irresistibly cherubic toddler wreathed in golden curls who suddenly became a man of accomplishment, wisdom, wit, and tremendous integrity, now a father himself and not too far removed from the fortieth anniversary of his arrival in our lives. As I look back on things, one of my greatest regrets is that too many of the entries on my résumé may have been purchased with forgone opportunities to watch him roar around on his Hot Wheels or try to give him a run for his money at Pac-Man, or simply to spend more time together, doing whatever he wanted to do. His dad's occasionally misplaced priorities notwithstanding, to his everlasting credit, as an adult Ben Cobb has remained not only everything a father could ask for in a son but a source of much merriment and laughter in the lives of parents who have tended now and then to get a little too serious about things in their old age. In light of that advancing age, it seems advisable that our little boy get a dedication page of his very own before his name starts to slip my mind. So here it is, Son, and before you ask, it's the book that's dedicated to you, not the royalties.

To Benjamin Chandler Cobb

CONTENTS

Introduction

"You Ain't in the United States Now"

Summing up his impressions after spending six years in Alabama, New Yorker Carl Carmer confirmed many a Yankee's perception of the South in 1934 when he observed, "The Congo is not more different from Massachusetts or Kansas or California." Therefore, Carmer explained, he was writing of Alabama "not as a state which is part of a nation; but as a strange country in which I once lived but from which I have now returned." A year later, Alabama native Clarence Cason was forced to admit that the entire South was actually "self-conscious enough and sufficiently insulated from the rest of the country to be thought of as a separate province." Meanwhile, up in North Carolina, as he grew increasingly obsessed with the threat of Nazism in Europe, W. J. Cash struggled to pull together his sweeping analysis of the enduring peculiarity of a southern white "mind." The most dangerous characteristic of this mind, Cash contended, was a "savage ideal" of communally enforced conformity of thought mandating intense hostility to any suggestion of change or criticism of the South. Such was the dominance of the savage ideal, Cash believed, that conditions in his native region invited comparisons with "Fascist Italy…Nazi Germany [or]…Soviet Russia." Thus it was hardly surprising that, when it appeared some ten months before Pearl Harbor, *The Mind of the South* seemed to echo Clarence Cason, as Cash pointed to the "profound conviction" shared by northerners and southerners alike at that point that "the South is another land," so sharply "differentiated" from the rest of America as to constitute "not quite a nation within a nation, but the next thing to it."[1]

These assertions of the South's "otherness" would soon be echoed again and again as World War II dispatched millions of Americans on their first visit to the region for training at a number of mammoth military facilities scattered from North Carolina to Texas. Northern GIs were struck not only by the abysmal poverty and ignorance they observed among both blacks and whites but by the brutal rigidity of the omnipresent color line. Reports that German POWs were dining in southern cafés with their white military guards while black soldiers traveling with them were required to eat out back were especially jarring for a great many Americans born outside the region. The same was true of their responses to individual and mob attacks on black soldiers on or near southern military bases.

The South clearly held no monopoly on wartime racial hostility, of course. Not only were black troops denied service at restaurants from Kansas to California, but large and deadly conflicts had erupted between blacks and whites just weeks apart in Detroit and Harlem in 1943. There were also a number of violent incidents the following year, including one at Fort Lawton in Seattle that sprang from perceptions that Italian POWs were being treated like royalty in comparison to black troops. "There ain't no North any more. Everything now is South," lamented an elderly black woman in Detroit in 1943. Perhaps not all black servicemen would have gone quite that far, certainly not Johnnie Stevens, who believed that "to be a black soldier in the South in those days was one of the worst things that could happen to you." Surely many African Americans who were down South for the first time would have had little difficulty grasping what the black Marine meant when he wrote, "You ain't in the United States now. This is North Carolina."[2]

Journalist John Gunther had traveled throughout the country during the war, gathering observations and insights for *Inside U.S.A.*, his comprehensive survey of contemporary conditions and attitudes in America. Gunther confessed that as he made his way through Dixie "once or twice," he, too, had begun to feel that he "wasn't in the United States at all, but in some utterly foreign land." Yet Gunther also understood that the South's peculiarities were more than anything matters of degree. It was better understood, therefore, not as a separate place but as the "problem child of the nation" because "more than any other region, the South highlights almost every American problem." At roughly the same time political scientist V. O. Key joked that the Democratic Party in the South was responsible for conducting its "'foreign relations'…with the rest of the nation." Key quickly added, however, that "the South after all is a part of the United States," and thus "in its shortcomings" it had "all the failings common to the American states." To some extent, for all of Gunther's and Key's emphasis on the South's obvious and disturbing deficiencies, in acknowledging the fundamental Americanness of those imperfections both anticipated by nearly twenty years scholar-activist Howard Zinn's contention that the South "contain[ed], in concentrated and dangerous form, a set of characteristics which mark the country as a whole" and thus merely "crystallize[d] the defects of the nation."[3]

Gunnar Myrdal, a Swedish sociologist, had made a similar point in *An American Dilemma*, his massive and influential 1944 study of race relations in America. Like Cash, Myrdal saw "the white South" as "something of a nation within a nation." Yet though he found racial attitudes and practices decidedly more at odds with the "American Creed" in the South than elsewhere, he also understood that the "Negro problem" was not merely a southern phenomenon or concern but rather what he called "*a problem in the heart of the American*" because whites outside the region not only practiced their own forms of discrimination against the relatively small number of black people among them but salved any guilt they may have felt over this by comparing "the favorable treatment of Negroes in the North with that of the South."[4]

When forced to rationalize their tolerance for the more egregious abuses that their fellow white citizens were heaping on their black fellow citizens down South, northern whites could do little but point to their ancestors, who after all had fought in the Civil War to secure "full citizenship" for southern blacks. In the main, though, Myrdal quickly discerned, "the Northerners want to hear as little as possible about the Negroes, both in the South and in the North," the result being "an astonishing ignorance about the Negro on the part of the white public in the North." However, the day was fast approaching, Myrdal warned, when northern whites could not "afford any longer to let the white Southerners have their way with the Negroes as they have in the past."[5]

Myrdal's admonition would prove prophetic. World War II not only brought unprecedented opportunities for economic and physical mobility for black Americans but made them increasingly restive as they were called to join the fight for democracy and freedom abroad when both were still in such short supply in many of their own lives. One of the war's primary consequences, Myrdal believed, was that "the North is getting prepared for a fundamental redefinition of the Negro's status in America." Although he insisted there had been "a slow but visible decrease of discrimination" against southern blacks in recent decades, Myrdal understood full well at that point that, unless compelled by force, the overwhelming majority of white southerners would not accept any truly meaningful improvements in the civil and political status of black southerners. Ultimately, he concluded, the success of efforts in this direction would come down to the simple fact that "the North has much more power than the South."[6]

In practical terms, for Myrdal and his contemporary commentators, the South's distinguishing racial, economic, educational, and political traits did not actually isolate it so much as make it "a national problem" or, as Gunther put it, "a problem child to the nation." By the end of the war, with its budding aspirations to free-world leadership clearly incompatible with continued tolerance of blatantly undemocratic and repressive racial practices within America itself, the nation could deny its "problem child" no longer. Rather, the South would have to be brought to heel and remade in the image of its more advanced and enlightened sibling, the North, which, since the early stages of nationhood, had actually been for many outside the region all but synonymous with the idea of America itself. Though some hopeful postwar observers could already see the South beginning ever so gradually to change, many others, North and South, foresaw a protracted, bitter, and possibly bloody struggle to force recalcitrant white southerners to bring their region's racial practices—and ultimately its economic, political, and educational systems as well—even minimally in line with northern, and therefore American, norms.[7]

At the middle of the twentieth century few could have imagined that the backward and scorned South would within scarcely more than a generation seem not only to catch up with the North, but briefly even eclipse it in the eyes of some influential liberals eager to believe that Dixie had actually become the embodiment of a vibrant "New America." With one of its own in the White House, a racially cleansed, economically invigorated South supposedly stood poised to inspire the entire nation to rise from the rubble of the Vietnam and Watergate debacles and reclaim its moral hegemony in the world. The liberal vision of a redeemed and redemptive South would fade quickly, however, as, in the wake of Jimmy Carter's troubled presidency, the region's white voters quickly resumed their more traditional, rabidly conservative posture. Moreover, it would soon be clear that perceptions of the South's apparent convergence with the North rested not only on truly heartening advances in its own racial practices and economic fortunes but on sorely disappointing discoveries of corresponding deficiencies above the Mason-Dixon line as well.

Those deficiencies had been there all along, of course, languishing as the nation's attention became steadily more focused on solving the seemingly more pressing "southern problem." Yet concerns about what had suddenly gone wrong with the North would only intensify in the 1980s as whites throughout the country joined white southerners in tilting hard to the right. With their enthusiastic vision of an emergent liberal South now gone with the wind, so to speak, a number of commentators would quickly begin to bemoan the "southernization of America," as if, like a hyperaggressive supervirus released by terrorist infiltrators, Dixie's alien and pernicious values had suddenly broken regional containment to infect the hearts and minds of northern whites. With the South's overall economy continuing to prosper and its population (and therefore its congressional delegations) swelling in response to a steadily accelerating influx of northern in-migrants, in 1996 Peter Applebome saw Dixie not only "rising" but bending the nation's political institutions and even its cultural values to its rigidly conservative will. By 2002 Joshua Zeitz would go even further, insisting that "Southern culture today enjoys far more national influence than it has at any time since a Virginian was given command of the Continental Army."[8]

The durability of what Zeitz called "Dixie's victory" in national political and cultural affairs would soon begin to look a bit suspect, however. In fact, both the 2006 congressional voting and the 2008 general election suggested that, as the principal regional holdout in a national retreat from far-right politics, most of the region had begun to stand out as a strikingly red island in an increasingly blue sea. It is difficult to tell at this juncture if the South is simply suffering a temporary slippage in its widely presumed centrality to national politics and affairs, or whether it might soon be relegated to a peripheral position reminiscent of the one it occupied some six decades ago. Readers may or may not be troubled by the prospect of a South that is once again characterized primarily in terms of its perceived differences from the rest of the country. In either case, however, the following discussion of the profound changes in the region and its relationship with the nation over the past three generations should at least convey the sense that, however tempting or convenient it may be to emphasize the disparities, in the future as in the past neither the South nor America can ever be truly understood as anything but a part of the other.

1

"The Democracy They Fought For"

The Postwar Assault on Jim Crow

America's racial winds had clearly started to shift even before World War II began. During the previous decade NAACP litigation had pushed the U.S. Supreme Court to revisit the "separate but equal" doctrine introduced in *Plessy v. Ferguson* in 1896 and affirm in several rulings that, contrary to prevailing practice practically everywhere in the South, separate accommodations and facilities for blacks should in fact be equal to those available to whites. Although President Franklin D. Roosevelt was reluctant to offend the ardent white supremacists who represented the rigidly segregated South in Congress, First Lady Eleanor Roosevelt had made no secret of her desire to see dramatic improvements in the status and prospects of black Americans, and nowhere more so than in the South. Regardless of how they felt about it, by 1944 a great many southerners had come to agree with Gunnar Myrdal's prediction, "There is bound to be a redefinition of the Negro's status as a result of this war." In the summer of 1941 black labor leader A. Phillip Randolph had threatened to assemble 100,000 marchers to protest discrimination against African Americans in the rapidly expanding defense industry, relenting only when President Roosevelt issued an executive order outlawing such discrimination in federal defense industries and training programs. *Richmond Times Dispatch* editor Virginius Dabney observed in 1944 that "the war and its slogans have roused in the breasts of our colored friends hopes, aspirations and desires which they did not formerly entertain, except in the rarest instances."[1]

In fact, Dabney might have added bitterness and cynicism to the list of black emotions stirred by the war. An old black sharecropper who slyly told his landlord, "I hear the Japs done declared war on you white folks!" only began to reveal the mixed feelings of black southerners at the outset of the war. "I've been so used to pulling for the underdogs," confessed a North Carolina teacher, "that I all but root for the Japs." Growing up in Gulfport, Mississippi, made Wilson Evans think, "If the Japs took America...I might fare better." Seeing few differences between racism in Nazi Germany and in his own country, even after fighting as an infantryman at the Battle of the Bulge, Evans admitted that, so long as the Germans left his mother's home alone, if "they wanted downtown Gulfport...as far as I was concerned, hell, they could have it." Refusing a white New Orleans bus driver's order to sit in the seats designated for blacks, a young serviceman responded angrily, "They tell me I'm supposed to fight for democracy. I may as well start here."[2]

Such attitudes did not escape the notice of whites, including Birmingham's hard-nosed commissioner of public safety Eugene "Bull" Connor, who warned President Roosevelt of an impending race war because blacks were becoming "impudent, unruly, arrogant, law breaking, violent and insolent." Sensing growing white anxiety and antagonism, a black minister in North Carolina confessed in 1943, "[I am] worried for my people. They have grown restless. They are not happy....There is a new feeling among them—something strange, perhaps terrible." After surveying southern race relations in 1944, sociologist Charles S. Johnson affirmed the clergyman's judgment, concluding, "The great majority of southern negroes are becoming increasingly dissatisfied...and want a change."[3]

These aspirations were not confined to black soldiers or civil rights leaders and intellectuals. Sociologist Samuel Adams saw a more overt spirit of assertiveness and pride emerging among blacks in the Mississippi Delta during the war as enhanced mobility and higher wages bolstered self-confidence and ambition. An aspiring local poet even exhorted his fellow blacks not to "think because you're a nigger, you just can't get no bigger." A young black man told Adams forthrightly, "I can't get nothing out of what no white man do, but, boy, I get a thrill out of what the colored do." Other researchers in the same area found, "Negro leaders are becoming more fearless and ready to state what they believe to be the basic rights of the group," and "even down to the sharecropper there is a feeling of discontent and a growing consciousness of exclusion from social, economic, and political participation." As if to validate these observations, blacks in Coahoma County, Mississippi, even staged a brief strike in 1945 when local planters tried to limit the earnings of local cotton pickers.[4]

As World War II moved into its final stages, a black activist pointed ahead to what would be an even more critical conflict for African Americans: "If the Negro can't get what he wants through this war, he will get it when the boys come home. The Negro will fight for it. We might as well prepare for it because it is going to happen." In reality, the emergence and spread of black activism was neither immediate nor simultaneous nor uniform across the postwar South, but buoyed by the "Double V" campaign for victory over fascism abroad and racism at home, NAACP membership had expanded ninefold during the war and continued to grow in the first few years after 1945. There were only eight hundred NAACP members in South Carolina in 1939, but more than fourteen thousand by 1948. Georgia, which had fewer than ten NAACP chapters in 1940, boasted fifty new ones by 1947.[5]

Black voter registration in the South had risen gradually, from less than 1 percent of the adult black population in 1932 to 5 percent in 1944, when the U. S. Supreme Court concluded in *Smith v. Allwright* that excluding black voters from the Democratic primaries in Texas, a state where Republican opposition was so ineffectual that the outcome of a general election was never in doubt, effectively denied black citizens the opportunity to vote in the only state election that mattered. Therefore one of the fundamental pillars of Jim Crow politics in the South, the so-called white primary, was unconstitutional. By 1947 black registration across the region had reached an estimated 15 percent of the eligible black population.[6]

After the war a great many who led the effort to forge wartime black discontent on the home front into a viable force for racial change were veterans who came back determined to change a South that constantly made a mockery of the principles of freedom and democracy they had risked their lives to defend. Born in North Charleston, South Carolina, William Carter believed the war had taught him "to be a man," and when he came home he still had "the same feeling: 'I'm a man. I'm not a boy no more.'" Wilson Ashford recalled, "You were always taught that you can't do, you can't do." Ashford went on to become both an NAACP leader and, in 1950, one of Oktibbeha County, Mississippi's first black voter registrants since the turn of the century. He believed his wartime military service had been "where the change come in...where you would feel you could do it." Seriously wounded in combat, Georgian Doyle

Combs had "lost a portion of my body to protect my own rights," and he served notice that he was ready both "to die...for my rights" and to "kill for my rights." Not all returning black soldiers were as forthright as Combs, but because they felt that "the democracy they fought for [was] worth working for here at home," a number of Georgia's black veterans fell in step with the Georgia Veterans League, which launched an all-out effort to encourage registration and voting in the upcoming statewide Democratic primaries.[7]

To their surprise black veterans-turned-activists actually found some whites sympathetic to their efforts and message. A white Texan who had never given the matter much thought before the war came home insisting that whites should not "abuse the colored people any more. After all, blacks as well as whites had given their lives for this country." Another white veteran noted that the LSTs that returned from Normandy on D-Day had brought the bodies of "many negroes, some burned to a crisp," and asked how the army could mistreat "part of its men because the color of their skin is darker than some others." Americans outside the South were not alone in their disgust at reports that proprietors of some Louisiana restaurants had given German POWs preference over black American soldiers. Such behavior was "a disgrace to a democratic nation," Cpl. Henry Wooten charged, and it had made him "none the more proud of my southern heritage....Are we fighting for such a thing as this?" he demanded, observing rather pointedly, "A lot of us, especially in the South, should cast the beam out of our own eyes before we do so in others across the seas."[8]

Stationed in Cairo during the war, Hodding Carter, the editor of the Greenville, Mississippi, *Delta Democrat Times*, had seen firsthand the damaging effects of the racism underlying British colonial policy, and he came home urging his white readers at least to live up to their long-ignored obligations under the "separate but equal" doctrine. When local whites balked at honoring black as well as white veterans, Carter demanded, "How in God's name can the Negroes be encouraged to be good citizens, to feel that they can get a fair break, to believe that here in the South they will some day win those things that are rightfully theirs...if we deny them so small a thing as joint service recognition?"[9]

Racially moderate Mississippi congressman Frank Smith might have been referring to Carter or future activists such as Medgar Evers, Aaron Henry, Amzie Moore, and any number of other black veterans when he observed, "More young men came home from World War II with a sense of purpose than from any other American venture." Still, it did not follow that all veterans shared the same sense of purpose, for in many instances they clearly returned at cross-purposes with each other. Smith discovered this firsthand when one of his ardently segregationist fellow veterans told him in no uncertain terms that he had "just begun" to fight integration: "When I was on a beach in the South Pacific, I was fighting and I didn't know why. Now we know what we are fighting for and nothing is going to hold us back." Smith also recalled that at least half of his former Ole Miss student friends who survived the war later wound up affiliating themselves with the segregationist Citizens Councils, organized by veteran paratrooper Robert "Tut" Patterson.[10]

After the fact, at least, a few white veterans seemed to think that one of the fundamental principles they had gone to war to preserve was white supremacy, especially when they returned to find themselves competing with blacks for a limited number of jobs or decent places to live. Although fighting for their country would seem to have been the ultimate validation of their manhood, the absence of satisfactory jobs and housing appeared to challenge their masculinity and call their traditional roles as providers and defenders of their wives and families into question. As a result, white veterans also showed up prominently in the suddenly swelling ranks of the Ku Klux Klan and other hate groups such as the neofascist Columbians, whose leaders insisted, "Our heroes didn't die in Europe to give Negroes the right to marry our wives." Returning to Clarksdale, Mississippi, after "jumping in and out of foxholes in five battles" and wearing the decorations to prove it, black veteran Dabney Hamner was welcomed back by a white man who professed to be impressed by the "spangles on [his] chest," but quickly added, "Don't you forget...that you're still a nigger." This scene played out hundreds of times across the South in the first months after the war. The refusal of black veterans to step back into second-class citizenship upon their return made them vulnerable to violent reprisals, such as the "Moore's Ford" lynching in which a white mob brutally gunned down two black couples in Walton County, Georgia, in 1946. Referring to one of the victims, George Dorsey, one of Dorsey's accused slayers explained many years later, "Up until George went into the army, he was a good nigger. But when he came out, they thought they were as good as any white people."[11]

Black leaders in Georgia had been encouraged when the more moderate Ellis G. Arnall managed to oust the viciously racist incumbent governor Eugene Talmadge in 1942. The decidedly relative nature of racial moderation in the South of this era came through, however, when black leader A. T. Walden declared Arnall "as liberal as it is possible for a white man to be and hold office in the South," even though Arnall had boasted in 1942 that "if a nigger ever tried to get into a white school in my part of the state, the sun would never set on his head." Still, in an era marked by mounting black agitation against Jim Crow, the fact that only one lynching had been recorded during Arnall's gubernatorial term as compared to eighteen during the previous decade actually seemed to suggest that Georgia might have turned a corner and moved into an era of greater racial tolerance.[12]

Georgia had repealed the poll tax in 1945, and more than 125,000 black Georgians, roughly 20 percent of the adult black population, were registered to vote in the 1946 gubernatorial primary. Needless to say, blacks felt they had a lot at stake in this election because the volatile white supremacist Talmadge was seeking his fourth term. Moreover it would be their first opportunity to vote in the state's Democratic primary

Eugene Talmadge, campaigning for governor, 1946. Courtesy of Richard B. Russell Library for Political Research and Studies, Herman E. Talmadge Collection, The University of Georgia Libraries, Athens, Georgia.

The South and America since World War II

since it and others throughout the South had been stripped of their racial exclusions by the U. S. Supreme Court in 1944. Incensed that black voters would actually have a say in whether he returned to the governor's mansion, Talmadge practically yelled himself hoarse about a "nigra takeover" and warned ominously that "wise Negroes will stay away from white folks' ballot boxes." Only three blacks in Talmadge's own Telfair County had cast a ballot by afternoon on election day, but that was three more than voted over in Schley County, where, lacking Talmadge's subtlety, the local state legislator had simply stood outside the polls with a shotgun, declaring flatly, "If a nigger votes in this election, he'll be a dead nigger." It was small wonder, perhaps, that the brutal slaying of the two black couples in Walton County came just eight days after the racially charged 1946 campaign ended in a Talmadge victory.[13]

Black optimism surrounding the 1946 Georgia primary had failed to take account of the growing sense of alarm among white southerners

Funeral service for two victims of the Moore's Ford lynching, Walton County, Georgia. Bettman/Corbis.

who were convinced that only a last-ditch, no-holds-barred defense of white supremacy could save them from the unimaginable horror of not only political and economic but social equality with blacks. Although many reform-minded white veterans had supported business executive James V. Carmichael in his race against the virulently racist Talmadge, others had seen "ol' Gene" as the only thing standing between them and "a dictatorship like Germany, Russia, Italy, and Japan...under...a bunch of fools in the Congress and 'Negroes lovers' in the Supreme Court."[14]

The racial animosities and anxieties laid bare in Georgia in 1946 had been building across the South for at least a decade. Determined that their constituencies would get their share of desperately needed federal largesse, until the latter half of the 1930s southern politicians had maintained a nervous but superficially friendly relationship with President Roosevelt's New Deal. The agenda of the national Democratic Party had begun to show more of a northern orientation, however, in response to the demands of both organized labor and African Americans who had left the South in great numbers during the previous two decades and given Roosevelt the majority of their votes in 1936. Increasingly frustrated by what he saw as judicial and congressional efforts to derail the New Deal, the president had frightened some white southerners when he sought the power to appoint additional justices in order to liberalize the U. S. Supreme Court through his ill-fated 1937 "court-packing" plan. When he moved the following year to unseat certain conservative Democrats in the South in his equally ill-considered "purge" campaigns, the New Deal's unlikely marriage of convenience with southern white conservatives had definitely begun to unravel.

With the return of relative prosperity during the war, the need for Washington's assistance was not so urgent, and southern Democrats like Senator James O. Eastland of Mississippi quickly served notice that they were prepared to make a stand in defense of their region's racial and political hierarchy. Anti-Roosevelt insurgencies broke out in Texas, Mississippi, and South Carolina in 1944, and rather than endorse FDR, disenchanted delegates from seven southern states cast a total of eighty-nine votes for Senator Harry F. Byrd of Virginia at the party's convention, where southerners led the successful charge to replace liberal vice-presidential incumbent Henry A. Wallace on the ticket with a presumably more conservative Senator Harry S. Truman of Missouri.[15]

Most southern Democrats would soon be lamenting their support for Truman as Wallace's replacement, however. As FDR's successor, not only did he appoint a high-profile President's Committee on Civil Rights, but after some deliberation he endorsed the committee's extensive recommendations for federal action against racial discrimination on an expanded front. In 1948 Truman issued executive orders ending segregation in the armed forces and forbidding racial discrimination in government hiring. The party of his forefathers, fumed Alabama governor Frank Dixon, had become nothing but an "unholy alliance of left-wingers, pseudo-liberals and radicals of as many hues as Joseph's coat." Always one to cut to the racial bottom line, Mississippi's Eastland thundered that "the organized mongrel minorities" who "control[led] the government" were determined to "Harlemize the country."[16]

Dixon and Eastland would have found substantial grist for their propaganda mill in a memo by Truman's advisor, Clark Clifford, written a year before the 1948 election. "Unless there are new and real efforts (as distinguished from mere political gestures which are today thoroughly understood and strongly resented by sophisticated Negro leaders)," Clifford warned, "the Negro bloc will go Republican." Truman therefore should "go as far as he feels he could possibly go in recommending measures to protect the rights of minority groups." The administration's "no compromises" strategy would be purely for the benefit of black voters of course, and premised on the supposition "that it will get no major part of its program approved." There would be no need to worry about adverse southern white reaction, Clifford assured the president: "As always, the South can be considered safely Democratic. And in formulating national policy it can be safely ignored."[17]

Had southern political leaders seen this bit of White House strategizing, they would have found it strikingly straightforward confirmation of their worst fears and suspicions, but that came soon enough as it was. The majority vote at the Democratic convention to include a pathbreaking civil rights plank in the party's campaign platform in 1948 was all the proof many white southerners needed that the Democratic Party had turned its back on nearly a century's worth of their all but unswerving loyalty in order to curry favor with liberal northern whites and African Americans. Clifford's confident assurances that this loyalty was unshakable soon rang hollow, however. When Minneapolis mayor Hubert Humphrey delivered an impassioned speech on behalf of the party's pro–civil rights stance, delegates from Alabama and Mississippi walked out of the national convention. This move led ultimately to a meeting in Birmingham, where disaffected southern Democrats formed the States' Rights Democratic Party, known popularly as the "Dixiecrats," and chose South Carolina governor J. Strom Thurmond as their presidential candidate, with Governor Fielding Wright of Mississippi as his vice-presidential running mate.

That the disgruntled southerners who refused to support the national Democratic ticket and platform called themselves States' Rights Democrats was no accident. Their strategy centered on gaining control of southern state Democratic organizations in order to have their candidates designated on the ballot, not as the standard-bearers of a third party, but as the duly ordained representatives of the Democratic Party within each state. Ultimately the Dixiecrats managed to pull this off only in Alabama, Mississippi, South Carolina, and Louisiana, and these were also the only states they were able to carry come election time. Listed on the ballot only as a third party, they captured 20 percent of the vote in Georgia but less than half that in North Carolina and Texas.[18]

Overall, the Dixiecrat ticket of Thurmond and Wright had collected more than a million votes, showing its greatest strength in counties with large concentrations of nonvoting blacks that were dominated by the white elites whose interests and ideas the Dixiecrats most clearly represented. Because of their hostility to organized labor, they had also drawn strong support from representatives of some southern businesses and industries intent on keeping unions out and wages low. On the other hand, the Dixiecrats' message generally did not resonate quite so well among metropolitan whites or those outside plantation counties. They had also clearly underestimated the enduring strength of partisan Democratic attachments among many of the region's most influential politicians, such as Georgia senator Richard B. Russell, who had been the Dixiecrats' first choice as presidential nominee before he declined the honor. Much as a century earlier the proponents of "King Cotton" had banked on the rest of the nation's economic dependence on the South, the Dixiecrats had set out to demonstrate the Democratic Party's political dependence on white southerners. In the end, Truman's rather surprising reelection may have suggested that their efforts had fallen short, but their insurgency was nonetheless a sobering testament to how frayed the party fabric had become as a result of just a few preliminary efforts to address some of the nation's racial wrongs.[19]

In reality, these efforts and the general sense that the South's racial practices might be coming under attack even caused some consternation among whites who had once called for giving southern blacks a fairer shake. In the eyes of many observers the South had become a veritable hotbed of liberal activism in the 1930s as a combination of New Deal idealism and "critical realism" set off what Ralph McGill described as a "mighty surge of discussion, debate, self-examination, confession, and release." Mighty as it may have seemed to McGill, this surge had done little to shake the foundations of racial separation in the South. In keeping with leading New Deal thought of the era, southern liberals of the 1930s had largely skirted the segregation issue by insisting that the sustaining forces behind Jim Crow were not racial but economic. Formed in 1938, the Southern Conference for Human Welfare was the region's most aggressive advocate of racial reform, but activist-writer Stetson Kennedy summed up the SCHW'S stance nicely when he observed, "The Southern Negro must be emancipated economically and politically before he can be emancipated socially." Likewise, when it was organized in 1944, the Southern Regional Council epitomized what Morton Sosna called the "separate-but-equal liberalism" that still defined the racial vision and agenda of most enlightened white southerners at the end of World War II.[20]

This is actually less surprising than it might appear, because regardless of how cruel and anachronistic it seemed to critics at the middle of the twentieth century, when legally mandated racial separation emerged some fifty to sixty years earlier, not all whites had seen it simply as a means of holding down blacks. Rather, some more racially moderate advocates of *de jure* segregation embraced it as a way of simply holding blacks at a distance sufficient to minimize their contact with whites and therefore reduce the likelihood of racial violence against them. Other whites, less concerned about black welfare, championed segregation largely because they believed that any sort of violence or racial turmoil would be extremely bad for business at a time when Henry Grady and other "New South" apostles were busily courting northern industrialists with promises of an abundance of cheap and orderly labor. At the outset at least, the dedicated proponent of segregation was less likely to be an incendiary, race-baiting advocate of lynching like Benjamin R. Tillman of South Carolina than an image-conscious urban booster or a thoughtful paternalist like Rev. Edgar Gardner Murphy of Alabama, who saw keeping the races apart as a way "not to condemn the negro forever to a lower place but to accord him another place," where he could develop his own leadership and institutions and find a respected, albeit inferior, position for himself in the new southern order.[21]

The more moderate advocates of segregation had soon learned, however, that *Plessy v. Ferguson*'s stipulation of equal facilities notwithstanding, with blacks stripped of the vote and consigned indefinitely to the bottom rung of the economic ladder, segregation afforded them little protection from white violence, much less access to institutions and accommodations even remotely equivalent to those available to whites. Nearly fifty years after *Plessy*, leading moderates like journalists Hodding Carter and Ralph McGill persisted in believing that segregation could be made humane and just if only they could persuade their fellow whites simply to live up to the court's stipulation that separate must be equal. Even this restrained position earned them little more than a constant barrage of threats and invective, however, and beleaguered separate-but-equal liberals suffered what Sosna called another "rude jolt" when, as the war drew to a close, a number of prominent black southerners began to demand an immediate end to racial segregation in any form.[22]

In 1943 University of North Carolina Press director W. T. Couch had asked African American historian Rayford W. Logan to assemble a collection of essays by prominent black intellectuals focusing on "what the Negro wants." Although he considered himself a liberal, Couch was taken aback when even the most conservative contributors, such as Tuskegee Institute president F. D. Patterson, condemned segregation as "inconsistent with the guarantees of American democracy" and called for its immediate destruction. "If this is what the Negro wants," an angry Couch wrote Logan, "what he needs and needs most urgently is to revise his wants." Even if ending segregation were desirable, Couch added, this could not possibly be achieved overnight and might even require from fifty to a hundred years. The volume finally appeared in 1944, but only after Couch, unable to get Logan and his contributors to back off their demands, had added a publisher's introduction in which he insisted that an immediate end to segregation would be "disastrous for everyone." Disgusted by Couch's response, black writer Langston Hughes sneered that the South's liberals seemed to be "crowding Hitler for elbow room."[23]

The most notable exception to the general reluctance of southern liberals to distance themselves from segregation was Georgia's Lillian Smith. Smith's unrelenting attacks on the injustice and hypocrisy of the Jim Crow system and her forthright explorations of the repressed guilt and sexuality that festered within the southern white psyche had taken her well beyond where any but a very few whites were willing to go on

The South and America since World War II

the race issue in the 1940s. Smith's 1944 novel, *Strange Fruit*, was a hard-hitting tale of interracial sex, brutal violence, and moral cowardice in which an innocent young black man, Henry McIntosh, is burned alive by a lynch mob. Henry was accused of murdering Tracy Deen, his white former playmate, who was actually slain by the brother of the young black woman whom Tracy had made pregnant and then tried to marry off to Henry. After the lynching two elderly white women compare the smell of Henry's sizzling flesh to barbecue, and a poor white man who lost both his legs in a sawmill accident finds renewed sexual potency in recalling the incident. Smith's heavy-handed symbolism presented lynching as a manifestation of what she would later call the "composition of hate and guilt and sex hunger and fear, created by our way of life in the South." Although (or perhaps because) it was banned in Boston as "obscene," *Strange Fruit* was selling thirty thousand copies a week at its peak.[24]

Perhaps the greatest obscenity depicted in Smith's novel was not the illicit sex or shocking violence but the severe emotional trauma the

Lillian Smith surveys her vegetable garden, 1940s. Courtesy of Georgia Archives, Vanishing Georgia Collection (Rab 356), Atlanta, Georgia.

Jim Crow system inflicted on both white and black children. Smith captured brilliantly that stunning, never-to-be-forgotten real-life moment in the "haunted childhood" of anyone who grew up in the Jim Crow South when they are finally forced to confront the difference between being white and being black. After seven-year-old Tracy and eight-year-old Henry collide with a little white girl, knocking her from her bike, they both laugh, but Henry's mother, Mamie, who is the Deen family's housekeeper, is not amused. Realizing she must impress on her son the life-and-death necessity of avoiding even a hint of aggressiveness toward white females of any age, she whips him mercilessly, warning repeatedly, "You can't look at a white gal like dat, you can't tech one, you can't speak to one cep to say yes mam and thanky mam. Say it after me. Say it!" After a squalling Henry finally manages to repeat his mother's warning three times, he races to their cabin and crawls under the bed "like a shamed dog." Meanwhile, Tracy has been unable either to watch the whipping or leave the scene, and when, with the innocent concern of a child, he finally speaks to a silently sobbing Mamie, she screams, "Go to your own folks," leaving him stunned and "cut to the bone by the new strange words."[25]

Stung by the negative reaction of Hodding Carter, Ralph McGill, and others of a more gradualist inclination to her trenchant but unforgiving analysis of the White South in *Killers of the Dream*, Smith complained in 1949 that "75 percent of the 'liberals' in the South seem to favor segregation." She exaggerated but little. When the Southern Regional Council finally went on record as being officially opposed to segregation, the membership base shrank from 3,400 in 1950 to 1,800 four years later. Across the South, as external and internal criticism of segregation mounted, reform-minded public figures of the 1930s like journalists Virginius Dabney and John Temple Graves had become defenders of the racial status quo, Graves to the point of actually supporting the Dixiecrats in 1948. Whatever their personal feelings, most influential southern white moderates seemed absolutely convinced that any federally initiated attempt to destroy segregation could end only in a racial holocaust. Segregation was an "iron taboo" that southern whites would "not in any foreseeable time relax," warned David Cohn in 1944, and should there be any attempt to end racial separation by "federal fiat," he had "no doubt that every southern white man would spring to arms, and the country would be swept by civil war."[26]

A similar warning came from William Faulkner's long-winded lawyer Gavin Stevens, who insisted in Faulkner's 1948 novel *Intruder in the Dust* that the white southerners who "genuinely regretted the black southerners' shameful condition and would improve it" would respond to northern efforts to force the issue by moving "willy-nilly into alliance" with rabidly racist whites, "with whom we have no kinship whatever in defense of a principle which we ourselves begrieve and abhor." Struggling and squirming, Faulkner himself would say much the same thing on a number of occasions, none more memorable than the interview in which he insisted that if he were forced to choose, he would "fight for Mississippi against the United States even if it meant going out into the street and shooting Negroes." Although this dramatic— and if Faulkner is to be believed, drunken—statement surely shocked most southern liberals, Faulkner's presumption of such a violent reaction from his fellow southern whites surely did not. Like Faulkner, the South's white moderates generally premised their positions not on what should be done but on what they believed the mass of white southerners would accept. Because they feared that any more aggressive approach would ultimately force them to make the kind of agonized decision that Faulkner described, most sought what he called "a middle road," which actually led nowhere.[27]

Black voter registration had grown significantly by this point, but this progress had come primarily in the immediate wake of the U.S. Supreme Court's invalidation of the white primary in 1944. Supreme Court or not, white supremacists showed no intention of giving in to black voting without a fight. Eugene Talmadge was by no means the only white politician who blatantly encouraged whites to use violence and intimidation to keep blacks away from the ballot box. Facing a reelection challenge in 1946, Mississippi senator Theodore G. Bilbo urged "every red-blooded American who believes in the superiority of the white race to get out and see that no nigger votes.... AND THE BEST TIME TO DO IT IS THE NIGHT BEFORE."[28]

Those who lacked the stomach for such a direct approach opted for measures like Alabama's Boswell Amendment, approved in 1946 to allow registrars to require any prospective voter to "understand and explain" any section of the U.S. Constitution. So empowered, registrars were free to ask potential black voters questions about the most trivial and obscure sections of the Constitution and, regardless of their response, declare their answer unsatisfactory. Such a system, in which Alabama's black educators and doctors could be denied the opportunity to vote by whites who had not finished high school was acceptable, according to former state bar association president Horace C. Wilkinson because "no Negro is good enough, and no Negro will ever be good enough to participate in making the laws under which the white people in Alabama have to live." For all the progress in black voter registration in some states, in Mississippi and Alabama only 1 percent of the adult black population was registered in 1947, and in Louisiana the figure was less than 3 percent. One in six blacks may have been registered throughout the South in 1948, but fewer than one in ten had actually managed to cast a ballot. Four years later, blacks accounted for only 6 percent of the southern presidential vote.[29]

Although the Dixiecrat insurgency had not cost Truman the White House in 1948, it had made Democratic Party leaders acutely aware of the unflinching determination of white southerners to resist interference in their racial affairs. The Democrats had also regained control of Congress in 1948, thereby restoring southerners to their powerful positions as chairs of several strategic committees. The Truman administration continued to talk about a fair employment bill, but with most observers on both sides aware that the chances of collecting the necessary votes for it were well-nigh nonexistent, such talk was relatively cheap. With the onset of the Korean War and Wisconsin senator Joseph R. McCarthy's reckless campaign to capitalize on fear of communist subversion on the home front, the president made it clear that he would launch no more civil rights initiatives. For the time being further advancements toward racial equality would depend on the actions of the judicial rather than the executive branch.

After the fashion of the South's white moderates, the NAACP's legal assault on racial discrimination had concentrated at first not on overthrowing the 1896 *Plessy* decree but on convincing the Supreme Court to enforce it fully by demanding strict adherence to the second half of the separate-but-equal principle. The Court had moved in this direction in 1938, when it rejected the State of Missouri's attempt to avoid admitting a black applicant, Lloyd Lionel Gaines, to the University of Missouri Law School simply by paying the additional tuition required for him to pursue his legal education out of state. In the absence of an in-state law school for blacks, the justices ruled Gaines was entitled to the same access to the state university's law school enjoyed by any white Missourian.[30]

A decade later, however, the Court had swallowed Oklahoma's transparent subterfuge of roping off a section of the state capitol and hiring three lawyers to teach black law school applicants like Ada Sipuel. In a similar effort, the State of Texas had tried to keep a black letter carrier, Heman Sweatt, out of the University of Texas Law School by quickly throwing together an equally suspect "law school" for blacks in Houston. Meanwhile, although the courts had forced the University of Oklahoma to admit George McLaurin to its graduate program in education, university officials required him to sit in a room adjacent to his actual classroom, and he was assigned both a separate work area in the library and a designated eating space in the cafeteria.

When NAACP lawyers again challenged these tactics, the Supreme Court was more sympathetic than it had been in the *Sipuel* case. Heman Sweatt, the justices concluded, could never have the same experience in three basement rooms with three hastily appointed part-time teachers as he would have at the University of Texas Law School, with its huge law library and abundant opportunities to interact with its large faculty and student body. Likewise, the justices also ruled that although George McLaurin was technically a student at the University of Oklahoma, by virtue of his being effectively segregated within the campus environment, he had been denied the full educational interaction available to his white fellow students. Not only were the *Sweatt* and *McLaurin* rulings unanimous, but they were both handed down on June 5, 1950, a day on which the high court threw in for good measure its finding in the case of *Henderson v. U.S.* that the Southern Railway Company could no longer restrict or curtain off seating for blacks in its dining cars.[31]

In all these cases the justices had made it indisputably clear that from now on "separate" would at least have to be equal. Although at the end of what seemed a banner day for the proponents of racial equality, the fundamental validity of legally mandated segregation of the races was still intact, in both the *Sweatt* and *McLaurin* cases NAACP attorney Thurgood Marshall managed to get statements on the record that blacks were injured not just by the inferior quality of their separate facilities but by the "badge of inferiority" that the separation itself implied.[32]

The justices had focused their deliberations in *Sweatt* and *McLaurin* only on the issue of whether the separate-but-equal standard had been met, but Marshall was determined to put the very principle of segregation itself on trial. The opportunity to do so seemed to present itself in a case that originated in Clarendon County, South Carolina. Clarendon's all-white school board had consistently refused to provide buses for black students, even those who had to travel several miles on their own to get such education as was available in the county's ramshackle, often overcrowded black schools. The background for *Briggs v. Elliott*, the case that would lead to the most momentous civil rights ruling of the twentieth century, was the story of a people who, after enduring generations of injustice, rose up with a courage and resolve that ultimately changed the course of race relations not just in the South but in all of America.[33]

At the beginning of the 1950s Clarendon County, whose population was 70 percent black, was spending annually more than four times as much per white pupil as was spent on a black pupil. The county also owned and operated thirty buses for 2,375 white students, while 6,531 black students were left to get to school the best way they could. When a group of black parents asked for a single bus for their children, however, the chairman of the board of education informed them, "We ain't got no money to buy a bus for your nigger children." The black parents, few of whom had more than four years of schooling themselves, had scraped up enough to buy an old bus in hopes of sparing some of their children what could turn out to be a nine-mile walk to school, but even then the school board refused to help purchase gasoline for the utterly decrepit vehicle.[34]

When the NAACP revealed an interest in taking the county to court over its blatantly discriminatory bus policies, Rev. Joseph A. DeLaine became one of the pivotal local figures who would step forward again and again at crucial times in crucial places throughout the civil rights movement. A fierce believer in the paramount importance of education, DeLaine had earned his bachelor's degree in theology only through protracted slaving and sacrifice. As a fourteen-year-old, DeLaine had left Clarendon County rather than take a whipping from whites for defending his sister when she was shoved by a white boy, and he was widely respected by local blacks both as a minister of the gospel and a man of great courage and conviction.[35]

Ultimately it fell to DeLaine to recruit twenty local blacks to serve as plaintiffs in the NAACP suit. This was no trifling assignment in a county where few black students made it past the fourth grade, barely 6 percent of the black families earned as much as $2,000 in 1950, and the overwhelming majority of the remainder were economically dependent on whites in one way or another. One of DeLaine's recruits was Harry Briggs, whose name, thanks to the legal custom of naming a multiplaintiff case according to the first plaintiff listed alphabetically, would forever be associated with the legal action that eventually toppled

Jim Crow. A World War II veteran in his early thirties, Briggs had spent fourteen years pumping gas and fixing flats. He had recently taken out a loan to build a small house, and it was in his parlor that many of the NAACP plaintiffs actually put their names, and a great deal more, on the line. When his white employer urged him to take his name off the suit, Briggs had responded, "I'm doin' it for the benefit of my children." The day before Christmas in 1949 the boss handed Briggs a carton of cigarettes and his walking papers, explaining, "I want me a *boy* and I can pay him less than you." Briggs's wife also lost her job as a maid, and he was eventually forced to take work in Florida, returning on weekends when he could to see his family.[36]

Among the other signers, teachers were fired and sharecroppers evicted, and credit dried up overnight for any plaintiff who depended on whites for any sort of financing. A veteran of Iwo Jima and Okinawa, John Edward McDonald could not get a loan for the tractor he needed to work his 100-acre farm. Creditors even threatened to seize the mules of complainants whose notes they held, and the crowning absurdity came when Briggs's cow was effectively "arrested" for trespassing on a cemetery plot belonging to a prominent white family. Needless to say, in addition to seeing his church burned down, not to mention braving gunfire and all manner of threats and harassment, both DeLaine and his wife lost the teaching jobs that supplemented his meager ministerial income.[37]

Painfully aware of his obligation to people who had so little to begin with and had lost much of that in the simple pursuit of their rights, NAACP Legal Defense Counsel Thurgood Marshall faced a dilemma. Before a sympathetic Judge J. Waties Waring, a Charleston aristocrat turned unlikely racial maverick, Marshall felt confident that he could win a judgment requiring equalization of Clarendon County's school facilities. On the other hand, Marshall had recently convinced NAACP higher-ups that it was time to move beyond simply asking the courts to force southern states and communities to live up to the *Plessy* doctrine and begin petitioning them to overturn that doctrine on the grounds that legally imposed social separation could never be truly equal. In order to use the *Briggs* case to attack *de jure* segregation, however, Marshall would have to make his arguments not only to the sympathetic Waring but to a three-judge federal panel on which Waring's single vote would surely be neutralized by that of George Bell Timmerman Jr., an ardent segregationist and future South Carolina governor, with the third judge likely voting Timmerman's way as well. Marshall opted initially to focus on the inequality issue and argue only before Waring, while insisting that his challenge to the broader practice of segregation itself was implicit in his argument. Yet acting with the encouragement of the NAACP's executive secretary, Walter White, the judge finally persuaded Marshall to revise his approach so that his objections to the doctrine behind *Plessy* would be clearly and prominently stated.[38]

When the case came to trial in May 1951, South Carolina's head defense counsel, Robert M. Figg, shocked Marshall and his NAACP team by conceding up front that there were definite inequalities between black and white schools in the state. However, in a response that would recur repeatedly in other southern states finally facing a judicial ultimatum to live up to the separate-but-equal standard laid down for them a half-century earlier, South Carolina lawmakers had enacted a 3 percent sales tax and committed themselves to bringing black school facilities up to par. Accordingly, Figg insisted, the courts should be willing to accept the unavoidable delays attendant to doing what whites had already been refusing to do for fifty years and tell the plaintiffs that the equality they had so long sought must be deferred yet again. Marshall dismissed this argument as an irrelevant distraction from his contention that even with equalized facilities, enforced segregation was simply incompatible with equality of citizenship. He introduced expert witnesses such as social psychologist Kenneth Clark, whose experiments using dolls with black children ages three to seven showed "an unmistakable preference" for white dolls over brown ones. Such testimony would eventually be incorporated into the Supreme Court's assessment of the inherently damaging aspects of segregation, but in the short term the judicial trio in Charleston voted unanimously to order equalization of educational facilities in Clarendon County and two to one against any effort to overturn segregation per se.[39]

Contesting this latter point, Marshall and his team would take *Briggs et al.* to the Supreme Court on appeal. Their journey would be one of fits and starts and frustration, and by the time *Briggs v. Elliot* made it to the high court, it had been bundled with other, similar cases from Virginia, Delaware, the District of Columbia, and Kansas. In the process, despite being the first major court challenge to *de jure* segregation, the South Carolina case lost its primacy to *Brown v. Board of Education of Topeka, Kansas.* As the Supreme Court Justice Tom Clark later explained, "We felt it was much better to have representative cases from different parts of the

The South and America since World War II

country, and so we consolidated them and made *Brown* the first so that the whole question would not smack of being a purely southern one." The Court scheduled its first hearing on the case in December 1952, and after nearly eighteen months of pleadings, hearings, and rehearings featuring testimony from historians, social scientists, and experts on education as well as law, the justices concluded unanimously—and, to say the least, momentously—on May 7, 1954, that separating black children "solely because of their race generates a feeling of inferiority... that may affect their hearts and minds in a way unlikely ever to be undone." It followed then that "separate educational facilities are inherently unequal" and therefore an unconstitutional denial of "the equal protection of the laws guaranteed by the Fourteenth Amendment."[40]

2

"For Us or Against Us"

Massive Resistance and the Civil Rights Awakening

The justices who made history with the *Brown v. Board of Education* ruling may have hoped that their decree would not be construed as "purely southern" in its implications, but as soon as it was announced, most Americans and many others throughout the world immediately fixed their eyes on the South and waited for the fireworks. As though determined not to disappoint, the next day *Jackson [Mississippi] Daily News* editor Fred Sullens ran a front-page editorial, bordered in black and titled "Blood on the White Marble Steps," declaring that "in the fight for white supremacy...there will be no room for neutrals or non-combatants...if you are a member of the Caucasian race.... You Are For Us Or Against Us."[1]

In reality, however, despite the earlier defiant posturing of so many southern political leaders in response to growing fears of federal intervention in their region's racial affairs, the immediate response of whites to the decree was generally less explosive than might have been expected. To be sure, Governor Herman Talmadge of Georgia charged that the Court had reduced the Constitution to "a mere scrap of paper." Yet Governor Lawrence Wetherby of Kentucky announced that his state would "do whatever is necessary to comply with the law," and Virginia governor Thomas Stanley called for "cool heads, calm study, and sound judgment" in responding to *Brown*. The *Louisville Courier-Journal* assured its white readers that "the end of the world has not come for the South or the nation," and the *Miami Herald*, *Dallas Morning News*, and *Norfolk (Virginia) Pilot* showed similar restraint. Even James J. Kilpatrick, the segregationist editor of the *Richmond News-Leader*, initially told readers,

"We accept the Supreme Court's ruling. We do not accept it willingly, or cheerfully, or philosophically. We accept it because we have to."[2]

The relatively mild early reaction to the *Brown* decision may have stemmed in part from the justices' decision to hold back on issuing a final order for implementing school desegregation until they had heard further arguments from all parties to the process during the next session of the Court. There was certainly an immense challenge in integrating schools across a vast array of local settings where dozens, hundreds, or even thousands of students might be affected and varying degrees of cooperation or resistance might be expected. Hence many observers of both races saw virtue in giving white southerners a little time to get used to the idea.

However, if the aim of the Court in delaying implementation was to give southern whites a chance to come around on desegregation, it was soon apparent that this strategy was not working. Less than six weeks after Governor Stanley's call for calm, thoughtful reflection, he was pledging to "use every legal means at my command to continue segregated schools in Virginia." As other southern leaders weighed in and several states filed official briefs with the Court, they consistently stressed the dire consequences of attempting to use immediate, unyielding federal compulsion to force such a radical alteration of southern society. Proponents of the "not yet" approach also pointed to striking disparities in the current educational attainments and capabilities of black and white pupils, never once acknowledging that these discrepancies were largely attributable to the inequities of the very system whose demise they were trying to postpone.[3]

Florida's brief, which urged the Court to "restrain the use of coercive measures where necessary until the hard core of public opinion was softened," and Virginia's, which suggested that "an indeterminate period" be allowed to pass before actual integration began, were fairly typical. Lawyers for the Eisenhower administration, whose lack of enthusiasm for enforcing *Brown* would soon become obvious, urged the justices to stay away from any fixed timetable for desegregation. Ultimately the Court took this advice to heart, and on May 31, 1955, a year and two weeks after its initial decree, Chief Justice Warren reaffirmed the earlier opinion that "racial discrimination in public education is unconstitutional" and declared that "all provisions of federal, state, and local law requiring or permitting such discrimination must yield to this principle." Warren did not, however, set a deadline for acquiescence to said principle. Instead he directed that when segregated local systems were brought before them, the lower courts were to require them to "make a prompt and reasonable start [toward] compliance with our May 15, 1954, ruling." Although he set no deadline, this was to be accomplished, Warren concluded famously, with "all deliberate speed."[4]

Not surprisingly, the *Brown II* ruling disappointed activists hoping for immediate desegregation. Some have argued that its almost studied ambiguity actually intensified rather than defused southern white resistance by conveying just the sense of federal uncertainty and aversion to confrontation that the South's hard-core defenders of Jim Crow needed to convince more skeptical whites that they might actually succeed. On the other hand, having ventured into a racial no-man's-land, the justices had found themselves confronting the fierce and effectively solid opposition of southern whites from Congress down to the courthouse, with no sense whatsoever that the executive branch had the stomach, much less anything approaching actual enthusiasm, for enforcing their mandate. President Dwight Eisenhower had opposed the desegregation of the armed forces and indicated more than once that he found "social mingling" of the races personally distasteful. Shortly before *Brown* he had revealed his empathy for southern segregationists when he explained, "All they are concerned about is to see that their sweet little girls are not required to sit in schools beside some big overgrown Negroes." Not unlike his two-time Democratic opponent, Adlai Stevenson, who also believed that white attitudes toward blacks in the South were too deeply ingrained to be changed by law, the president warned that "prejudice" would not "succumb to compulsion," and he declared to a speechwriter, "The fellow who tries to tell me that you can do these things by FORCE is just plain NUTS." Eisenhower refused to endorse the Court's decision publicly; privately he blamed it for "[setting back] progress in the South at least fifteen years."[5]

In recent years some historians and legal scholars seem to have come surprisingly close to agreeing with Eisenhower on this latter point, arguing that by engendering a white backlash against federally imposed racial change the *Brown* ruling may have slowed or even reversed the progress in southern race relations that had supposedly been the inevitable by-product of postwar industrialization, urbanization, and mounting black political influence. Yet although there were clear signs of economic and demographic change and a sharp increase in black activism in the South in the decade prior to *Brown*, a few scattered local

The South and America since World War II

examples of truly voluntary and uncoerced efforts by southern whites to fundamentally alter the Jim Crow system hardly stacked up against the towering evidence of white determination to prevent such alterations at all costs.[6]

Several generations of research into the intense hostility of most white southerners to any perceived challenge to their racial supremacy have pointed not to a single cause but to a variety of factors, frequently operating in such close interaction that they were all but indistinguishable from each other. At the most elemental level, many whites in the South (and elsewhere as well) still harbored strong feelings of physical aversion toward blacks that could be traced all the way back to the earliest European contact with Africans in the sixteenth century. This reaction may have been primarily emotional, but it was remarkably durable nonetheless, manifesting itself even at the middle of the twentieth century in continuing complaints about how blacks looked, sounded, and smelled. God himself had given blacks a disagreeable odor, a white Alabaman complained in 1957: "No one wants there [sic] child to go to school with stinking [Negroes] they stink they all do. God Put that Sent [sic]on them."[7]

Even in the 1950s, the comparisons of blacks with apes offered by the South's more virulent racists were eerily similar to comments by early European visitors to Africa who reported that the black natives resembled "orang-outangs" and even suggested that the Africans might actually have interbred with them. The same was truer still of the hoary notion of black men's abnormal sexual urges and, as a seventeenth-century English traveler put it, the "large propagators" he observed on African males. More than three centuries later, in 1954, a Virginian who considered himself "a student of physical anthropology" explained to Governor Stanley that "a skull about 40% thicker than normal" and other features typical of "primitive man" were linked directly to a black man's "sexual maturity at a very early age, and sexual organs of exaggerated size with a corresponding intense sex-urge difficult to control."[8]

Better-educated white southerners generally shied away from such graphic references, but a number of them still struggled to get past their ingrained distaste for intimate physical contact with blacks. Despite his racially paternalistic upbringing, as a North Carolina teenager in the early 1950s, Melton McLaurin had already begun to harbor doubts about the Jim Crow system. Yet when he inadvertently put a needle used to inflate a basketball in his mouth immediately after it had been in the mouth of his black friend "Bobo," it was all he could do to resist "the urge to gag, to lean over and vomit out any trace of the black saliva that might remain to spread its contamination throughout my body."[9]

Despite his own inclinations to question the southern racial system, as a teenager McLaurin could not free himself entirely from the dominant prejudices of a society where practically all whites were apparently convinced that "nothing could change the status of blacks," who were intellectually incapable of conducting themselves according to white standards. "'You can educate a nigger all you want, boy,'" McLaurin was often reminded, "'but he's still just a nigger. Ain't nothing you do ever gonna change that.'"[10]

McLaurin's experience illustrated the almost seamless transfer of an exceedingly toxic bundle of racial prejudices from one generation of white southerners to the next. These indelibly imprinted beliefs in the intrinsic inferiority of all blacks regardless of their conduct or achievements survived the test of time and prevailed against an ever-accumulating body of evidence to the contrary by serving the very practical purpose of sustaining white economic and political advantage while doubtless affording many white southerners, poor and otherwise, their primary reassurance of self-worth. Although as he matured McLaurin himself would succeed in casting aside this most onerous element of his birthright, as Earl and Merle Black observed, "through the cues of their parents, other adults, and their peers," the typical white youth of that era had simply "absorbed the region's dominant values [and] would fervently believe that racism was altogether 'natural, proper, and sacred,' a belief that ordinarily would not be reconsidered for the rest of his or her life." In 1958, after investigating local white attitudes toward desegregation in Guilford County, North Carolina, sociologist Melvin Tumin and his associates affirmed both the breadth and depth of white beliefs in black inferiority. Nearly 75 percent of those interviewed believed that blacks had a less fully developed sense of responsibility than whites, and 66 percent found blacks similarly lacking in morality and ambition. Almost 60 percent felt that blacks were inferior to whites in intelligence, and only 16 percent saw them as the equal of whites in all these categories—all of this despite the fact that whites in Guilford County, which included the city of Greensboro, enjoyed income and educational levels well above the regional average.[11]

This firmly fixed and rarely reconsidered core of racial attitudes was by no means the sole force behind white southerners' rabid determination to preserve Jim Crow, however. For a great many whites, maintaining their racial supremacy was also a simple but seldom acknowledged matter of dollars and cents. With whites moving into new industrial jobs that were frequently not available to blacks, the gap between the percentages of the black and white male labor forces employed in agriculture had widened sixfold between 1900 and 1950. In South Carolina 90 percent of new manufacturing jobs created between 1940 and 1964 had gone to whites. Black southerners who did find work in southern factories could generally count only on jobs that many whites would not accept, most requiring long, backbreaking hours at low pay under the intense scrutiny of white supervisors demanding every possible ounce of effort they could give. When fifteen-year-old Mary Mebane went to apply at an American Tobacco plant in Durham, North Carolina, in 1948, she knew that the better jobs on the "cigarette side" of the plant were reserved for whites. Nonetheless she found a large crowd of black women so desperate for work that they stood in the hot sun all day to watch only a few women get jobs and all but mobbed the personnel manager whenever he came out of the office.[12]

When Mebane was finally hired at the plant, she spent hour after frenetic hour choking on tobacco dust while she struggled under the unsympathetic eyes of white male foremen to keep pace with the relentless conveyor belt that she and her coworkers were feeding with bundles of tobacco. Knowing that they could be replaced immediately by anyone among the throngs who came seeking work each day, the women worked like relentless automatons. On the day when a visit from the "big boss," said to be "mean as the devil," was expected, they were coerced to even greater exertions. Mary was amused initially to see that the "big boss" was actually a short little fellow wearing clothes and a hat that were clearly too big for him. He quickly lived up to his reputation, however, when he noticed that Flora, a hard-bitten little woman given to occasional surliness, had not sped up her movements to match the pace of others on the line. Mebane flinched when the man remarked that Flora was working as if she was "half-dead," but Flora did not. Instead she simply stood motionless and stared back at him before finally placing her tobacco bundle on the belt. Instead of firing her, to Mary's surprise, the big boss just moved on to another line, because, Mary later surmised, Flora's look had "told him she was another mean one like him, and if he got started, he was going to get a good cussing out . . . right there in front of his subordinates." Flora had "won" on that occasion, but her "protest" brought no improvement in the extremely "hard and mind-numbing" routine of the black women working with her, and young Mary was actually pleased when she was laid off some time later.[13]

Arduous and exploitive as it might have been, a great many other black southerners would obviously have jumped at the chance to have a job like Mebane's. As it was, a general pattern of hiring all- or overwhelmingly white workforces in industrial plants translated into an abundance of black men willing to work for any wage they were offered doing day labor or such occasional odd jobs as they could find. In Jim Crow–era Greenville, Mississippi, David Cohn recalled, "a colored boy mowed the lawn for a quarter, stoked at noon with a pork chop sandwich, and a jug of cold buttermilk provided by his employer." Likewise, left with little or no option, black women cooked, cleaned, washed, ironed, and babysat for whatever their white employers were willing to pay. Black domestic servants in Birmingham earned a median income barely in excess of $10 per week in 1950. Steeling themselves against the indignities they faced, many black women did remarkable things with their meager earnings as domestics. Martha Calvert recalled that her mother "brought up fifteen kids to finish high school, mainly ironing clothes." This was "pre-food-stamp days," but Calvert had no memory of feeling "poor" until her mother paid for her first semester of college with "$333 in dimes and quarters" that she had somehow managed to save.[14]

Whites seemed to justify the meager wages of someone who worked so hard to keep them comfortable and well-fed by allowing their maid to "tote" whatever leftover food she could carry home to her own family at the end of a long and very hard day. In all likelihood that family lived in a rundown shack in a rundown neighborhood where municipal services might be minimal or even nonexistent. Why, after all, should whites pay higher taxes to provide expensive amenities like sewers and paved streets since, as most whites contended, practically no blacks paid taxes? In any case, as long as so few blacks were allowed to vote there was little incentive for local officials to spend money addressing the deplorable conditions over in "niggertown." This was a classic illustration of the symbiotic relationship between prejudice and discrimination: not only was black disfranchisement protecting white economic advantage, but it was reinforcing white prejudices by allowing politicians to cite the effects of this discrimination in the form of the appalling appearance or smell of black neighborhoods as simply more evidence that blacks were not as "clean" or as fastidious as whites. Certainly as the second half of the twentieth century began there was still no end in sight for the discriminatory hiring practices that rendered southern blacks so read-ily exploitable as domestics or day laborers and ultimately consigned them to life in the slums. A 1958 survey of 402 local white employers in Greensboro, North Carolina, which was considered one of its state's more progressive cities, showed scarcely 13 percent of them favored color-blind hiring policies.[15]

In addition to the economic advantage, Jim Crow also afforded whites what anthropologist John Dollard called an ego-boosting "pres-tige" gain. In a rigidly white supremacist society, the emotional perks of prejudice and discrimination were often too substantial and seduc-tive for even otherwise thoughtful and sensitive white southerners to resist. Cheap and relatively pliable black domestic and farm labor was a definite plus, but the sense of power, status, and self-esteem derived from living among dutifully deferential "inferiors" could be absolutely intoxicating. Although white employers insisted that their black maids were like members of their families, the maids encountered constant reminders that the color line ran right through the houses where they worked. "They even had separate bathrooms! Oh no, you didn't go in the bathroom they went in," recalled Aletha Vaughn. "You ate out of certain dishes, and your particular plate and fork and spoon went in a certain place.... But I had to work, so I did the work. But now I wouldn't do it no more if I had to eat lizards for a meal."[16]

Meanwhile, few whites entertained the possibility that the tenuous circumstances of their black employees forced them not only to sup-press their resentment of racial protocol but to actively affirm whites' feelings of superiority with elaborate assurances of affection and grat-itude for even the slightest show of benevolence or concern on their part. Reflecting on his boyhood in Yazoo City, Mississippi, in the 1940s and early 1950s, Willie Morris confessed that his attitude and behavior toward black people had ranged from "a kind of unconscious affection, touched with a sense of excitement and sometimes pity," to "sudden emotional eruptions of disdain and utter cruelty." Though he had felt temporary pangs of guilt about the latter, he had simply taken it for granted that "even Negro adults I encountered alone and had never seen before would treat me with generosity and affection." Even more than Morris, Virginia patrician Sarah Patton Boyle had begun in childhood to expect not only deference but affection from blacks. Not perceiving that her family's black retainers had little choice in the matter of how they treated her, Boyle believed firmly that "between Negroes and my whole stratum of southern society there was a continuous flow of understanding, love, tenderness, and well-being." To Boyle and generations of white southerners before her, even in adulthood, the South's hierarchical and strictly observed code of racial etiquette meant that all blacks were constantly available sources of "comfort, love, and security."[17]

Clearly even sympathetic white southerners like Boyle had trouble imagining blacks in any but the roles and personae that the Jim Crow South had imposed on them. Although novelist Walker Percy had defied the Klan by speaking out against segregation in Louisiana, after forming an acquaintance with black writer Albert Murray and finally reading Ralph Ellison's *Invisible Man*, Percy admitted, "It's really hard for me to accept the fact that you and Ellison are for real."[18]

Nobody bore the emotional brunt of white southerners' stereotyping and indiscriminate discrimination against their race more heavily than African Americans whose personal accomplishments made them persons of note and status outside the region but counted for little or nothing within it. In 1941 historian John Hope Franklin had joined W. E. B. Du Bois as only the second African American to receive a doctorate from Harvard. Franklin had published two well-regarded books by 1949, when, in his capacity as Southern Historical Association program chair, his friend C. Vann Woodward asked him to become the first black scholar to present a paper at the group's annual meeting, which was to be held that year in Williamsburg. When word of Franklin's impending participation in the program leaked out, there was great consternation among some of his white fellow historians over where he would eat, sleep, and use the toilet, since the city's nicest hotels were open only to whites. Woodward pointed out that the same circumstances might attend if the meeting were scheduled for the Pennsylvania Hotel in New York, or the Mayflower in Washington, or the Parker House in Boston, and Franklin's decision to stay with a local white friend and avoid any of the dinner meetings helped to assure that this unprecedented event came off smoothly. Franklin's paper drew a warm response, but he was not actually allowed to attend the banquet that traditionally accompanied the SHA's presidential address until three years later, and then only because Woodward, as president, insisted that the affair be moved from the host hotel in Knoxville, which had made it clear it would not serve a racially integrated group.[19]

Outwardly Franklin seemed to suffer these affronts with humor and grace, doubtless out of consideration for his white friends who were working to end the group's traditional adherence to the Jim Crow practices of host cities and hotels. In 1970 the Southern Historical Association would become the first of the nation's three major historical organizations to select Franklin as its president. He was still not seeing much progress in 1954, however, and he gave a rare glimpse into his personal frustrations after he was invited to serve on the program committee for that year's SHA meeting in Memphis. Officials of that city's fabled Peabody Hotel had promised that although no African Americans were allowed to stay there, all of the group's meetings and official dinner functions would be open to blacks. Yet Franklin refused to "subject myself to the inconvenience and risk of humiliation involved in attending the meeting" because Memphis was "a terrible town with the most rigid patterns of segregation." He would be "literally stranded at the hotel all the time," he explained, because "white taxicabs will not ride Negro passengers," and "Negro taxicabs don't like to go into 'the white part of town' since return fares are impossible." The enduring strength and inflexibility of Jim Crow's grip on Memphis had thus put Franklin in "the anomalous position of helping to plan a meeting that will be interesting, valuable and most attractive," though "not...attractive enough to draw me to Memphis!"[20]

The patent absurdities of Jim Crow made it an affront to the intelligence of both races, but whites who spoke out against it could expect physical threats and verbal abuse, and at the very least they could count on a steely, unremitting social ostracism that set them and their children outside their traditional community, whether at work, school, church, or the supermarket. Sarah Patton Boyle soon found herself persona non grata among the other faculty wives when she innocently sent what she regarded as a merely pro forma welcome note to a young black man who enrolled in the Law School at the University of Virginia in 1950. Boyle's chastisement for her affront to racial propriety was trivial compared to that meted out to Clifford and Virginia Durr in Montgomery. Their support for the bus boycott and his legal assistance to Rosa Parks not only put his law practice in jeopardy but, Virginia Durr complained, it also turned their children into "pariahs and outcasts" among their peers. The Durrs had already been hounded mercilessly by Mississippi Senator James Eastland during hearings on the integrationist and allegedly subversive Southern Conference Educational Fund, and though she admitted, "Trying to make a living here and raise children in such an environment is difficult, to put it mildly," the feisty Virginia was squarely in accord with her husband's decision to stay, simply because being "run out" meant "a victory for Jim Eastland, that lowdown skunk."[21]

By the end of the 1950s sociologist and social psychiatrist Herbert Blumer was arguing that for southern whites the "color line" was not a single barrier or demarcation but rather "a series of ramparts like the Maginot Line, extending from outer breastworks to inner bastions." In reality, Blumer's schematic for understanding southern racial discrimination consisted merely of three concentric circles, with the "inner citadel" dedicated to the last-ditch defense of the absolute taboos against social interaction and physical, especially sexual, intimacy, ringed by a larger "economic subordination and opportunity restriction" line that assured cheap and abundant black labor, limiting occupational and social mobility by denying blacks the benefits of better jobs, better schools, and better places to live. This intermediate line of discrimination was itself circumscribed by an outer circle representing refusal to allow blacks "free access to public accommodations and public institutions, the enjoyment of the franchise, the equal protection of the laws and equal rights as consumers."[22]

In general, Blumer believed, these encircling "color lines" grew increasingly easier to breach as one moved out from the center. After all, whites' inner emotional aversion to certain intimate interactions with blacks was seemingly beyond the direct reach of law, but as *Smith v. Allwright* in 1944 and *Brown v. Board* ten years later had already shown, maintaining the integrity of the outer political and economic circles was more difficult because it typically meant justifying blatant denials of the legal and constitutional rights of black Americans. When it was actually under attack, however, Jim Crow's concentric defense network tended to coalesce almost instantly into a single unitary circle of resistance as propagandists cast every assault on the outer political and economic breastworks of white supremacy as a direct and critical threat to the sacred "inner citadel" of social and physical exclusion. Hence from the disfranchisement campaigns of the late nineteenth century to resistance to black registration efforts in last half of the twentieth, the sanctity of the ballot box could readily become synonymous with the sanctity of the bedroom, so much so that an outraged white man in Mississippi would attack a black voter registration worker yelling, "You sonofabitch, you sonofabitch, you'll never marry my daughter." Likewise, in the rhetoric of massive resistance, the crusade for integrated schools made racial "mongrelization" or "amalgamation" a swift and terrible certainty.[23]

In such an atmosphere, white politicians with even modest inclinations toward elevating the circumstances of black southerners were obliged to proceed very gingerly. In the wake of *Smith v. Allwright* the actual communications between more racially moderate white office seekers and the black citizens whose votes they sought were typically low-key and could even be secretive, conducted not in public gatherings and forums but privately through black ministers and other intermediaries. Despite their common fondness for alcohol and the company of women other than their wives, in the first decade after the war Governors Jim Folsom in Alabama and Earl Long in Louisiana had enjoyed a measure of success by emphasizing the need to improve and expand state services for the poor and working people of both races. Preaching a simple gospel of fairness, Folsom noted that blacks made up 35 percent of Alabama's population and questioned whether they were "getting 35 percent of the fair share of living," meaning "their share of democracy, the same opportunity of having a voice in the government under which they live." Long meanwhile scoffed at the "fakers" trying to use the race issue to "befuddle the people." Yet although both men spurned the traditional rhetoric of white supremacy, neither came close to publicly challenging legal segregation or left behind much in the way of major advancements or safeguards for black rights. Critics would later blame the 1954 *Brown v. Board of Education* desegregation ruling for igniting an angry white backlash that quickly sent the political fortunes of white moderates like Folsom and Long into a tailspin, but it may well have simply been that prior to the *Brown* decree most southern whites did not believe such politicians posed much of a threat to the racial status quo in the region.[24]

That status quo itself had become an impediment to the nation's cold war aims and objectives, however. With the Soviet Union and the United States in competition for the allegiance of the world's "developing nations," especially those in Africa, some strategists had begun to suggest that curtailing the South's racial abuses might be critical to preserving American credibility abroad. On the other hand, in the context of rampant cold war fears of communist subversion, anyone who forcefully agitated for racial change or supported an organization that did could easily be branded as an agent of the Kremlin bent on overthrowing the U.S. government. Former University of North Carolina president Frank Porter Graham and Florida's Claude Pepper were among the South's most racially moderate leaders, though neither advocated racial integration nor forcefully endorsed the *Smith v. Allwright* ruling. Still, both were ousted from their Senate seats in 1950 by opponents who harped not only on their racial liberalism but on their alleged ties to communism. Pepper's opponent, George Smathers, even dubbed him "the Red Pepper."[25]

Members of the Southern Conference for Human Welfare were forced to endure merciless harassment by the House Un-American Activities Committee, which, when it failed to find any real evidence of communism in their ranks, ingeniously concluded that the group was "perhaps the most deviously camouflaged Communist-front organization" in the nation. When the Young Men's Business Club of New Orleans condemned the SCHW's "communistic tendencies," it required no more proof than the group's support for "repeal of the poll tax, the passing of the FEPC bill [to prevent racial discrimination in federal hiring practices], better living conditions for the working man, civil liberties, racial equality, and more." Elsewhere, the Senate Internal Security Subcommittee declared the Southern Conference Education Fund, an SCHW offshoot, a communist-front organization. Finally, despite the NAACP's sworn opposition to communism, segregationist politicians insisted that the blueprint for its legal offensive against Jim Crow had been drawn up in Moscow.[26]

As pivotal as they may seem in retrospect, as of the mid-1950s the NAACP's hard-won legal victories still seemed far removed from the realities of life for many southern blacks caught in the iron grip of poverty and racial repression. Anne Moody was fourteen years old before she first learned of something called "the NAACP." After overhearing Mrs. Burke, her white employer in Centreville, Mississippi, discussing the group with her friends, Moody asked, "Mama, what do NAACP mean?" only to have her frightened mother hush her with a warning not to "ever mention that word around Mrs. Burke or any other white person, you heah!" When the teenager asked one of her teachers about the NAACP, the woman explained, "The NAACP is a Negro organization that was established a long time ago to help Negroes gain a few rights," but she quickly added, "I shouldn't be telling you all this, and don't you dare breathe a word of what I said. It could cost me my job if word got out I was teaching my students such."[27]

Fully aware of what they were up against, NAACP leaders nonetheless urged individual chapters to file petitions asking their local school systems to comply with *Brown*. The Yazoo City, Mississippi, chapter was one of sixty or so that acted on this request, and the fifty-three petitioners quickly faced severe reprisals when local papers published their names. Most of those identified were black professionals and businessmen, but their economic independence from whites was far from complete. To a person they faced the loss of credit or the opportunity to pursue business transactions of any kind with whites. Angry whites also pressured the tenants and laborers in their employ to stop purchasing goods and services from these NAACP upstarts. Several signees later withdrew their names or were forced to leave the community altogether.[28]

This sort of repression and coercion was the specialty of the Citizens Council, which was formed in July 1954 in the heart of the Mississippi Delta at Indianola by World War II veteran and plantation manager Robert B. "Tut" Patterson and some local businessmen and politicos. The council organizers had been inspired by a speech by Judge Tom Brady, also a Mississippian, who called on southern whites to mount an organized resistance campaign against the Supreme Court's integration decree. The Council spread across and ultimately out of Mississippi, generally attracting the white economic and political elites of the Deep South's Black Belt counties but later making some inroads among blue-collar whites in the cities as well.[29]

Citizens Council membership may have reached a regionwide total of 300,000 at one point, but the group's political influence varied considerably from state to state. It was strongest by far in Mississippi, where the Council worked closely with the publicly funded State Sovereignty Commission to spy on, harass, and undermine not only those thought to favor integration but those whose attitudes toward it were simply unclear. Pugnacious editor and publisher Hazel Brannon Smith, who would win a Pulitzer Prize in 1964 for her editorial assaults on the Citizens Council, described the atmosphere in Holmes County, Mississippi, when the group's power was at its peak: "The councils said that if we buried our heads in the sand long enough, the problem would go away. It was the technique of the big lie, like Hitler: tell it often enough and everybody will believe it. It finally got to the point where bank presidents and leading physicians were afraid to speak their honest opinions, because of this monster among us." Smith went toe-to-toe with both the Citizens Council and abusively racist local law enforcement officers even as her newspapers were, as she put it, being "bombed, burned and boycotted." A frustrated local legislator condemned her as a "female crusading scalawag domiciled in our midst," and when her printing plant was torched by arsonists, the utterly resolute Smith managed nonetheless to get out a smaller version of her paper in which she warned readers, "When I am no longer free to print the truth unafraid, then you are no longer free to speak the truth without fear."[30]

Outside Mississippi the councils grew strongest in Alabama, Louisiana, and South Carolina, while Virginia boasted a powerful variant known as the Defenders of State Sovereignty and Individual Liberties. The movement was notably less successful in both Arkansas and Georgia, where rural white elites seemed more confident of their influence on state politics and thus may have felt less need to organize a separate organization dedicated to their particular racial preferences.[31]

In soliciting new members and financial contributions, the councils mounted a strong propaganda campaign aimed at nurturing white segregationist unity. The weapon of choice in their propaganda arsenal quickly proved to be Judge Brady's pamphlet, *Black Monday* (referring to the day the *Brown* decision was announced), which trumpeted the segregationist mantra that mixed schools were a final and irrevocable step onto the slippery slope leading directly to the pit of horrors that was racial amalgamation. To ensure that future generations remained wedded to segregation, the councils' propaganda machine was soon offering other "educational" materials for use in the public schools: "One of the main lessons in our Bible is that your race should be kept pure.... A friend had 100 white chickens and 100 reds. All the white chickens got to one side of the house and all the red chickens got on the other side of the house. You probably feel the same way these chickens did whenever you are with people of another race. God meant it to be that way."[32]

In trying to make good on their pledge to maintain white supremacy, the councils did their best to intimidate blacks who might think about challenging the status quo and to make painful examples of those who did. Perched atop the local economic pyramid, the councils' white elites could seriously reduce if not cut off entirely the flow of commerce and credit, not to mention employment, to blacks who got out of line. Council leaders typically made it a point to see that the names of any black persons who had attempted to register to vote or signed petitions for school desegregation made their way to the local newspapers so that whites in the community would know which blacks to fire, turn off their tenant farms, or deny credit. An Alabama council member summed up his group's aims quite candidly when he explained, "We intend to make it difficult, if not impossible, for a Negro who advocates desegregation to find and hold a job, get credit, or renew a mortgage."[33]

Such tactics often succeeded, but not always. The Citizens Councils movement reached South Carolina shortly after the NAACP filed a petition in August 1955 calling for immediate integration of the Orangeburg County School District No. 5. Council chapters quickly sprang up in Orangeburg and Elloree and set about recruiting "every white man in the area" to join the group and "fight the leaders of the NAACP from ditches to fence posts to keep Negroes out of white schools." Less than a year later the state boasted fifty-five Council chapters, many of them concentrated in the Low Country, where the largest number of blacks was also concentrated. Meanwhile, the Orangeburg Council had begun propaganda and pressure campaigns aimed at rallying whites to their cause and intimidating any blacks who might be inclined to challenge the status quo.[34]

As their counterparts elsewhere did so frequently and effectively, the Orangeburg Council launched a wave of economic reprisals against petition signers and known supporters of the NAACP. Black service station owner Jim Sulton lost his credit and his Coca-Cola and ice cream concessions. Standard Oil refused, however, to cut off Sulton's gasoline supply, and he managed to stay open, even defiantly organizing a relief drive to support others victimized by the Council. Council leaders clearly counted on their economic leverage to maintain white supremacy, but they had underestimated both blacks' determination and, in a county that was 60 percent African American, the countervailing economic pressures that might be brought to bear against them. Local blacks organized a boycott of their own, targeting the products of Coca-Cola, Sunbeam Bread, and other companies that had succumbed to Citizens Council pressure to stop supplying black merchants who supported the petition. They also refused to patronize the businesses of Council members or of blacks who caved in to Council pressure. Within a few weeks supplies were suddenly flowing to black businesses regardless of whether their owners had signed the petition, and white entrepreneurs began working quietly to try to win back the black customers who had spurned them. The Council meanwhile began to lose both membership and momentum in Orangeburg and across the state.[35]

If Mississippi gave birth to the Citizens Councils, it was Virginia that contributed the ideological premise, however flimsy, for what the Councils and their affiliates or clones were trying to do. Segregationist forces in Virginia issued a call for "massive resistance" to the Court's ruling, reaching back to the Nullification Crisis of 1832 to resurrect the hoary theory of "interposition," whereby the state could invoke its sovereign will to prevent allegedly unconstitutional actions by the federal government from infringing on the rights of its citizens. Urged on by the state's long-entrenched U.S. senator, Harry F. Byrd, the Virginia legislature approved an interposition resolution in February 1956, pledging to "take all appropriate measures honorably, legally, and constitutionally available to us, to resist this illegal encroachment on our sovereign powers." They also urged their "sister states" to follow suit, believing that, as Senator Byrd explained, "If we can organize the southern states for massive resistance to this order... in time the rest of the country will realize racial integration is not going to be accepted in the South."[36]

Five other "sister states" were quick to oblige. The Mississippi legislature even went so far as to declare the *Brown* decree null and void and "of no lawful effect within the confines of the State of Mississippi" and ordered all public employees to "prohibit the implementation or the compliance with the Integration Decision." On the day after Georgia lawmakers put themselves on record in a similar statement, they also approved a new state flag bearing the Confederate battle flag insignia in order to, as one die-hard defender of white supremacy put it, "show that we in Georgia intend to uphold what we stood for, will stand for, and will fight for."[37]

Buoyed by such attempts at interposition, the journalistic point man of massive resistance, James J. Kilpatrick of the *Richmond News Leader*, predicted that if the southern states could "hold out" against integration for ten years, they could "yet win the war." The key to victory, most argued, was a rock-ribbed, regionwide commitment to massive resistance because, in the long run, the prospects for "holding out" rested not on the persuasiveness of the interposition theory so much as the realities of the judicial system. If whites in every community simply forced integrationists to fight their way through layer after layer of litigation and appeal, battling obfuscation and deliberate delay every step of the way through a court system whose lower echelons were dominated by southern-born segregationist judges, NAACP resources and resolve would surely wear thin before any meaningful racial mixing had been achieved.[38]

Georgia's folksy but fervent segregationist governor Marvin Griffin promised, "If we in the South band together and present a unified front, they'll never get to us." In an effort to generate and, where necessary, coerce such a show of regional unity in Washington, Virginia's Byrd and his senatorial colleague, South Carolina's former Dixiecrat standard-bearer, J. Strom Thurmond, led the way in drawing up a "Declaration of Constitutional Principles" in March 1956. As it was signed by 19 of 22 senators and 82 of 106 representatives from the Old Confederacy, the final version of the "Southern Manifesto" did not endorse interposition, but it commended "the motives of those States which have declared the intention to resist forced integration by any lawful means" and pledged the signers to using "all lawful means to bring about a reversal of this decision which is contrary to the Constitution and to prevent the use of force in its implementation."[39]

Although Citizens Council members preferred straw hats and seersucker suits to robes and hoods and forswore violence of any sort, their dire prophesies of "mongrelization" and warnings that "desegregating the schools will lead to rape" clearly inflamed white racial passions. A number of key defenders of segregation talked out of both sides of their mouths on this point. Citizens Council stalwart James Eastland took to the floor of the Senate ten days after the first *Brown* decision and insisted with a straight face that there was "no racial hatred in the South" and that "the Negro is not an oppressed race." At the same time, back in his own Sunflower County, Mississippi (where blacks accounted for 70 percent of the population), and wherever else whites gathered to hear his segregationist harangues, Eastland's supporters circulated handbills declaring, "When in the course of human events it becomes necessary to abolish the Negro race, proper methods should be used. Among these are guns, bows and arrows, sling shots and knives: We held these truths to be self-evident that all whites are created with certain rights, among them are life, liberty, and the pursuit of dead niggers."[40]

White Mississippians were busily engaged in this pursuit in 1955. In May, shortly before the Supreme Court released its ruling in *Brown II*, Rev. George W. Lee was killed by a shotgun blast in Belzoni after registering to vote and urging his congregation and other black citizens to do the same. On August 13 Lamar Smith, a World War II veteran who had also encouraged black voter registration, was shot dead in broad daylight on the crowded Brookhaven courthouse lawn. No arrests were made in the Lee case, and though the sheriff had seen a white man leaving the scene "with blood all over him," Smith's accused slayer went free when no witnesses would come forward.[41]

Two weeks after Smith was killed Mississippi produced yet another racial slaying, this one so brutal and heinous that it would begin to awaken the world to the savagery of some white southerners' racial passions and the hopeless vulnerability of blacks who lived virtually at the mercy of those passions. On August 24, 1955, Emmett Till, a fourteen-year-old black youth visiting from Chicago, tried to impress his southern cousins by, according to varying accounts, either whistling at a white woman or saying "Bye, baby!" to her at a country store at Money in the Mississippi Delta. Four days later, in the early morning hours, the teenager was taken from his bed at his great uncle Mose Wright's house and first beaten and then shot by J. W. Milam, whose wife he had ostensibly offended, and Milam's half-brother, Roy Bryant. After shooting Till the two used barbed wire to tie a seventy-five-pound cotton gin fan around his neck before tossing his body into the Tallahatchie River. Already under arrest for kidnapping after, to their surprise, Mose Wright turned them in to the sheriff, Milam and Bryant were charged with the murder three days later, when the boy's body was plucked from the river. Distraught but purposeful, Till's mother, Mamie, not only insisted that her son's remains be returned to Chicago for burial but decided to open the casket so mourners could see his swollen, mangled, and beaten body for themselves.[42]

When *Jet* magazine and other publications ran photos of Emmett's bloated corpse, complete with a bullet hole in his head and a missing

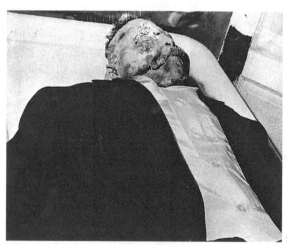

Emmett Till in his casket, Chicago, Illinois, 1955. Courtesy of the *Chicago Defender*.

eye, many black southerners seemed to react with a profound unease that quickly gave way to anger and resolve. In Louisville, Cassius Marcellus Clay felt a "strange kinship" with his fellow fourteen-year-old with a "swollen and bashed in" head and "eyes bulging out of their sockets." Obsessed with Till's murder, the future Muhammad Ali feverishly sought "a way to get back at white people for his death" by throwing rocks at an "Uncle Sam Wants You" poster before planting stolen shoe trees on a railway track and successfully damaging a train. For others who would go on to organize civil rights protests and voter registration drives, Till's murder was a critical, life-changing event. Growing up in Denmark, South Carolina, future SNCC activist Cleveland Sellers was three years younger than Till, but he "identified" with him and tried to "imagine what he was thinking when those white men took him from his home that night." Sellers recalled that blacks in Denmark were no strangers to racial atrocities, "but there was something special about this one. For weeks after it happened…it was impossible to go into a barber shop or corner grocery without hearing someone deplore Emmett Till's lynching." Both the photographs of the corpse and the story of his brutal slaying provoked national and international outrage that soon coalesced into a demand for justice.[43]

Justice for black people was hard to come by in the South of that era, however. Many whites in Mississippi had initially expressed regret about the atrocity and shown little support for the accused men, who at first even had difficulty securing defense counsel. Yet, as they faced a billowing firestorm of northern criticism, many local whites quickly grew surly and defiant, rallying around Bryant and Milam, who soon had the best local lawyers available. Despite a substantial body of incriminating evidence against them the two men were acquitted after an all-white jury "deliberated" for barely an hour, and only that long, so one juror admitted, "to make it look good."[44]

Clearly the verdict itself did not look particularly "good" to the nation and the world at large. Swamped by a torrent of criticism, whites in Mississippi and throughout the South were quick to point to bloody, wholesale racial violence in major northern cities where an influx of black migrants threatened to overrun previously all-white neighborhoods and facilities. A favorite example was Emmett Till's Chicago, where wartime and postwar overcrowding had fueled a number of brutal incidents, including, not long after Till's death, an attack by more than 6,000 whites on 500 blacks who had attempted to use a portion of Calumet

Park previously thought to be off-limits to nonwhites. Such efforts to put their accusers on the defensive gained little traction, however, as white southerners continued to face condemnation aplenty from every corner of the nation and the world in the wake of the Till verdict. The outrage only intensified after Bryant and Milam sold their stories, in which they confessed to the crime, to writer William Bradford Huie, who published them in *Look* magazine.[45]

For southern blacks the outcome of the Till case was a vivid reminder of just how tenuous even their already deprived and down-trodden existence really was. In addition to "hunger, hell, and the Devil," the Till murder had brought "a new fear" into Anne Moody's adolescent world, "the fear of being killed just because I was black": "This was the worst of my fears. I knew once I got food, the fear of starving to death would leave. I also was told that if I were a good girl, I wouldn't have to fear the Devil or hell. But I didn't know what one had to do or not do as a Negro not to be killed. Probably just being a Negro period was enough, I thought."[46]

As it would with Cleveland Sellers, Julian Bond, James Forman, and a host of others, Moody's fear soon hardened into the anger and resolve that would transform her into a civil rights activist. In the wake of the Till case, she reflected, she had begun "to hate people," including not only "the white men who murdered Emmett Till" but those who had committed the "countless murders" that her teacher had told her about or "those I vaguely remembered from childhood." At the same time, however, Moody realized she also "hated Negroes . . . for not standing up and doing something about the murderers": "Negro men were cowards, smiling in a white man's face, addressing him as 'Mr. So-and-So,' saying 'yessuh' and 'nossuh' when after they were home behind closed doors that same white man was a son of a bitch, a bastard, or any other name more suitable than mister."[47]

Two months after Till's murderers were set free, it became clear that black southerners had finally suffered one injustice too many. Rosa Parks, a Montgomery, Alabama, seamstress with a history of NAACP activity, later admitted she had "thought of Emmett Till" when she refused to yield her seat near the front of a bus so that a white passenger would not have to sit in the same row as a black one. Parks's arrest sparked a year-long boycott led by a young local pastor, Rev. Martin Luther King Jr., although discussions had actually been going on for some time about a boycott similar to one that had enjoyed a measure of success in Baton

Rouge, Louisiana, in June 1953, well before the first *Brown* decision. In Montgomery boycott organizers formed themselves into the Montgomery Improvement Association, led by Reverend King, whose work in leading the boycott would catapult him to national prominence as a civil rights leader. Although King became the face of the boycott, nobody stood more squarely at its heart than Jo Ann Gibson Robinson, who taught English at all-black Alabama State University in Montgomery. Robinson had endured humiliation at the hands of a racist bus driver herself, and as leader of a black group, the Women's Political Council, she had written the mayor warning of a possible boycott of city buses even before the Rosa Parks incident. After Parks's arrest Robinson spent the entire night mimeographing some thirty-five thousand leaflets calling on Montgomery blacks to join the mass action the following day.[48]

After seeing numerous empty buses on December 5, 1955, the first day of the boycott, Reverend King rejoiced that "the once dormant and quiescent Negro community was now awake," but later that day a number of black ministers in the group wanted to end the boycott at that point and effectively quit while they were ahead. In response an angry Rev. E. D. Nixon demanded to know, "What's the matter with you people? Here

Rosa Parks after her arrest during the Montgomery Bus Boycott, 1956. Courtesy of Montgomery County Archives, Montgomery, Alabama.

you have been living off the sweat of these washerwomen all these years, and you have never done anything for them. Now you have a chance to pay them back, and you're too damn scared to stand on your feet and be counted! The time has come when you men is going to have to learn to be grown men or scared boys." That night a mass meeting brought a unanimous vote to continue the boycott, which, despite legal subterfuge and extralegal harassment and threats from whites, lasted until the day after Christmas the following year. A well-organized "private taxi" system ferried boycotters to and from their jobs, and peer pressure to hold fast remained strong. In one oft-repeated story a white bus driver who had just let off a lone black passenger saw an elderly black woman with a cane hurrying toward the bus, and he opened the door to reassure her, "You don't have to rush, Auntie, I'll wait for you." "In the first place," the old lady replied, "I ain't your auntie. In the second place, I ain't reshin' to get on your bus. I'm just trying to catch up with that nigger who just got off, so I can hit him with this here stick."[49]

Maintaining morale as well as day-to-day coordination required Herculean effort from boycott leaders like Jo Ann Robinson, who chose to stay in the background rather than risk her job and those of some of her colleagues at Alabama State. Ultimately it was not the protracted boycott itself that actually broke the back of segregation on city buses, but a federal court ruling declaring that practice unconstitutional. Nor did the end of the boycott signal the end of racial conflict in Montgomery. Buses now occasionally drew sniper fire; there was a wave of bombings at private homes and black churches; and an unexploded bomb was found on Reverend King's front porch. Still, through their courage and perseverance King and his followers had won a major strategic victory and established collective action as an effective means of overturning Jim Crow in the South.

King's work was clearly cut out for him, however. In February 1956, when the Montgomery boycott was still in its early stages, less than a hundred miles away in Tuscaloosa Autherine Lucy, a black woman from rural Marengo County, Alabama, had entered the University of Alabama by court order only to face a raging hate-filled mob variously estimated at five hundred to several thousand whites. Cries of "Lynch the nigger!" and "Hit the nigger whore!" rang out as Lucy and her escorts were pelted with gravel, rotten eggs, and produce, while on the fringe of the crowd a silver-haired white lady swung a sweater over her head while screaming, "Kill her, kill her!" Security precautions were far from adequate because,

Rev. Martin Luther King Jr. after his arrest during the Montgomery Bus Boycott, 1956. Courtesy of Montgomery County Archives, Montgomery, Alabama.

university officials insisted, they had not anticipated such outrage. Yet rather than stand fast in the face of mob lawlessness, the school's board of trustees voted that afternoon to ban Lucy from the campus for the time being for her own safety.[50]

Outraged at this apparent capitulation to mob rule, Lucy's NAACP legal team filed suit for her immediate readmission but erred badly in suggesting that in order to thwart the integration decree university officials had engaged in a conspiracy with those who threatened their client. The conspiracy charges were utterly unprovable, and the upshot was that when the court ordered Lucy's readmission, within a matter of minutes the university's trustees met to approve a resolution expelling her because of her "baseless, outrageous, and unfounded charges of misconduct on the part of university officials." After the readmission order but before Lucy's expulsion was announced a white supremacist agitator, Asa Carter, called for a massive protest rally of "more than 15,000 persons," and the state legislature demanded that Lucy's lawyers appear before them so that the NAACP's communist ties could be explored. Another resolution urged Congress to provide funds to relocate blacks outside the South, and members of the lower house of the legislature also threatened to cut off appropriations both for all-black Tuskegee Institute and for out-of-state scholarships for black students who sought professional training they could not receive in segregated Alabama.[51]

Scoffing at the notion that Autherine Lucy's dismissal had brought "peace" to the Alabama campus, Reverend King stood in the pulpit at Montgomery's Dexter Avenue Baptist Church and condemned any peace "purchased at the price of allowing mobocracy to reign supreme over democracy" as the type of peace "that stinks in the nostrils of the Almighty God." "If peace means a willingness to be exploited economically, dominated politically, humiliated and segregated," King added emphatically, "I don't want peace."[52]

Peace would be a scarce commodity indeed as the lofty political rhetoric of interposition and the disingenuous strategy of delay gave way to the bitter confrontations that marked the integration of Little Rock's Central High School in the fall of 1957. Shortly after the *Brown* decision in 1954, Little Rock school officials had announced their intentions to comply with the Court's decree. They had proposed to do so through a carefully controlled plan of admitting a small, selectively screened group of black students to Central High, with integration then proceeding gradually down through the earlier grades. Central High's students were primarily from working-class families, many of whom resented the school board's plan to target their children's school rather than the city's more affluent, socially elite Hall High School.

As a loose coalition of Citizens Council and other segregationist agitators and the resentful and resolute Mothers' League of Central High roiled the racial waters in Little Rock, the state's governor, Orval Faubus, at first did his best to keep his distance from what he saw initially as a political "no win" situation for him. Born in the Ozark Mountains, Faubus had cut his political teeth as a pro–New Deal, economic development–oriented Democrat with little taste for race-baiting. Trying desperately to avoid having to take sides in the conflict over segregation, he pledged that he would use his authority neither to compel desegregation nor to resist it.[53]

Such a promise did not oblige him to intervene in Little Rock, where official compliance with *Brown*, although token and protracted, had been nonetheless voluntary. However, as the September opening date for public schools approached, the agents of massive resistance turned up the heat, warning of angry and perhaps even armed segregationists converging on Little Rock by caravan. When Faubus sought assurances of federal peace-keeping support in case of violence, he found the Eisenhower administration no more eager to jump into the middle of a social and political firestorm than he was. Finally, anticipating a strong segregationist bid to deny him a third term in 1958, Faubus activated the Arkansas National Guard on the premise of keeping the peace, not by standing guard over the integration of Central High but by preventing it altogether.

At this point interposition became a matter not just of legalistic and political bluster but of deliberate defiance of national authority by a governor using a state military organization (which was also part of the U.S. Army and thus ultimately under the command of President Eisenhower) to prevent compliance with a federal court order. Finally, Federal District Judge Ronald Davies instructed the Justice Department to seek an injunction to stop Faubus from using the Arkansas National Guard to block integration at Central High. When the injunction was issued, however, Faubus immediately removed the guardsmen rather than leave them in place to keep the peace as integration proceeded.

With the city in transition to a manager-commission form of government, the lame-duck incumbent mayoral administration declined to step into the breach to maintain order, leaving a hapless contingent of state policemen little choice but to evacuate Central's first-ever black students when as many as a thousand angry whites gathered at the school. Before she left, Melba Patillo looked out the window in her shorthand class: "The ocean of people stretched farther than I could see—waves of people ebbing and flowing, shoving the sawhorses and the policemen who were trying to keep them in place." Meanwhile, Daisy Bates, a long-time black activist and NAACP state chapter head who had served as the nine black students' sponsor, mentor, and, insofar as possible, protector, found her own house bombarded with rocks and gunfire and her lawn adorned with a burning cross.[54]

A few local whites privately expressed their dismay over this turn of events, but publicly the silence was deafening. President Eisenhower, who faced off against a Democratic Congress six of the eight years he was in office, may have thought that he could ill afford to alienate the powerful, entrenched southerners across the aisle if he hoped to get any Republican bills into law. Still, Eisenhower's refusal prior to the Little Rock crisis to endorse the *Brown* decision as the law of the land and his expressed sympathy for southern whites terrified by the prospect of racial amalgamation had surely stiffened the backs of resistance forces in Arkansas and elsewhere.

A year before the Little Rock crisis, whites in Mansfield, Texas (where there was but a single black teacher for eight grades and black high schoolers were bused some twenty miles to Fort Worth each day), had also defied a court order to integrate. When several hundred segregationist demonstrators gathered at the school, Governor Allen Shivers sent in the Texas Rangers, not to enforce the law but, like Faubus in Arkansas, to support the segregationists. In this case the White House had ignored the affair altogether, leaving local NAACP leaders no choice but to withdraw their demands for integration. A year later, however, when both Faubus and local officials abdicated their responsibilities to maintain law and order in Little Rock, President Eisenhower had no choice but to federalize the Arkansas National Guard and bring in additional regular troops from the 101st Airborne Division to maintain a tensely integrated peace.[55]

Although the troops were there for the ostensible protection of the nine black students at Central High and some teachers and administrators did try to be supportive, the 1957–58 school year was an all but seamless sequence of ugly confrontations and painful abuse, both physical and emotional, for these young civil rights pioneers. Kicked, punched, shoved, spat upon, doused with hot soup, and splattered with ink they faced an unending chorus, either shouted or murmured, of "Nigger, Nigger, Nigger!" Some white students, females as well as males, were both the eyes and ears as well as the fists of the screaming segregationist mobs outside. The only senior among the "Little Rock Nine," Ernest Green recalled, "Walking up the steps that [first] day was probably one of the biggest feelings I've ever had.... I figured I have finally cracked it." Actually Green did not really "crack it" until May 27, 1958, when, with Reverend King in attendance, he walked across the stage as the first black graduate of Central High School and became a symbol of the ultimate futility of massive resistance when blacks simply refused to abandon their demands for integration.[56]

The Little Rock crisis also demonstrated that, especially when pushed by black citizens determined to claim their rights, Washington's tolerance for continuing, outright defiance of the *Brown* decree clearly had its limits. In the first two years after *Brown II*'s somewhat equivocal insistence on integration at "all deliberate speed," the percentage of southern whites who believed integration was inevitable fell from 55 to 43. A year after federal intervention in Little Rock, however, a majority of white southerners again saw no hope of preventing desegregation.[57]

The South and America since World War II

At that point the Little Rock crisis was still far from over, how-ever. With the full encouragement of Governor Faubus, who had just won reelection with 70 percent of the vote, the state legislature quickly passed a law in August 1958 empowering him to close any school facing integration under a federal court order. Faubus proceeded to shut down Central and three other Little Rock high schools, a move endorsed by some 70 percent of the voters in a local referendum, but not by the Women's Emergency Committee to Open Our Schools, formed by some of the city's most prominent white women a few days after the closings were announced. The entire school board resigned after the emphatic public rejection of their position on keeping the schools open, but the WEC quickly mounted a vigorous lobbying effort, warning local busi-nessmen of the dire economic consequences of the school closings. In the December 1958 special election to choose a new school board, for-mer Chamber of Commerce executive Everett Tucker headed a "busi-nessmen's slate" of candidates who favored segregation but also pledged their support for open, stable public schools. Hesitantly, and often inef-fectually, local development leaders had tried to persuade Governor Faubus to moderate his actions throughout the crisis, fearing that the economic momentum generated by a newly created "industrial district" and their success in attracting a new air force base to the area might be lost. Tucker and two of his colleagues won seats on the school board, but the election of three arch-segregationists led only to stalemate.[58]

In May 1959 after the three businessmen left a deadlocked meeting, the three segregationists on the school board voted to terminate the con-tracts of forty-four teachers and administrators whom they suspected of integrationist sympathies. This action outraged supporters of public education throughout the city, leading to the formation of STOP (Stop This Outrageous Purge), a group of young businessmen and profession-als. With the now thousand-member strong Women's Emergency Com-mittee providing critical guidance and organizational and promotional support, STOP launched a petition drive for a recall election to oust the offending board members. Finally, with four thousand black voters making the difference, this was accomplished on May 25, 1959, paving the way for the schools to be reopened some three months later.[59]

Hailed as a victory for moderation, this reopening was no less a triumph of tokenism, for it came with only six black students in previ-ously all-white schools, fewer than had entered Central High two years earlier. Even then segregationists staged raucous protests, and on Labor

Day Eve in 1959 bombs destroyed the fire chief's car and damaged administrative headquarters. As a follow-up, a caller left a message for Chamber of Commerce President Grainger Williams warning, "We got some dynamite for him, too, if he doesn't keep his damned mouth shut." With this, however, it seemed a shocked public had finally had enough; the local radical segregationist establishment fell quickly into disfavor, especially after the WEC released a sobering report on the sharp decline in Little Rock's housing, business, and population indicators since the crisis began.[60]

As the conflict in Little Rock was unfolding, Melvin Tumin and his colleagues found 75 percent of the whites in Greensboro, North Carolina, also wanted to keep their schools segregated. When Tumin and his colleagues analyzed their interview material, however, they found some significant variation in the intensity of this sentiment. In fact, Tumin was able to establish three reasonably distinct categories of white attitudes toward integration. Twenty-five percent of the white respondents struck Tumin as "hard core" segregationists who seemed ready even to use violence to prevent mixed-race schools. On the other end of the spectrum were the 33 percent of whites who either actually opposed segregation or were not so wedded to it that they were unwilling to compromise. In between lay the middle 42 percent who clearly preferred segregation but were not prepared to resort to violence or coercion to maintain it. If they were forced to choose between closing the schools or integrating them, the middle would sooner or later vote for integration, but until such a choice was required, they were content to remain silent on the finer details of their priorities. The hard-core segregationists were anything but silent about theirs, of course, and Tumin's findings suggested that so long as the courts and the Eisenhower administration refrained from pressing the matter, the dominant voices on this issue were bellicose and defiant. However, when, as in Little Rock, the executive and judicial branches of the federal government finally forced them to choose, the white middle opted, however belatedly, for the moderate (albeit token) response rather than allowing the hard-core segregationists to destroy public education and perhaps their city's economic future as well.[61]

Events in Little Rock had shown that in the face of the right combination of black determination and federal resolve, Jim Crow's outer defenses, which by then included the massive resistance movement, were ultimately insufficient to keep the system intact. Beyond that, the Little Rock crisis also produced the first hard evidence of the economic repercussions of racial conflict. It would be 1961 before the city attracted another industry. In fact, the only businessman who appeared to have benefited at all from the affair was a local mover who claimed to be "moving families away from Little Rock faster than ever." This "lesson of Little Rock" would soon become a strikingly potent weapon in the arsenals of both civil rights activists and concerned business and civic leaders across the South.

Harry S. Ashmore, the progressive editor of Little Rock's *Arkansas Gazette*, was one of the latter. A few months before Ernest Green claimed his diploma in 1958, Ashmore had published *An Epitaph for Dixie*, in which he concluded that white southerners simply could no longer resist the powerful forces that were beginning to transform their region into just another part of America. Ashmore pointed to rapid economic modernization and emerging indications of a viable Republican challenge to the South's traditional one-party politics. This meant that the only pillar of Dixie's stubbornly peculiar identity still standing was its system of legalized racial segregation, and he had just seen that beginning to crumble right before his eyes in Little Rock. Predicting that all the hastily erected legal and pseudo-legal barricades that had been thrown up all along Jim Crow's southern defense line would soon be breached, Ashmore was fully confident that nothing could "turn back the forces that are reshaping the Southern region in the nation's image." Clearly welcoming this transformation, he insisted, "For better or worse, the South must now find its future in the national pattern." Though he shared none of Ashmore's enthusiasm for this prospect, South Carolina conservative Henry Savage could only agree; at that point it seemed "irretrievably foreordained that, year by year, the South will be more American and less southern."[62]

3

"The Dominant Psychology...Is No Longer Agrarian"

From Farm to Factory and Town to City

The forces that seemed to be propelling the South toward the American mainstream had clearly gotten a major boost from World War II, which represented the culminating event of a roughly thirty-year "turning period" in the South's economic history that spanned the invasion of the boll weevil, the "Great Migration" northward of as many as 1.5 million blacks out of the region between 1916 and 1930 alone, the economic devastation of the Great Depression, and the transformation of southern agriculture set in motion by New Deal farm policies. Landowners who had reduced their crop acreage in return for government payouts from the Agricultural Adjustment Administration (AAA) found their labor requirements reduced as well. Although AAA rules ostensibly forbade them from evicting tenants, many AAA recipients ignored this restriction with impunity. Meanwhile, government checks had allowed them to double the number of tractors per 1,000 acres of cropland in some states during the 1930s, further reducing their manpower needs and providing additional incentive to rid themselves of even more tenants. Nearly one-third of the region's sharecroppers were pushed off the land over the course of the decade, and in peak labor periods when their remaining croppers could not do all the work that was required, planters simply dispatched trucks into nearby towns and cities each morning to round up day laborers, many of them displaced tenants, who were employed only on an as-needed basis, with no assurances of future work or the long-term support accorded sharecroppers.[1]

By rendering thousands of tenant families superfluous, New Deal acreage-reduction incentives had not only made some landlords rich but strengthened their hands in dealing with an expanded labor surplus.

World War II had reduced this advantage, however, by siphoning off some 400,000 farm workers either for military service or attractive jobs in defense plants and projects. Some landlords had little choice but to offer better wages, which more than tripled in some areas during the war, in order to get the labor they needed. This unwelcome pressure for higher wages proved to be a critical incentive for planters to renew their push for a mechanical cotton picker, which finally became widely available at the end of the 1940s.[2]

The want of such a picker had been one of the major impediments to a complete shift away from sharecropping, because so long as cotton still had to be harvested by hand, landlords were forced to retain at least enough of their tenant families to guarantee a solid cadre of workers come picking time each fall. With even the early one-row mechanical pickers said to duplicate the work of forty humans, surging demand for these machines in the perennially productive alluvial plantations of the

Cotton picker in use on a Georgia farm, 1950s. Courtesy of Georgia Archives, Vanishing Georgia Collection (Hab 024), Atlanta, Georgia.

Mississippi Delta led International Harvester to open a commercial production facility in Memphis in 1948. The mechanical picker was already common on larger cotton plantations across the South by the late 1950s, and most of these would be fully mechanized, from planting to harvest, well before the end of the 1960s.[3]

With the major obstacle to full-scale mechanization now removed and farm laborers moving to better jobs in industry both in and out of the South, tractors had quickly become a fixture on the southern agricultural landscape. There were already roughly twenty-two thousand of them on Mississippi farms in 1947 and nearly eighty-two thousand by 1954. Tractors only enhanced the relative advantages of farming on a larger scale, and as fleets of them rolled into the field at one end, plowmen leading their mules made their exits from the other. The aggregate mule population in the Carolinas, Georgia, Alabama, and Mississippi fell by some 350,000 in the decade after the war.[4]

On the eve of World War II roughly two in three southerners still lived on the land or in towns of fewer than twenty-five hundred, and manufacturing employment in five southern states was even lower in 1939 than it had been thirty years earlier. That changed quickly enough as the rural population shrank by more than 20 percent during the war alone, while the number of industrial workers swelled by nearly 60 percent. In economically marginal rural areas like eastern Kentucky, the population drain was beyond severe. This corner of Appalachia lost roughly 20 percent of its people between 1940 and 1942 alone, more than wiping out the gains of the entire preceding decade. This number included 25 percent of the men between fifteen and thirty-four, leaving a local teacher to observe, "Our young manhood has moved out en masse," and to predict, quite correctly, "Never again can this section be the same." About half of those who left had entered the military, and most of the rest had been drawn away by the promise of good jobs in the reinvigorated factories of the Ohio Valley and Great Lakes regions. Rural Appalachians continued to leave in huge numbers over the next several decades. Leslie County, Kentucky, lost 98 percent of its farmers during the 1950s, and Swain County, North Carolina, 80 percent. By 1960 only 6 percent of the South's mountain population continued to make their living as full-time farmers, while across the South as a whole the percentage of people living on farms represented scarcely one-third of the 1940 figure.[5]

The political and ideological restraints on federal spending had effectively fallen away when America's priorities shifted from relieving economic distress to shoring up national defense, and wartime defense expenditures played a key role in fueling southern economic growth. The South accounted for 27 percent of the U.S. population in 1940, but roughly 36 percent of total spending for military facilities (more than $4 billion) during the war. Another $5 billion poured into defense plants. The latter figure was only 18 percent of the total expenditures in this category and fell well below the region's share of the population, but it represented a tremendous increase over prewar totals.[6]

In a sense wartime federal spending was like another and considerably more generous New Deal to a South that had remained economically stagnant and severely cash-strapped at the end of the 1930s. Overall employment in manufacturing had increased by 50 percent by 1945, and the war finally brought competition for workers to what had long been a labor-surplus region. Per capita income in the South stood at 47 percent of the national average in 1929 and 64 percent in 1948, but over half of this gain had actually come between 1940 and 1945. In addition to pulling people into southern cities, the war also triggered massive outmigration; 1.6 million people left the region between 1940 and 1945, and 2.2 million (three-fourths of them black) over the course of the decade. The 1950s would see nearly 1.5 million additional whites and 2 million more blacks abandon the South, so that by 1960 well over 10 million people—a number amounting to more than one-fifth of the region's remaining population—who had been born in the South no longer lived there.[7]

For many of those who stayed, the lure of the city had proven well-nigh irresistible, and the region's urban population swelled by 33 percent during the war alone. Over the course of the decade some 75 percent of young people had left the farm upon reaching adulthood. After 1945, however, the defense industry began to cut back sharply, while a rapidly mechanizing agricultural sector also required fewer workers. With thousands of mustered-out veterans demanding more and better economic opportunities from communities they had risked their lives to defend, business and professional leaders in the region's cities and towns launched all-out campaigns to bring more jobs to their area. As Samuel Lubell put it, "the fever for new industry" had infected "the young lawyer searching for clients, the college graduate seeking a supervisory post in the mills, merchants and salesmen with something to sell," as well as bankers eager for new investments, doctors looking to build their practices, and speculators hoping "the cities they live in will grow out to the land they own and strike them rich."[8]

Southern states and communities had been pursuing industry on an ad hoc basis since the late nineteenth century, but the decline in agricultural jobs that had begun in the 1930s and accelerated in the 1940s soon dictated a more organized and structured approach to industrial development. Mississippi was a pioneer in this field, with its 1936 Balance Agriculture with Industry program that provided new plants with free buildings financed by special municipal bond issues. Foreshadowing what would become a regional and ultimately national trend, in the wake of World War II Kentucky, Tennessee, and Alabama quickly adopted bond subsidy programs similar to Mississippi's, sometimes supplemented by tax exemptions for new industries as well. With so many communities desperate for jobs, the practice caught on quickly, to say the least. Well over half of the 168 new industries locating in fifteen Tennessee cities between 1945 and 1953 had received some form of subsidy. Municipally owned and financed buildings were built with low-interest, tax-free bonds and were exempt from local property taxes. These benefits were passed along to their industrial occupants in the form of low rental rates that could be promptly written off as operating expenses. It quickly became a rule of thumb that poorer communities severely in need of payrolls were more likely to offer tax exemptions to new industries despite their equally desperate need for the revenue to improve local institutions and services.[9]

Critics charged that no industry worth having would be swayed in its location decisions by a subsidy, and it was true that the promise of a tax exemption or a subsidized building was most attractive to "footloose," labor-intensive firms that could basically operate anywhere there was an adequate pool of low-wage workers. Even these firms, however, were at a premium across a region where farming was no longer a viable option for most people. Both industrial interest in subsidies and community willingness to provide them were evident in a memorandum circulated by the Louisiana Department of Commerce and Industry concerning a "well-rated" clothing manufacturer likely to hire 250 female workers at an annual payroll of "about $250,000." The company's executives wanted to avoid any location where they would have to compete for "white female labor," and they had already received "offers" from two communities in both Arkansas and Mississippi in addition to one from

Alabama and one from Louisiana. In each case the community or some of its "interested citizens" had agreed to provide a suitable building on a ten-year lease at an annual rental rate of "four percent of building costs." Commerce and Industry officials urged local development leaders to move quickly, for the company in question wanted to make a decision within ten days.[10]

This feeler doubtless drew a number of prompt responses, for Louisiana communities were no less rabid in their pursuit of industry than any others in the South. Through its program of tax exemptions for new plants, Louisiana gave up nearly $12 million in revenue in 1948 alone, a figure approximating 20 percent of its total property tax collections for the year. As competition for payrolls grew more intense, Louisiana, Alabama, Mississippi, South Carolina, and Kentucky handed out roughly $144 million in tax exemptions between 1958 and 1961 alone.[11]

Many economists bemoaned such practices, and both labor union leaders and politicians, such as Senator John F. Kennedy of Massachusetts, complained, with some justification, that by dangling such enticements before northern employers, the southern states were essentially engaging in industrial piracy. The Textron Corporation, for example, had fifteen plants in northern states in 1954 and nine in the South. Three years later all the northern plants were gone. Southern leaders were unapologetic, even defiant on this point, however. When the governor of Rhode Island complained of industrial "raiding" by southern governors in 1952, Georgia governor Herman Talmadge escalated the rhetorical combat, vowing, "If he wants war, we'll give him war." Back home the state's newspapers reported excitedly on the governor's industry-seeking forays to the North, much as if he were a latter-day Jeb Stuart conducting a daring raid behind enemy lines.[12]

The rewards for such audacity could be sweet. When local leaders chipped in $42,500 to entice a garment manufacturer to Lafayette, Tennessee, the payoff was a plant employing 350 people, enough to stem the tide of outmigration that threatened the entire local economy. Buoyed by this and several subsequently successful subsidy ventures, business leaders got behind an effort to form the Macon (County) Industrial Corporation, which succeeded in bringing in a large shirt factory by sweetening the pot with a $400,000 building leased to the company for thirty years at an aggregate charge slightly less than the construction cost. Reflecting on Lafayette's experience, the town's mayor advised fellow members of the Tennessee Municipal League in 1957, "The little town that wants industry to stop the flow of young people away from its surrounding rural area does what is called 'buying industry' or it does not get any." One of his colleagues concurred: "If you are wise, you do whatever it takes to get the plant, and I mean just that, whatever it takes." There were clearly a lot of southern community leaders who agreed, judging by the continuing spread and increased size of industrial bond issues.[13]

In addition to a variety of other financial or in-kind subsidies, such as free or discounted land, water, or electric power, southern leaders talked incessantly of the need to maintain a "favorable" business climate. Opening their arms wide to new industry, the southern states began cutting their average corporate tax rates dramatically in the early 1950s, and lawmakers were considerably more sympathetic to expenditures to facilitate industry and commerce than to those for welfare or other forms of public assistance. Hence, based on per capita income, Mississippi, the nation's poorest state, spent twice the national average on highways in 1965, and every state but North Carolina at least exceeded that average. At the same time twelve southern states lagged well behind the national standard for welfare expenditures per capita. Development-oriented leaders like Governor Luther Hodges of North Carolina might support modest hikes in certain levies to support improvements in education, but increases in corporate taxes were anathema, and public welfare expenditures were typically the first target when the budget had to be cut. Likewise, when labor strife erupted Hodges did not hesitate to bring in state troopers or national guardsmen to break a strike.[14]

Because the centerpiece of the South's appeal to new industries was still its large pool of cheap workers, labor unions could be demonized as nothing less than a mortal threat to industrial development efforts. Despite strong employer resistance, under the protection of the War Labor Board, union membership in the South had more than doubled, from 500,000 to more than a million, between 1938 and 1948. This led a government labor economist to observe that there was some "evidence...that workers among both races are beginning to realize that economic cooperation is not only possible but desirable," although he warned, presciently as it turned out, "Much of the present organization, of course, has developed during very recent years, [and] its stability in many cases has yet to be tested." This became apparent when, hoping to hold onto their wartime advances, both the AFL and the CIO launched much-trumpeted recruiting efforts in 1946. By October the more moderate AFL was already claiming 500,000 new southern members, and a year later leaders of the more activist CIO's "Operation Dixie" were bragging, with obvious exaggeration, of some 400,000 new recruits. Both these campaigns had met with bitter opposition from local leaders and law enforcement officials, however, and as they found themselves competing for new members while grappling with the practical aspects of managing Jim Crow, both attempts soon began to falter. To say the least, they found few friends within the ranks of southern congressmen, and certainly not in Representative John Gibson of Georgia, who condemned efforts by the AFL and the CIO to unseat him as "the nefarious and dastardly attempts of the Communist to fool the lower classes, and especially the American Negro, into embracing them as savior and liberator." Gibson warned that "all labor, including the classes just mentioned, would be subjected to absolute slavery if and when they force their form of government over this country."[15]

Along with practically all his southern colleagues in Washington, Gibson showed great enthusiasm for any measure designed to clip organized labor's wings after its fortunes had soared majestically during the war. The most critical of these was the Taft-Hartley Act, which, with strident backing from the southern congressional contingent, was passed over President Truman's veto in 1947. With its prohibition of the "closed shop" (where union membership was a condition of employment) and its provision for states to pass "right-to-work laws" outlawing the "union shop" (where unaffiliated employees could be forced to pay union dues nonetheless), Taft-Hartley was a dagger to the heart for organized labor's hopes for future expansion in the South. Five southern states had enacted right-to-work laws before the end of 1947, joining three others that already had similar provisions in place. A decade after the war only Kentucky and Oklahoma lacked such a statute. Union membership among nonagricultural workers in the South had stood at 17 percent in 1946. Seven years later, despite two major organizing drives, the figure was essentially unchanged.[16]

Much of the local resistance to unions was actually illegal, extralegal, or both. In addition to police harassment and the willingness of law enforcement to look the other way when union opponents resorted to physical violence against labor organizers, some communities actually tried to keep unions out by blatantly discriminatory local ordinances. In 1955 Sandersville, Georgia, adopted a statute requiring "any organization, union or society" to pay $2,000 for a permit and $500 per new member recruited. After Star City, Arkansas, voters approved a $150,000 bond subsidy for a new garment plant, the city council imposed a daily license fee of $1,000 on all union organizers. Star City's mayor explained that officials of the new company had made it clear that "if the union ever got into the plant here, they might have to close up." With the $150,000 bond obligation hanging in the balance, he explained, "We've got too big a stake in this to let anything like that happen."[17]

Playing on sectional and racial prejudices as well as cold war anxieties about communist subversion, antiunion propaganda warned white workers, "This outside influence is just a bunch of pot-bellied Yankees with big cigars in their mouths, and the dues they collect will just go up North.... If they come in you will share the same restroom with Negroes and work side by side with them. It comes right out of Russia and is pure Communism and nothing else." In the face of such over-the-top propagandizing and numerous legal and extralegal impediments, it was not exactly surprising that in 1964 only Kentucky, with its strong United Mine Workers presence, approached the national average of 29 percent union membership among nonagricultural workers. No other southern state had as many as 20 percent of its workers in unions, and for the two Carolinas the figure was less than 8 percent.[18]

Industrial developers insisted their emphasis on low wages was working as employment in manufacturing grew by 18 percent in the southeastern states between 1947 and 1953. Yet the South's share of the nation's manufacturing jobs still stood at only 15 percent in 1953, just about where it had been in 1939. Compared to their counterparts elsewhere, the region's workers actually lost ground wage-wise after the war. Employees in southeastern manufacturing plants, who had received 28 percent less than workers in other parts of the nation in 1947, actually saw the gap widen to 35 percent by 1953, leaving an overall net improvement of only 3 percent since 1939. In 1959 a typical New Jersey production worker earned half again as much as his North Carolina counterpart, with fringe benefits and disability and unemployment payments registering a comparable disparity. The South's industrial mix was dominated by low-paying, labor-intensive operations. In the early 1960s more than three-fourths of the workers in nearly half of Georgia's 159 counties were employed in the textile, apparel, or lumber and wood industries.[19]

The heavy concentration of female employment in the apparel industry (80 percent nationwide in 1960) and the proliferation of apparel or "sewing" plants across the southern countryside challenged traditional gender roles both in and outside the household. Many a one-time farmer now found himself no longer the family's breadwinner but a mere "go-getter," whose chief responsibility each day was to take his wife to work in the morning and then "go get 'er" in the afternoon. Though they tried to laugh it off, for a great many southern men of this generation, when farming finally played out, the reality of being a "go get 'er" was anything but pleasant, for it signified failure not simply as a farmer but as a man. Meanwhile, her new status as the primary provider for the household relieved the go-getter's wife of none of her domestic duties as cook, housekeeper, laundress, and mother, and at the plant the pressure of making the so-called piece rate by sewing the requisite number of pieces for drawing full pay gave rise to a variety of stress-related conditions, ranging from "sick headaches" to nervous breakdowns. Rosalie Tucker, who led an organizing drive for the International Ladies Garment Workers Union at the Butte Knit plant in Spartanburg, South Carolina, believed, "The union got in because of the piece rates. If they set it at 100 pieces for eight hours, you had to make over a hundred to make any money. If you done more than they set the piece rate at, they'd up the rate."[20]

For all their zeal for bringing new private employers into the region, southern leaders were no less committed to attracting public payrolls as well. Even as white southerners condemned the federal government's interference in their racial affairs, they were reaping the benefits of a dramatically expanded federal economic presence in their region after World War II and doing their best to expand and enhance that presence wherever and however possible. In 1940 federal grants had accounted for 14 percent of total state revenues in the South; by 1955 that figure had risen to 20 percent, which was 40 percent higher than the national average. Whenever possible this federal money was used to improve the region's infrastructure with an eye to encouraging economic growth. Perhaps William Faulkner exaggerated just a bit when he declared in 1953, "Our economy is the federal government," but his words certainly suggested where the South seemed to be heading.[21]

Because state and local representatives in the South hoped to rake in as much federal money as possible without putting up any more local revenue than was absolutely necessary, they typically reserved their greatest enthusiasm for programs where funding came with few strings—or matching requirements—attached. When resentful northern politicians whose states had largely financed the construction of their own infrastructures objected to Washington's role in subsidizing the South's modernization, powerful and cagey southern leaders like Senate Majority Leader Lyndon B. Johnson of Texas managed to keep the money flowing southward by avoiding a specific regional focus while simply earmarking assistance programs for states and communities most in need of economic help. Because the South accounted for so many of these, the region continued to receive a disproportionate share of federal aid.[22]

The southern states also enjoyed a substantial boost from cold war military expansion in the region. Here again politically astute southern congressional perennials used their seniority and skill to transform the nation's least democratic region into the arsenal of American democracy. No southern politician proved more adept at maximizing the local bang of the defense buck than Congressman L. Mendel Rivers of South Carolina, who used his position on the House Armed Services Committee to, as one journalist put it, "transmogrify Charleston into a microcosm of military industrial civilization." For his district alone Rivers procured both air and naval bases, a missile maintenance center, a naval shipyard, a submarine training station, a naval hospital, a mine warfare center, a Coast Guard station, and the Sixth Naval District headquarters. Not surprisingly defense contractors McDonnell-Douglas, Avco, General Electric, and Lockheed all opened plants in Rivers's district while he chaired the committee. Some guessed that as much as one-third of the income and half the employment of his constituents was defense related. Across the river in Georgia, Representative Carl Vinson worked with powerful Senator Richard B. Russell to bring in fifteen military installations and make the U.S. Defense Department the state's largest employer.[23]

Primarily because of the sheer number of military bases it boasted, the South led the nation in defense salary expenditures by the mid-1950s. The nondefense jobs generated by southern military installations fell primarily in the lower-paying service sector, however. The region lagged behind California and other areas in the value of typical defense contracts, with a large portion of the South's production contracts centering on such rudimentary items as food, textiles, tobacco, and coal rather than high-technology, high-dollar necessities purchased from suppliers elsewhere in the nation. Even so, the military and civilian salaries paid by the federal government accounted by themselves for roughly one in every ten dollars of personal income in the South in 1955. Defense

Ft. Benning, Georgia, 1960s. Courtesy of Georgia Archives, Vanishing Georgia Collection (Mus 027), Atlanta, Georgia.

expenditures were primarily responsible for the fact that by 1960 the South provided only 12 percent of all federal tax revenue but received 25 percent of all federal spending. The federal government accounted for more than 20 percent of income growth in Mississippi from 1952 to 1962 and for at least 10 percent or more of such growth in Texas, Alabama, Georgia, Florida, North Carolina, and Virginia.[24]

Offered ostensibly as a means of assuring the speedy movement of troops across the national expanse, the Federal Highway Defense Act of 1956 triggered a profusion of interstate highways in the region. Atlanta and other cities that were located at the juncture of two or three of these superhighways stood to benefit enormously, of course. So, too, however, did remote and formerly well-nigh inaccessible areas of the South. Now southbound manufacturers eager to escape the higher taxes and greater likelihood of unionization in large urban locations could fan out across a countryside brimming with eager, docile, fresh-off-the-farm workers, not to mention grateful local officials offering free land and buildings and promising minimal taxation and interference with their community's new industrial benefactors.

By taking cheap electric power into the rural countryside, federal programs like the Rural Electrification Administration and the Tennessee Valley Authority further encouraged the dispersion of southern industry. In the early 1960s more manufacturing jobs were appearing annually outside than within the region's metropolitan areas. Between 1963 and 1965, 80 percent of new manufacturing jobs in Tennessee were created in rural counties; in Virginia the figure was 66 percent. By 1969 nearly 40 percent of the industrial plants in ten southern states (excluding Texas, Oklahoma, and Kentucky) were operating in rural or small-town settings; for South Carolina the figure was 61 percent.[25]

The sheer number of plants dotting the rural landscape was considerably more impressive than most of the plants themselves, however. Leaders of the region's small county-seat towns were managing to fill some of the void left by a rapidly constricting agricultural base with garment factories or other exceedingly low-wage, low-value-added operations. Yet in terms of overall economic significance, and ultimately political significance as well, the real growth momentum in the postwar South had clearly shifted by the end of the 1950s to larger urban areas, with their growing concentrations of new, better-paying industries, such as chemicals, electrical machinery, transportation equipment, and fabricated metals. On the eve of World War II only one in ten southerners had lived in cities larger than 10,000, as compared to one in three nationally. For the first time, however, during the 1940s southern cities larger than 10,000 people had begun to grow faster than those that were smaller. The metropolitan populations of Miami and Tampa had nearly doubled, while Dallas–Fort Worth swelled by 67 percent, Houston by 58 percent, and Atlanta by 51 percent.[26]

Spurred by defense spending and expanding consumer markets, bigger cities offered more and better jobs to people who saw no future either in staying on the farm or in the stagnant small towns whose economies were still dependent on farming. With the urban South's new industries, which were likely to be branch plants of major national firms, came executive, managerial, and high-level production personnel who were well educated and relatively well paid. Urban growth also meant attractive opportunities in wholesale and retail trade—which, with some 1.5 million new jobs between 1940 and 1960, represented the South's fastest growing employment category—as well as law, finance, and an expanding government sector. The 418,000 new government jobs created across the region between 1940 and 1960 represented nearly twice the total for the low-wage apparel industry. By 1960 four in ten southerners pursued some white-collar occupation. If there was a better life to be had, the city—the real city, not just a dusty town dreamily aspiring to be one—was the place to find it. Although Arkansas, Mississippi, and the Carolinas still lagged behind, by 1960 the South had become a region with more urban than rural residents, and most of these lived in larger cities. Metropolitan Houston, Dallas, and Atlanta now boasted at least a million residents each, and a dozen more cities had surpassed half a million.[27]

The postwar South's economic and demographic transformation from rural to urban foreshadowed a corresponding shift in political momentum. At the end of the war antiquated systems of election and representation, sometimes dating back to the turn of the century or earlier, still assured that political power resided in the country rather than the city. Georgia's outrageously inequitable county-unit system amounted to a miniaturized and seriously skewed version of the electoral college, in which elections were decided not by the popular vote but by the number of "unit" votes a candidate received. Even the tiniest of the state's 159 counties was accorded two unit votes in statewide races, while the largest wielded only six. Thus in 1960, taken together, voters in the state's three smallest counties, with a combined population of less than 7,000, effectively had as much say in electing the governor as the more than 556,000 residents of Fulton County, where Atlanta was located. The county-unit system explained why a self-styled rustic like Eugene Talmadge had been elected governor of Georgia four times while bragging that he had never campaigned in a county with a streetcar in it and why he invited rural Georgians to join him on the porch of the governor's mansion for a communal urination on any Atlanta "city slicker" foolish enough to come in range. No southern state had anything directly comparable to the county-unit system, but several, including Alabama and Tennessee, maintained constitutions whose antiurban apportionment plans reflected conditions as they had existed more than a half century earlier.[28]

With political influence so decentralized, much of the real power in southern politics at the middle of the twentieth century still resided with what Ralph McGill called "a certain type, small-town rich man," who, depending on where he lived, owned "the gin, the turpentine works, the cotton warehouses" or "the tobacco warehouses." Typically he was not only a director of the bank, but also owned the area's largest store, where most of the locals went for "fertilizer, plows, machinery, food, fencing, seeds, patent medicines, poultry and livestock." As often as not either he or a relative operated the town's automobile agency as well. With his thumb on the flow of credit, the small-town rich man "knew the financial predicament of every man in his section of the county," information that he did not hesitate to use or act upon when he needed local political contests to go a certain way.[29]

The small-town rich man also knew his state's senators personally, and as a close friend of his congressman he could, if so disposed, use his pull in Washington to get someone a job or another such favor. Needless to say, he always had the ear of the governor, perhaps because he seemed to have a knack for contributing to the right candidate, although in close races he was not above writing a check to both contestants. No decisions about patronage in his county were final without his approval, and he either "advised" or simply "selected" the men who represented the county in the legislature. His politics were generally racist and reactionary but always consummately self-interested and aimed primarily at preserving a status quo from which he benefited quite handsomely. In South Carolina, State Senator Edgar Brown and House Speaker Solomon Blatt of rural Barnwell County were the kingpins of the "Barnwell Ring," which jealously guarded the planting, textile, and banking interests in their area while maintaining a virtual stranglehold on state politics for more than a generation. On his own the small-town rich man might have seemed like little more than a big fish in a small pond, but multiplied by several hundred such ponds these men had a great deal to say about what went on in the big pond that was southern politics at the middle of the twentieth century.[30]

One of the first indications that the imbalance of political power in the South might be shifting away from these long-entrenched local kingpins had come when World War II veterans in several states came home demanding more opportunity and better government and rallied to the banner of political reform in what quickly became known as "GI revolts." In Hot Springs, Arkansas, Sid McMath, a highly decorated Marine officer who would soon claim the governorship, led a campaign to oust an entrenched political ring controlled by local gambling interests. In 1946 veteran J. Strom Thurmond won the South Carolina gubernatorial race by promising to modernize government and schools and bring new jobs to the Palmetto State. In Augusta, Georgia, veterans spearheaded the Independent League for Good Government's ouster of the "Cracker Party," a machine headed by state and local political boss Roy Harris. With the support of fellow veterans DeLesseps S. Morrison succeeded in ousting machine politician Robert Maestri as mayor of New Orleans in 1946, and in Tennessee former GIs lent crucial support to Gordon Browning, who captured the governorship, and Estes Kefauver, who won a U.S. Senate seat. The Browning-Kefauver victories came as the result of a revolt against the vast political machine of E. H. Crump, which was centered in Memphis but statewide in its influence. These political uprisings turned violent in a number of Tennessee counties and communities, such as Athens, where the "Battle of Athens" featured a shootout between veterans and local law enforcement officers.[31]

Such incidents underscored the determination of returning veterans to change the way things were done in state and local politics and government, but the motivation for their insurgency was hardly as radical as the accompanying fireworks sometimes made it seem. Against the backdrop of its Operation Dixie organizing push, the CIO had supported certain veteran slates, such as the Browning-Kefauver challenge in Tennessee, but among the local citizenry and many veterans themselves, an affiliation with organized labor was not always a plus. The veterans' demands for more job opportunities quickly ignited a renewed and expanded commitment to recruiting new and more dynamic industries that offered more attractive, better-paying jobs. Labor union leaders also called for higher wages and improved working conditions, but growth-oriented GI reformers understood that most potential employers were eyeing the South in the first place precisely because they wanted to avoid union pressure and potential disruption of the workplace.

In 1946 Alabama congressional candidate and veteran Laurie C. Battle defeated the CIO's candidate, Luther Patrick, by vowing to fight the labor unions with as much ferocity as he claimed to have mowed down Japanese soldiers with his machine-gun. His opponents charged that Battle's only real "battles" were fought with the typewriter he used as an army clerk, but he made good on his promises by voting for every antilabor measure that came along during the next eight years. In North Carolina congressional candidate Thurmond Chatham, a veteran and wealthy industrialist, committed himself to "more business in government and less government in business" and charged that opponent John

H. Folger's ties to the CIO put him "on the side of those who would bring all wheels of industry to a halt."[32]

The pro-business, development- and efficiency-oriented political philosophy of the reformist veterans marked them as what historian Bruce Schulman called the postwar South's "New Whigs." Rather than reach out directly to those in the lower economic strata, the New Whigs stressed the trickle-down effect of economic modernization as the ultimate solution to southern social ills. In this sense their thinking largely foreshadowed what political scientists Earl and Merle Black would describe some forty years later as "the reigning political philosophy of the new southern [white] middle-class," with "its emphasis on low rates of taxation, minimal regulation of business, and resolute opposition to unions and redistributive welfare programs for the have-nots and have-littles." (This connection was fitting because the political odyssey of the first postwar generation of Democratic politicians would see them go on to embrace the ascendant Republicanism that held sway in the South by the 1980s.) This is not to say that at the end of the 1940s the veterans were simply serving up more of the same old standpatism that had been so much a staple of southern politics. Like the business progressivism that had emerged after World War I, the modernizing reform ethos of the late 1940s acknowledged that expanded public investment in education, health, and infrastructure would be necessary to achieve more rapid and beneficial industrial and commercial growth.[33]

Some of the benefits of initiatives in these areas eventually made their way down to black southerners, but regardless of how displeased they were with the status quo in other respects, the politically insurgent white veterans of World War II generally showed no particular interest in challenging the fundamentals of the racial status quo. The veterans who spearheaded the Independent League for Good Government in Augusta, Georgia, spoke for many of their reform-minded peers across the South when they swore that they stood for "honesty, decency, and clean government" but "bowed to no one in the love for and loyalty to the traditions of the South." Elsewhere, pro-business veteran congressional candidate Thurmond Chatham insisted that it was the South's "natural social segregation" that allowed "each of the two races to live side by side comfortably."[34]

On the other hand, veterans or not, by and large the new pro-business leaders who entered southern politics after the war at least offered recently reenfranchised black voters more respect and less race-baiting

and thus proved a much more palatable option than the incendiary dem-
agogues they had known far too long and all too well. For black voters in
Georgia determined to cast a ballot for governor in 1946, between James
V. Carmichael, a former Bell bomber plant executive who simply swore
to uphold segregation if elected, and Eugene Talmadge, who threatened
physical harm if they even tried to vote, the choice was so clear as to be
no choice at all. Likewise, for the rising, growth-oriented white middle class, the need for more responsible, businesslike leadership simply
ran counter to the wild-eyed racist rants of a Talmadge or a Theodore
G. Bilbo, whose crude, embarrassing behavior was hardly suggestive of
a state with its eye on the future.

Elected lieutenant governor in 1952, North Carolina's Luther
H. Hodges became governor when incumbent William B. Umstead died
in 1954, and he won the office outright two years later. A self-proclaimed
"Businessman in the Statehouse," Hodges made industrial development
"with all its advantages to the people and the state…the number one
goal of my administration." Though he made no secret of his opposition
to the *Brown* decision, Hodges toned down his rhetoric when he began
to fear it might be undermining his industrial recruitment efforts. Columnist Ralph McGill reported in 1959 that when industrial executives
who had tentatively decided to locate a plant in Alabama decided to
visit Governor John Patterson to ask about the state's schools, Patterson
had vowed without hesitation to close them all rather than see them
integrated. Rethinking their decision, the executives eventually chose a
North Carolina site after Governor Hodges assured them that his state's
schools would not only remain open but would receive a boost in funding. Rupert Vance observed quite aptly in 1955, "The dominant psychology of the South is no longer agrarian; it is Chamber of Commerce."
Friendly to business but hostile to organized labor, committed to better government without bigger taxes, still preferring segregation but
squeamish about racial agitation and violence, the South's urban elites
were ultimately more attuned to the upbeat rhetoric of progress than
the angry rearguard propaganda of the Citizens Councils that often still
held sway in the small towns of the countryside.[35]

In fact, one of the principal factors distinguishing city from town
in the South at the end of the 1950s was a pervasive boosterism that
had even crept into what Erskine Caldwell called "wealthy, urban, large-
membership churches," supplanting the old evangelical fervor still common among worshippers in smaller, rural churches. Ministers "make

use of the name of God sparingly, if at all, from the pulpit" in these "modernist," big-city churches, Caldwell observed, noting sarcastically, "Instead of threatening sinners with the wrath of God, a cautious and perceptive pastor will offend no one, and at the same time, endear himself to the congregation, by recommending serenity as...the ideal way to obtain a comfortable religious feeling."[36]

A North Carolina pastor of just such a persuasion, whose fast-growing flock numbered more than a thousand well-heeled worshippers, boasted that, owing to his fund-raising prowess, his church had not only gobbled up surrounding property but was now building a new educational wing and a nursery. "Surplus funds," meanwhile, were under the supervision of an "investment committee," which favored low-income housing units that, whether for "Negro or white," offered "about the best yield obtainable these days." Having to evict tenants was "unfortunate," but "something that has to be taken in stride when you're responsible for the safety and yield of money put into collection baskets in good faith by the congregation." Most of his members, after all, were "well to-do and many are wealthy" and "would be critical and disapproving if we made investments yielding only the ordinary five and six percent." Describing himself as "not only a go-getter but also a hurry-upper and a do-it-nower," the pastor was pursuing the presidency at two Baptist colleges, where his salary would be higher and his benefits fancier. For this the minister made no apology: "There's no reason why any man shouldn't accept the good things in life when they are put within his reach."[37]

Not everybody found the environment in these upscale houses of worship particularly welcoming. A furniture worker who attended services at one such church reported that he had been "stared at the whole time I was there," and even though he tried "to be friendly and nice...the people just acted like they didn't want to have nothin' to do with me cause I wasn't in their class." Such churches clearly catered more to those whose economic fortunes were on the upswing, for their religion, Caldwell explained, was more akin to the "'boosterism' of such businessmen's civic organizations as Kiwanis, Rotary, and the Junior Chamber of Commerce."[38]

Though he foreswore any desire for personal gain, the eloquent and charismatic North Carolinian Billy Graham came to epitomize the marriage of evangelical Protestantism and the ambition and acquisitiveness of the rapidly expanding urban white middle class. From his beginnings after World War II as a youth organizer and proselytizer against juvenile delinquency and communism, Graham had risen rapidly to national prominence as an evangelist, thanks in part to the favorable exposure afforded him by media magnates William Randolph Hearst, who tersely ordered his subordinates to "puff Graham," and Henry Luce, who put him on the cover of *Time*. Both men were impressed with Graham's ardor for capitalism. For Graham the cold war conflict between capitalism and communism was, quite simply, a "battle to the death" between "Christ and anti-Christ": "Either communism must die or Christianity must die." To individual capitalists Graham stressed the merits of having God as "a working partner" and posited a beneficial relationship between prayer and profits. His sentiments on labor-management conflicts came through clearly enough in his description of the Garden of Eden as a place with "no labor unions, no snakes, [and] no disease."[39]

In secular affairs it fell to elected officials to articulate the message of economic growth, good government, political conservatism, and moderate support for segregation. Yet it was hardly a secret that real power resided increasingly in the boardrooms and private clubs of the urban South's captains of commerce, industry, and finance. In a famous study of the Atlanta power structure in the early 1950s, Floyd Hunter identified forty people, only one of them female, as the city's real decision makers. Twenty-eight of the forty came from the highest echelons of the local commercial, industrial, and financial hierarchy, but only four held elected office. One member of the group, chamber of commerce president and future mayor Ivan Allen Jr., later admitted in his memoirs, "When you talked about the 'power structure' or the 'establishment' in Atlanta, you were really talking about the leaders of the top fifty or so businesses in the city." Much the same could be said of Dallas, where the Citizens Council, an organization of leading businessmen that antedated their segregationist counterpart, was the dominant voice in local politics and government. A similar pattern had also emerged in smaller cities from Oklahoma City to Charlotte.[40]

No individual better personified the South's new business-oriented, racially moderate urban leadership than Atlanta's William B. Hartsfield, who, as mayor from 1942 until 1961, solidified the city's reputation for the aggressive pursuit of economic growth coupled with fiscal responsibility and racial moderation. Hartsfield spearheaded an annexation campaign in 1952 that more than tripled Atlanta's size while bringing in 100,000 new residents. He also presided over the construction of a modern expressway system and the opening of several new parks. For all his visible manifestations of moderation, Hartsfield remained a segregationist, and neither facilities nor opportunities for blacks in Atlanta were anywhere near equal to those available to whites. Still, once the white primary went down, the always pragmatic mayor foresaw the powerful electoral potential of a large population of black voters, and he promised black leaders that if they could raise black registration from slightly less than seven thousand to ten thousand voters before the July 1946 primary election, he would listen to what they had to say about the city's programs and services. When they managed to more than triple black registration in less than eight weeks, making blacks more than a quarter of the Atlanta electorate, Hartsfield began working immediately to remove some of the city's barriers to black well-being and advancement.[41]

Building and sustaining biracial support soon became fundamental elements of Hartsfield's political strategy as he pushed an agenda of good government and continued growth. When he learned of an impending court order to desegregate the city's public golf courses in 1955, he managed to avoid an embarrassing clamor for closing the courses by having

Atlanta mayor William B. Hartsfield, 1952. Courtesy of Lane Brothers Photographers Photographic Collection, 1920–76, Special Collections, Georgia State University Library, Atlanta, Georgia.

The South and America since World War II

the order issued during the Christmas season, a time when white Atlantans were likely to be distracted and perhaps a bit mellowed by holiday good cheer. Thus Atlanta retained its reputation for racial moderation, a reputation that Hartsfield would reinforce by dubbing it "The City Too Busy to Hate." Whether this description was by any means accurate remained to be seen as the 1950s drew to a close, but no one was busier trying to make it seem so than William B. Hartsfield.[42]

Like Houston and Dallas, as one of the region's million-plus metropolitan centers, Hartsfield's Atlanta entered the 1960s poised to take its place as one of America's most dynamic large cities. Many of the South's smaller cities were booming as well. John Westbrook observed that investments in the oil, rubber, aluminum, and chemical industries had made Baton Rouge the nation's fastest growing city with over 100,000 people and, he believed, a place of such strategic importance that it could claim the dubious distinction of being Russia's "atomic target number one." At this point Baton Rouge was but one of a number of second-tier southern cities, including Charlotte, Raleigh, Richmond, and Oklahoma City, that were boasting median family incomes at or above the national average and populations in which college graduates were significantly better represented than in the nation at large. As the population profiles of these cities approached or surpassed the national norm, however, the gap between them and the remainder of their state's population only widened. In all of them median family incomes ranged from 20 to nearly 40 percent higher than the state norms, and median educational attainment ran from 15 to 33 percent higher.[43]

As economic momentum swung rapidly to the urban areas, pro-growth, image-conscious boosters and politicians were clearly looking to steer their cities into the nation's economic mainstream. With a long-awaited economic breakthrough finally seeming less like a dream than an actual possibility, although they would have been loath to admit it publicly, some urban spokesmen now seemed even to be pondering the unthinkable: if it meant jeopardizing a chance for further and more rapid growth, the price of maintaining Jim Crow at all costs might ultimately prove higher than they were willing to pay.

"If they are left to their own resources and given...local autonomy," the economist William H. Nicholls observed in 1960, "the South's cities can ameliorate the race problem as its semifeudalistic rural areas yet cannot." Nicholls's prediction rested on an exceedingly rosy assessment of white racial attitudes in an urban South where six years after *Brown*, save in Oklahoma City and a very few other scattered and limited cases, school segregation still survived largely unscathed. Beyond that, he also pointed to a big "if" indeed when he suggested that in order to "ameliorate the race problem" southern cities would have to enjoy "local autonomy" in the matter. At this point, the South's increasingly anachronistic but still powerful small-town rich men largely stood united and determined against any compromise that might undermine white supremacy, and the die-hard segregationists who still dominated Deep South legislatures seemed ready to shut down the schools statewide rather than see a single system integrated. The pragmatic moderates of the cities would soon have their work cut out for them, especially as the leaders of the civil rights movement adopted a new, more aggressive and confrontational strategy aimed at discrediting the very image of progress, order, and restraint that white urban leaders were working so hard to construct and maintain.[44]

4

"From a Thousand Streets in a Hundred Towns"

How the Civil Rights Movement "Overcame"

With so many white leaders now obviously intent on making their state or community look good in the eyes of potential employers and investors, civil rights leaders began to move toward a more direct approach that would grab bigger headlines and illustrate the moral injustice of Jim Crow more dramatically. Prior to the Montgomery boycott, polls had shown racial discrimination well down the list of concerns for most white Americans. Sensing that what he and his colleagues accomplished in Montgomery had not only pushed civil rights considerably farther up that list, but also "demonstrated a revolutionary change in the Negro's evaluation of himself," Rev. Martin Luther King Jr. believed the time was ripe for a broader, more aggressive campaign of mass action. Accordingly he and several other black ministers joined forces with veteran activists like Bayard Rustin and Ella Baker to form an "indigenous, black-led organization" that could provide "a small disciplined group of non-violent volunteers" capable of inspiring community protests and black voter registration activity across the South. This new group officially became the Southern Christian Leadership Conference (SCLC) in August 1957, and though its members represented a variety of perspectives, its governing board was dominated by Baptist ministers who pursued a somewhat autocratic approach under the leadership of Reverend King. Fusing Christian doctrine with militant nonviolence, King promised whites to meet "physical force with soul force" and awaken their "moral consciousness" to the reality and injustice of racial segregation.[1]

Despite the SCLC's ostensible desire to avoid competition with the NAACP, relations between the two groups soon grew strained. NAACP leaders clearly had the SCLC newcomers in mind when they insisted, "We need only one national organization to speak for Negroes." For all that the NAACP had accomplished, however, younger African Americans in particular had shown growing impatience, especially after even the charismatic Dr. King's new SCLC struggled initially to gain traction against entrenched white resistance. Five years after the first *Brown* decree, less than 1 percent of the South's school-age black children attended integrated schools. Beyond that, although Congress had reaffirmed the Fifteenth Amendment's protection of black voting in the Civil Rights Act of 1957, after well-publicized voter registration drives by the NAACP and other groups, the number of southern blacks on the voter rolls had increased by only 3 percent between 1956 and 1960, and the approximately 4 million registered black voters in the region represented just 28 percent of its adult black population.[2]

Among the many African Americans, young and old, who were dismayed by the apparent loss of momentum on civil rights matters were four students at all-black North Carolina A & T College in Greensboro. Ezell Blair Jr., Franklin McCain, Joseph McNeil, and David Richmond had brooded about this state of affairs throughout their freshman year of 1959–60. With some encouragement from Ralph Johns, a local white storekeeper and NAACP member of Syrian descent, the four friends had decided to make something happen themselves by challenging the local Woolworth's refusal to serve blacks at its lunch counter. In the parlance of the day, Woolworth's, which was part of a national chain, was a "five and dime" or "novelty" store, offering a variety of less expensive merchandise. Its lunch counter was also downtown Greensboro's busiest daytime eating spot, where hungry white shoppers could dine on soups and sandwiches, including the ever-popular tuna melt, consisting of tuna salad topped with a slice of melted cheese. Black shoppers were welcome to spend their money on Woolworth's merchandise, but hungry or not, they were banned from eating at its lunch counter.

Determined to rectify this, the anxious but determined young collegians sat down and ordered coffee at the Greensboro Woolworth's counter on February 1, 1960. Although their actions would ultimately take on monumental significance, the black students' presence on the lunch counter stools initially brought only a polite refusal of service from the white manager and a sharp but somehow not so stinging rebuke from a black dishwasher, who informed the boys that "rabble-rousers" such as they were the reason blacks "can't get anyplace today." Later there were some scattered curses from whites, and finally some truly unexpected encouragement from two elderly white ladies who whispered, "You should have done this years ago." In the end the young men left, elated and proud of what they had done, and they were soon delighted to learn of their sudden, meteoric rise in status among their fellow students, some twenty of whom joined them at the lunch counter the next day. In the days to come their numbers would grow steadily as even local white college students joined the movement, which would eventually spill over to lunch counters at S. H. Kress and Walgreens and then to other Greensboro dining venues.[3]

As the sit-in strategy spread rapidly across North Carolina and the rest of the South, white hostility to sit-in participants came through in a variety of responses, ranging from smoldering, angry silence to curses and racial epithets to showers of hot soup and scalding coffee to direct physical assault. Sit-ins at southern retail outlets of major national chains like Woolworth's soon drew sympathy protests and pickets at stores and company offices in other locations. It would not be long before the threat of boycotts and bad publicity nationwide began to make the price of respecting Jim Crow in Dixie suddenly seem potentially too steep. Fretful corporate financial officers could not overlook reports that Woolworth's profits in Greensboro were off by 50 percent for the year. When both Woolworth's and S. H. Kress finally opened their lunch counters to blacks in July 1960, it was clear that direct action had the potential to generate the kind of economic and political pressure that could topple Jim Crow much faster than any legal brief or even a court order. The Greensboro sit-ins had propelled the civil rights movement into what would be a decidedly more dynamic and dramatic phase.[4]

In April 1960 Ella Baker, who had grown tired of the "cult of personality" that had arisen in the SCLC around Dr. King, presided over the formation of another new group, geared toward younger blacks who had been chafing under the tactical restraints imposed by both the SCLC and the NAACP. The Student Nonviolent Coordinating Committee (SNCC) quickly showed itself ready to adopt more confrontational and sometimes controversial strategies to speed up the pace of racial change, and its members eventually played a key role in energizing lower-income blacks who were often uncomfortable with the NAACP's decidedly middle-class makeup and orientation. After SNCC came on the scene, the list of sit-in targets expanded to include theaters, drugstores, and drive-ins. The movement soon spun off tactics such as

Jackson, Mississippi, sit-in, 1963. The woman seated at the right is Anne Moody. Bettman/Corbis.

"wade-ins" at swimming pools, which frequently led simply to the pools being closed to all swimmers and sometimes even filled in and covered with cement.[5]

There were also "pray-ins" at all-white churches, but the achievements of these were generally token or temporary at best. Although some would-be agents of integrated worship received death threats, the face-to-face response was more typically a polite but definitive rejection. Most southern whites simply declined to acknowledge the contradiction between their professed fidelity to the egalitarian teachings of Jesus Christ and their refusal to put them into practice in their own houses of worship. In the mid-1950s Hodding Carter's openness to integrating St. James Episcopal Church in Greenville, Mississippi, cost him and a like-minded associate reelection to the vestry. Later when the issue came up at Greenville's Presbyterian Church, a young man in favor of admitting blacks to worship services reportedly asked his agitated mother, "What do you think Jesus Christ would do if he were standing at the door of the First Presbyterian Church?" when a black would-be worshipper arrived. "I know exactly what he would do," she replied without hesitation, "and he would be wrong." Another, perhaps apocryphal but still entirely plausible anecdote had the leader of a black delegation that had just been refused entry to Sunday services at a large urban Baptist church asking one of the white deacons, "Brother, don't you believe we'll all be together in heaven?" only to hear in response, "Yes, but we prefer to wait until them."[6]

The stilted civility that met many a black delegation to a white church was eminently preferable to the way some whites responded to the "Freedom Riders," who made their way south from Washington, D.C., in April 1961 to test the U. S. Supreme Court's recent extension of its earlier ban on segregation in commercial interstate travel to include all related terminal facilities, including lobbies, restaurants, and rest rooms. The idea for this exceedingly dangerous journey had come from the Congress of Racial Equality (CORE), which had actually been staging direct-action protests since the 1940s, and a number of the young SNCC members had responded to the call for volunteers. The Freedom Riders vowed that, when arrested, they would remain in jail rather than pay their fines, hoping not only to generate public opinion pressure but, by filling the local jails, to make such segregation simply too expensive and unwieldy to maintain. These "sit-ins on wheels" went fairly smoothly until May 9, when the riders reached Rock Hill, South Carolina, where ducktailed white hoodlums in leather jackets reacted to future Georgia congressman John Lewis's attempt to use the "whites only" restroom by punching and kicking him bloody. Police were on hand but took no action until some of the women in the group were knocked down.

Rock Hill proved to be a picnic compared to what awaited the Freedom Riders in Alabama. In Anniston angry whites armed with blackjacks, tire irons, and chains surrounded the first bus. When the vehicle's slashed tires went flat a few miles farther on, a pursuing mob firebombed it. Local white medical personnel refused treatment to the injured, and those cut by flying glass or overcome by smoke were finally rescued by an armed caravan of cars organized by Rev. Fred Shuttlesworth of Birmingham. When the second bus arrived in Anniston, a white male boarded and began beating the riders, leaving one near death and with permanent brain damage.[7]

Birmingham's Trailways bus terminal was only a short distance from the office of the city's openly racist police commissioner, Eugene "Bull" Connor, but not a single policeman was in sight when a mob of white toughs grabbed the Freedom Riders and began beating them with anything they could find. Investigators later discovered that Connor himself had promised local Klansmen fifteen minutes to do as they wished with the demonstrators before the police arrived. It was some time before the group could find a driver willing to take them on to Montgomery. When they finally did, their police car and helicopter escorts simply faded away as they reached the Birmingham city limits.

Upon arrival at the Montgomery terminal, what had seemed initially like a ghost town was suddenly alive with whites pouring out of buildings, and true to the tradition of Alabama hospitality, a gang of whites was soon beating the riders with pipes and baseball bats to the delight of onlookers yelling, "Git 'em! Git 'em!" As he lay in a pool of blood suffering from a concussion, John Lewis was handed a state court injunction forbidding mixed-race travel in Alabama. Urged by angry bystanders to "kill the nigger-loving son of a bitch," the mob beat white Freedom Rider James Zwerg mercilessly, kicking out his teeth and injuring his spinal cord. Zwerg later denied that he had done anything heroic, especially in comparison to "the black man who probably saved my life": "This man in coveralls, just off of work, happened to walk by as my beating was going on and said 'Stop beating that kid. If you want to beat someone, beat me.' And they did. He was still unconscious when I left the hospital. I don't know if he lived or died." When the police finally showed up, it took them an hour to quell the violence, but an unrepentant Montgomery police commissioner made it clear that he and his forces had "no intention of standing guard for a bunch of troublemakers" who had invaded their peaceful city.[8]

Although John F. Kennedy's phone call to Coretta Scott King when her husband was jailed in Atlanta in 1960 had won him some additional black support in the 1960 presidential election, he had otherwise shown relatively little interest in the civil rights cause up to this point. Several members of the Kennedy administration saw the Freedom Rides as a public relations disaster in light of their ongoing diplomatic efforts to shore up America's credentials for free world leadership. The president's initial response had been "Tell them to call it off. Stop them!" Attorney General Robert F. Kennedy even wondered if the Freedom Riders had "the best interest of their country at heart." The attorney general might better have raised the same question about the lawless mobs who brutalized and terrorized the activists at every stop in Alabama, but apparently fearing the loss of crucial southern support in Congress and in the 1964 presidential election looming three years down the road, he never did.[9]

Even as his aides urged black leaders to observe a "cooling off" period before attempting to complete the Freedom Rides through Mississippi and Louisiana, President Kennedy himself revealed little but hesitation and angst in trying to get southern whites to moderate their behavior. Finally, the Kennedy administration made a pact with Senator James Eastland and Governor Ross Barnett of Mississippi that the riders would not be abused physically but simply arrested and jailed, this despite the fact that the demonstrators were clearly acting within their legal rights. More than 350 Freedom Riders went to jail in Mississippi, many of them spending part of their summer in the state's notorious Parchman Penitentiary. Winonah Beamer, a student at Central State University in Ohio, refused CORE's offer of bail, spending four of her six months of incarceration in Parchman, where she was permitted no visitors, allowed to write only one letter a week, and given ten minutes outside her cell twice a week to shower. When some of the imprisoned Freedom Riders persisted in singing despite warnings not to do so, they were denied toilet paper and given only one meal a day.[10]

The Freedom Rides quickly thrust SNCC and CORE into the national spotlight and gave added momentum and a sense of purpose to what was now a full-fledged student movement. Hoping to channel civil rights efforts away from direct-action protests, the Kennedy administration promised funding and federal protection (far more than was ever delivered) for initiatives to register more black voters. If administration officials truly hoped that voter registration campaigns would prove less violent and confrontational than direct protests against segregation, they were soon disappointed. Trying to persuade uneducated, impoverished blacks to present themselves before a glowering registrar in rural backwater counties dominated by antagonistic whites accustomed to having their way could test the commitment of even the most zealous activist. The difficulty they faced actually went far deeper than the mere matter of getting blacks to register, however. Young SNCC and CORE workers soon realized that, as SNCC's Charles Sherrod put it, they were "engaged in a psychological battle for the minds of the enslaved." Regardless of his socioeconomic standing, exhorting a black southerner to challenge a system he had accommodated so long as a simple matter of survival amounted to, as one Voter Education Project worker put it, "demanding a confession that his life up to now had been lived upside down." Though they sometimes grew frustrated with the reluctance of black southerners to stand up to local whites, the civil rights activists learned quickly from stories such as that of Louis Allen, who had agreed to testify against a Mississippi politician who had murdered a black man for trying to register, provided he was given federal protection. Despite the Kennedy administration's promises of support, the Justice Department not only refused protection but informed the local authorities of Allen's request. After a severe beating by a deputy sheriff, Allen then agreed to become a defense witness in the case, but he was nonetheless a marked man who went to his death at the hands of parties unknown in 1964.[11]

If poor blacks trying to register had precious little hope of legal protection for their lives or property, they were even more vulnerable to the kind of economic coercion practiced by the Citizens Councils. White creditors often adopted the stance that "if you can afford to vote, you don't need a loan," and suffice it to say, showing up at the registrar's office did little to enhance one's prospects for getting—or keeping—a job. Although it might seem that the South's most down-and-out blacks had little to lose, those who had moved up the ladder a bit were another matter. Charles Sherrod grew particularly impatient with black educators "who refuse to think further than a new car, a bulging refrigerator, and an insatiable lust for more than enough of what we call leisure."[12]

All of these obstacles confronted workers in SNCC's Southwest Georgia Project in November 1961 when they launched the "Albany Movement," demanding desegregation of public facilities and transportation and an end to racially discriminatory hiring in this predominantly rural area's largest city. The Albany Movement spawned a series of mass protests that saw five hundred demonstrators arrested during the first month. At that point, the local movement's leader, Dr. William Anderson, decided to invite Reverend King to Albany. Though the two were long-time friends, King accepted only reluctantly and with no apparent intention of becoming personally involved in the demonstrations. When he gave in to requests that he take part in one of the protests, King was one of two hundred blacks arrested, however, and he declined bond, vowing to spend "Christmas in jail" and asking "thousands to join me."[13]

King's arrest seemed to reinvigorate the Albany effort, but when local blacks negotiated the release of King and other demonstrators while securing little else in the bargain, the movement seemed to fizzle. King's return for his trial and his subsequent incarceration sparked new excitement, leading one of the growing number of his critics in SNCC to concede that despite skepticism about King's tactics and style, "one has to admit that he can cause more hell to be raised by being in jail one night than anyone else could if they bombed city hall." Local whites realized this as well, and after an anonymous figure paid King's bond without his consent, the charismatic civil rights champion remarked that this was the first time that he had been "thrown out of jail."[14]

King would be jailed in Albany yet again in August 1962 for leading a prayer meeting in front of city hall, but with more than a thousand fellow protestors already behind bars, leaders of the Albany Movement decided to forgo further organized demonstrations. Not only had Police Chief Laurie Pritchett disproven the old maxim "They can't arrest everybody" by farming his prisoners out to jails in surrounding counties, but by making the arrests with restraint, at least until those arrested were out of public view, he had also denied the nonviolent demonstrators the newsworthy violent response they needed to gain widespread public sympathy for their cause. The real object of such nonviolent protests, King would later admit, was to "precipitate violence" by making "people inflict violence on you." By refusing to go for the bait, Pritchett had both outwitted King and revealed that, without the high drama of a morality play in which the denied and downtrodden were openly assaulted and blatantly abused by their oppressors, the simple day-to-day reality of racial discrimination itself was insufficiently compelling to generate or sustain widespread public outrage against it.[15]

Pritchett had been what Calvin Trillin called a "smart" segregationist, but fortunately for King and the civil rights movement in general, there was an abundance of the other kind, particularly in Alabama, which, according to Trillin, would prove to be "world headquarters for dumb segs." If the propensity of many white Alabamans to turn what might have been minimally dramatic encounters into lead stories on the evening news was not fully evident in Alabama's brutal and lawless response to the Freedom Riders, it would surely become so in 1963. George C. Wallace, the self-described "fightin' little judge" from Barbour County, used his January inaugural address as governor to set the tone for the year's events in the state. In his remarks the new governor drew a "line in the dust," tossing "the gauntlet before the feet of tyranny" and vowing, "Segregation now, segregation tomorrow, segregation forever." Anything but dumb himself, Wallace knew by then that neither he nor anyone else could save Jim Crow, but he was counting on the fact that the majority of the sovereign electorate of Alabama (which, all told, included less than a quarter of the black adult population at that point) knew no such thing. When it came to the fine art of cynical, reckless manipulation of the race issue, Wallace would soon put more than a century's worth of his southern political predecessors to shame.[16]

Shame appeared to be in short supply among white Alabamans in 1963, however, especially in Birmingham, where there had been more than fifty reports of bombings directed at African Americans since 1947. According to Rev. Fred Shuttlesworth, the city was "very close to hell itself" for black people, who hardly had more to fear from the local KKK and its murderous thugs than from the city's police department, overseen with Gestapo-like ruthlessness and cruelty by Commissioner Bull Connor, who had engineered the beating of the Freedom Riders in 1961. Wallace knew Connor's confrontational style was good for his own political career, which depended on maintaining his image as an overmatched but game segregationist David standing up to the bullying integrationist federal Goliath, and in the spring of 1963 he embraced Connor's mayoral candidacy with gusto.[17]

When, Wallace's endorsement notwithstanding, Connor was defeated by a reluctant moderate, Albert Boutwell, many local black leaders hailed the dawning of "a new day" in Birmingham. Fearing that further demonstrations at that point might undermine recent gains, more established local black leaders hung back in early April 1963, when King and his associates launched a new series of protests against segregation and discrimination. King's arrest for violating a court order against further demonstrations became the premise for his famous "Letter from Birmingham Jail," which explained why blacks could wait no longer to gain their rights as Americans. Yet even King's skillfully choreographed response to his incarceration failed to replenish the thinning ranks of protestors. With the media losing interest, the prospect of total failure loomed large until some of King's subordinates began recruiting hundreds of black teenagers for a massive "Children's Crusade" that soon filled the streets and then the jails with what seemed like an inexhaustible flow of young bodies. With Governor Wallace fulminating against the communist "agitators, integrationists and others" who wanted to "destroy the freedom and liberty of Americans everywhere," Connor, who had thus far shown what was for him uncharacteristic restraint, seemed to snap. In what would prove to be one of the most crucially wrongheaded decisions of the civil rights era, the enraged commissioner brought in police dogs and rolled out the fire hoses in a desperate, determined effort to "get the niggers off the streets." The result was some of the most dramatic photographs and news footage the civil rights movement would produce. When one of the hoses slammed fiery civil rights champion Fred Shuttlesworth into the wall of the Sixteenth Street Baptist Church and he was carted away in an ambulance, Connor could only lament that he had not witnessed the event personally, adding, "I wish they'd carried him away in a hearse."[18]

Shuttlesworth had gone to the area to try to calm blacks who had started to retaliate against police brutality with bottles and bricks. With no end to the daily confrontations in sight, cooler white heads than Connor's saw a city in economic free fall and perhaps even on the brink of a race war. The result, on May 10, was a negotiated settlement that promised a halt to the protests in exchange for assurances that downtown businesses would be desegregated and hire more black employees within the next three months.

Men trying to avoid high-pressure spray from fire hoses during a demonstration in Birmingham, Alabama, 1963. Bettman/Corbis.

The Birmingham campaign marked the most significant local victory of the civil rights movement to that point, but its immediate impact on race relations in the area was anything but salutary. Just two days after the settlement was finalized, the explosion of two bombs, one at the home of King's brother and the other at the Gaston Motel, which had been King's headquarters, triggered a night of violence by hundreds of angry blacks who had just exited some of the bars in the area. Governor Wallace blamed the outbreak on the "so-called biracial negotiating groups of appeasers" who had signed an agreement with "mobsters" like King and on the Kennedy administration, which had given "sympathy and tacit approval" to "Negro mobs." A week after the Birmingham accord was reached, a disgusted Wallace told President Kennedy by phone that King and Shuttlesworth were less interested in solving Birmingham's problems than in seeing "who could go to bed with the most nigger women."[19]

A few weeks later Wallace's tightly orchestrated "stand in the schoolhouse" door failed to prevent the integration of the University of Alabama, but it allowed him to cast himself as a hero for standing up to "the Kennedys." Meanwhile, at long last, John F. Kennedy was genuinely revulsed both by the blatant dishonesty and cynical politics of Wallace and his counterparts, such as Mississippi's Ross Barnett, not to mention the violent fruits of their reckless manipulation of white racial emotions. On the evening of June 11, the day that Wallace pulled his staged step-aside in Tuscaloosa, Kennedy made what was clearly his most impassioned address to date on the issue of civil rights, telling a national television audience that the country was confronting "a moral issue" every bit "as old as the Scriptures and...as clear as the Constitution itself." No longer could other Americans expect blacks to "be content with counsels of patience and delay." It was time for government at all levels to assure that "all Americans are...afforded equal rights and equal opportunities." To that end, he announced plans to ask Congress the following week to make a "commitment...to the proposition that race has no place in American life or law" by enacting a new civil rights bill "giving all Americans the right to be served in facilities which are open to the public—hotels, restaurants, theaters, retail stores, and similar establishments."[20]

Later that very evening, Mississippi civil rights leader Medgar Evers was shot from ambush while in his carport and died with his horrified wife and children looking on. Evers's murder only fueled growing public outrage that would actually make securing congressional action in behalf of racial justice less difficult than it might otherwise have been. Two and a half months later, on August 28, 1963, more than a quarter-million people, perhaps 20 percent of them white, gathered at the Lincoln Memorial during the March on Washington. The scene suggested that a great many Americans now shared Reverend King's dream that "one day this nation will rise up and live out the true meaning of its creed."[21]

Such a day still seemed a long way off in Alabama, however. Determined that the Kennedy administration would have to use troops to enforce court-ordered school integration in his state, on September 9, 1963, Governor Wallace called out the National Guard to prevent black students from entering schools in Mobile, Birmingham, and Tuskegee. As he anticipated, the president quickly federalized the Alabama Guard. Wallace had vowed, "We will never surrender," but with the state's guardsmen no longer answerable to him and the federal courts rejecting his every stall and subterfuge, he ultimately staged yet another orchestrated retreat, protesting bitterly, "I can't fight federal bayonets with my bare hands."[22]

Although Wallace had come out on the short end of two confrontations with the federal government over integration, his artful show of defiance had definitely boosted his political stock with Alabama whites. In stoking the anger of some of the state's and region's most zealous white supremacists, Wallace had also fostered an environment in which violence and bloodshed were less a cause for concern than an outright certainty. Historian Dan T. Carter observed that in his efforts to encourage racial extremists to create the public confrontations that he claimed integration would inevitably produce, Wallace had probably sought "disorder" rather than "bloodshed." Yet by inciting these single-minded "hate-mongers" for his own political purposes, the governor had kindled animosities whose temperature he could not control. On September 6, 1963, in the midst of the school integration crisis, even Wallace complained that society was "coming apart at the seams," although he blamed those who were trying to force integration on southern whites. "What this country needs," he declared, "is a few first-class funerals"—including "some political funerals, too."[23]

Wallace's menacing reference proved darkly prophetic slightly more than two months later, on November 22, when President Kennedy was assassinated in Dallas. It would be only a matter of days, however, before Alabama would reap the harvest of rage Wallace had helped to sow in his own backyard. On Sunday, September 15, an explosion at Birmingham's Sixteenth Street Baptist Church killed four young girls who were about to participate in a special 11 a.m. youth service. Doris Maddox recalled that although her own congregation felt the shudder from the bomb all the way over on Forty-Fifth Street, "we continued with church.... I guess we had got used to bombings." Even before the bodies of Addie Mae Collins, Denise McNair, Carole Robertson, and Cynthia Wesley were dug out of the rubble, Pastor John Haywood Cross had commandeered a fireman's bullhorn to encourage his congregation to be "forgiving, as Christ was forgiving." Cross was asking a lot, especially after two whites rode a motor scooter into a black neighborhood and shot and killed Virgil Ware, who was riding his bicycle with his brother. Shortly thereafter other white youths ignored a sheriff's department plea to cancel a pro-segregation motorcade and cruised the area where the bomb had exploded, blowing their horns in celebration. When some men and boys from the neighborhood began pelting the cars with rocks, police opened fire with shotguns, killing one sixteen-year-old with a blast in the back as he attempted to flee.[24]

Apparently a great many Americans agreed with Oregon senator Wayne Morse's assessment that the scenes from Birmingham would "disgrace" even such hellholes as "a Union of South Africa or a Portuguese Angola." Overall, there were four times as many civil rights protests recorded in 1963 as the year before. In the last seven months of the year, after millions of television viewers had seen Bull Connor's fire hoses and police dogs savaging young and old alike in Birmingham, more than 100,000 Americans had demonstrated in behalf of civil rights, and nearly 15,000 of them had been jailed as a result. Polls showed that after the Birmingham demonstrations and the violence they triggered, as many as 50 percent of all Americans believed civil rights was the nation's "most pressing problem," as compared to only 5 percent who had felt this way before the protests began.[25]

A great deal more blood would be spilled, but the events in Alabama in 1963 had galvanized American public and political opinion in behalf of civil rights as never before. President Kennedy's assassination would also provide powerful emotional leverage for Lyndon B. Johnson, who came to the presidency both committed to the ideal of racial equality and superbly equipped as a former Senate majority leader to see to it that Congress did the right thing in spite of itself. After months of cajoling, coercing, and political horse trading, Johnson made good on

Kennedy's pledge when he overcame a last-ditch filibuster by a bloc of southern senators. On July 2 he signed the Civil Rights Act of 1964, the most far-reaching civil rights legislation since Reconstruction, making it illegal to deny the use or enjoyment of any public accommodation or to discriminate in employment or the operation of any federal programs on the basis of race, sex, religion, or national origin. The bill also banned the unequal application of voter registration requirements and authorized the attorney general of the United States to file suit to force school desegregation. Although Johnson was proud and pleased, immediately after signing the bill into law, he remarked to an aide, "We have lost the South for a generation." By "we" Johnson meant the Democratic Party, and by "South" he meant white southerners. His observation was prophetic, even if it underestimated the long-term political price the Democrats would ultimately pay in the South for embracing the cause of civil rights.[26]

If Johnson had thought to get ahead of African American demands for equality with the passage of the Civil Rights Act, he failed to take full account of the new determination and sense of urgency that was driving the civil rights movement as younger, more militant organizers committed themselves to bringing both political and personal empowerment to the South's most deprived black residents. When they arrived in a community, SNCC workers had often sought the advice and support of older local NAACP leaders who, like Clarksdale, Mississippi, pharmacist Aaron Henry, were frequently middle-class black businessmen and professionals and therefore somewhat less vulnerable to white economic pressures. Yet through their persistent organizing efforts at the grassroots level, SNCC and its cohort ultimately brought into the movement a group of blacks who had thus far managed only to eke out a tenuous living as sharecroppers and day laborers, subject always to the white man's needs and whims, but never relinquishing their dreams that a better, more just existence was possible.

If it seemed that such people had little to lose, that little was also all they had. Up to the time she attended a "mass meeting" with SNCC organizers in August 1962, Fannie Lou Hamer's adult life in the Mississippi Delta had been one of unremitting toil after a childhood scarred by poverty and racial persecution. When she was eleven or twelve, her sharecropper parents had managed to purchase their own implements, livestock, and even a car, only to have a resentful white neighbor dash their hopes of self-sufficiency by poisoning all three of their mules and both their cows. Shortly after the death of the mother she adored, Hamer underwent surgery for a cyst in her stomach; later she discovered that she had also been given a hysterectomy and thus was sterilized without her consent.[27]

Fannie Lou Hamer claimed that until she heard SNCC workers tell a black audience of their constitutional rights, including the right to vote against politicians like the Delta's own Senator Eastland, who did their best to keep them in subjugation, she "had no idea that blacks were legally entitled to vote.... We didn't even know what was going on in the rest of the state even,...much less in other places." Yet when the organizers encouraged those at the meeting to try to register, Hamer was one of the first to volunteer, and she urged others to do the same. As the group began to sing freedom songs like "We Shall Overcome" and "This Little Light of Mine," she realized that SNCC workers "really wanted to change the world.... They wanted Blacks to have some say about their destiny." Although this commitment impressed Hamer tremendously, by this time she was, at the very least, already an activist-in-waiting. She had always believed that "hard as we have to work for nothing, there must be some way we can change things.... There must be something else."[28]

In the short run, Hamer's pursuit of "something else" came at the cost of her job as timekeeper on a plantation where she had begun as a sharecropper eighteen years earlier. After she refused to withdraw her voter registration application, she was also thrown off the plantation. Ten days later a hail of bullets struck the house where she was staying. She and her husband, "Pap," could find no employment anywhere around her hometown of Ruleville, and she was the target of constant threats and hurled obscenities. Their home was invaded by white intruders on more than one occasion, and in the crowning absurdity, she and Pap received a $9,000 water bill for a house that had no running water. Hamer had only six years of what passed for "formal" schooling for blacks in the Mississippi Delta in that era. Yet she went on to become an eloquent, compelling embodiment of a crusade that was now not only "for" the people but increasingly "of" the people as well.[29]

As inspiring as it might sound, this transition was troubling for some within the movement, as well as for many who supported it from the outside. SNCC organizer Bob Moses admitted that "Jackson [Mississippi] Negroes are embarrassed that Mrs. Hamer is representing them—she is too much a representative of the masses." Beyond that, impoverished and ill-educated black southerners like Hamer often came into the movement with an exceedingly straightforward, almost absolutist sense of right and wrong. Having experienced so much of the latter for so long, they were inclined to see any compromise with whites as either simply unreliable or a "sellout" by the movement's more established and economically secure leadership. This class-based difference in perspective on dealing with whites was more than apparent when Hamer, as part of a delegation from the Mississippi Freedom Democratic Party, an outgrowth of SNCC's Mississippi Project, traveled to the National Democratic Party convention in Atlantic City in August 1964. The MFDP cohort was there to challenge the seating of the all-white delegation chosen by Mississippi's regular Democratic organization, some of whose leaders had already expressed their outright hostility to the national party and its aims. As loyal Democrats, many of whom had been denied their right to vote their convictions in regular elections and all of whom had been excluded from the delegate-selection process, the MFDP's representatives argued that the state's convention seats rightly belonged to them. Ultimately this challenge simultaneously exposed and widened the fissures within the Democratic Party establishment and the civil rights establishment as well.[30]

Hamer's testimony before the convention's Credentials Committee was as emotionally riveting a first-person account of southern racial injustice and brutality as the era would produce. She shared the details of the threats and persecution she had endured simply for attempting to register to vote, and she graphically described the beating she had endured in a Winona, Mississippi, jail because of her voter registration efforts. According to Hamer, the beating had actually come at the hands of two black prisoners under the orders and supervision of state troopers. After her first assailant had worn himself out beating her and the second took the blackjack and continued the blows, Hamer "began to scream, and one white man got up and began to beat me on my head" in an effort to silence her. As she lay down on a bunk, writhing in pain under a hail of blows, Hamer's dress had "worked up high," and a white man walked over to pull her dress down, only then to pull it "back, back up." With perhaps half the room in tears by then and millions soon to be watching a replay on the evening news, Hamer declared, "All of this is on account of us wanting to register, to become first-class citizens and if the Freedom Democratic Party is not seated now, I question America, is this America, the land of the free and the home of the brave where we have to sleep with our telephones off of the hooks because our lives be threatened daily because we want to live as decent human beings, in America?" Afterward, weeping but obviously relieved, she explained, "I felt just like I was telling it from the mountain."[31]

Clearly Hamer's testimony instilled no such sense of exhilaration in an angry and frustrated Lyndon Johnson, who had tried desperately to keep it off the airwaves by staging an impromptu presidential press conference at the same time. Johnson saw the MFDP group's persistent demands for recognition at the convention as a mortal threat to any remaining hopes of holding on to southern white voters after passage of the Civil Rights Act of 1964, and he brought all manner of pressure against the MFDP group and its supporters. Dangling the number-two slot on the ticket before Minnesota senator Hubert H. Humphrey, the crafty Johnson dispatched him to negotiate with the insurgents. When Humphrey arrived, sweating profusely and clearly discomfited, Hamer recalled telling him, "Senator Humphrey, I know lots of people in Mississippi who have lost their jobs for trying to register to vote.... Now if you lose this job of vice-president because you do what is right, because you help the MFDP, everything will be all right. God will take care of you. But if you take it [the vice-presidential nomination] this way, why, you will never be able to do any good for civil rights, for poor people, for peace, or any of those things you talk about." This was hardly what Humphrey, who considered himself a civil rights pioneer dating back to the Truman era, wanted to hear, of course, and when he announced Johnson's token offer of two delegate seats to the MFDP contingent, he made it a point to inform the group that the president had said "he will not allow that illiterate woman [Hamer] to speak on the floor of the Democratic Convention."[32]

Before her disillusioning experience with Humphrey, Hamer had already suffered what she called "blow number one" when NAACP leader Roy Wilkins approached her with a condescension bordering on disdain to say, "You people have put your point across... [but] you don't know anything about politics. I [have] been in the business over twenty years.... Why don't you pack up and go home?" They may not have understood "politics" as Wilkins defined it, but when, despite the efforts of Reverend King and other civil rights leaders to persuade them otherwise, Hamer and her colleagues firmly rejected Johnson's compromise, they nonetheless recognized that the arrangement they were offered would have trivialized the cause they had come to plead and all the hardships they and others had to endure just to get there in the first

The South and America since World War II

place. "We didn't come all this way for no two seats," Hamer snorted, after reportedly telling Aaron Henry that she would "cut your throat" if he accepted Johnson's offer. The MFDP group eventually managed to take over the seats allotted to the regular Mississippi Democratic delegation, but by the time they did, all but three of the regulars had gone home in a huff, upset by even the token offer of two seats to their MFDP challengers.[33]

Differences in philosophy and strategy had been there all along, but the saga of Atlantic City also revealed class cleavages that had always been a part of African American life and were now emerging within the civil rights movement itself. Afterward Fannie Lou Hamer, who became increasingly bitter toward middle-class blacks, recalled learning in Atlantic City that "everybody who would compromise in five minutes is the people with a real good education.... Them folks will sell you, your mama, they mama, anybody else for a dollar." In a sense the MFDP challenge foreshadowed a future in which the movement would seem close to splintering as its leaders and the various factions they represented sometimes appeared to be fighting each other as much as the remaining vestiges of white resistance. There remained, however, one last epic confrontation between oppressed and oppressor that would once again shake the national conscience and culminate in another historic and arguably revolutionary advancement for many black Americans in the South.[34]

Roughly 40 percent of black adults were registered to vote across the South in 1964, although there was considerable variation from state to state (Mississippi's black voter percentage was only 6.4 percent) and from place to place within a state. Blacks accounted for more than half of Selma, Alabama's population but only 3 percent of its registered electorate in 1964. Not only was Selma Bull Connor's hometown, but it had hosted the state's first White Citizens' Council meeting. Conditions were even worse in nearby Lowndes County, where 75 percent of the population was black, but not a single black person was registered to vote, and so far as anyone knew, none had even attempted to register at any point during the twentieth century. Selma had Dallas County sheriff Jim Clark, however, a brutal, bad-tempered man known to informally "deputize" like-minded civilians and lead them on racist vigilante forays into Birmingham and Oxford, Mississippi, or wherever blacks were challenging white supremacy.[35]

On his own turf Clark was especially violent and volatile, and he often seemed wholly unmindful of the consequences of his actions.

When provoked, neither the age nor the gender of the object of his ire seemed to matter in the least. In January 1965, when protesting black teachers marched silently around the courthouse, Clark and his deputies came after them with billy clubs and electric cattle prods. Three days later, as he was shoving and otherwise attempting to intimidate blacks lined up to register under the ostensible protection of a court order, Clark received a brief comeuppance when a rather large black woman informed him, "There ain't nobody scared around here." Clark pushed her, but rather than falling she regained her balance and landed two blows that flattened him instead. After dispatching the deputies who grabbed her, she felled Clark once more. By the time three deputies managed to pin her to the ground, a crowd of photographers and reporters had gathered, but showing no hesitation or restraint whatsoever, Clark sat on her stomach and clubbed her till she lost consciousness.[36]

Like Bull Connor's excesses, Clark's ready resort to billy clubs and cattle prods would soon serve only to provoke a louder national outcry. The sheriff and several of his men were on hand the evening of February 18, when local officers, state troopers, and white civilians wielding axe handles and clubs set upon a group of marchers and reporters in nearby Marion after the streetlights had been extinguished and the camera lenses of newsmen spray-painted. Clubbed with an axe handle, NBC correspondent Richard Valeriani reported that "local police simply stood by while they beat us." As the violence escalated, twenty-six-year-old pulpwood worker Jimmie Jackson was beaten and shot by a lawman. After Jackson died seven days later, hundreds of mourners showed up for his funeral, and talk began almost immediately of a march to Montgomery to confront George Wallace. "We had decided we were going to get killed or we was going to be free," local black leader Albert Turner explained.[37]

Upon hearing that a march from Selma to Montgomery was to begin on March 7, Governor Wallace first seemed grudgingly amenable to a moderate response that would avoid further adverse publicity, but after consulting with legislators from counties in the area of the proposed march, he reconsidered, telling aides, "I'm not going to have a bunch of niggers walking along a highway in this state as long as I'm governor." The fateful consequences of Wallace's hard-line stance would play out on Selma's Edmund P. Pettus Bridge that "Bloody Sunday" of March 7, 1965, leaving millions of Americans aghast and sickened for days and ultimately even years thereafter.[38]

More than four decades later, the very mention of Selma still evoked the imagery of burly lawmen swinging billy clubs, thrusting with cattle prods, and flinging canisters of powerful, nausea-inducing C-4 tear gas as they set on the marchers. With Sheriff Clark urging them to "get those goddamn niggers," his mounted posse also charged, swinging bullwhips and ropes and filling the air with rebel yells. These cries merged with shouts of encouragement from white bystanders, but they did not prevent reporters' microphones from picking up the persistent thudding and thwacking of billy club against flesh and bone. There had been a great outcry against the "white niggers" who were participating in the march, and they found themselves targeted by troopers for special abuse. However, what happened on the bridge at Selma that day proved a powerful emotional catalyst for literally thousands of other whites and blacks who, after witnessing these scenes on television, either rushed to airports or gassed up their cars and headed straight to Selma to join the protesters.[39]

The national uproar intensified even more after some local whites attacked three white northern ministers, one of whom died from his

John Lewis, beaten by Alabama law enforcement officers on "Bloody Sunday," Selma, Alabama, 1965. Bettman/Corbis.

head wounds. Telegrams flooded the White House, and sympathy demonstrations were the order of the day throughout the country. Just over a week after Bloody Sunday, President Johnson asked a joint session of Congress for a voting rights bill because "what happened in Selma is part of a far larger movement which reaches into every section and state of America.... This cause must be our cause, too. It is not just Negroes, but all of us who must overcome the crippling legacy of bigotry and injustice. And we shall overcome."[40]

Within a week three thousand people joined Rev. Martin Luther King Jr., who was intent, once again, on marching from Selma to Montgomery. As they drew closer to Montgomery, their ranks were swelled to thirty thousand by celebrities of all sorts and stripes, ranging from conductor Leonard Bernstein to boxer Floyd Patterson to entertainer Sammie Davis Jr. "Selma has become a shining moment in the history of man," King told an assembled throng upon the march's triumphant conclusion. "Like an idea whose time has come, not even the marching of mighty armies can halt us."[41]

This did not mean that all southern whites would suddenly stop trying. After King's speech Viola Liuzzo, a Detroit resident who, with so many others, had been drawn to Selma by the horrors she had seen on television, was shot and killed by a carload of Klansmen as she returned to Montgomery after ferrying some marchers back to Selma. Like so much of the racist savagery that white Alabamans had so frequently and matter-of-factly put on public display, however, Liuzzo's murder simply fueled further demands for federal action. A disgusted editorial writer for the segregationist *Alabama Journal* had foreseen this outcome only a few days after the brutal confrontation on the bridge. Assailing the "stupidity" of state officials and law enforcement personnel who had created a scene "beyond the wildest dreams of King," the writer bemoaned the fact that "by dumb, cruel and vastly excessive force we have made new civil rights legislation, not considered likely earlier, almost a virtual certainty." Sure enough, on August 6, almost five months to the day after Bloody Sunday, Lyndon Johnson signed the Voting Rights Act into law.[42]

Scarcely a week later, on August 14, federal examiners who had been dispatched to Selma under the terms of the new act added 381 blacks to the voter rolls, more than had been allowed to register over the previous sixty-five years. As a sullen Jim Clark looked on, a steady stream of applicants continued to file in, and by November 1965 nearly eight hundred new black registrants were eagerly anticipating their first opportunity to vote in Dallas County, Alabama.[43]

Over in similarly recalcitrant Leflore County, Mississippi, the story was much the same. For all their strenuous, courageous efforts over several years, SNCC organizers had managed to get only three hundred black names on the Leflore rolls. Yet less than two months after the examiners showed up, the county had roughly five thousand new black registrants. A year after the Voting Rights Act took effect, the share of the adult black population registered in the five states (Alabama, Georgia, Louisiana, Mississippi, and South Carolina) to which examiners had been assigned stood at 46 percent, roughly twice what it had been a year earlier. Follow-up studies showed that, although Voter Education Project efforts had clearly helped, the crucial factor in black-registration gains was the presence of federal representatives. The Voting Rights Act had effectively taken down the literacy test, and with Congress (via the Twenty-fourth Amendment) and the Supreme Court moving to eliminate the poll tax where it had not already been abolished by state action, black registration in the states of the old Confederacy, which had stood at 29 percent in 1960, had risen to 63 percent by 1968.[44]

This breakthrough seems all the more remarkable in light of the fact that while federal examiners made the act of registering itself less dangerous, in rural Black Belt counties especially, voting organizers, not to mention those who answered their call, were still forced to overcome both deep-seated economic dependence and entrenched patterns of overt deference to local whites. Scholars and other liberal observers who saw the desire for control of black labor as a sustaining force behind the Jim Crow system had assumed that the government acreage-reduction and subsidy programs that encouraged mechanization in southern agriculture would give whites less incentive to maintain their rigid dominion over blacks who were no longer needed as laborers. Yet as demand for black farm workers continued to shrink in the late 1940s and 1950s, mounting pressures for racial change had actually led whites to tighten rather than relax their chokehold on black freedom and opportunity. Some whites responded to the demise of the white primary in 1944 by redoubling their efforts to develop an effective mechanical cotton picker, which, they reasoned, would render their newly enfranchised black workers economically expendable and, hopefully, force them to leave the region before they could mount a challenge to white political supremacy. As one Yazoo–Mississippi Delta planter put it, "Mechanized farming will require only a fraction of the amount of labor which is required by the sharecropper system thereby tending to equalize the white and Negro population which would automatically make our racial problem easier to handle." Sure enough, as mechanization gained momentum in the 1950s, a number of Delta counties registered net outmigration rates near 20 percent, but at the end of the decade, all of the counties in the area still retained a substantial black majority.[45]

By 1967 over 90 percent of southern cotton was picked by machine, and where there had been some 283,000 black farm tenants in 1954, by 1969 the number was down to 18,000. Some in Washington had predicted that mechanizing southern agriculture would simply free former sharecroppers for more lucrative work in the South's expanding manufacturing sector. Yet continued emphasis in promotional materials on a large pool of "Anglo-Saxon" labor made it clear that black employment was not exactly a priority for those charged with bringing more industrial payrolls to southern communities. In light of the recently enacted Voting Rights Act of 1965, in Yazoo County, Mississippi, where blacks outnumbered whites by more than five thousand, local development officials candidly admitted that they were interested in creating new jobs only for whites.[46]

In addition to making little effort to provide employment opportunities for blacks, support for those who could not find jobs or were physically unable to work was meager at best. Unemployment payments in southern states typically ran from 30 to 40 percent below the national average, and disability benefits were even lower. Some local officials made no secret of their desire to encourage black outmigration when they began to publicize the comparatively generous welfare benefits available in northern states. Across the region, most states appeared to premise their participation in the Aid to Families with Dependent Children program on the minimal outlay of state revenues required to receive federal matching funds. On average, over 70 percent of state expenditures for public assistance in the South came from federal funds in 1965, as opposed to 54 percent nationally. Yet save for Oklahoma, with its large American Indian population, no southern state reached 75 percent of the national average amount for monthly payments to dependent children per family, and five of them provided less than 50 percent, including Mississippi, the nation's least charitable state by a wide margin, where these payments came to less than one quarter of the national figure.

The South and America since World War II

To make matters worse for suddenly superfluous farm workers, many rural southern counties with large black populations simply did not participate in federal food assistance programs. Even in those that did, the situations of many low-income black residents became even less tenable after 1964, when these programs began to shift from the direct distribution of flour, canned goods, and other federal commodities to the Food Stamp Program. Although the food stamp initiative promised more choice and dietary variety, the program's eligibility criteria were also much stiffer, requiring participants to document their poverty to the satisfaction of local white officials who generally took none too kindly to applicants believed to be engaging in civil rights activities of any sort. Food stamp recipients were also expected to pay what was supposed to be little more than a nominal fee for the stamps, which could then be used to purchase groceries.[47]

Nominal proved to be a relative term, however. A 1966 survey showed that in order to participate in the plan even minimally, 33 percent of the poor families in Mississippi would have to dedicate more than a third of their total income to food. The figure was 27 percent in South Carolina and 26 percent in Alabama, as compared to a national average of only 13 percent. "You've got to have money to buy the food stamps, and if you don't have any, you can just go and starve to death," a Beaufort County, South Carolina, woman complained in 1968. "If it wasn't for the little we grew and the fact that we all try to look after each other, we'd be dead right now."[48]

The combination of the cost of the stamps and tighter white control over eligibility helped to explain why when Leflore County, Mississippi, went from commodities to food stamps in 1965, the number of people receiving food assistance plummeted from 20,000 to 8,300. In nearby Sunflower County, where approximately 6,000 families lived in poverty, only 3,250 of them had received commodities, and when the food stamp plan was implemented, the number of recipients shrank by nearly 50 percent. By the end of the 1960s, participation in the food stamp program was down 67 percent in Georgia in comparison to the commodities program and by more than 50 percent in Alabama and Virginia as well.[49]

Not convinced that the promise of greater welfare support up North would pull enough blacks away, some whites decided to do a little extra pushing. In 1964 the Mississippi House of Representatives even passed a bill aimed at stemming what one backer called "this black tide that threatens to engulf us" by making it a felony to become the parent of a second illegitimate child and mandating either a one- to three-year prison term or an agreement to submit to sterilization. "When the cutting starts, they'll head to Chicago," chortled one of the black-majority Delta's white legislators who had sponsored the bill. Although the sterilization provision was eventually deleted and the offense was reduced to a misdemeanor, the measure that eventually passed still mandated a thirty- to ninety-day jail term or a $250 fine.[50]

Aware of the enormous economic and social leverage they could bring to bear against blacks who showed signs of demanding the rights that the courts had decreed should be theirs, the architects of massive resistance had spoken with great confidence in 1956 when they announced their plan to preserve white supremacy by forcing civil rights leaders to take to the courts to secure every inch of ground they gained. A decade later, however, that strategy lay in tatters because crusaders for black rights had decided to circumvent the tangled and tortuously slow legal process by taking their case directly and dramatically into the proverbial court of public opinion instead. They had risked their lives and livelihoods, but in the end, by forcing millions of whites across the nation to look repeatedly on the ugly face of American apartheid, they managed to speed up the creaky wheels of law and government that were at long last finally turning in their direction.

In a real though truly perverse sense, civil rights leaders were actually indebted to recalcitrant, short-sighted "dumb seg" antagonists like Bull Connor and Jim Clark, whose violent overreactions unwittingly facilitated their efforts. SCLC strategist Wyatt T. Walker observed, "There never was any more skillful manipulation of the news media than there was in Birmingham." The Birmingham campaign "would have been lost," Walker admitted, if Bull Connor had just "let us go down to the city hall and pray," but he added, "we had calculated for the stupidity of a Bull Connor [and] knew that he would inevitably do something to help our cause." Later, in Selma, the SCLC's C. T. Vivian persisted in goading Jim Clark, daring Clark to hit him until Vivian was indeed struck in the face, an act for which Clark was happy to claim credit, but one that made "vivid television" for propaganda purposes. "Every time it appears the movement is dying out," an SCLC staffer confided to reporters, "Sheriff Clark comes to our rescue." Likewise, when the Connors and the Clarks lived down to their reputation through acts of violence against civil rights activists, a cadre of courageous and determined journalists were typically there to record and report on them. Their critical video footage, photographs, and written accounts of the bitter, bloody, almost surreal scenes that played out in the South between the Emmett Till slaying in 1955 and the violent confrontation nearly ten years later on the bridge in Selma had effectively offered the rest of the nation a decade-long spectacle of southern white savagery on parade.[51]

In the end, of course, civil rights leaders understood that someone had to be willing to brave this savagery and precipitate such a spectacle in order not just to get Washington on their side but to pressure white southerners into abandoning their resistance to Washington's laws and decrees. It was here that the emerging emphasis on economic development that had swept across the South in the wake of World War II proved critical. This growth impulse was most potent in the larger cities, and when demonstrators took to the lunch counters and streets to demand integration and their right to vote, white business and political leaders were ultimately forced to weigh their commitment to segregation against their desire to see their communities—and themselves—continue to prosper. Rev. Martin Luther King Jr. criticized the protest strategy in Albany because it focused on elected officials rather than businessmen and merchants, and in city after city civil rights leaders learned quickly that the weak spot in Jim Crow's armor could usually be found in the vicinity of his pocketbook. By late 1961 boycotts, sit-ins, and other sorts of demonstrations or the threat thereof had already brought the desegregation of at least some public facilities in ninety southern cities. Not only did protests and the violent responses they so often elicited disrupt commerce on a daily basis, but they threatened long-term damage as well by marring the city's image in the eyes of potential investors and tourists.

Hoping to persuade community leaders across the South that diehard resistance to desegregation and black voting was truly bad for business, the liberal activists of the Southern Regional Council had launched the Southern Leadership Project to hammer home the bitter "lesson of Little Rock" in order to encourage business leaders to avoid a similar lapse into economic stagnation by supporting a speedy and nonviolent end to Jim Crow practices in their cities. Some learned this lesson more readily than others. In Virginia, the birthplace of massive resistance, Governor J. Lindsay Almond Jr. had vowed in early 1959 to close the public schools rather than allow integration to subject Virginia's white children to the "livid stench of sadism, sex, immorality, and juvenile pregnancy infesting the mixed schools of the District of Columbia and elsewhere." After several schools were forced to shut down in the face of court-ordered desegregation, however, Almond was flooded with letters warning that "industry surely will not come to a state where education is in the fix it is in Virginia," and six months after his vow of last-ditch resistance, the governor announced a striking change of heart, insisting rather melodramatically, "No error could be more grave. No mistake more costly, no travesty more tragic, no curse more productive of woe than to succumb to the blandishments of those who would have Virginia abandon public education and thereby consign a generation of children to darkness and illiteracy, the pits of indolence and dependency, and the dungeons of delinquency."[52]

The lesson of Little Rock also took a while to sink in with white leaders in New Orleans. In the face of court-ordered desegregation in 1960, Mayor DeLesseps S. Morrison had warned that "ugly, irresponsible incidents" could tarnish the city's image as "a thriving center of commerce and industry," but like many other southern political leaders of the era, he did so while still promising to resist integration. When the school board chose to begin desegregation in two schools in low-income neighborhoods where whites were already feeling economic pressure from blacks, segregationist agitators saw their chance and seized upon it. As a result, New Orleans exposed a cringing nation to racism in the raw as a group of working-class white women, quickly dubbed "the cheerleaders," gathered daily in front of television cameras to shower obscenities and threats on the black children and those who escorted them into their new schools. In hopes of avoiding just such an outcome, Mayor Morrison had appealed to the city's economic elite to make a call for peaceful acceptance of integration, but when it became apparent that his plea had fallen largely on deaf ears, he vowed, "If these SOB's aren't going to do anything, I'll be damned if I'm going to do anything." Finally, after three and a half months of disastrous publicity, with tourism and retail spending in sharp decline, 105 of the city's business and professional leaders took out a full-page ad in the *New Orleans Times-Picayune*, calling for order. Belated as it was, their action proved to be a key factor in gradually defusing the crisis.[53]

After seeing their apprehensions about losing jobs and trade because of racial conflict confirmed in Little Rock and New Orleans, Atlanta business leaders stepped up their calls for a proactive approach, lobbying successfully to persuade the state legislature that pursuing a local option policy would be preferable to an across-the-board provision to automatically close any public school facing a desegregation order. When the courts compelled Atlanta schools to desegregate in the fall of 1961, local business leaders followed the lead of longtime mayor William B. Hartsfield, who had already insisted his city was "too busy to hate." With the support of influential businessmen such as Chamber of Commerce President Ivan Allen Jr., banker Mills B. Lane, and the editors of the *Atlanta Journal-Constitution*, Hartsfield managed to make the integration of the city's schools, which initially involved only ten black students, so uneventful that the flock of reporters in town to cover this historic event actually had little or nothing to do, giving the tireless booster Hartsfield a chance to take them on a tour of the city, emphasizing such bragging points as its many "fine Negro homes."[54]

Although liberals tried to establish Atlanta as the region's role model for handling desegregation, even after the New Orleans and Little Rock debacles not all southern economic leaders were ready to throw their weight behind racial moderation. As the crisis over integration at the University of Mississippi loomed in September 1962, Mississippi's top businessmen showed little inclination even to attempt to rein in the alternately buffoonish and incendiary segregationist governor Ross Barnett. The bloody campus riot that left two dead and dozens injured on the eve of James Meredith's registration as the first black student at Ole Miss reverberated throughout the nation and the world that autumn, affirming an already widespread perception that Mississippi represented the South at its ignorant, bigoted, unredeemable worst. In the aftermath of the Ole Miss uprising, an executive of Work Wear of Cleveland, Ohio, informed a Magnolia State developer that his firm would not "consider expanding in Mississippi again until the state and its people join the Union again," and a *New York Times* report claimed that one small factory had actually been moved just across the state line into Louisiana just to avoid having a Mississippi mailing address.[55]

At that point, most white business leaders in Birmingham seemed just as committed to defending the racial status quo as their Mississippi counterparts had been. At the end of World War II, Birmingham had seemed poised to challenge Atlanta for the distinction of being the South's most "modern" and dynamic city, but during the 1950s Atlanta's population had grown by 40 percent, more than three times faster than Birmingham's. United States Steel dominated the local economy, and its executives saw little reason to support efforts to recruit new employers who might compete for their labor. As a result, when the steel industry turned toward automation, rising unemployment bred rising fear and uncertainty among local whites already known for their proclivities for racial violence. The city had been close to landing a large steel products plant when the violent reception it accorded the Freedom Riders hit the front pages and television screens. The steel products company quickly backed off, choosing a Tennessee location even though the steel it used would still have to be shipped from Birmingham. A disgusted local businessman complained, "We let twenty-one college kids looking for trouble come into our town and make half a million of us look like damn rednecks—besides losing us a lot of money, time and jobs."[56]

Fearing a string of such setbacks after hearing George Wallace's "Segregation forever" inaugural speech in January 1963, Henry C. Goodrich, an industrial location specialist who was also vice president of the Birmingham Rotary Club, informed the new governor that he and others in the local business community feared Wallace's defiantly segregationist stance would "lead to economic disaster": "I cannot emphasize this too strongly because I have already had many such reactions from prospects in the North who might have considered Alabama. Their files are now closed." In response, Wallace brushed off Goodrich's concerns, lecturing him on the importance of maintaining state sovereignty lest Alabama degenerate "to a complete welfare state" where "Washington will be taking care of us" and assuring him that there would be "no major problem in bringing industry into the state of Alabama." Not all business-oriented Birminghamians agreed with Goodrich, of course. The president of the Chamber of Commerce assured Wallace that, like the governor, he was "unalterably opposed to desegregation." Another Wallace supporter actually urged him to find a way "to stop those Yankee corporations from putting pressure on those third-rate Babbits in these Chambers of Commerce to surrender to these Negroes."[57]

Although Wallace had promised Goodrich that his segregationist stance would not undermine industrial recruitment efforts, several prospects clearly got cold feet in the wake of the Birmingham bombings in September 1963. As a result, when tensions began to escalate in Selma, Wallace was doubly determined to see Hammermill Paper Company commit to building a plant there. To sweeten the pot, in addition to cheap labor the state of Alabama offered Hammermill cheap land, cheap water, a 50 percent property tax deduction, speedy approval of its waste disposal plans, and a personal pledge from Wallace to begin

The South and America since World War II

work immediately on a new bridge to handle the additional traffic that would be generated by the new plant. In the wake of the Pettus Bridge violence, Hammermill took a lot of flak in the media and from the National Council of Churches and other liberal organizations, but company executives stood by their decision, assuring critics that they would follow a color-blind hiring policy and arguing that by bringing new jobs to "the economically depressed central Alabama area," they would be "making a positive contribution to the pressing national problems of race relations."[58]

The willingness of Hammermill's executives to locate a plant in so racially troubled a community as Selma rested primarily on economic considerations. Perhaps things might have been different if Hammermill's deal with Alabama had not already been in the works before Selma's day of shame, for despite the resolutely positive public posture maintained by its company leaders, they were severely embarrassed by what had transpired on that bridge. Prior to that point, on the other hand, these same executives had not been terribly troubled by the blatant and long-standing denial of black voting rights in Selma that had set the stage for Bloody Sunday. A 1969 survey of 308 corporate executives who chose to locate plants in Tennessee revealed that in making their decisions only four of them had given any weight whatsoever to a community's actual progress in race relations. Overall, save for Hammermill's decision to stick with Selma, there was remarkably little reason to dispute former Arkansas governor Winthrop Rockefeller's assertion that "the industrial prospect doesn't give a hoot whether your schools are segregated or not, but he wants no part of disorder and violence."[59]

Accordingly, though he preached nonviolence to his followers, Reverend King's capacity to elicit a violent response from his white antagonists made him a fearsome figure among image-conscious southern white community leaders. In Augusta, Georgia, Mayor Millard Beckum quietly capitulated to black demands for desegregation of local lunch counters and theaters in the face of threatened protests during the Master's golf tournament in 1962. "We were afraid they would bring in Martin Luther King," Beckum later explained. Elsewhere, his strife-torn city would be all right, a Birmingham leader insisted in September 1963, "if we can just get Martin Luther King, Governor Wallace, and John F. Kennedy out of here and keep them out." As St. Augustine hemorrhaged tourist dollars in the midst of boycotts and demonstrations in June 1964, the owner of a sightseeing boat warned, "If Martin Luther King doesn't stay away, the whole summer will be lost."[60]

There was anecdotal evidence aplenty that many southern white leaders eventually became convinced that racial strife was bad for business, but it is difficult to gauge just how bad it actually was because there are too many other variables that may have contributed to differences in growth rates. Still, it is difficult to dismiss statistics showing that employment in Little Rock grew by less than 2 percent in the 1950s while rising by 35 percent in Atlanta. Likewise, in the following decade the number of jobs in Atlanta and Charlotte grew by 6 and 26 percent, respectively, while shrinking by 7 percent in New Orleans and 8 percent in Birmingham over the same period. Finally, there is certainly good reason to suspect that the relative intensity of Mississippi's racial turmoil may help to explain why employment grew by only 5 percent statewide in the 1960s in comparison to roughly 25 percent in both Georgia and North Carolina.[61]

Whatever might be made of their moderating influence, however, once the "crisis" of initial, typically token desegregation had passed, growth-conscious local business and development leaders generally showed little inclination to push for accelerated or expanded integration unless their city faced the threat of further court orders or renewed protests, either of which might lead to conflict or turmoil. Despite Greensboro's status as the titular birthplace of the sit-in movement in February 1960, it took well over three years for black activists to achieve a truly significant breakthrough in desegregating the city's restaurants, hotels, and other businesses. Even this came only in the wake of massive, unrelenting protests, leading to Mayor David Schenck's June 7, 1963, appeal to businessmen to "immediately cease selection of customers purely on the basis of race" because "when our image in the nation is damaged, for whatever reason, our citizens of all races suffer." Schenck was willing to make such a statement only after meeting with Greensboro's leading corporate and financial executives, who had assured him of their support. The pattern in Greensboro up to this point had been one of fits, starts, and stalls in which business leaders did no more than absolutely necessary to get black leaders to temporarily suspend their protests. Even in the wake of Mayor Schenck's plea, in the absence of immediate pressure from blacks, the city's economic leaders were clearly in no hurry to facilitate further desegregation, leading a local activist, William Thomas, to conclude, "The Negro won't ever get any more than he pushes and presses for."[62]

In reality, whereas businessmen and economic boosters had at least sought to exert a moderating influence on politicians during the conflict-ridden early 1960s, by the middle of the next decade, these roles were frequently reversed. Though now much more beholden to black voters in many cases, white political leaders were still not terribly enthusiastic about busing or affirmative action, but surveys showed them to be notably more receptive to such measures than their counterparts in business, whose fiscal conservatism also made them more leery of government assistance programs that might benefit severely disadvantaged blacks.[63]

Still, regardless of how self- or class-interested their actions may have been at the time, when the South's growth-oriented business moderates pressured segregationist politicians to consider the potential economic consequences of their recalcitrance and rabble-rousing, they gave them the respectable, politically plausible out for which some of them had actually been searching for some time. The severely limited scope of initial school integration in Atlanta, Charlotte, and other cities stuck in the craw of more than one observer, but none could argue that the nauseating scenes of brutality and hate that played out in places like Birmingham and Oxford were preferable.

It might well be that George Wallace and other posturing segregationist diehards could hardly have behaved otherwise and remained in office. Figures showing that only 9 percent of a group of 720 southern white voters surveyed in 1964 favored desegregation surely suggested as much. Still, an Alabama official recognized that Wallace was not simply "the product of the times so much as the times were a product of Wallace.... Wallace fanned the flames. Sure, there were flames there to begin with, but how the populace responds to changing times and conditions is influenced to a very great extent by leadership." Evoking Melvin Tumin's research on the large percentage of Greensboro whites who preferred segregation but did not favor extreme measures to maintain it, a white Arkansas woman revealed how important some timely, politically courageous moderate white leadership might have been. After expressing her preference for segregation over integration, she clarified her response for survey researchers by explaining, "You asked me what I favor, not what I will accept graciously; not what I thought was right."[64]

Certainly a preference for segregation and a willingness to accept integration were not mutually exclusive. In fact, where individual white southerners stood on such matters sometimes had less to do with their personal feelings about blacks than considerations of career and livelihood, considerations that often reflected the attitudes that pre-vailed among their clients, customers, and business associates. A Geor-gia attorney who kept his integrationist sympathies to himself admitted, "I know I should be out there taking a stand...but I can't. It means ruin-ing my practice and losing everything I've worked a life to build. So I just nod with them, and to tell the truth, if the conversation gets to a point that I have to commit myself, I go along with them. Later, when driving home, I talk to myself and say, 'You're a coward and a liar.'" On the other hand, in growth-conscious Atlanta another lawyer confessed in 1961, "I was born a segregationist, and I'll die one, but I was born a lot of things and right now I think my family and job mean more to me than keeping a few niggers out of a school or a restaurant." Two years later he was calling a friend who still clung to his diehard segregationist views an "eccentric" and noting that the man was becoming an "outcast." Meanwhile, with the University of Georgia embroiled in an integration crisis that might lead to its being closed, white students who had the opportunity to express themselves anonymously generally put getting their diplomas ahead of maintaining segregation. "Integration is com-ing, period," one wrote, "and the sooner it is done and forgotten about, the better off everyone will be."[65]

Although white southerners rarely acknowledged the economic advantages they enjoyed from the Jim Crow system, once its defenders began to sense that it might be costing them more money than it was saving them, many an absolutist became an accommodationist. "The nigras, we have to get them to cooperate with us, like everybody else, if we're going to get more industry here and keep the city booming," a once-committed segregationist told Robert Coles. "How can you say 'never' one year, then 'yes' the next? It wasn't just that we obeyed the law. I guess it was really because we finally got it through our heads that it was in our own best interests to do it." Behind such rationaliza-tions, Coles surmised, was the reality that for all of their oaths of fealty to total segregation, most white southerners actually cared less about their "beliefs" than "the comfortable continuity of their lives." When that comfort and continuity were jeopardized more by defending segrega-tion than by accepting at least a measure of integration, they proved a bit more accommodating and flexible than the rhetoric of massive resis-tance had suggested.[66]

William Chafe might as well have been referring to the entire South when he observed that "the surge for racial justice in North Carolina came not from the City Hall in Greensboro nor from the State Capitol in Raleigh" but "from a thousand streets in a hundred towns where black people, young and old, acted to realize their vision of justice deferred." There is no denying either the central importance of this surge or the courage and determination of those who took to the streets, but neither should we forget that the success of their efforts frequently depended on their capacity to send shockwaves through not only the South's chambers of government, but its chambers of commerce as well. When they were finally forced to choose, some of the region's most influential white leaders concluded, however belatedly or begrudgingly, that their desire to keep the South racially southern must give way to their goal of making it economically American.[67]

5

"The Whole United States Is Southern!"

The Politics of Backlash, North and South

The protest phase of the civil rights movement had focused largely on voting rights and access to public accommodations, but for all that was accomplished in these areas, when Lyndon Johnson signed the Civil Rights Act of 1964 into law, save for some purely token desegregation, mostly in the cities, southern schools were generally no more integrated than they had been ten years earlier, when the first *Brown* decision came down. However, Title VI of the new law mandated that school districts receiving federal assistance must submit acceptable desegregation plans or see their funds cut off. In their initial response to federal guidelines on desegregation, white school officials typically adopted "freedom of choice" plans, giving parents the option of enrolling their children in any school within the system. This approach placed the burden of integration squarely on black parents, who would obviously be forced to brave white wrath and economic coercion if they opted on their own to put their children in formerly all-white schools. Meanwhile, it was presumed that few, if any, white parents would voluntarily enroll their children at an all-black school. Because it offered an escape route for whites whose children attended schools where black pupils did happen to enroll, freedom of choice was geared much more toward keeping whites out of integrated classrooms than putting blacks into them.

Finally, fed up with such tactics, Judge John Minor Wisdom of the Fifth Circuit Court of Appeals decreed in 1966 that in order to be in full compliance with *Brown,* school systems were required not simply to end formal practices of segregation but to take "affirmative action" to promote integration of student bodies, faculties, facilities, and school events.

Because urban housing patterns were so typically a reflection of the spatial separation of the population by race, the key step in the integration process, Wisdom indicated, was to begin assigning students to schools within a system on the basis of race rather than place of residence.[1]

Wisdom's reasoning won, U. S. Supreme Court affirmation in 1968. Noting that three years after a freedom-of-choice plan was introduced in New Kent County in rural Virginia, 85 percent of African American students were still in all-black schools, the Court declared that the *Brown* decrees had made it an "affirmative duty" to establish racially "unitary" schools. Therefore the responsibility fell on the school board "to provide a [desegregation] plan that works *now*" (emphasis added). Here again the justices suggested that using race as the basis for assigning students was an appropriate method of achieving integration. With the courts applying heavy pressure, the percentage of southern black children attending racially mixed schools quickly shot up from 32 in 1968–69 to 79 by 1970–71, meaning that 44 percent of black students were now enrolled in white-majority schools in the South, as opposed to 28 percent in the North and West.[2]

Across the rural South resistance to integration generally remained strongest among whites in school districts with substantial black populations. When desegregation could be staved off no longer in these areas, most white parents who could afford it—and quite a few who could not—enrolled their children either in established private schools or in hastily organized all-white "seg academies" that often convened classes in church basements or old, unused public school buildings. Regardless of their opposition to integration, many white public school teachers were simply loath to abandon the higher salary, better benefits, and greater security that their current positions offered and move to underfunded, underequipped private schools whose future was anything but certain. In a number of the new schools the faculties cobbled together were an amalgam of experienced teachers unwilling to teach in an integrated setting and local college graduates of various sorts, many of them lacking formal training, much less certification, in the subjects they were actually assigned to teach.

For some parents, however, the impulse to place their children in private schools, even those with markedly inferior faculties and facilities, was a matter not simply of racial attitudes but of social standing. In Holmes County, Mississippi, Melany Neilson's mother had assured her that the family's maid, Elsie, was "like family," but trying to stay abreast of the sometimes frenetic social swim in the Yazoo-Mississippi Delta had taxed that family's finances even before school integration became an immediate prospect. After the public schools were desegregated in 1967 and her parents enrolled Melany and her siblings at Central Holmes Academy, not only did their partying fall off precipitously, but, family or not, they also had to let the beloved Elsie go.[3]

Southern rural counties and small towns had been the breeding grounds for the Citizens Councils, but because they were the nation's least physically segregated areas by race and transporting children by bus was already standard practice, these locales actually presented the fewest administrative and logistical obstacles to school integration. In large metropolitan areas the growing inner-city-suburban racial disparity posed a more serious problem. White parents with adequate financial resources simply moved their families to the suburbs in hopes of avoiding anything more than minimally integrated schools. The white population of the City of Atlanta, for example, shrank by 20 percent between 1960 and 1970 alone. With the courts now insisting that racially concentrated residential patterns could no longer be accepted as a limiting factor in determining how integrated a school system must become, anxious white parents in most of the South's larger metropolitan areas faced the prospect of seeing their children transported by bus to distant and likely inferior schools.[4]

New York Times writer James Wooten observed in 1970 that although integration had progressed nicely in recent months in "traditionally recalcitrant areas like rural Mississippi and Louisiana," in Atlanta, Charlotte, Birmingham, Jackson, Memphis, Nashville, Columbia, "and almost any other city of any size in the South," new court orders for integration had met with "angry cries of protest." Apparently turning a deaf ear to this massive antibusing outcry, the U.S. Supreme Court sent shock waves reverberating throughout the nation in 1971 when it ruled in *Swann v. Charlotte-Mecklenburg Board of Education* that transporting students over a reasonable distance was an acceptable means of achieving racially balanced schools. This ruling meant that Charlotte's inner-city black children might be bused out to schools in the suburbs, and white suburban children to predominantly black schools within the city. The response was an angry chorus of protests and threats and a firebomb that exploded at the office of Julius Chambers, a black attorney who had been instrumental in pursuing the *Swann* case.[5]

In the long run, however, as Robert J. Norrell pointed out, "Where it was tried extensively, busing usually succeeded or failed on matters of demography and geography," and because Charlotte was so centrally located within its metropolitan area, whites found it harder to escape to suburbs in other districts. Moreover, the population of the school district was only 29 percent black, and none of its schools had reached the traditional 40 percent black tipping point that typically prompted wholesale white flight. With image-conscious local leaders stressing strong and orderly schools as the key to future growth, whites had become noticeably more resigned to the *Swann* decree by the mid-1970s. The story was quite different up in Richmond, however, where the school system was already 65 percent black before busing began. With two all-white systems lying nearby, white enrollment in Richmond's public schools had fallen below 20 percent by 1976.[6]

Although black gains in education varied considerably from one locale to another, for the region as a whole the pace of progress was impressive. Only 35 percent of southern blacks age twenty to twenty-four were high school graduates in 1960; by 1977 this figure had more than doubled. Meanwhile, black college enrollment had stood at 84,000 in 1960 and was concentrated overwhelmingly in predominantly black institutions. By 1976 the South boasted 426,000 black collegians, 57 percent of them studying at predominantly white schools.[7]

Anyone who wondered whether integration was really worth all the trauma it so often inflicted on the individual black children who broke the color barrier at previously all-white schools could have learned much from the story of Ruby Bridges. Psychiatrist Robert Coles began observing Ruby in 1960, when she was a six-year-old braving the fearsome, hateful mob that gathered daily to curse and threaten her as one of the first black pupils to attend a New Orleans grammar school. In her early crayon drawings, Coles noticed, Ruby typically made white characters larger and more fully detailed in their features and appendages than her black characters, who often lacked eyes, fingers, or toes. Coles was also struck by Ruby's propensity to draw black figures without mouths, while giving them extraordinarily large ears. When sketching specific black individuals Ruby took pains with details only in depicting her grandfather, an independent, landowning farmer whom Ruby's mother described as "the strongest man you can find."[8]

Ruby Bridges escorted from her grammar school by U.S. Marshals, New Orleans, Louisiana, 1960. AP Photo.

As time passed in her new, integrated setting, however, Ruby's drawings of black people gradually began to take on the same detail and definition as her drawings of whites, because, she explained, over time her pioneering experience as one of the first few black pupils in what had been an all-white school had not only taught her to be less intimidated by whites but made her more aware of "my own people" and given her reason to be "proud of them instead of ashamed." At the same time, Ruby's white classmate, "Jimmie," had initially sketched her as little more than a shapeless mass. Actually he had no real idea what Ruby looked like because, Jimmie confessed, "I don't look at her close if I can help it." A year or so later, however, Jimmie was drawing much more detailed portraits of Ruby, which suggested that he had learned a great deal about her appearance and her habits and activities as well.[9]

Although it was difficult to measure the civil rights movement's impact on the way individual blacks and whites actually saw themselves and each other, there could be little doubt about its effect on the behavior of the white politicians who suddenly found themselves with a substantial black constituency they could no longer ignore. As long as so few, if any, of the black people whose interests they were supposed to represent could actually vote, white officeholders were under little pressure to accord them even a measure of respect, much less address any of their substantive grievances and concerns. The impact of adding 1.7 million new black voters to the rolls during the 1960s was soon apparent, however, in the remarkable change in operating styles among white elected officials and representatives who might now be answerable to significant black populations. Studying the impact of the civil rights movement in Panola County on the edge of the Yazoo-Mississippi Delta, Frederick Wirt found that by the end of the 1960s white politicians had already made it a point to identify the most influential local blacks and cultivate their support. Blacks who had long since given up hope of getting their streets repaired or improved suddenly noticed maintenance and even paving crews in their neighborhoods, and some rural dirt roads were graveled for the first time anyone could remember. Both the police and sheriff's departments also moved, albeit slowly, to hire a few black officers. New signs of respect or at least recognition of a black presence emerged in the content of the local newspaper, which for the first time began to run stories about black Panolans and their activities within the community. Moreover, these newspaper references now employed the courtesy titles "Mr." and "Mrs.," once so pointedly withheld by whites talking either to or about blacks.[10]

Across the South white politicians who had once sworn fealty to the Citizens Councils now visited black churches and locked arms with ministers and congregants to sing "We Shall Overcome." Concerned that some whites might see them as suddenly too attentive to blacks, white politicians sometimes walked a tightrope in trying to convince white voters that their interests remained paramount. To explain his support for sewer construction in a black residential area, one quick-thinking local politico told white constituents, "We got to get rid of those mosquitoes. We can't let them carry that contaminated blood from those folks throughout the [white] community."[11]

The ultimate goal for recently registered black voters, of course, was electing their own representatives who would advance and protect their interests without apology or equivocation. Southern whites responded to this prospect with a variety of tactics and subterfuges, ranging from gerrymandering to at-large elections for city council or county commission. Nowhere was white resistance to black office-holding more pronounced than in Mississippi, where as late as 1964 only 6.7 percent of the black voting-age population were registered and only six blacks held any sort of elected office anywhere in the state. Three years later nearly 60 percent of Mississippi's black adults were on the voter rolls when Robert Clark became one of twenty-two blacks elected to county-level offices by unseating longtime incumbent J. P. Love as state representative from Holmes County. Clark, a former teacher and administrator, ran as the candidate of the Mississippi Freedom Democratic Party. More than 70 percent of eligible blacks were registered in this black-majority county, where official totals also showed more than 100 percent registration by whites. On his first day in office Clark strode by a statue of the notorious race-baiter Theodore G. Bilbo to take his seat, which was isolated from those of his legislative colleagues, some of whom refused to eat with him at the opening day legislative luncheon. Still, Clark's victory was a great symbolic triumph for blacks in Mississippi, for it came in a rural county noted for rabid white resistance to racial change.[12]

By 1971 blacks accounted for roughly 30 percent of Mississippi's electorate and held a solid electoral majority in twenty of its eighty-two counties. Hoping to build on the gains of 1967, more than three

A new voter taking the oath from a federal examiner, Prentiss, Mississippi, 1965. Courtesy of Mississippi Department of Archives and History, Jackson, Mississippi.

hundred black candidates sought county-level posts across the state, and the controversial and erratic Charles Evers, the brother of slain civil rights leader Medgar Evers, ran for governor on an Independent ticket. In a disappointing showing Evers received only 22 percent of the vote, and Clark was the only successful black candidate among twenty-nine who had sought legislative seats. Overall, only one in six black office seekers were successful, and other than Clark these gained only minor posts, leaving Mississippi still without a black sheriff or school superintendent, much less state senator. On the other hand, only six years after the Voting Rights Act, Mississippi had 117 black elected officials, more than any state in the nation, and there and elsewhere throughout the Deep South major gains in black political influence were too obvious to deny.[13]

Although the economic benefits of the civil rights movement were not always readily apparent to blacks still struggling to hang on in the old plantation belt, for those in the region's industrializing areas the payoffs were more immediate and dramatic. Historically, racial discrimination had operated either by jobs within particular southern plants or by entire industries. The South's "blackest" industrial workforces were in timber and steel, which as of 1966 were the only southern industries where blacks accounted for more than 12 percent of the employees.[14]

In industries that employed both white and black workers, jobs paying anything above entry-level wages were rarely available to blacks. (This explained why, in 1958, 35 percent of white workers in rural Louisiana and Mississippi plants earned more than $45 per week, whereas less than 2 percent of black workers did this well.) A survey of North Carolina manufacturers in 1965 showed that scarcely 1 percent of factory foremen were black, and blacks still performed the great majority of the most onerous and arduous jobs in poultry processing plants and the timber industry. With the Jim Crow system still securely in place, for blacks, the very act of applying for any job other than janitor in a plant that also employed whites had required not only courage but savvy. Although he was a high school graduate, James Fields recalled that when he applied for a job as a laborer with Union Bag in Savannah in the 1940s, he had "put ninth grade instead of twelfth, because I figured they didn't want...no smart black man."[15]

Though he was a common laborer, "A. C.," a black worker at a relatively new steel mill in South Carolina, drew far better wages and enjoyed benefits that had never been available in his previous job cutting pulpwood. Yet even in the early 1960s the familiar pattern of discrimination by job was holding fast. "None of us could weld or nothing.... All we could do was be a helper.... All the better jobs were all white, all white." When A. C. put in for a welder's position his white employers told him, "You can't pass no test," but he replied, "Sign me up, anyhow. If anybody else can pass it, I can pass it." When a white supervisor encouraged A. C. and helped him prepare for the test "the other whites stopped liking him 'cuz he was helpin' me." A. C. passed the test, but "they give me another one. All the whites didn't have to pass but one, but I had to take two. I passed both of 'em. I was the first black qualified to weld. I paved the way for about ten more."[16]

Across the South the doors to textile plants had remained so firmly closed to blacks that counties with high levels of textile employment typically also showed high levels of black outmigration. Gavin Wright has pointed out that prior to the Civil Rights Act of 1964 blacks held only 5 percent of the textile jobs in South Carolina. By 1970 the figure was 20 percent. Where blacks had been able to claim only one in ten of the new jobs in South Carolina between 1940 and 1964, by the end of the 1970s they were filling roughly one in three of the new positions. The story in North Carolina was much the same, as the portion of the rural black labor force employed in textiles rose from 3 percent in 1960 to 21 percent a decade later.[17]

Laughter erupted on the House floor when the archconservative Howard Smith of Virginia tried to torpedo the Civil Rights Act of 1964 by tacking on an amendment that banned employment discrimination on the basis of sex as well as race. Smith's hopes that his amendment would help to derail the bill came to naught, however, and with Title VII of the Civil Rights Act eventually helping to clear the way, increasing numbers of black women soon joined the manufacturing workforce as well. Even typically recalcitrant companies like J. P. Stevens opted to bring their hiring practices into line with federal law when they came under scrutiny from the federal Equal Employment Opportunity Commission.[18]

Not all the credit for this turnabout should go to Washington, of course. Economists had argued for several generations that the South's courtship of low-wage industry would have been even more fruitful had development leaders encouraged more prospective employers to take advantage of the economically desperate black workers who represented the region's very cheapest labor. In reality, the general and long-standing availability of ample numbers of whites eager for work at essentially the same starting wages as blacks meant that it typically cost southern employers practically nothing to hire only whites. By the mid-1960s, however, as more and better jobs became available to whites, labor market conditions began to force employers who had refused to hire blacks to choose between labor shortages and the higher wages that would be necessary to hold onto white employees. With only 16 percent of North Carolina's rural white workers still in textile jobs in 1970, it seemed clear that many new black textile workers had come in behind whites who, with the state's industrial economy on the upswing, had been able to move into better positions in newer plants.

For textiles and other traditionally lily-white industries that were losing large numbers of white workers to the more attractive job opportunities that became available during the 1960s, the civil rights movement was, as more than one plant manager admitted, "a blessing in disguise": "The government gave us a nice way to facilitate it, and if anybody wanted to complain about it, white people who would say 'hey why are you hiring all of these black people,' you'd say 'because the government forces us to do this,' you could place the blame on the government."[19]

Federal antidiscrimination legislation had obviously set the stage for dramatic gains in the workplace. One study showed that the mean earnings ratio between black and white workers in southern industry rose from 53 percent in 1968 to 65 percent in 1979, while falling from 76 to 72 percent outside the region. A pioneering black textile worker in West Point, Georgia, Floyd Harris had worked as a porter at a mill for several years, delivering mail to a white receptionist who persisted in calling him "boy" even though he was in his midthirties. By 1970 Harris had won a seat on the local city council and a promotion to assistant personnel manager of the mill, giving him the quiet satisfaction of serving as the woman's superior. Harris understood the importance of federal authority in forcing what many of his black coworkers called "the Change," but he knew that marchers and protestors had also been critical to bringing it all to pass: "I was active in the social revolution that went on from the fifties, through the sixties and early seventies, so I was aware of what the black leaders were talking about. We wrote the laws and they passed the Civil Rights bill, and I knew that if the federal government made it a law it'd have to be followed. Our management here is smart, and they knew it too. Besides, that was the only way they could survive."[20]

Alfred Dawkins had worked in maintenance outside the Reeves Brothers Chesnee Mill in the South Carolina Piedmont, but when dependence on federal contracts forced his employers to integrate their plant's workforce in the 1960s, Dawkins became the first black employee to "go inside" as a production worker. His wife, Alaree, soon joined him, and though both met some early resistance from white supervisors and coworkers, Alaree, who had worked as a maid before going into the mill, continued to work there until it closed, some thirty years later. "I think it was a good job," she reflected. "We made what everybody else made. . . . It put you in the middle class, I guess. It was good because we were making as much as the whites."[21]

The civil rights movement not only facilitated black upward mobility, but inspired it as well. Watching Rev. Martin Luther King Jr.'s funeral as she sat in the house where she cleaned and cooked for someone else, Essie Favrot suddenly thought, "This man is there in Memphis and lost his life trying to upgrade the black people. And I'm sitting here making five dollars a day just as satisfied, and I said, 'Lord, have mercy, Jesus, if it's your will, I'm going to get out here and do better.'" After a two-year night-school nursing course, Favrot could find no work as a nurse's aide, but she went on to become an executive housekeeper, supervising fifteen workers at a hospital.[22]

While some black leaders expressed disappointment with the initial pace of both political and economic change, many anxious and resentful white southerners reacted strongly to what they saw as rapid and revolutionary black advances. In the first half of the twentieth century white voting in presidential elections in the one-party South seldom reached half the turnout levels elsewhere, and scarcely 60 percent of eligible whites were even registered in 1960. That changed quickly after 1965, however, as whites descended in huge numbers on local registrars throughout the region. In fact, a key reason blacks failed to claim more elective offices in the immediate aftermath of the Voting Rights Act was that while registration among adult blacks in the old Confederacy shot up from 36 to 65 percent between 1964 and 1969, white registration also rose significantly, from 73 to 84 percent. Because the adult white population outnumbered the adult black population by about four to one, even though the South had gained 1.8 million new black voters over the course of the decade, the white electorate had actually swelled by 4.7 million during the 1960s. Population growth accounted for roughly 60 percent of the white increase, but it seems safe to conclude that most of the rest did not register for the first time in order to vote for black candidates in local races. Nor did they show much inclination to support a national Democratic Party that, in their view, had rewarded nearly a century's worth of their all but unshakeable loyalty by turning their racial world upside down. Indeed, angry white southerners were about to retaliate by turning the Democrats' political world upside down as well.[23]

The ascendant hero of the Republican Party's right wing, Senator Barry Goldwater of Arizona, had been a favorite of southern whites since he expressed reservations about the Kennedy administration's handling of the Ole Miss integration crisis in 1962. Needless to say, his vote against the Civil Rights Act of 1964 had done nothing to diminish his stature in diehard segregationist circles. Mississippian Florence Sillers Ogden had written as early as 1962 in her syndicated column, "Dis 'n Dat," that "a southerner cannot be a conservative and a Democrat, too." By 1964 she was calling for all loyal white Mississippians to "forever break with the National Democratic Party." Ogden made no bones about her own intention to vote for Goldwater, and she was confident not only that her father would approve, but "so would my two Confederate grandfathers."[24]

The key to understanding the explosive growth of Republican voting in Augusta, Georgia, lay in a Democrats for Goldwater group organized by one-time local political kingpin Roy E. Harris, a segregationist mainstay of the old Talmadge machine who published an openly white supremacist newspaper. Some Republican organizers had insisted that they were not trying to capitalize on a "white backlash" against the Democrats, but when GOP vice-presidential candidate William Miller came to Augusta for a speech, a more candid Republican activist bragged to a reporter that "there was only one nigger in the crowd" and predicted, "If Johnson comes in here, it'll look like a checkerboard out there." Sure enough, on election day Johnson appeared to collect practically every black vote cast in Augusta, while Goldwater swept the city's predominantly white wards, including Ward 5, where working-class whites gave him 75 percent of the vote after producing a narrow majority for Democrat John F. Kennedy only four years earlier.[25]

Across the South the story was much the same. The Republican candidate made good on his vow to "go hunting where the ducks are" by courting southern whites who were disenchanted with the Democratic Party's pro–civil rights stance, and he did so openly and blatantly, while showing not so much as a pretense of interest in winning black support. Thus he effectively got none while amassing huge white majorities in areas where substantial black populations had yet to be enfranchised by the Voting Rights Act. The counties of the southern Black Belt, home to the South's most racially conservative whites and large numbers of unregistered blacks, had given 58 percent of their votes to Democrat John F. Kennedy in 1960 only to go for Goldwater by a slightly higher proportion four years later. Where blacks could vote the outcome was stunning in its racial polarity. Goldwater averaged over 90 percent in Jackson, Mississippi's white precincts and over 80 percent in Mobile, Alabama, where he received less than 1 percent of the black vote. Overall, he racked up white majorities in every southern state except Lyndon Johnson's Texas. In dragging Alabama, Georgia, Louisiana, Mississippi, and South Carolina into the Republican column (all save Louisiana for the first time since Reconstruction), Goldwater also helped to elect seven new GOP congressmen from the Deep South, five of them from Alabama alone.[26]

Goldwater's success in their region made a serious impression on Democratic congressmen, especially those from deepest Dixie; and 86 percent of them opposed the Voting Rights Act the following year. Fervent, racially coded opposition to federal intervention quickly became the best hope for southern Democrats looking to punch their return tickets to Washington, particularly those representing largely rural districts. With candidates of both parties scrambling to get to the right of each other on racial and social issues in general, black voters typically deemed even a conservative Democrat preferable to a Republican. Hence the key for the GOP congressional candidates in 1966 was to use the Democrats' greater appeal to black voters against them by suggesting that their opponents would roll into office already beholden to a black "bloc" vote unless whites effectively voted as a bloc themselves on behalf of the Republicans. Because this appeal to white solidarity was more compelling in counties where whites were likely to feel most threatened by growing black political clout, Republican candidates in the Deep South actually fared better in districts where the black population was greater than 15 percent. In 1966 all but one of the GOP's six Deep South congressional victories came in districts with black populations of 30 percent or more. In the border-state South, where white solidarity was harder to muster, Republicans claimed only one of their eighteen victories in a district with a black population of this size and only six of them where the black population exceeded 15 percent.[27]

The South and America since World War II

Although no southern Republicans had gained statewide office in 1964, the days of counting on steadfast support for any Democratic candidate were clearly a thing of the past. While two-thirds of southern whites still saw themselves as Democrats in 1964, by 1968 that number had fallen to one-half, a trend reflected in the election of Republican governors in Arkansas, Florida, Kentucky, and Oklahoma in 1966 and 1967. Kentucky Republican John Sherman Cooper retained his U.S. Senate seat in 1966, and Howard H. Baker Jr. joined him from Tennessee.[28]

In addition, Howard H. "Bo" Callaway, a segregationist Georgia Republican who had ridden Barry Goldwater's coattails to a congressional seat in 1964, won a slim 3,000-vote plurality in the 1966 Georgia gubernatorial race. Yet Callaway's failure to capture a majority of the vote put the decision into the hands of the state legislature, whose Democratic majority showed no hesitation whatsoever in handing the keys to the governor's mansion to Callaway's opponent, Lester G. Maddox, the axe-handle-wielding Atlanta who had closed his fried chicken restaurant rather than serve blacks. Maddox had bested the more moderate former governor Ellis G. Arnall in the Democratic primary, amassing a 64 percent majority, courtesy, in large part, of racially conservative white voters in the Georgia countryside. Like that of Lurleen Wallace, anointed by her husband, George, as his stand-in successor in Alabama in 1966, Maddox's improbable ascent to the governorship suggested that, despite a dramatically expanded black share of the electorate, for Democrats who aspired to political office in the Deep South, the very appearance of racial liberalism, even in moderation, was still ill-advised.[29]

In light of his staggering defeat nationwide, white southerners' enthusiasm for Goldwater in 1964 might have seemed like nothing more than further evidence of their affinity for lost causes. In forthcoming presidential elections, however, their partisan as well as ideological stances would actually put them closer to the American political mainstream than they had been for several generations. Convinced that northern whites shared many of the racial and status anxieties of their southern counterparts, Governor George Wallace of Alabama had stunned liberal pundits by grabbing 34 percent of the 1964 Democratic presidential primary vote in Wisconsin, 30 percent in Indiana, and a whopping 43 percent in Maryland. At that point Wallace began to talk about a third-party candidacy, but lacking funds as well as a broad organizational base, he also let it be known that he was available to serve as Goldwater's running mate. When his overtures were summarily rebuffed, Wallace had little choice but to put his presidential plans on hold until 1968.[30]

As the 1968 campaign approached, the Republicans seemed poised to expand on Goldwater's five-state Deep South breakthrough in 1964, but where Wallace had been forced to abandon his campaign four years earlier, he was now in the race as the candidate of the American Independent Party and committed not only to sweeping the South but to making a race of it nationally as well. Such an idea might have seemed far-fetched if not ludicrous in 1964, but over the intervening four years a "white backlash" against black advances had clearly surfaced above the Mason-Dixon line. The explosion of violence in the Los Angeles ghetto of Watts in August 1965 and similar conflagrations in Detroit and Newark two years later not only exposed black anger at racial conditions in northern cities but sparked white anger and anxiety as well. The same was true of the Black Power movement and ideology so aggressively articulated by Stokely Carmichael in 1966, after James Meredith was shot before completing a symbolic walk from Memphis to Jackson. Needless to say, Carmichael's denunciation of black soldiers serving in Vietnam as "traitors" to their race and his insistence that when a black soldier was issued a weapon with orders to "shoot his enemy... if he don't shoot Lurleen and George [Wallace] and little junior, he's a fool," did little to defuse racial tensions in the South or elsewhere.[31]

Meanwhile, northern whites had shown little enthusiasm when civil rights leaders began to take their campaign for racial equality beyond the South. Reverend King's efforts to call attention to poverty and segregation in Chicago culminated in an August 1966 march to Marquette Park, located in an area inhabited by the first-generation descendants of European immigrants. A great number of locals turned out to shout greetings to "Martin Luther Coon" and bombard him and his entourage with a hail of bricks (one of which knocked the civil rights leader to his knees), bottles, and additional racist invective. Afterward a shaken King remarked that he had "never seen such hate, not in Mississippi or Alabama as I see here in Chicago." The rioting that exploded in several major cities in the wake of King's assassination in April 1968 further stoked racial resentment among northern whites, as did the wild and ugly melee in the streets outside the Democratic convention in Chicago a few months later.[32]

In short, the entirety of America had become much more fertile ground for a naturally gifted rabble-rouser and polarizer like George

Wallace. A 1968 Gallup poll showed Wallace to be the seventh most admired man in America, placing him just ahead of the pope. Even so, the Wallace campaign faced a major challenge in some states, especially California, where third parties had to register at least 1 percent of the electorate as members in order to get their candidate on the ballot. For Wallace's American Independent Party, this meant collecting almost sixty-six thousand signatures in a state where even the conservative press had heaped vituperation on Wallace's head. A condescending *Los Angeles Times* writer who confidently predicted "Wallace will never make it" simply failed to understand how well the Alabama governor's unsubtle racial message resonated with white audiences, especially in working-class neighborhoods. Wallace obviously touched a nerve when he asked, "How would you Californians like it if you were told you would have to bus your children out of your neighborhood?" and when he ridiculed left-wing "pseudo-intellectuals" who "explain it away" when "someone goes out and burns down half a city and murders someone…by saying the killer didn't get any watermelon to eat when he was 10 years old." Finally, he connected with voters in California who were upset by campus anti-war protests and other demonstrations at Berkeley and elsewhere by condemning "pro-Communist, long-haired hippies" who were trying to take over their "tax-supported" universities while spouting "the academic freedom talk that allows people to call for Communist victory."[33]

In the end, after securing 100,000 signatures, well over the required 66,000, Wallace enjoyed the last laugh at the expense of the naysayers who had dismissed his prospects of even getting on the California ballot. Nationwide, the Wallace campaign collected some 2.7 million signatures on ballot petitions despite having to operate on alien turf with few or no local contacts. The campaign also raised $9 million; this included an estimated $250,000 to $300,000 in cash stuffed into a briefcase, courtesy of Texas billionaire Bunker Hunt, and three $10,000 checks from actor John Wayne, the last supposedly inscribed "Sock it to 'em, George." Such high-profile donors and supporters notwithstanding, more than 80 percent of Wallace's contribution total came in increments of $50 or less solicited by mail or at fund-raisers or rallies where "Wallace girls" simply passed the bucket.[34]

Wallace clearly had no real prospect of capturing enough votes to win the presidency outright, but he reasoned that if the race between Republican Richard Nixon and Democrat Hubert Humphrey proved to be as tight as expected, he might have a good chance of throwing the election into the House of Representatives and even winning an electoral vote plurality. If he simply carried the same Deep South states as Goldwater and won the border states as well, he would have already collected 177 electoral votes, and eking out a narrow victory in a few states like Indiana or Ohio might actually make him the frontrunner. Congress, so Wallace managed to convince himself, would not dare elevate a second-place finisher to the presidency.[35]

Outraged by Wallace's mere presence on the ballot, northern commentators made no effort to conceal their contempt for him or his campaign entourage, even as they ducked the issue of his obvious appeal to many voters in their supposedly enlightened city or region. Gary Wills compared Wallace to "a B-movie idol" playing "a handsome garage attendant who comes out rubbing his hands on an invisible garage rag (most of the pit grease out of his nails), smiling and winking....His hair still wet from careful work with comb and water in the gas station's cracked mirror." Northern reporters delighted in listing and detailing "Wallaceisms," such as "Electorial college" and "stastistics," some of them uncertain whether the governor actually knew no better or simply "mashed" such words deliberately in order to show his contempt for those who pronounced them crisply and correctly.[36]

Scorning Wallace as "the racist candidate" in February 1968, the New York Times fretted at the outside chance that he might do well enough to propel the presidential selection process into congressional hands, but predicted, "Since Mr. Wallace is an ignorant, mean-spirited adventurer without personally attractive or socially redeeming qualities…the longer he campaigns the weaker he will become." A few weeks later a Gallup poll showed Wallace with 11 percent support nationally, but that figure rose to 14 percent by early May, leading George Gallup to warn that if the election "were being held today" there was "a strong possibility" that Wallace "would deny either major party candidate the electoral votes needed to win." By mid-July Wallace's support had edged up to 16 percent.[37]

Much to the dismay of northeastern liberals, Wallace found common ground with many whites in Massachusetts by taking issue with the National Advisory Commission on Civil Disorder's emphasis on white racism as a primary cause of recent racial violence in major cities. "They're trying to tell all of you that you're guilty," he insisted, "[but] the country's not sick, the Supreme Court is sick." His attacks on "lawlessness and crime" represented "the kind of thing that the little people

The South and America since World War II

George Wallace, campaigning in Illinois, 1968. Bettman/Corbis.

like me are worried about," a young Connecticut woman admitted, insisting she was not "an extremist or a nut, and I grew up right here in Wethersfield. But I talked around some, and I think you'll find lots more Wallace support up North than they say." Charging that "liberal newspaper editors" were criticizing him for saying "what the people want to hear" as if "what the people want is bad," Wallace delighted a crowd in Hammond, Indiana, by asking "the little folks" to help him bring down "the smart folks in Washington who have been looking down their noses at you." He also found a receptive audience among whites in Michigan who competed with blacks for jobs in the automobile industry.[38]

Wallace seemed to come across especially well with turf-conscious and somewhat xenophobic northern ethnic voters. Covering a Wallace rally at Milwaukee's Serb Hall, gonzo journalist Hunter S. Thompson looked on in amazement as Wallace delighted his audience with his vicious attacks on civil rights "agitators," "hippies," "Communists," and various criminals who had "turned to rape and murder 'cause they didn't get enough broccoli when they were little boys." All but transfixed by Wallace's performance, Thompson felt almost as if he were witnessing the political equivalent of "a Janis Joplin concert": "The bastard had somehow levitated himself and was hovering above us."[39]

Not all Wallace's northern audiences were totally enthusiastic. In fact, television news crews at his rallies took to setting up with one camera focused on the podium and one pointed at the audience, where confrontation and disruption were all but guaranteed. Wallace was right in his element in Milwaukee when 250 black protestors positioned themselves in the midst of 5,000 whites, stomping their feet in unison and taunting the speaker with shouts of "Sieg heil." He quickly turned the situation to his advantage, however, urging cameramen to focus on his antagonists and noting with a smirk, "I usually talk about anarchy, but I don't have to tonight, you can see it."[40]

Wallace consistently denied being a racist even as he employed all of his considerable cunning in appealing to the racism of his northern audiences. Many members of those audiences were not so constrained by the niceties of public discourse. "Now let's get serious a minute," a Polish American man in Webster, Massachusetts, demanded of Wallace's strategist Tom Turnipseed. "When Wallace gets elected president, he's going to round up all the niggers and shoot them, isn't he?" Thinking the man was joking, a laughing Turnipseed replied, "No, nothing like that. We're just worried about some agitators. We're not going to shoot anybody." Turnipseed quickly realized his grim-faced questioner was genuinely disappointed, however, when the man responded, "Well, I don't know whether I'm for him or not." In one of the many ironies generated by the Wallace campaign outside the South, his organizers were frequently shocked and dismayed by the open, unfettered racism and advocacy of violence they encountered among those who volunteered to support their efforts.[41]

Back in February the *New York Times* had editorialized that Americans in general were too enlightened and smart to embrace an "ignorant" candidate like Wallace, but by mid-September, with some polls suggesting that he might get as much as 20 percent of the vote in November, the *Times* was lamenting the "Wallace Sickness" that was "abroad in the land." The writer pleaded with Americans "to ask themselves whether their discontents are so fierce, their grievances so woeful that they are prepared to follow this apostle of violence and anger as he leads them they know not where." Did northern white workers really resent recent black advances enough to "vote for this smooth-talking adventurer"? Did the young northerners who attended Wallace rallies really see him even remotely approaching "the integrity, the intellectual breadth, the charity or the compassion required of a President of the United States"? Mystified as to how such "an evil phenomenon" as the Wallace movement had become "a major factor in national politics," the writer clearly believed that many Americans outside the South had simply taken temporary leave of their senses. How else could one explain their attraction to this man who was merely "the political expression of the school burners and the church bombers and the night riders"?[42]

Reporters who saw Wallace's appeal to northern campaign audiences firsthand were less likely to see him as simply the carrier of a contagion of southern bigotry and belligerence. Wallace had gained standing as a "national candidate," wrote Ben A. Franklin, "not because he has abandoned the attitudes of the South but because the rest of the country more and more embraces them." It remained, however, for veteran journalist Douglas Kiker, a southerner himself, to sum up the Wallace campaign's appeal in the North with the observation that Wallace had made the startling discovery that whites in the North were not all that different from whites in the South: "They all hate black people, all of them. They're all afraid, all of them. Great God! That's it! That's it. They're all Southern! The whole United States is Southern!"[43]

For most of the campaign, no voters seemed more southern than the white factory workers of the nation's old industrial belt, many of whom saw themselves competing directly with blacks for jobs and promotions. A number of locals either endorsed Wallace or refused to endorse Democratic nominee Hubert Humphrey. As a UAW official saw it, "The men in the plants want to zap the Negroes by voting for Wallace. It's as simple as that." Actually it was a bit more complicated. The Wallace supporters among the unions' rank and file also wanted to "zap" labor leaders who seemed routinely to ignore the wishes of many of their constituents by endorsing the kind of liberal candidates and policies that Wallace was so busy condemning. Still, union officials suspected that their members' enthusiasm for Wallace was both exaggerated and transitory. Even as he peaked in the national polls, a nationwide survey showed only 16 percent of unionized workers outside the South actually intended to vote for him. This did not prevent labor leaders from unloosing a withering counterattack against a self-styled champion of the "little man" who had consistently opposed unions, higher wages, and better benefits for workers in a state that ranked forty-eighth in per capita income. An AFL-CIO pamphlet put it bluntly enough for any northern worker to understand: "George Wallace could cost you one thousand dollars a year."[44]

The anti-Wallace union fusillade was only one of his problems as the campaign moved into the final weeks. Seeking a running mate, Wallace had first asked A. B. "Happy" Chandler, a former governor of Kentucky and one-time commissioner of major league baseball. As baseball commissioner, however, Chandler had presided over the integration of America's pastime in 1947 and therefore seemed insufficiently adamant in his opposition to black progress to suit many influential, hard-core Wallaceites. To say that Wallace's decision to drop Chandler and go with the notoriously trigger-happy General Curtis LeMay instead proved to be disastrous is to flirt with understatement. At a fateful October 3 press conference, the general made it clear why he was known as "Bombs Away! LeMay," horrifying Wallace (but making things a lot more interesting for the small crew of reporters on hand) by bemoaning the American public's "phobia about nuclear weapons," which he attributed to "the propaganda that's been fed to them." Presumably to alleviate these fears, LeMay reassuringly cited conditions in the Bikini Atoll, where numerous nuclear tests had been conducted, but now the fish, the birds, the coconut trees, indeed every living thing seemed to be flourishing— except the "land crabs," which the general reluctantly conceded "might still be a little hot."[45]

Not surprisingly, the incident triggered a chorus of "I told you so's" from those who had argued that Wallace was both too reckless and too inexperienced to be taken seriously as a presidential candidate. Ultimately polls showed that the fiasco hurt him far more outside the South than within it, especially with women voters. Meanwhile, he also faced a vigorous counterassault from the Nixon camp, which warned southern whites that by supporting Wallace they could wind up electing Humphrey. As of September many believed that Wallace might actually deny Nixon any of the old Confederate states, and the GOP strategy seemed simply to concede to him the Deep South states that had gone to Goldwater in 1964, save for South Carolina, where Senator Strom Thurmond, the old Dixiecrat turned Republican, was expected to hold the state for his new party. Otherwise, the Nixon plan was to contest the Upper South states by avoiding the bluntly antiblack, anti–civil rights rhetoric of Goldwater while still making it abundantly clear to apprehensive white parents that a Nixon administration would oppose "forced busing" to achieve school integration.

Nixon's selection of Maryland governor Spiro T. Agnew as his running mate struck most observers as an overture to southern white voters. Agnew had won Nixon's favor by blaming "caterwauling, riot-inciting, burn-America-down" black leaders for five days of rioting in Baltimore following the assassination of Reverend King in April 1968. Agnew showed no qualms about using deadly force to deter rioting, suggesting that all looters should be "shot down by police." When the Republican vice-presidential candidate threatened rioters and verbally pummeled bleeding-heart white liberals, Agnew got the point across that Nixon would be just as quick as Wallace to restore "law and order" by saying the things that Nixon himself could not say if he wanted to present himself as a like-minded but more moderate and responsible alternative to the rabble-rousing Alabama governor.[46]

As what Dan Carter called "the master of the wink, the nudge, the implied commitment," Nixon himself two-stepped more than once on civil rights issues. He promised to enforce Title VI of the Civil Rights Act of 1964, which provided for the denial of federal funds to school districts still practicing outright segregation, but vowed not to do so simply to achieve a "radical balance" of the races in the public schools. Likewise, he pledged that his administration would be open to freedom-of-choice plans, provided they were not simply subterfuges for maintaining segregation—this despite recent court rulings suggesting that such plans were at best inadequate vehicles for achieving integration. Nixon had made it clear, even as he pursued southern delegates at the GOP convention, that he would take a minimalist approach to enforcing pro–civil rights court decisions and be in no hurry to "satisfy some special civil rights group or something like that." In the waning days of the campaign, by reiterating his lack of enthusiasm for implementing such rulings, Nixon forced Hubert Humphrey to renew his pledge to enforce them fully and vigorously. This undercut Wallace's contention that there wasn't "a dime's worth of difference" between the candidates of the two major parties and demonstrated why white southerners should think twice about voting for Wallace, lest they wind up electing Humphrey.[47]

In the end Nixon captured seven southern states, all of them, except South Carolina, in the upper South. Wallace racked up a majority of the votes in Alabama and Mississippi and carried Arkansas, Georgia, and Louisiana as well. Humphrey was a pariah to southern whites, including many Democratic politicos, but owing to the influence of native son Lyndon Johnson, who had declined to seek reelection himself, he narrowly bested Nixon in Texas. Overall, Nixon captured 36 percent of the southern popular vote compared to 33 percent for Wallace and 31 percent for Humphrey, whose totals closely approximated black turnout. Nationally Wallace had stood at 20 percent in the polls as late as the end of September, but the LeMay fiasco and Nixon's clear signals that he had no great interest in civil rights enforcement sent Wallace's candidacy swooning in early October, and he finished with 13.5 percent of the total vote, with more than half of his ten million ballots coming from the South.[48]

Political analyst Kevin Phillips saw the 1968 election as the harbinger of "a new American Revolution," driven by an "emerging Republican majority" that would be fueled by middle- and lower-middle-class whites in the South and West. In positioning himself as a more moderate and responsible alternative to Wallace, Nixon had captured the votes of suburban upper-South whites who were nervous about busing and urban violence but likely to be a bit uncomfortable with Wallace's outright segregationism and crude threats to run down antiwar protestors who tried to block his way. Once in office Nixon continued to suggest that white southerners were being singled out unfairly to bear the burden of school integration: "Let's just stop this hypocrisy that the problem in our schools is only in the South....The time has come to quit jerking the South around."[49]

Nixon revealed no real personal desire to roll back the fundamental accomplishments of the civil rights movement, but from a political standpoint it clearly made sense for him to give southern whites the impression that he was trying to do just that. In reality, however, as Phillips, the original architect of Nixon's southern strategy, pointed out in 1969, "The Republicans would be shortsighted if they weakened enforcement of the Voting Rights Act. The more Negroes who register as Democrats in the South, the sooner the Negrophobe whites will quit the Democrats and become Republicans. That's where the votes are."[50]

Up to this point, meanwhile, gross racial imbalances in northern schools had largely escaped judicial scrutiny because they were said to be products not of unconstitutional southern-style *de jure* school segregation but merely incidental to supposedly *de facto* residential segregation. Yet by the end of the 1960s some activists had begun to ask if southern school systems were obligated not simply to end long-standing formal policies of segregation but to eliminate the racial imbalances created by those policies, why should systems outside the South be any less obliged to rectify similar conditions in their own schools, regardless of the causes. Beyond that, by the early 1970s some jurists were also beginning to affirm claims by the NAACP and parents groups in other regions that school segregation in their cities was actually the de jure result of official municipal or school board policies and practices relating to public and private housing, zoning, school construction and placement, and pupil assignment. Therefore, these judges reasoned, northern officials also had a responsibility to integrate their schools even if busing was required to achieve that end.

At the time, the northward shift in judicial scrutiny and pressure seemed to raise the curtain on a more expansive phase of the civil rights movement that would lead to a comprehensive effort to achieve greater racial balance in public schools throughout the country. In retrospect, however, the real future of court-ordered busing was actually foretold in an extensive October 1969 *Newsweek* report titled "The White Majority," which pointed to a Gallup poll showing 98 percent hostility to busing nationwide. There was also considerable predictive power in the fact that the antibusing statutes approved by several southern legislatures at that point were actually all but verbatim copies of a New York law decreeing that no student could be "assigned or compelled to attend any school on account of race, creed, color, or national origin or for the purpose of achieving equality of attendance or increased attendance or reduced attendance at any school."[51]

To the disappointment and anger of both black and white southerners who had laid lives and careers on the line in support of school integration, many northern liberals in Congress were now protesting that busing should be used only to rectify racial imbalances that had been caused by generations of legally mandated segregation in the South. Although she had once criticized President Eisenhower for his failure to support school desegregation efforts in the South, Oregon congresswoman Edith Green recoiled from the prospect of busing in her own state. Sounding for all the world like many a southern white parent, Green complained, "We cannot go back 100 years to correct the errors that may or may not have been made by our ancestors." However, when Mississippi senator John C. Stennis introduced a proposal that would have applied federal desegregation guidelines "uniformly in all regions of the United States without regard to the origin or cause of such segregation," he drew unexpected support from liberal Connecticut senator Abraham Ribicoff. "A child in the third grade who goes to an all-black or all-white school—whether in Mississippi or New York

City—has not the slightest idea that there is a difference between *dejure* and *defacto*," Ribicoff insisted. "If segregation's bad in Alabama, it's bad in Connecticut." When Ribicoff's squirming northern colleagues refused to accept Stennis's proposal or Ribicoff's own plan to gradually integrate schools in northern suburbs, he scolded them for their "hypocrisy," accusing New York's Jacob Javits of lacking "the guts to face your liberal constituents who have moved to the suburbs to avoid sending their children to school with blacks."[52]

Having used all manner of subterfuge and obstruction to maintain school segregation themselves, white southerners in Congress had no trouble seeing through arguments by northern liberals that applying the same school integration standards nationwide would undermine support for maintaining desegregation pressures in the South. They were not alone. *New York Times* reporter David Rosenbaum observed matter-of-factly in January 1972, "The tide in Congress began to shift dramatically against school desegregation last year, just as Southern congressmen have always said it would, when the courts began to require the same disruption of traditional school assignments in the North that had been forced on the South throughout the 1960s." If this perception required further confirmation, it came shortly thereafter, when, with Detroit officials facing Federal District Judge Stephen J. Roth's order for busing on an unprecedented scale, George Wallace won the majority of votes in the 1972 Michigan Democratic presidential primary. Roth's decree had earned him a chorus of death threats and the kind of calumny once reserved only for integrationist judges in the South. Not coincidentally, Wallace's standard campaign fare at that point included withering denunciations of federal judges who issued "asinine busing decisions."[53]

In 1972 the Civil Rights Commission reported that 98 percent of the black children in Chicago attended schools that were more than 50 percent black, and the figures for Los Angeles, Philadelphia, and Detroit were all above 90 percent. While northern whites continued to express strong support for school integration in principle, a 1973 Gallup Poll found 63 percent of them opposed to sending their own children to predominantly black schools. The prospect of busing had sparked school bus bombings in Pontiac, Michigan, and even fueled noticeable Klan activity in and around Detroit.[54]

The most shocking revelation of northern whites' hostility to forced integration in their own schools came in the fall of 1974, when a federal judge ordered the busing of seventeen thousand students to break down racial concentrations in Boston, where over half the black pupils were in schools that were at least 90 percent black. In its jaw-dropping ugliness and sheer ferocity, the response from whites in Boston surely equaled, if not exceeded, anything seen in Little Rock or New Orleans. Black students bused in to South Boston High regularly faced a hail of rocks and racial epithets, both in the parking lots and on the buses themselves, and every incidence of racially mixed one-on-one violence seemed to mushroom into a larger confrontation. With ubiquitous graffiti proclaiming "FUCK NIGGERS!" and "KEEP SOUTHIE WHITE!" a protest march of five thousand angry whites through the South Boston area drew local white politicos of every stripe, each looking to outdo the others in denouncing busing. Meanwhile, a wholesale exodus of twenty thousand white students gave Boston a majority-minority school system in short order. This uproar in the birthplace of the abolitionist movement, the hometown of the Kennedys, and a supposed stronghold of contemporary liberalism forcefully demonstrated once again that for many northern whites ending segregation in southern schools was one thing, but in their own schools quite another.[55]

When she spoke with Robert Coles in 1966, a woman of Irish descent who lived in a mixed Irish-Italian working-class neighborhood revealed the same sort of resentment toward Boston's upper-class suburban whites that white southerners had reserved for holier-than-thou northerners who were forcing them to accept integration: "It's the rich, out there in the suburbs, who keep on telling us what we should do. They preach at us to take them [blacks] here and let them live there, and act this way to them, and that, and so on until you get sick hearing it all.... They stepped all over us, and kept us out of everything, the Yankees and the college people over there at Harvard did.... Now...they're all excited and worried about people, but only the Negroes get their sympathy, only them. Talking about prejudice, that's what we face, prejudice against us."[56]

A young white lawyer from a low-income white neighborhood agreed: "The suburban housewives and the Ivy League students, they've gone poor-crazy, but only for the colored poor. They've been pushing us around all these years before the Negroes started coming up from the South, and now they have someone to do it for them.... It's a two-faced business if you ask me and it's becoming worse now that they talk about juggling our kids around so that they're 'integrated.' That's when you'll get the explosion here, when they try to move our kids across the city, or bring all those little darkies here."[57]

Such southern resentments coming out of northern mouths made for a political no-brainer for Richard Nixon, whose southern strategy now seemed to have genuinely national possibilities. Back in July 1969 Nixon's Justice Department had petitioned to delay court-ordered desegregation of local school districts. The move had solidified Nixon's standing with southern white voters, and its rejection by the courts had also affirmed the villainy of liberal judges in the eyes of many whites in the South and elsewhere. Suddenly, the new president's judicial appointments seemed all the more crucial. With southern white voters primarily in mind at that point, Nixon nominated South Carolinian Clement F. Haynesworth Jr. to replace departing, U. S. Supreme Court Justice Abe Fortas in August 1969. Liberal Democrats succeeded in blocking Haynesworth's confirmation on the grounds that he had voted against a desegregation order in the high-profile Prince Edward County, Virginia, school case and, in addition to amassing a strong pro-management record in labor disputes, had also ruled in a case involving a company on whose board he served. Nixon then nominated Floridian G. Harold Carswell, whose history of segregationist politics and efforts to block the integration of a Tallahassee golf club rendered him unacceptable in short order. For many, however, the Haynesworth and Carswell defeats merely affirmed Nixon's repeated suggestions that white southerners were often singled out unfairly for special scrutiny by self-righteous, regionally biased northern Democrats.

Despite the Haynesworth and Carswell setbacks, Nixon soon delivered on the judicial relief he had promised southern whites, ultimately much to the delight of many white northerners as well. In 1974 Nixon appointees Warren Burger, Harry Blackmun, Lewis F. Powell Jr., and onetime *Brown* decision critic and future chief justice William Rehnquist provided four of the five majority votes in *Milliken v. Bradley*, which overturned the earlier lower court ruling that required a desegregation plan for Detroit that would encompass eighty-five suburban districts and require massive busing. Finding no suburban responsibility for current patterns of school segregation in Detroit, the majority opinion held that "dismantling a dual school system" need not entail "any particular racial balance" in a specific "school, grade, or classroom." This ruling, complained a dissenting Justice William O. Douglas, "means that there is no violation of the Equal Protection Clause though the schools are

The South and America since World War II

segregated by race and though the black schools are not only separate but inferior." Also dissenting, Justice Thurgood Marshall lamented a ruling that he saw as "a reflection of a perceived public mood that we have gone far enough in enforcing the Constitution's product of neutral principles of law."[58]

Marshall was right on target, of course, and the "public mood" that shaped this and subsequent similar decrees and essentially put the brakes on aggressive federal efforts to protect and extend minority rights was not merely southern but truly national in scope. The effort to integrate America's classrooms had rightly begun in the old Jim Crow South, where it had finally met with considerable success after taking on the trappings of a long overdue crusade for justice, pitting northern virtue and enlightenment against the stubborn, provincial bigotry of white southerners. When the judicial mandate to eradicate school segregation "root and branch" wherever it might be found steered the desegregation crusade northward, however, the campaign for school integration had quickly ceased be one of enlightenment and virtue and become one of impractical idealism run amok.

In short order the uproar over busing outside the South promised to transform the Republican southern strategy of promising to pull back on enforcing desegregation into a message likely to appeal to white voters throughout the country. Still covering all his bases, however, Nixon continued to commiserate with white southerners about the "double, hypocritical standards of those Northerners who look at the South and say: 'Why don't those Southerners do something about their race problem?'" Nixon knew that in a two-way race he had little to fear in the South from any Democratic opponent in 1972, but as late as mid-1970 he had scribbled and underlined in his notes, *"Need to Handle Wallace."* Knowing that if Wallace ran as an independent practically every vote he received would come at Nixon's expense, the administration had tried to thwart his presidential plans by derailing his bid to reclaim the Alabama governorship in 1970. This entailed funneling some $400,000 in campaign funds to his opponent, Albert Brewer.[59]

When that effort failed to keep Wallace out of the governor's office, the Nixon camp apparently decided to make him an offer he could not refuse. In January 1972, a week after the Justice Department announced that it was dropping its investigation of Wallace's brother Gerald (and potentially even Wallace himself) for accepting illegal personal and political payoffs from state contractors, the Alabama governor shocked supporters and detractors alike by announcing that he would be pursuing the presidency in 1972 as a Democrat rather than an Independent. Suspicions of a backroom deal were rampant and probably well-founded, but nothing could be proven, and Wallace's nominal return to the Democratic field further enhanced the already strong prospects of Nixon's return to the White House. With Wallace effectively out of the way even before he was disabled by a would-be assassin's bullet during the presidential primary season, Nixon went on to reunite the white southern vote, claiming every southern state as he routed his hapless Democratic opponent, George McGovern, in November 1972.[60]

The Republican conquest of the South was still incomplete, however, because despite its recent presidential successes in the region, the GOP's efforts to capture offices farther down the ticket had not gone so smoothly. Nearly a century's worth of dominance in state politics had created strong, entrenched statewide networks of Democratic officials in practically every southern county courthouse. The Republicans, meanwhile, were practically starting from scratch in counties beyond their state's metropolitan areas. Beyond that, in a number of states the Democrats stood ready to offer a number of appealing, well-educated, politically savvy candidates who managed not only to learn from what the Republicans had done in presidential politics, but in some respects to turn it against them. In fact, the 1970 gubernatorial races showed remarkable Democratic resilience as several successful candidates managed to bring together the blue-collar whites who had flocked to Wallace and the black voters who had supported Humphrey, sometimes adding a surprising number of suburban white voters who seemed a much more natural fit for the GOP.

Reubin Askew came out of the Florida Panhandle to defeat the erratic right-wing Republican incumbent governor Claude Kirk, who had ordered some school districts to defy desegregation decrees and praised the combative Spiro Agnew as "our gladiator [against] the Philistines, the ultraliberal and wild radicals." Promising racial moderation and vowing to restore political stability and pursue economic growth, Askew won the backing of former Wallaceite blue-collar whites in northern Florida as well as more moderate whites in the suburbs. His Democratic colleague Lawton Chiles captured a Senate seat from Florida with much the same approach after kicking off his populist campaign with a well-publicized, thousand-mile "walk" from one end of the state to the other. In Arkansas, Dale Bumpers promised fairness and moderation en route to winning the governorship in 1970. In South Carolina, Lieutenant Governor John C. West moved up to the governor's office, overcoming Goldwater Republican Albert Watson's crude, racially charged appeal to whites after promising to destroy all vestiges of racial discrimination in state government and rejecting "all forms of extremism and demagoguery that seemingly motivate our opposition." In reality, though, even some successful Republican candidates, such as Winfield Dunn in Tennessee and Linwood Holton in Virginia, pursued a decidedly more restrained approach than their party's national strategy suggested.[61]

Several historians have argued that the results of the 1970 elections represented a defeat for the GOP's race-centric southern strategy, but it is easy to overlook how closely the successful Democratic candidates followed the Wallace model in appealing to white voters. For example, if this surge of victorious southern moderates served clear notice that the era of standing in the schoolhouse door to defy court orders was definitely over, the newcomers' positions on school busing ranged from steadfastly critical to promises of outright resistance. In Georgia the self-described peanut farmer and former state senator Jimmy Carter sometimes sounded like a Wallace impersonator as he won the governorship in 1970 by successfully wooing the blue-collar whites who had catapulted the defiant segregationist Lester Maddox into the governor's mansion in 1966 and then rallied behind Wallace in 1968. Openly critical of forced busing, Carter skillfully contrasted his own image as a hard-working farmer and agribusinessman with that of his chief opponent, the moderate and urbane Democratic insider Carl E. "Cufflinks Carl" Sanders.

Still, although Carter's victory suggested that just a whiff of the old-style southern politics might still pay off for Democratic candidates with white voters, his oft-quoted inaugural announcement that "the time for racial discrimination is over" indicated that Carter the governor would be different from Carter the candidate. The crusty segregationist politico Roy Harris complained that Carter "got elected by saying, 'I'm just like Lester Maddox and George Wallace,' [but] he turns out to be one of the most liberal governors in the South." Carter's racial egalitarianism was very much in the mold of his fellow Democratic moderates of the early 1970s such as John West in South Carolina and Reubin Askew, who told Floridians, "The law demands, and rightly so, that we put an end to segregation in our society."[62]

At the same time, however, West was also in tune with his moderate cohort in promising African Americans "no special status" because this new generation of Democrats was both too skeptical of social welfare programs and too fiscally conservative to spend heavily on them in any event. For that matter, their approach to black poverty and racial disparities in income was not unlike Richard Nixon's "bootstrap" plan, which stressed the need to create more jobs and see to it that these jobs were filled without regard to an applicant's color. In fact, save for renouncing segregation, these new moderates called to mind the early World War II veterans' campaigns to promote economic growth and improve education while making government more responsible, honest, and efficient.[63]

In this sense, once in office this new breed of southern governors was far more bureaucratic than populist, supporting both constitutional and governmental reform and soliciting far more input from businesspeople and manufacturers than from the people who worked for them, much less the people who struggled to find any work at all. When Jimmy Carter drew up his plan to reorganize state government he relied heavily on corporate executives and academicians, and in selling the plan to the public he called on top media executives and specialists as well as representatives of the Georgia Chamber of Commerce. From budgeting to bidding, the fiscally cautious Carter emphasized consistency and economy. Meanwhile, he joined his gubernatorial contemporaries throughout the region in ardently courting new industry not just within the United States but throughout Europe and Asia as well.[64]

For all their relative conservatism on monetary and constitutional matters, however, the region's new leaders of this era were clearly far more restrained and realistic on racial matters than their predecessors had been. The sense of a new day in Democratic politics in the South had begun to surface after Virginia's architect of massive resistance, Senator Harry F. Byrd, announced his retirement in 1965 and Georgia's staunchly segregationist senator and longtime southern congressional caucus leader, Richard B. Russell, died in 1971. In both the Senate and the House, death, defeat, and retirement soon thinned the ranks of the old "Dixieland band" of longtime segregationists considerably, and Arkansas's Orval Faubus and his one-time Louisiana gubernatorial contemporary Jimmie H. Davis, both of whom had been at the forefront of southern white defiance in the 1950s, had their bids for political comebacks summarily crushed by voters in 1970 and 1971, respectively.

The South and America since World War II

Once-stalwart segregationists like Mississippi's John Stennis and James Eastland, Georgia's Herman Talmadge, and Arkansas's John McClellan continued to prowl the U.S. Senate, of course, but the times were clearly changing. McClellan was defeated in 1978 and Talmadge in 1980, and the still unapologetic Eastland chose to retire in 1978. On the other side of the aisle, after witnessing the disastrous results of Albert Watson's race-baiting campaign against John West in 1970, South Carolina's Strom Thurmond, who had once vowed that "there aren't enough troops in the Army" to force southern whites to accept integration, not only moderated his rhetoric but added a black aide to his Senate staff.[65]

Southern Republicans like Thurmond hardly expected to win black votes in huge numbers. Yet overt appeals to racism or suggestions that the *Brown* decision or the Civil Rights Act of 1964 or the Voting Rights Act of 1965 might somehow be undone were now outside the comfort zone of many of the South's metropolitan whites. Still, for Democrats an exceedingly delicate balancing act would be required to keep the GOP at bay over the long term. Somehow they must be responsive enough to the concerns of black voters to convince them that their loyalty to the party was not taken for granted without having to embrace expensive social welfare and entitlement programs that stirred the status anxieties of working-class whites in the countryside or threatened the pocketbooks of their more affluent counterparts in the suburbs.

In the 1976 presidential election, with Jimmy Carter bidding to become the first president from the Deep South since Woodrow Wilson, the Democrats rolled out a southern strategy of their own. In essence their battle plan consisted simply of holding together the combination of blacks, blue-collar whites, and a significant minority of upper-income whites that had fueled the moderate triumphs of 1970 in the South. As an economically conservative Southern Baptist who had announced the end of racial discrimination in Georgia and hung a portrait of Rev. Martin Luther King Jr. in the Georgia state capitol, Carter was peculiarly equipped to execute this strategy, and he did so to near perfection. To be sure, Carter's cause benefited significantly from Gerald R. Ford's preemptive pardon of Nixon, who had resigned in the face of his certain impeachment and possible removal from office in the wake of the Watergate scandal. An ineffective campaigner at best, Ford had been hampered further by an economic slowdown in the months before the election as well as by a convention challenge from rising right-wing star Ronald Reagan.

For all this, as Carter's campaign manager Hamilton Jordan explained at the outset, his chances depended on the southern states" which gave Carter "a base of support that cannot be taken for granted or jeopardized": "The Republicans cannot win if they write off the South." The essence of Carter's southern strategy became apparent when he sought and won the simultaneous endorsement of Rev. Martin Luther King Sr. and George Wallace. Carter's decision to place a portrait of King's son in the Georgia capital scored big with black voters, and as a born-and-bred Southern Baptist and longtime Sunday school teacher, he was well-versed in the pulpit-pew dialogues so common in black churches, where he was both relaxed and extremely effective.[66]

Showing an agility and flexibility as a candidate that he would often seem to lack as president, Carter maintained his ties to blacks while simultaneously pursuing the Wallace vote at every opportunity, even claiming a special affinity with NASCAR fans and showing up to ride the track at the annual Darlington 500 race. At a rally in Birmingham Carter paid tribute to a beaming Governor Wallace, who sat on the platform in his wheelchair while Carter asserted, "We Southerners believe in work, not welfare," and promised to balance the federal budget without undermining a strong national defense. In response Wallace confessed with what seemed genuine fervor, "Oh, how I have longed to see a Deep Southerner like you and me and Jimmy Carter in the White House."[67]

Carter did not hesitate to appeal directly to white southerners' sense of grievance and pride. One television spot announced, "On November 2, the South is being readmitted to the Union. If that sounds strange, maybe a southerner can understand. Only a southerner can understand years of coarse, anti-southern jokes and unfair comparison. Only a southerner can understand what it means to be a political whipping boy. But, then, only a southerner can understand what Jimmy Carter as President can mean." Texas-born writer Larry L. King captured the significance of Carter's candidacy for millions of white southerners when he simply exulted, "We ain't trash no more!" Upon encountering Carter's armor of southern honor and pride, Republican charges that he was an "ultraliberal" or merely a "Southern-fried McGovern" seemed to glance harmlessly away. On the eve of the election Anthony Lewis of the *New York Times* emphasized that white southerners would interpret the next day's balloting as a referendum on whether the rest of the nation was ready to accept a bona fide representative of a decidedly "new South." In reality, the circumstances surrounding the 1976 election made it difficult to determine whether the 170 electoral votes (57 percent of his total) that Carter picked up elsewhere meant that Americans outside the South had actually accepted him or had simply rejected his opponent and his scandal-plagued party. In either case, by that point it was apparent that much of the rest of America was looking at the South through very different eyes.[68]

6

"A Foretaste of the New America"

The South Rejoins the Union, and Vice Versa

More than one observer saw Jimmy Carter's victory in 1976 as a sign that his once ostracized region had at long last rejoined the Union. In reality, however, even when the South's differences with the rest of the country had seemed most pronounced, southern tastes and influences had remained a vital part of an evolving national culture. This was never more apparent than during the first generation after World War II when, despite the intensifying conflicts that threatened to widen and deepen the South's racial divide, a group of young performers managed to create an exciting, even exhilarating fusion of changing black and white tastes and styles that would place southern cultural values at the very heart of American popular music.

Born in the confluence of an African heritage and an American experience, the blues began as an expression of the feelings of black southerners who had escaped the horrors of slavery only to face the crushing disappointments of emancipation. When southern blacks responded to the freedom, opportunity, and allure of the city, they brought along the raw, individualized sound of the country blues. In the city, country blues would encounter the diverse instrumentation and more sophisticated stylings of urban blues. After World War II the fusion of these two would produce the hard-driving, electrified beat of rhythm and blues, which would in turn become the defining component of the revolutionary new sound known as rock 'n' roll.

One of the most successful country blues performers to make the transition to rhythm and blues was McKinley Morganfield, a.k.a. "Muddy Waters," who left Coahoma County in the Mississippi Delta in

1943 and headed straight for Chicago, where he bought an electric guitar and quickly acquired a local following. In 1948 Waters recorded "I Can't Be Satisfied" for a new independent company that eventually became Chess Records, a mainstay label for rhythm and blues performers and fans. Featured on other hit recordings like "Hoochie Koochie Man" and "Rolling Stone," Waters's electrified blues proved a formative influence in the early days of rock 'n' roll in general (and later on performers such as The Rolling Stones in particular).[1]

Waters's fellow Mississippian, Chester Burnett, a.k.a. "Howlin' Wolf," had rubbed shoulders with country blues pioneers like Charley Patton and Robert Johnson before forming his own band in West Memphis, Arkansas, after he returned from World War II. A hulk of a man at 6 feet 4 inches and 270 pounds, Wolf not only howled, but groaned and growled his electrified blues on KWEM in West Memphis. Before joining Muddy Waters in Chicago and signing with Chess, he made his first record in 1951 at the Memphis Recording Service, which would soon become Sun Records. Sun was owned and operated by Sam Phillips, a white former disk jockey who had played the records of both black and white artists while working in Muscle Shoals, Alabama. Phillips also collaborated in 1951 with another local rhythm and blues group, Ike Turner and the Kings of Rhythm (recording under the pseudonym Jackie Brentsen and the Delta Cats), to produce "Rocket 88," a song that reached back to Robert Johnson's "Terraplane Blues" and paid homage to the blues tradition of using references to automobiles and their parts as euphemisms for sex or the male sex organ:

> Yes, it's great, just won't wait,
> Everybody likes my Rocket 88 . . . .
> Taking my Rocket on a long, hot run
> Ooh, going out,
> Oozing and cruising along.[2]

"Rocket 88" rose quickly on the pop music charts in 1951, and it would later be designated the first true rock 'n' roll song, not in Ike Turner's version but as it was recorded a short time later by white artist, Bill Haley. Haley would gain fame with "Shake, Rattle, and Roll," another cover of a rhythm and blues song, this one by Joe Turner, and in 1954 he would also record "Rock around the Clock," which became rock 'n' roll's first truly big hit. Although he grew up in Pennsylvania, Haley was clearly influenced by his banjo- and mandolin-playing, Kentucky-born father. He began his musical career performing with country and western bands such as The Four Aces of Western Swing and The Saddlemen, who would eventually form the nucleus of his famous rock 'n' roll band, The Comets. Haley's musical odyssey reflected the postwar progression of styles and influences that had reshaped the rural white sound of country music and set it on course for the intersection with the urban black sound of rhythm and blues that would eventually produce rock 'n' roll.[3]

World War II had taken country music (known as "hillbilly music" to an earlier generation that had witnessed its commercial emergence in the 1920s) to a much wider national and international audience, thanks in part to the geographic dispersal of white southerners who took their music with them when they went to war or up north to work in the defense plants. Armed Forces Radio also spread country music around the world by broadcasting a segment of Nashville's famous *Grand Ole Opry* show each week. Stories that some Japanese troops who intercepted these broadcasts defiantly charged American positions yelling "To Hell with Roy Acuff" instead of "Banzai" may well be apocryphal, but when a poll asked GIs their preference between Acuff and Frank Sinatra the country star bested the pop crooner by a 15 percent margin. By 1944 *Billboard* found six hundred country radio broadcasts in the United States with an estimated audience of 40 million. The "Texas Troubadour," Ernest Tubb, even took country music to Carnegie Hall in 1947. By 1951 there were some fourteen hundred radio shows devoted to country music, and five years later the *Wall Street Journal* reported that annual sales of country records had reached $50 million.[4]

During World War II the acoustic instruments and delicate, high-pitched vocal harmonies of the popular hillbilly string bands of the twenties and thirties had begun to give way to the heavier, twangy, steel guitar–enhanced honky-tonk sound that flourished in the boisterous, rough-and-tumble beer joints of a wartime South. Freed at last from Prohibition and the economic constraints of the 1930s, many white southerners were eager to put aside, on Saturday nights at least, the stern religious moralism that had long put a severe crimp in their dancing and drinking, especially in public. Honky-tonk songs often recounted scenes that played out in the honky-tonks themselves: men, and occasionally women, led astray by the temptations of the flesh or the bottle, turning their back on the love and comforts of home and family for a few stolen hours of fleeting, dissolute pleasure, only to reap the bitter fruit of their transgressions in a harvest of heartbreak for themselves and their loved ones. In broader perspective honky-tonk songs such as Ernest Tubb's "Walkin' the Floor over You" and Floyd Tillman's "Driving Nails in My Coffin" reflected the stresses of a society steeped in the moral absolutism of evangelical Protestantism but tossed and tilted by the upheavals of war, urbanization, and economic transformation.

Some performers weathered this period of tumult and change better than others. Still in their teens when they made their first recording for RCA's Victor Records in 1936, Bill and Earl Bolick, the Blue Sky Boys, had made their way out of the western North Carolina hills down to Atlanta, where they became a fixture on radio station WGST with their *Farm and Fun Hour*, which offered a mixture of old-time gospel tunes like "Sister Mary Don't You Weep" and traditional ballads like "Banks of the Ohio," rendered in the soft, seamless harmonies that became their trademark. Although they were accompanied by a fiddler on radio, their recordings on Victor's Bluebird label featured only Bill's mandolin and Earl's guitar, both of which were carefully subordinated to the duo's delicate vocals. World War II interrupted the Bolick brothers' career, but their appeal with postwar radio and live audiences remained strong. Although they disdained the new honky-tonk style, under pressure from Victor the brothers agreed to add some fiddle accompaniment in their later studio sessions. Country music in general was moving rapidly to a bigger and more complicated sound, however, and RCA executives also began to urge the Bolicks to add an electric guitar to their recordings. Bill and Earl resisted this coercion for a while before finally opting in 1951 simply to end their performing careers. Bill eventually found employment at a post office in North Carolina, while, fittingly enough, Earl took a job near Atlanta, working for Lockheed, one of the industrial behemoths whose appearance in the South seemed to signal the end of a way of life that the music of the Blue Sky Boys had captured with such fidelity.[5]

Not all the old-style performers went the way of the Blue Sky Boys after World War II, but the more successful survivors were generally those who were willing to adapt their sound and repertoire to the changing times. A case in point was Kentuckian Bill Monroe, who is credited with reworking the old string band stylings of the prewar era into a faster paced, more modern sound that drew its name from Monroe's band, the Bluegrass Boys. A gifted mandolinist, Monroe had made his name performing with his guitarist brother, Charlie, in the 1930s, but after he and Charlie split up, Bill's Bluegrass Boys featured not only a mandolin and a guitar, but a fiddle and ultimately a banjo. Bluegrass music did preserve many elements of an older string tradition, but it drew relatively little attention until the old clawhammer style of strumming the banjo gave way to a much more dynamic three-finger picking or rolling technique first popularized by Earl Scruggs, who joined the Bluegrass Boys in 1945. With the continuous driving sound generated by Scruggs's picking style, the banjo could join or supplant the fiddle or mandolin as the lead instrument. The result was a sound, illustrated by Scruggs's rendition of "Foggy Mountain Breakdown" and later the theme music for *The Beverly Hillbillies* television show, that one commentator described as "folk music with overdrive." The rudiments of this banjo technique had been part of the local musical tradition when Scruggs was a boy in western North Carolina, but when integrated with the old string band style, it gave bluegrass a much more contemporary sound without the addition of electric instruments or amplification. By any objective standard, the lyric content and instrumental stylings of bluegrass music retained a markedly more traditional character than the more commercially successful mainstream country sound. Still, in a very real sense bluegrass was also yet another prominent example of southern musical adaptation. Unlike the Blue Sky Boys, performers like Bill Monroe and Earl Scruggs, who, along with Lester Flatt, left the Bluegrass Boys in 1948 to form their own, even more successful act, not only survived but prospered by embracing change rather than resisting it.[6]

Other postwar country musicians began to experiment with a variety of new sounds and styles. Alabama-born Alton and Rabon Delmore had incorporated some blues influences into their otherwise traditional duet stylings before the war. After the war the Delmore Brothers offered a more dynamic blend of blues and country in their "Hillbilly Boogie" (1946) and other numbers, while using harmonicas to achieve the bluesiest country sound yet in their biggest hit, "Blues Stay Away from Me" (1949). Blues as well as jazz were also fundamental elements of western swing as it was perfected and popularized in the postwar years by the legendary Bob Wills and his Texas Playboys.[7]

Like so many successful country singers, Hank Williams had been influenced by a black musician during his hardscrabble Alabama childhood, and as a performer he helped to bridge the gap between the war-born pedal-steel twang of honky-tonk and what would become the more youthful rockabilly sound of Carl Perkins, Jerry Lee Lewis, and Elvis Presley. Williams's 1947 recording of "Move It On Over" fore-shadowed the heavy, aggressive bass that would mark so many Presley recordings. After Williams signed on with MGM Records, Charles Gillett observed, "He shook all these black-influenced styles together using as strong a beat as his recording supervisor would sanction." In some ways, Williams's performing style also foreshadowed Presley's, although he moved his legs rather than his pelvis in sway with the music, some-times deliberately lowering the microphone so that he could bend over it while swinging his legs from side to side.[8]

Williams's "Cold, Cold Heart" was a number-one hit for pop crooner Tony Bennett, and several of his songs became mainstream favorites when covered by pop artists, but Williams himself remained strictly a country artist until his untimely death on New Year's Day 1953. Other artists of the early 1950s also pushed the boundaries of country toward pop music and what would become rockabilly and ultimately rock 'n' roll. East Tennessean Carl Smith cut his musical teeth on the honky-tonk style of Ernest Tubb, but after the war Smith raised not only eyebrows but the hackles of Grand Ole Opry traditionalists like Roy Acuff when he decided to use drums to give his up-tempo songs like "Go Boy Go" a heavier, driving beat. By the mid-1950s his music, Smith explained, was "somewhere between rock 'n roll and western swing": "I used to do 'Shake, Rattle, and Roll' on the stage and songs like that before Elvis started kickin'. The audiences got a kick out of it—It was pretty rockin'."[9]

With millions of southerners abandoning the farm for the city, in both a literal and figurative sense, the backdrop for these changes in southern musical styles was definitely "country comes to town." Black rhythm and blues bands like the Red Tops, who played up and down the Mississippi Delta at school and country club dances, had been playing for more affluent white audiences for a long time. Yet it was only in the move to Memphis to work in its Firestone Rubber or International Harvester plants that whites who aspired to make their names as performers would see and hear for themselves how this "nig-ger music" that was so popular with the teenage crowd was actually made. "Going Negro" by affecting black accents, inflections, and man-nerisms was a popular fad among young whites of the post–World War II generation, and white teenagers responded enthusiastically when rhythm and blues performers grew more expressive and experi-mental in their stylings. Rhythm and blues got another boost from the wartime proliferation of jukeboxes and the postwar spread of smaller recording studios that featured both black and lesser known white performers on the newly introduced 45-rpm singles that were perfect for the jukebox format. As the 1950s began, jukeboxes at diners, drug stores, and swimming pools rocked with the pounding, reverberating rhythms of black artists, much to the delight of affluent white kids who believed their preference for black music bespoke their worldliness, unlike the country and western "hillbilly" music they associated with the unsophisticated tastes and narrow provincialism of their lower-class white counterparts.[10]

In 1948 the white owners of Memphis's struggling new radio station, WDIA, made a bold move by hiring a local black high school teacher, Nat D. Williams, to host his own rhythm and blues show. The phenomenal following that Williams soon attracted convinced the station's management that there was money to be made in appealing to black listeners and advertisers. The proof of their conviction came soon enough as WDIA quickly became the first station in the region to gross $1 million. Williams recruited other black deejays, including Riley "B. B." King, whose work on WDIA helped to launch his virtuoso career as a rhythm and blues artist.

Still marveling many years later at WDIA's racially integrated work environment, King recalled, "When you went in there, it was no more 'yes sir, no sir' and this and that because people were white....You were just another person." WDIA also hired female program hosts and offered gospel and religious as well as public affairs programs oriented toward black Memphians. The station also made "goodwill announcements," inquiring after wayward cows and even missing false teeth. Meanwhile, over at WHBQ, Memphis's most popular and influential disc jockey, Dewey Phillips, was playing rhythm and blues and country boogie music for a large young white audience six nights a week on his *Red, Hot and Blue* show.[11]

Flocking to Memphis in search of day jobs to tide them over until they made their music breakthrough, aspiring young white performers were fascinated by the new reckless and raunchy rhythm and blues sounds they heard on local radio or encountered directly, sometimes in the same small independent studios where they cut their own records. They soon realized that the key to making a name for themselves was finding a way to make their own music appealing to the same record-buying, upscale white teenagers who spurned the hillbilly music they

B. B. King as a young performer and D.J., Memphis, Tennessee, 1948. Michael Ochs Archives/Corbis.

associated with working-class whites. Among the more than 100,000 people who poured into Memphis as the city's industrial economy boomed in the late 1940s were Vernon and Gladys Presley, who moved up from nearby Tupelo, Mississippi, in 1948, hoping to find a better life for them and their son. In July 1953 that son, now a bashful eighteen-year-old, dropped by Sam Phillips's Sun Studios in Memphis and paid $3.98 to record two songs, "My Happiness" and "That's When Your Heartaches Begin," for his mother. In January 1954, now working as a truck driver, Elvis Presley again stopped by and recorded two more songs. Phillips liked the young man's voice, and some six months later he called Elvis to tell him he had set up a studio session for him with ace guitarist Scotty Moore and accomplished bassist Bill Black. Moore thought with a name like Elvis Presley the young neophyte must be "something out of science fiction," and when he saw Elvis's "black shirt, pink pants with black stripes, white shoes and…greasy ducktail" his initial reaction seemed to be right on the money.[12]

Ultimately, however, it was not the way Elvis dressed but the way he sounded that would set him apart. This much was evident in the very first formal session at Sun, which resulted in a cover version of "That's Alright, Mama," a rhythm and blues number previously recorded by a black artist, Arthur "Big Boy" Crudup. This time the singer was a white performer who simply "sounded black." In a pattern that would hold for Presley's other early Sun recordings, the flip side of "That's Alright, Mama" was a country song, "Blue Moon of Kentucky," released earlier by the famed bluegrass artist Bill Monroe.

Within a week of its first airplay on WHBQ, Phillips had received some six thousand orders for Presley's first Sun recording, and the record soon hit the charts across the South. In addition to country music, Elvis's singing style and repertoire were heavily influenced by gospel music, although few of the screaming young women set off by the sight of him thrusting and wiggling his pelvis as he sang onstage seemed to be pondering their eternal fate at the time. At the apex of McCarthyite paranoia, Presley's suggestive stage gyrations provided ample ammunition for those who condemned rock 'n' roll as part of an insidious communist plan to destroy the moral fiber of American youth. Likewise, with the courts and the NAACP clearly taking aim at the South's repressive racial system, the sexually charged lyrics and black "feel" of rock 'n' roll made it easy for segregationist whites to see this new musical craze as a harbinger of things to come if integration were allowed to destroy the protective barriers separating their daughters from the lustful advances of black men. (The term *rock 'n' roll,* after all, had originated as a blues euphemism for sex.) Elvis represented "a new low in spiritual degeneracy," a Jacksonville minister claimed, although what Nick Tosches called the "hellish persona" and "wicked, wicked ways" of the spectacularly uninhibited singer and piano player Jerry Lee Lewis made Presley seem downright tame by comparison. At any rate, the outraged preacher would have gotten no disagreement from the Citizens Council polemicists who saw this new "jungle music" as part of a plot to bring whites down to the abysmal moral level of blacks.[13]

Of all his attributes, the exaggerated masculinity of the typical white rock 'n' roll performer was hardest to miss. Country artists had never been shy about expressing their maleness through references to fighting, working, or driving trucks or trains. With Elvis and other young white rock 'n' rollers like the hedonistic Jerry Lee, however, this masculinity became much more narrowly and overtly sexual. As music historian Bill C. Malone wrote, "The good-natured hedonism and swaggering machismo of the rockabillies were deeply rooted in southern working-class culture, not hastily donned pretensions." The urbanization of southern life had simply "provided new outlets for the expression of aggressive masculinity, and the appropriation of black music, or its rough approximation, gave young [white] men a chance to strut their style and display their sexual energy."[14]

Elvis's almost frightening appeal to music-mad white teenagers quickly caught the attention of bigger record labels, and by the end of 1955 a financially strapped Sam Phillips had signed over the remainder of his star singer's contract to RCA, where Presley sold more than 27 million singles during the first year alone. Despite his overnight success and fame, Elvis was drawn back to the familiar, comfortable environment of the town where his career began. On December 4, 1956, he strolled into Sun Studios just as his friend Carl Perkins, who hailed from nearby Jackson, Tennessee, was wrapping up a recording session that also included Jerry Lee Lewis. At some point, another Sun artist, Johnny Cash, who hailed from Dyess, over in the Arkansas Delta, showed up as well. All of these soon-to-be rockabilly legends had grown up within roughly two hundred miles of Memphis, and after swapping a few stories they fell into a spontaneous jam session, during which the opportunistic Sam Phillips deliberately left the tape running.

The resulting tape of impromptu performances by what would later be called the "Million Dollar Quartet" revealed rock 'n' roll's eclectic origins with near-perfect clarity. Old-time gospel tunes predominated, along with a mix of country and bluegrass, but the group also tried to recreate black artist Chuck Berry's recently released "Brown-Eyed Handsome Man." Berry's style was heavily influenced by country music, and Perkins, who had just finished a tour with Berry, marveled at the rhythm and blues star's virtuosity. The most telling evidence of rock 'n' roll's interracial complexity came when Presley tried to imitate rhythm and blues singer Jackie Wilson's imitation of him. While he was in Las Vegas, Presley had learned that Wilson, then a member of Billy Ward's Dominoes, was performing his own version of Elvis's "Don't Be Cruel" in a local club, and after hearing Wilson the first time, Presley went back three nights in a row. Gathered with his fellow white artists in Sun Studios, Presley proceeded to offer his own imitation of Wilson, who had "sung the hell out of that song." In fact, Elvis claimed, Wilson's version of "Don't Be Cruel" was "so much better" than his own: "He cut me out. I was under the table when he got through singing."[15]

Gospel music had profoundly influenced not only country performers but rhythm and blues artists as well. Many of them had actually begun their careers singing in church and even moved on to commercial gospel groups. Born the son of a Holiness minister in Clarksdale, Mississippi, about seventy miles southwest of Memphis, Sam Cooke gained considerable attention performing church music during his youth, and in 1950, at age nineteen, he joined the popular gospel group The Soul Stirrers. Recordings such as "Jesus Gave Me Water" and "The Hem of His Garment" won Cooke a huge gospel following, but other listeners saw his even greater potential as a pop singer. His efforts to conceal his gospel identity by recording "Lovable" in 1956 as "Dale Cooke" failed miserably as listeners soon picked up on his mellifluous voice. When

The "Million Dollar Quartet" (from left): Jerry Lee Lewis, Carl Perkins, Elvis Presley (seated), and Johnny Cash, Sun Studios, Memphis, Tennessee, 1956. Michael Ochs Archives/Corbis.

executives at Specialty, a gospel label, balked at having an artist who also recorded rhythm and blues, Cooke left to become an extremely successful R and B singer and pioneering force behind soul music, a variant of rhythm and blues that drew less on instrumentation and more on individual vocal expressions of the raw emotions heard so frequently both in the blues and in the black church. Cooke's heavily gospel-accented "Bring It on Home to Me" became an instant soul classic.[16]

It was surely no mere coincidence that rhythm and blues came into its own as a dynamic, exuberant expression of black culture and identity in time with the sense of racial pride and determination for progress that accompanied the major accomplishments and breakthroughs of the civil rights era. In fact, the potential synergy between the biracial popularity of the music and the integrationist aims of the civil rights movement itself lay at the heart of segregationist opposition to rock 'n' roll in general. As with all such forms of popular music, however, the bottom line for rhythm and blues performers and producers was commercial rather than social or political. As deeply as they may have appreciated their loyal black fans, black artists understood that their financial independence and security ultimately depended more critically on securing and sustaining a large following among whites. Hence, from the financial standpoint there was something of a built-in deterrent to making one's music, performances, or public persona seem racially militant enough to discomfit one's white fan base. Nat King Cole's initial refusal to condemn the whites who physically assaulted him on stage in Birmingham in 1956 or to refrain immediately from performing for whites-only audiences branded him an "Uncle Tom" in the eyes of NAACP and other civil rights leaders, but from a career standpoint the most important color for Cole and many other African American performers of that era was not black but green. Critics would later attack Elvis and other white performers who profited handsomely from their cover versions of songs recorded by rhythm and blues artists, but Presley's even more flamboyant R and B contemporary "Little Richard" Penniman saw things differently. He and many other black artists of the era actually considered Elvis's success a "blessing," Penniman explained, because "they wouldn't let black music through. He opened the door for black music....I thank the Lord for sending Elvis to open that door so I could walk down the road."[17]

For white country performers as well, the primary concern was not preserving traditions but selling records. Since the introduction of country music into the commercial recording market after World War I, artists and recording executives alike had pursued the elusive goal of moving beyond its fundamentally rural southern base and tapping into the much larger and more lucrative national pop music market. In the mid-1950s, as rock 'n' roll began to take a huge bite of the record-buying dollar, country artists, writers, and arrangers stepped up the search for the right crossover formula before finding unprecedented success with the "Nashville sound" in the early 1960s. The principal architect of the Nashville sound was the virtuoso guitarist Chet Atkins. Atkins had begun his career playing traditional country before moving decidedly toward jazz and pop. Later, as head of RCA's Country Division, he performed in and presided over a number of sessions featuring smooth orchestral and choral backup and mellow, soothing lead vocals by artists like Patsy Cline, Jim Reeves, Ray Price, and the tuxedo-clad "Tennessee Plowboy," Eddy Arnold, who even recorded a yodeling cowboy song, "Cattle Call," accompanied by Hugo Winterhalter and his orchestra. Cline enjoyed striking success with crossover hits such as "I Fall to Pieces" and "Walkin' after Midnight" before her tragic death in a plane crash in 1963.

Reeves also died in a plane crash not long after Cline, but not before he had made his mark on the pop charts with his velvety renditions of songs like "Four Walls," in which a good-hearted man has lost his good-timing girl to the temptations of the night life: "Out where the bright lights are glowing, / You're drawn like a moth to the flame. / You laugh while the wine's overflowing, / While I sit and whisper your name." Here, as Bill C. Malone noted, was "a honky-tonk song without honky-tonk instrumentations" and, one might add, without the traditionally harsh nasal twang of the honky-tonk vocalist as well. Other truly successful crossover songs such as Pee Wee King's "Tennessee Waltz," sung by Patti Page, and Hank Williams's "Cold, Cold Heart," performed by Tony Bennett with an orchestral arrangement by Percy Faith, made it clear that not only was country music borrowing from popular music, but in the years after World War II, country themes had grown more resonant with mainstream audiences as well. Loneliness or regret over lost or illicit love and what Malone called a generally more "emotionally frank and simple" view of life had long been fixtures of country music, and they were now noticeably more common in pop music, where artists had once generally steered clear of these more personal experiences and sentiments.[18]

As for country music itself, thanks in no small measure to the success of the Nashville sound, things had never been better. In the first half of 1960, nine of the fourteen RCA Victor recordings in *Billboard*'s Top 50 and several from other labels were actually cut in Nashville. Not everyone was pleased with the Nashville sound's ardent courtship of pop fans. Honky-tonk pioneer Ernest Tubb had no problem with a band with "six fiddles," but "six violins" was another matter entirely. "Let 'em do what they want to do," Tubb complained, "but don't call it country." Not surprisingly, Tubb's lament fell largely on deaf ears in Nashville, where the recording industry was now pumping roughly $35 million into the local economy each year.[19]

The success of the Nashville sound in taking country music into the mainstream popular market foreshadowed a larger and much more significant trend. Scarcely half a decade after witnessing the horrific scenes from Selma that had seemed more in character for Germany in the 1930s than the United States in the 1960s, many Americans appeared eager to gather the South and its people and culture into an uncritical embrace. "Wherever one turned," wrote Lerone Bennett Sr. in a special 1971 issue of *Ebony* dedicated to the contemporary South, be it "in *Harper's*, in the *New York Times*, [or] in the *Atlantic Monthly*, there were rhapsodic litanies on the New South—a South that had turned its back on the horrors of the past; a South that was too busy to hate, a South that was hard at work outdoing the Yankees, a South of hustle and bustle, of new buildings, new roads and new factories."[20]

Georgia's brand-new governor, Jimmy Carter, made the cover of *Time* in 1971, and this sudden, uncharacteristic affinity for people and things southern reached epidemic proportions during his quest for the presidency In fact, the *New York Times*'s traditionally critical perspective on the South was little in evidence throughout the campaign, as its pages celebrated a risen, racially cleansed and economically resurgent Dixie, splashing happily in the American mainstream at last. Instead of backward and isolated, the South now came through in the media as the dynamic cornerstone of the ascendant Sunbelt, the lower tier of states that included all of the Old Confederacy and stretched all the way through California. Such positive treatments helped to unloose a flood of northern in-migrants drawn southward by the prospect of taking advantage, in some combination or another, of the region's vibrant economy, warmer climate, and less frenetic, congested, and complicated lifestyle. With Florida absorbing a little more than half of the newcomers, the entire South gained nearly three million people from in-migration between 1970 and 1976 alone. The region's economy had grown about 30 percent faster than the national average over the last quarter-century, and dramatic increases in per capita incomes suggested that regional differentials might soon be a thing of the past in some states.[21]

The Sunbelt South's gross regional product nearly doubled between 1960 and 1970 as well. Over the next five years, Texas alone added more jobs than Michigan, Illinois, Ohio, and Massachusetts combined, so that in 1976 its industrial output effectively equaled that of Australia. With southern plants producing one-third of the nation's electricity and southern wells pumping two-thirds of its petroleum, demand for energy was itself energizing the South's economy. This was a key to the miraculous Texas boom, especially in Houston, which attracted ninety-nine major industrial firms and their subsidiaries by the thousands between 1971 and 1978, not to mention a thousand new residents a week by the end of the 1970s. Thanks to the absence of state levies on either individual or corporate income, as they struggled with the stifling heat and humidity in their new home, New York transplants to Houston could console themselves with the knowledge that their move had cut their tax burden by roughly 80 percent. At the same time, capitalizing on defense facilities, other towns, such as Huntsville, Alabama, with the Marshall Space Center and the Redstone Arsenal, were able to win the hearts of high-end firms like IBM and Rockwell International.[22]

North Carolina's Research Triangle Park, situated within the immediate proximity of the state's three major universities in order to catch the eye of dynamic, research-oriented firms, was also flourishing. By the end of the 1970s, the RTP was home to twenty-eight research operations, including an IBM facility, the National Center for Health Statistics, and a key research branch of the Environmental Protection Agency. Although it was doubtless still a dubious claim to distinction in the eyes of many North Carolinians at that stage, the Triangle's favorite bragging point was a population that sported more PhDs per capita than any other metropolitan area in the nation.[23]

Northern newcomers obviously did not miss shoveling snow or paying the exorbitant heating bills brought on by the energy crisis of the mid-1970s, and air-conditioning had made their adaptation to sweltering southern summers a great deal easier. Air-conditioning was a relative novelty in the region prior to 1950, when the introduction of the window unit began to cool down southern homes and offices at a record clip. Two-thirds of the South's homes were air-conditioned by 1975, as were 90 percent of its office buildings and banks and 80 percent of its automobiles. Although one Florida woman condemned air-conditioning as "a damn fool invention of the Yankees" and declared, "If they don't like it hot, they can move back up North where they belong," most northern transplants seemed pleased with the southern hospitality they encountered. As *New York Times* reporter Roy Reed observed, "A hundred years ago, a Northerner in the South was called a carpetbagger. Ten years ago, he was called a meddling integrationist. In 1976 he is being called to come and have dinner."[24]

Yankee transplants even made the society pages on occasion; in 1970 a Boston native was elected president of the Atlanta Junior League. There were notable cultural and lifestyle adaptations as well. Newly arrived northerners took quickly to more casual business attire and developed a taste for bourbon, while southerners began to sip Scotch and watch in wonder as their children took to the ice on the rinks that were suddenly and improbably proliferating across the region.[25]

While the *New York Times* saw a South in transition, *Time* saw it as a timeless place where, despite "urban and industrial encroachments," people still lived close to nature, enjoying an "almost tactile empathy with the land" and savoring the "aphrodisiac-soporific" scent of the magnolia, "more potent in midnight bloom than overblown fiction can convey." In 1976 with the national media awash in the antics of the restrained, teetotaling presidential candidate's rambunctious, beer-swilling brother, Billy, *Time* assured readers that the southern "good ole boy" was not the stereotypical night-riding, Negro-hating "redneck" but rather a lovable, necktie-averse, pinball-playing reincarnation of Thomas Jefferson's peculiarly American agrarian everyman, whose "devil-may-care light-heartedness [masked] a strain of innate wisdom, an instinct about people, and an unwavering loyalty that makes him one friend you can turn to." The good ole boy's fun-loving ways were typical, the writer observed, of a people who "actively stalk pleasure in all its forms with all the avidity of a Yankee conglomerator bent on making billions." Gregarious, convivial, deeply attached to family, community, and place, southerners pursued their version of "the good life," never forgetting the virtue of the "good manners" that were "often neglected elsewhere."[26]

The South that captivated the national media in the mid-1970s seemed to represent the best of both worlds. Although many of its

Jimmy and Billy Carter, Plains, Georgia, 1976. Library of Congress, Prints and Photographs Division, Washington, D.C. (LC-U9-33315-31A [P8P]).

metropolitan areas appeared to be enjoying a warp-speed growth befitting the hottest spots in the nation's vibrant new region of opportunity, in most media portrayals at least, southerners had somehow managed to maintain the core of traditional values and beliefs that seemed largely to have slipped away from many of their fellow Americans. In fact, the South had gone from being a dismal swamp of ignorance and bigotry to a beacon of light and inspiration. With white southerners having owned up to their racial sins and seemingly begun to atone for them, the one-time regional outcast now seemed poised not simply to become part of the nation again but to serve as the embodiment of all that was good about America.

At the same time, the bloody riots in northern cities, not to mention bitter white resistance to busing and residential integration initiatives, revealed some fairly formidable motes in the eyes of white northerners who had long chosen to see racism and racial injustice as a purely southern characteristic. Meanwhile, the disappointing and divisive turn of events in Vietnam had dealt a devastating blow to the myth of American invincibility, a myth that southerners had found it difficult to embrace wholeheartedly for more than a century. Finally, on the heels of the Vietnam debacle came the Watergate affair, with its revelations of cynicism and political corruption at the highest levels of government, a revelation that, given their political history, hardly came as much of a shock to most southerners, white or black. "Watergate doesn't hold a candle to the way that Wallace runs this state," the publisher of the *Montgomery Advertiser* declared.[27]

Although white southerners were the least likely of all Americans to favor either withdrawal from Vietnam or the removal of Richard Nixon from the White House, they accepted both as faits accomplis, giving little indication of having been terribly traumatized by either. It was thus not as surprising as it might seem perhaps that Americans would turn to a humble but serenely confident white southerner for leadership in 1976, or that scholars, journalists, and pundits of all stripes seemed suddenly to believe that the long-lamented South was now peculiarly equipped to lead and inspire a nation that had somehow lost its way. Even the usually detached novelist Walker Percy observed that "the North saved the union the first time" and confessed to being "slightly optimistic that the South will save it a second time." The normally skeptical southern historian C. Vann Woodward was also inclined to think positively. "For 32 of the first 36 years of the republic," Woodward noted, "[the South had] managed to govern the country with some distinction, its burden of slavery and racism notwithstanding." With this burden removed and "both hands free," he dared to suggest, "it might do better should its chance come again." Writing almost simultaneously in the *New York Times,* Woodward's fellow southerner and historian David Donald expressed his hope that "a real South of goodness and decency" would provide the inspiration needed to "affirm this nation's humanity, its sense of community, and its deep dependence on the Almighty."[28]

The South's much-heralded moral and political ascent was only part of the story in the 1970s, for appealing portrayals of the region became a fixture of the nation's pop culture as well. Perhaps the first notable step in this direction had actually come when television's *The Andy Griffith Show* began airing in 1960. With Griffith as a wise, fun-loving sheriff surrounded by a cast of lovable eccentrics who comprised the citizenry of the tiny town of Mayberry, the show offered a welcome antidote to the all too real scenes of racial savagery that came out of the South during the first half of the 1960s. The program proved enormously popular throughout the country, reaching 42 percent of the total viewing audience, roughly 15.5 million homes, each week in 1967, its final year of live production, and reruns remained popular more than four decades later.[29]

Like *The Andy Griffith Show,* CBS's *The Waltons* countered the image of southern, poor-white depravity served up by Erskine Caldwell and William Faulkner (and by southern whites themselves in the 1950s and 1960s) with the solid, stable home life of a nurturing Virginia mountain family in the midst of the Great Depression. Soon after it premiered in 1972, *The Waltons* was reaching forty million homes, and the serious, sensitive, soft-spoken central character, eldest child John Boy Walton, even drew comparisons to an adolescent version of Jimmy Carter.[30]

Meanwhile, with a show about down-home southerners sitting near the top of the television rankings, the number of all-country radio stations had risen from just eighty in 1961 to well over eleven hundred by 1975, and country music's popularity was now indisputably national in scope. If the Nashville sound of the 1960s had demonstrated the real potential of country music's appeal to more mainstream audiences, the 1970s saw that potential more than realized by singers like Dolly Parton, who revamped her homey east Tennessee mountain style into something a bit more uptown in songs such as "I Will Always Love You" (1974) and "Here You Come Again" (1977). Parton enjoyed phenomenal success, but others, both newcomers and old-timers, succeeded by defying old stereotypes and presenting a new, more countercultural "outlaw" version of country music. When former Rhodes scholar and once-struggling Nashville songwriter and part-time janitor Kris Kristofferson began collecting awards for edgy, envelope-pushing songs like "Help Me Make It through the Night" and "Sunday Morning Coming Down," it became clear that country music was definitely not what it used to be.[31]

Much to the dismay of some self-styled traditionalists, some of country's more established performers, including Kristofferson's fellow Texans Waylon Jennings and Willie Nelson, suddenly saw the commercial wisdom in sporting long hair and beards and joining him in his musical outlawry. Jennings's early days performing with rock 'n' roll great Buddy Holly came through in the heavy, rocking beat of many of his most popular songs, including "Good Hearted Woman" (1972) and "I'm a Ramblin' Man" (1974). Jennings's friend Willie Nelson had to that point enjoyed much greater success with the songs he wrote for others

("Crazy" for Patsy Cline and "Hello Walls" for Faron Young, for example) than with those he recorded himself. When he was a member of Ernest Tubb's band, Nelson had always dressed conservatively on stage, but as the 1970s unfolded he opted for jeans and a red bandana encircling his long hair, and he began to perform at concerts that also featured rock 'n' roll acts. He scored his first number-one hit with "Blue Eyes Crying in the Rain" (1975) and followed that with a host of others, such as "Always on My Mind" and "On the Road Again." Nelson's ability to adapt a variety of pop classics such as "Stardust" and "Moonlight in Vermont" to his unconventional voice, singing style, and instrumentation only demonstrated how fuzzy the distinctions between country and pop music had become.[32]

Some seemed puzzled that Nelson and Jennings managed to achieve such popularity with the traditional country fan base while sporting the dress and casual affinity for controlled substances reminiscent of the much-despised hippie counterculture of the 1960s. This animus toward the draft-card-burning, bearded, sandal-shod rebels of the 1960s was the subtext for what began as an endearing tongue-in-cheek composition recorded by country star Merle Haggard in 1969. Many younger fans embraced Haggard's "Okie from Muskogee" as a spoof on small-town conservatism, but it proved even more popular perhaps with those

Willie Nelson, performing in concert, Athens, Georgia, 1999. Courtesy of Lyra M. Cobb.

who took it literally, especially blue-collar, hard-hat conservatives fed up with protests, long hair, and pot smoking and eager to defend the virtue of a place where folks shunned marijuana and were not ashamed to "wave Old Glory down at the courthouse." "Okie" won Haggard the admiration of both Richard Nixon and George Wallace, and despite his protestations that both men had misread his intentions, he quickly followed up with "The Fighting Side of Me," a warning that those who were "running down our way of life" had better be prepared to defend themselves. To some critical listeners these songs seemed to embody the jingoism, intolerance, and thirst for violence that white southerners had displayed so frequently throughout their history, although few who made this point seemed to notice how popular both of these recordings became throughout an ideologically polarized America in the late Vietnam era.[33]

By the same token, the war- and Watergate-weary national mood of the mid-1970s seemed perfectly suited to the relaxed, live-and-let-live musical stylings of the country music outlaws Nelson and Jennings, who had cleverly resurrected the escapist imagery of the cowboy that had been so popular in the 1930s and 1940s. Cowboy behavior was sometimes rowdy and unpredictable, but the sense of cowboy genuineness and honesty that came through in "Mamas Don't Let Your Babies Grow Up to Be Cowboys" suggested that such an outcome really might not be such a bad thing after all. Slightly less than a decade after Merle Haggard celebrated "Muskogee, Oklahoma, U.S.A." as a bastion of conformist conservatism, Jennings touted the tiny Texas hill country hamlet of Luckenbach as a place where escaping the conflicts and pressures of modern life required nothing more than abandoning the scramble for wealth and fame and pulling on the "boots and faded jeans" favored by the exceedingly laid-back locals. In little bitty Luckenbach, there was no feuding or, in fact, "nobody feelin' no pain" of any sort.[34]

For all its southwestern flavor, the image of the devil-may-care cowboy also meshed nicely with the similarly appealing portrait of the decidedly southern good ole boy personified by the irreverent, fun-loving "First Brother," Billy Carter. Jennings went on to record "Good Ol' Boys," the theme song for television's *Dukes of Hazzard*. The show's central characters were Bo and Luke Duke, a pair of lovable country boys who, while "meanin' no harm," were "fightin' the system like a true modern-day Robin Hood" and perpetually at odds with a more comical than sinister local political boss and his bumbling, hand-picked sheriff.

Inviting contrast to the sensitive social and political climate that had prevailed a decade earlier, at the end of the 1970s Bo and Luke roared over the back roads of rural Hazzard County in the "General Lee," a souped-up Plymouth that, despite its name and the Confederate flag emblazoned on its roof, seemed to convey no ideological or racial message whatsoever.[35]

Here, in the images of Bo and Luke, John Boy Walton, and the carefree cowboys of Luckenbach, was a South that was not just acceptable but actually appealing to other Americans, one they could admire and celebrate rather than fear and despise, a South that, at long last, seemed to represent something of the best their nation could offer rather than the worst. The broad-based emotional embrace of the South's new persona found its strongest, most exuberant expression in the pages of the *Saturday Review*, which not only welcomed it back "into the fraternity of states," but suggested that, with its soaring economic prospects and its ascendant progressive leadership, the South might now even represent "a foretaste of the New America."[36]

7

"Just What the More Ardent Confederates Always Wanted"

Poverty, Power, and the Rise of the Southern Rim

Appealing as it was in many respects, the South's rags-to-riches story was less a fairy tale than simply a cruel joke for those still in rags and struggling to survive in the economic backwaters where Sunbelt prosperity either did not reach or was, to say the least, unevenly distributed. Planters in the ten core counties of the Yazoo-Mississippi received 22 percent of all federal farm subsidy payments in excess of $50,000 in 1967. Yet whites in the Delta and Black Belt counties in general were notably less enthusiastic about Job Corps, Head Start, and similar federal anti-poverty programs, which they saw both discouraging outmigration and reducing their leverage over the remaining blacks who might still be needed as day laborers on occasion. Senator Ernest F. Hollings of South Carolina noted wryly that some of the large farmers in his state could pull in as much as $40,000 in federal incentives for not planting certain crops and yet remain "as red-blooded, capitalistic, free enterprising, and patriotic as ever before." On the other hand, "give the poor, little hungry child a 40-cent breakfast...and you've destroyed his character...[and] ruined his incentive."[1]

Strikingly true to Hollings's characterization, Mississippi congressman Jamie Whitten asked whether "when you start giving people something for nothing...you don't destroy character more than you might improve nutrition." Curiously Whitten showed no such concern about potential character damage among the 350 planters in his Mississippi Delta district who received Department of Agriculture crop-control subsidy checks in amounts of more than $50,000 in 1967, with sixty-nine of those payments topping $100,000 and some even running in excess of $200,000. In 1965 half the local poverty board in Coahoma County, Mississippi, resigned because they considered the county's $2 million antipoverty budget too big, but when the Department of Agriculture handed over the same amount to just twenty-seven local planters, none of them offered the slightest protest whatsoever. In nearby Sunflower County, planters cashed more than $10.2 million in cotton program checks in 1967, while federal food-relief expenditures totaled only $446,000 for the two-thirds of the county's population who lived below the poverty line. There was no federal food program at all in Clarendon County, South Carolina, where 70 percent of the population lived in poverty and 121 farmers had collected individual crop subsidy payments in excess of $5,000, adding up to a total of $1.6 million. There was also no food assistance available in Burke County, Georgia, where the poverty rate was slightly higher and 130 farmers received subsidy payments totaling well in excess of $1.9 million in 1967.[2]

Though white officials insisted that antipoverty programs were wholly unnecessary in some of the poorest counties in the nation, throughout the old southern cotton belt evidence of human neglect and suffering was both abundant and appalling. A pediatrician investigating Lowndes County, Alabama, in 1966 found that although "eighty percent of [the] children...had anemia sufficient to require treatment in any doctor's office anywhere in the country," 90 percent of them said they had never seen a doctor. An Alabama Black Belt mother whose two-and-a-half-year-old son still could not walk explained that her family went "half-hungry" year-round "because [the landlord] don't let us plant no greens nor keep no hens."[3]

In 1967 a team of physicians reported to Congress that they had found many black children in the Mississippi Delta living under "such primitive conditions that we found it hard to believe we were examining American children of the twentieth century." In "child after child" they detected "vitamin and mineral deficiencies, serious, untreated skin infections and ulcerations; eye and ear diseases, also unattended bone diseases secondary to poor food intake," and in "every county" they visited the doctors found children with "obvious evidence of severe malnutrition with injury to the body's tissues—its muscles, bones, and skin as well as an associated psychological state of fatigue, listlessness and exhaustion."[4]

Although health and nutrition conditions for poor blacks in the southern cotton belt repeatedly elicited comparisons to underdeveloped nations elsewhere in the world, these conditions prevailed in the midst of thoroughgoing economic and technological modernization. By the end of the 1960s practically all southern cotton was being picked by machine, thanks in part to enhanced federal cotton acreage-reduction incentives and a long-awaited 1967 minimum-wage law for agriculture, which mandated payments of at least $1 per hour. Liberal social scientists and other commentators had long believed such a law would prove enormously beneficial to black farm workers who had been at the mercy of an archaic system of credit and paternalism since Reconstruction, and $1 per hour surely sounded like a windfall for workers accustomed to receiving $3.50 for a twelve-hour day.[5]

Minimum-wage proponents presumed not only that planters would maintain day-labor employment at pre-1967 levels, but that the workers would fare better under a more economically modern arrangement than the old paternalistic one, in which they had been paid poorly but often received cash advances in times of direst need and were sometimes allowed to live rent-free in what had once been sharecropper cabins on the plantations. Prior to the new law, those displaced by mechanization had at least been assured of roughly thirty days' work chopping cotton (digging out grass that herbicides had missed) in midsummer. Once the minimum wage went into effect, however, cotton planters had greater incentive to rely more heavily on chemicals rather than continue to pay hand labor to keep their cotton clean. Suddenly at the mercy of what Nicholas Lemann called "the relentless logic" of modern capitalism, former sharecroppers were left with no expectation of part-time employment, housing, or other assistance from whites. As day laborers found their already marginal existence even more at risk, one complained, "A dollar a hour ain't worth nothing when, maybe they give you one day and then you're off for two weeks."[6]

Day laborers who could still find work also found themselves under much stricter supervision and scrutiny. A year after the law took effect, a Mississippi planter explained, "Hell, last year was the first time we really found out what labor efficiency could mean. We knew we couldn't use any more casual labor and now we're finding out we don't need as much specialized labor either." Encouraged by the new federal law to push his remaining workers harder, he added, "They can do better and they will."[7]

The Mississippi Delta and other parts of the Black Belt were not the only places where antipoverty and other federal programs and policies often seemed to benefit local political and economic elites more than the indigent and disadvantaged. Per capita income in Appalachia amounted to less than two-thirds of the national average in 1960, with one in three families living in poverty compared to one in five nationwide. Touring Appalachia that year, *Washington Post* writer Julius Duscher reported, "[From] the Blue Ridge Mountains of Virginia to the trail of the Cumberland Gap in Kentucky, tens of thousands of Americans live in appalling poverty. Live? No, they hardly exist." Sounding like visitors to the Delta, Duscher observed, "Much of the southern Appalachians is as underdeveloped, when compared with the affluence of the rest of America, as the newly independent countries of Africa." If anything, images of haggard, hollow-eyed whites living in crumbling tarpaper shacks without plumbing or running water seemed even more shocking than similar scenes from the Black Belt, and Appalachia seemed a prime candidate for the economic quick start envisioned by proponents of the Area Redevelopment Administration (ARA), which had been created in 1961 to provide low-interest industrial financing for local grants for public facilities and support for worker-training programs. Even ARA officials conceded theirs was a "trickle down" approach; by the very nature of the assistance offered, most of it flowed to private businesses in urban areas rather than directly into the suffering rural counties that lacked the rudimentary infrastructures and business bases required to meet participation requirements. Even before ARA's first birthday, the *Louisville Courier Journal* had already declared its efforts in eastern Kentucky "useless as oars on an airplane."[8]

Frustrated with the intractability of the area's economic problems, in 1964 the Johnson administration made Appalachia its unofficial ground zero for the War on Poverty, but much like earlier efforts of the ARA, many antipoverty programs would either be co-opted or thwarted by entrenched local economic interests and political machines. When Senator Robert F. Kennedy visited eastern Kentucky in 1968, he found conditions "intolerable, unacceptable, and unsatisfactory" and judged the federal antipoverty effort a dismal failure. As historian Ronald Eller noted, Kennedy heard one witness after another bemoan "manpower programs that didn't provide enough work, welfare programs that didn't provide enough help, and food programs that didn't provide enough food."[9]

In a refrain all too familiar down in the Delta, a former coal miner in Floyd County, Kentucky, who was suffering from silicosis, explained that his family often did not have even the $3 required to buy $82 worth of food stamps. Even when they could scrape together the money, the food seldom lasted more than two weeks, meaning "the rest of the month, it's nothing but bread and gravy." When Congress appropriated additional money to buy food stamps for families who had no cash whatsoever or had exhausted their provisions and were suffering severely from hunger, the funding was grossly inadequate. In 1969 local poverty officials serving Letcher, Leslie, Knott, and Perry counties in Kentucky had only $3,500 in additional food relief money available each month to distribute among more than thirty thousand residents whose families were struggling to survive on incomes of less than $1,500 a year.[10]

With so many residents unable to maintain a diet sufficient to stave off hunger, much less avoid malnutrition, visitors to the Appalachian region evoked visions of the Black Belt as they told again and again of encountering pallid, enervated, toothless (even in their thirties) adults and anemic, undersized children infected with parasites, perpetually ill from respiratory diseases and even showing a remarkably high incidence of gastric ulcers. As in Black Belt areas, the poor people of Appalachia were often seen as their own worst enemies, shackled by their own fatalism and lack of initiative. With less than half its adult population having advanced beyond the eighth grade in 1961, it was not surprising that Appalachia registered the nation's highest dropout and illiteracy rates in the 1960s or that many scholars and development experts believed the key to curing its numerous ills lay primarily in making its people less "backward" through education. Unfortunately, this cure would prove easier to prescribe than administer in places like central Appalachia, where only 12 percent of the population lived in towns. It had certainly seemed like progress when ramshackle one-room mountain schools gave way to modern consolidated facilities located in the more populous "growth centers" that were targeted to receive the bulk of federal funding in the area. However, school officials frequently had difficulty getting buses back into the isolated hollows, where parents suspicious of outsiders might not even let their children board them if they managed to make it through. Federal support helped to boost aggregate high school completion rates in the 1970s, but the most economically depressed areas still lagged well behind, and functional illiteracy rates among adults in Appalachia were still 50 percent higher than the national average in 1980.[11]

Shocking as they seem, such reports on the many dark spots in the Sunbelt seemed to gain remarkably little political traction. There were some, however, who steadfastly resisted the Cinderella story of a South rising kinder and gentler from its own degradation to help a shaken nation get beyond the multiple traumas of urban racial violence, bitter divisions over Vietnam, and widespread disillusionment over Watergate. Instead of celebrating the ascent of a beneficient Cinderella, these skeptics bemoaned the growing power and influence of a sinister, menacing South more reminiscent of her wicked stepsisters. Writing in 1975, journalist Kirkpatrick Sale grimly described a national "power shift" to the "Southern Rim," an area lying south of the 37th parallel as it ran from coast to coast. Sale was quick to point out that, thanks to the favorable flow of federal dollars and the payoffs from agribusiness, technological advances (including air-conditioning), oil, real estate, and the leisure industry, the gross economic product of the fifteen-state Southern Rim area would at that point have surpassed that of any foreign nation save for the Soviet Union. Not only were its brash and often ruthless entrepreneurs and industrialists bidding to wrest control of the nation's commerce, finance, and manufacturing sectors from the long-established economic titans of the Northeast, but the upstart wheeler-dealers of the Southern Rim seemed intent on a political takeover as well. Sale noted the preponderance of westerners and southerners in the cabinet and inner circles of the Nixon administration, for in its political, economic, and social outlook the dominant "cowboy culture" of the Southern Rim was aggressively conservative rather than liberal or even moderate.[12]

The Southern Rim's high-rolling, hard-riding business and industrial cowboys, such as the Texas multibillionaire H. L. Hunt, had little time for "live and let live." Their credo was closer to "I intend to get mine—and yours, too," and their reach also extended well into the upper echelons of Congress. Oklahoma senator Robert Kerr's identity as an oilman came through quite clearly in his votes on all issues petroleum-related, while House Ways and Means Committee chairman Wilber Mills of Arkansas seemed to find great merit in any legislation favoring either Gulf Oil or Texas computer giant H. Ross Perot.[13]

The religion of the Southern Rim was much more Old Testament fire and brimstone than New Testament love and forgiveness, and it was home to a host of rigid right-wing evangelical bastions such as Tulsa's Oral Roberts University and Bob Jones University in the South Carolina upcountry at Greenville. In its geography, culture, and mind-set, Sale's Southern Rim was nearly identical to the Sunbelt, which Nixon's southern strategist Kevin Phillips foresaw as the conservative cornerstone of an emerging Republican majority reflecting a pronounced shift in political influence both to the south and west. Though his take on "southernization" was not particularly ominous, historian David Donald offered little reassurance to nervous northerners when he observed that both the Southern Rim and the Sunbelt seemed "to be the Confederacy extended westward—just what the more ardent Confederates always wanted."[14]

To make matters seem even worse from the critical perspective of many liberals, there was little reason to think that whites elsewhere in the nation would offer much resistance to this southern political takeover. Introducing a fateful new addition to the liberal lexicon, Samuel Lubell warned in 1970 that George Wallace's 1968 campaign had raised the real prospect that "the North, as it changes, may become southernized." Three years later John Egerton suggested that, in addition to the ongoing "Americanization of Dixie," the "Southernization of America" might also now be well under way. Egerton noted the success of both Wallace and Nixon among northern white voters who were disenchanted with the conduct of the Vietnam War and convinced that both the civil rights movement and the War on Poverty had pushed the nation too far to the left. "Having failed for the first time to win at war, having found poverty and racism alive and menacing in its own house," Egerton observed, "the North has lately shown itself to be more and more like the South in the political, racial, social and religious inclinations of its collective majority." If what Sale and Egerton were describing was the face of a southernized "New America," it was the last face that liberal Democrats—and even some moderate Republicans—wanted to see. Over the last quarter of the twentieth century and well into the next, southernization would become the most widely and uncritically accepted explanation for why the rest of the country seemed suddenly to be succumbing to a contagion of race-tinged, right-wing politics, evangelical and fundamentalist religious fervor, outright hostility to social welfare programs, and other such afflictions previously associated with white southerners.[15]

In the mid-1970s, however, the sense of a South on the rise seemed more pronounced, and in some quarters certainly more ominous in the face of a concomitant sense of the North in decline. It seemed to James Wooten that "from Maine to the Great Lakes, the cities of the

The South and America since World War II

old Northern Crescent are steadily losing population, industry, jobs, payrolls, bank deposits, credit ratings, and tax bases. Meanwhile, from Virginia to the Pacific, the southern tier of America, the Sunbelt, is blossoming with new residents—a new prominence and place in the nation." An estimated two thousand people were leaving New York City's metropolitan area every day. Northern industrial cities were also reeling as the nation's once-vibrant Manufacturing Belt sagged and crumbled into the stagnant, sluggish Rust Belt, hemorrhaging jobs and people, many of them apparently heading for the warmer, more welcoming physical and business climates of the fast-growing South. Philadelphia lost an estimated twenty-five thousand residents in 1975 alone, and with smaller cities like Erie, Wilkes-Barre, and Scranton suffering proportionately, the population of Pennsylvania had already fallen by more than 400,000 people during the 1960s. In Ohio, with the southward shift of automobile manufacturing over the previous two decades, 50 percent of the jobs in Akron's tire and rubber industries had disappeared.[16]

Evidence of industrial decay and population decline became all the more frustrating to northern leaders in light of figures suggesting that taxpayers in their struggling communities might actually be underwriting the South's economic and population boom. In Alabama, where George Wallace had made a career out of defying and damning the federal government, Department of Defense expenditures totaled $1.2 billion in 1974, with the Department of Health, Education, and Welfare contributing another $1.5 billion. Meanwhile, the defense industry was the largest employer in Georgia, Louisiana, Mississippi, and Tennessee. The *National Journal* pointed out that while the southern states took in $11.5 billion more in federal funds than they paid out in federal taxes in 1975, ten Midwestern and mid-Atlantic states showed an aggregate federal funding deficit of $30.8 billion. In the Northeast, where the per capita federal tax burden was 12 percent higher than the national average, per capita federal outlays were 4 percent below it. In the South, although federal disbursements were 2 percent lower than the national figure, the average individual tax obligation was 14 percent below the national norm.[17]

Federal monies also played a key role in making the South more economically competitive by effectively subsidizing improvements in its educational systems. World War II had proved nothing less than a boon to southern higher education, injecting lethargic campuses with millions of defense training dollars and setting them aswarm with thousands of wartime trainees, followed by a postwar invasion of veterans funded by the GI Bill. Swelling enrollments meant more tuition money and increased state appropriations, a significant portion of which went into launching and expanding graduate education. Seventeen of the thirty-five southern schools offering PhDs in 1965 had launched their doctoral programs after World War II.

Allan Cartter of the American Council on Education observed in 1965 that the South could not "as yet boast a single outstanding institution on the national scene." Yet even though a number of these universities were still relatively new to the business of granting PhDs, the South's major universities were already raking in over 20 percent of federal research and development dollars annually. Even then these schools were seriously "on the make," as John Egerton put it, and as historian Clarence Mohr noted, the next decade would find them "fully engaged in a serious effort to equal or surpass their peer institutions in other areas."[18]

Certainly, when Cartter charged that southern leaders had traditionally "undervalued the economic benefits" of higher education, he was merely preaching to a choir of experts who were intent on linking education at all levels to industrial development. All the southern states had already launched programs to improve public elementary and secondary education as well. The result was higher standards for curriculum and instruction and better salaries for teachers, as well as school consolidation and administrative centralization aimed at making education more qualitatively sound and cost-effective. School officials also focused on the disparities between schools in urban and rural areas and, under growing federal pressure, those between black schools and white schools as well.

Although white officials often complained bitterly about this federal pressure, they seemed to have few qualms about accepting federal money for their schools. Mississippi's per-pupil expenditures had amounted to only 38 percent of the national average in 1950. The state had tripled its spending between 1950 and 1960, and the regional average for such expenditures had risen by 81 percent over the next decade. Still, with state spending on education increasing by 79 percent nationwide during the 1950s, the South began to register impressive relative gains only between 1960 and 1968, when the regional average rose from 71 to 78 percent of the national norm.[19]

It was no coincidence that this spike in southern school expenditures came during a period of dramatic expansion in federal spending on education, especially in the 1960s, when the tensions of the cold war and the so-called space race with the Soviet Union helped to inspire the National Defense Education Act and the Elementary and Secondary Education Act. In 1970–71 the southern states received more than 40 percent of all the funds provided by these programs. Nationally the average state drew on federal aid for 7 percent of its education budget, whereas southern states utilized money from Washington for from 9 to 22 percent of their school spending, and in some cases money ostensibly earmarked specifically for severely underfunded individual school systems simply disappeared into the stream of general operating revenue.[20]

The South's defenders argued that, as a percentage of personal income, the region's spending on education was close to national norms, but they seldom mentioned that a substantial portion of that funding actually came, not from state and local taxes, but from the federal government. Thanks to generous federal outlays, the southern states could provide modest upgrades for their schools without raising property taxes significantly or cutting back elsewhere. This was good news not only for individual taxpayers in the South but for corporate taxpayers as well. Although they seldom demurred publicly when southern development leaders insisted that better schools were crucial to the region's economic future, when representatives of textile, apparel, and other labor-intensive firms scouted for a new location, the quality of a community's public schools was far less important to them than its capacity to offer not only cheap labor but low taxes, and they feared the latter might easily be undermined by any educational improvement programs that had to be financed by local government revenue.

Nowhere were the concerns of such industrialists more influential than in Mississippi, and as the 1980s began, no state's educational system seemed to be in worse shape. The four-year high school dropout rate stood at 42 percent, and 35 percent of Mississippians attempting to join the U.S. Army flunked its basic intelligence tests. Both of these figures were approximately four times the national average. Yet when Governor William Winter launched his campaign to increase the severance tax on gas and oil in order to establish a statewide public kindergarten program and improve public education in general, opponents warned that any measure entailing a corporate tax hike was sure to undercut the state's appeal with the labor-intensive operations that accounted for the bulk of its industrial payrolls. Scoffing at Winter's argument that educational reforms were vital to bringing in more and better jobs, Meridian legislator Tommy Horne insisted in 1982 that improved schools were not necessary to bring industry to Mississippi: "We got plenty of cheap labor that doesn't take years to train. They can import the high-tech people from up North."[21]

Some observers blamed opposition to Winter's program on the lingering influence of the state's once dominant agricultural interests. One of the Winter plan's most ardent early opponents in the legislature was, in fact, house speaker and soybean farmer Buddy Newman, but Newman was also reportedly on retainer to a gas and oil pipeline company whose officials had in all likelihood noticed that Winter's initial proposal called for them to pay higher severance taxes. The public kindergarten provision was also a key sticking point with many white lawmakers who, regardless of profession, made little effort to conceal their aversion to using state money to provide what one characterized as "a damned babysitting service for blacks." Ultimately, in order to secure the kindergarten program, supporters had to agree to scrap the severance tax hike and finance the educational reform package primarily with an increase in the state's sales tax, which at 4 percent in 1982 was already one of the nation's most burdensome and regressive. "All of us should pay a part of the cost because all of us are going to benefit," explained state senator Ellis Bodron, a Vicksburg attorney. Bodron conceded that "a sales tax does exact a higher portion from those of limited means," but he added, "A gift is paternalism [and] …the unfortunate ought to be asked to be on the team." Bodron's rejection of "paternalism" was particularly striking, given that roughly one-quarter of Mississippi's education budget came courtesy of Washington at the time.[22]

Intensifying interregional competition for industry had already inspired talk of another War Between the States, and a dispute over the distribution of federal spending simply became another theater in that conflict. Those who contended that the South's economic gains were not coming at the expense of the northeastern and midwestern states pointed out that lower per capita tax burdens were simply a reflection of lower per capita incomes in a region where poverty was still far more widespread and intense than in the nation at large. They also argued that population growth in the Sunbelt South was more the result of a higher birth rate than an exodus of northerners to warmer—and

The South and America since World War II

cheaper—climes. Much the same could be said of employment growth, which actually stemmed more from the expansion of existing firms than the southward migration of northern industries.

Liberal critics, North and South, had spent several generations preaching that the South would not become more prosperous until it became more politically and socially progressive. These observers found it galling indeed to see the region's economy decidedly on the rise overall even as its politics had not only reverted to its traditional pattern of rock-ribbed conservatism but appeared to be pushing the rest of the nation sharply to the right as well. Cheered by the prospect of having one of their own in the White House, only 38 percent of Southern Baptists supported Gerald Ford against Jimmy Carter in 1976, but Republican Ronald Reagan claimed nearly half their votes four years later as an embattled Carter, already under attack for his handling of the Iranian hostage crisis, came under withering fire from television evangelist Jerry Falwell's recently organized "Moral Majority" for his stance on abortion and gay rights.[23]

Ronald Reagan seemed ready simply to pick up where the Nixon administration's southern strategy of appealing to white southerners' racial resentments had left off when he opened his 1980 presidential campaign in Neshoba County, Mississippi, the site of the brutal slaying of three civil rights workers in 1964. Offering a spirited defense of states' rights, Reagan's kickoff speech resurrected the racially coded rhetoric of the massive resistance era, and his pet campaign story about a "welfare queen" who supposedly fleeced the government for $150,000 a year was hardly free of racial overtones. "Obviously," a Reagan advisor conceded, "sitting around saying, 'We want to cut this,' is much more abstract than even the busing thing and a hell of a lot more abstract than 'Nigger, nigger.'" Essentily all Reagan had to do was "run in place on the issues he's campaigned on since 1964...fiscal conservatism, balancing the budget, cut taxes, you know, the whole cluster."[24]

Reagan's first term showcased his commitment to the "whole cluster," and his hostility to affirmative action, his indifference to voting rights enforcement, and his opposition to stripping all-white private schools of their tax-exempt status more than adequately affirmed and clarified his racial stance. This much was apparent in the racially polarized voting patterns that saw a triumphant Reagan claim an estimated 86 percent of the white vote in Mississippi in 1984, while his Democratic challenger collected 89 percent of the black vote. Across the South only 9 percent of all the ballots cast by blacks went to Reagan. His conservative economic stance doubtless contributed to his 77 percent showing among southern whites with incomes above $35,000, but given his opposition to wage hikes and other pro-labor policies, it was hard to see what, other than his across-the-board hostility to any programs seen as favorable to blacks, may have helped him capture 56 percent of the votes among southern whites with incomes less than $15,000.[25]

Still, for all its indebtedness to the old southern strategy, a more subtle and ultimately more formidable Republican message was actually in the making. Reagan's promise to "get government off peoples' backs" was simply irresistible to the great many southern whites who saw federal authority as merely the extension of northern will and the instrument of northern interference in their racial affairs. At the same time, by emphasizing his party's fervent opposition to "big government" liberalism, he was also scoring big with white voters across the nation who were fed up with expensive social welfare programs (seemingly lavished overwhelmingly on minorities) and meddlesome federal efforts to control their schools, neighborhoods, and other aspects of their lives.

For southern Republican congressional and gubernatorial candidates in 1984, the operative strategy was to cast themselves squarely in the Reagan mold while painting their Democratic opponents as clones of their party's big-government, big-spending, bleeding-heart liberal nominee, Walter Mondale. Perhaps the bitterest of these contests came in North Carolina, where ultraconservative segregationist Republican senator Jesse Helms managed to turn back a strong challenge from Democratic governor James Hunt by characterizing himself as "a Reagan conservative" and his opponent as a "Mondale liberal." Helms had led a losing fight against a national holiday honoring Rev. Martin Luther King Jr., and he issued campaign materials suggesting that Hunt was collaborating with Rev. Jesse Jackson on a plan to boost black voter registration. Across the South Republicans claimed nine new House seats in 1984, bringing them up to 37 percent of the region's total. After the elections Republicans also occupied 21 percent of the seats in southern legislatures, a 4 percent increase from 1982.[26]

Until the 1964 Goldwater campaign the Republicans had been the moderate alternative to Democratic conservatism in southern politics. When Reagan left office some twenty-five years later, the GOP was the conservative alternative to Democratic moderation. Under Reagan the

North Carolina Senator Jesse Helms (right) and Rev. Jerry Falwell, 1982. Bettman/
Corbis.

party had solidified its "natural" southern white-collar suburban base
while securing and extending Goldwater's and Nixon's inroads among
rural blue-collar whites. The most telling illustration of the Reagan
era's impact on southern politics may be that whereas only 40 percent
of southern white conservatives identified themselves as Republicans
in 1980, by 1988 that figure stood at 60 percent. Reagan's congenial-
ity, charm, and personal political skills doubtless played a key role in
accelerating this transformation, but the more fundamental elements of
the Republican Party's appeal for southern whites included its staunchly
conservative positions on race, taxes, welfare, anticommunism, and
moral and religious issues such as abortion and prayer in schools.[27]

Facing Massachusetts governor Michael Dukakis in the 1988 presidential race, Reagan's vice president, George H. W. Bush, pounced on
the liberal Dukakis's opposition to the death penalty, but his campaign
gained even more momentum by spotlighting the story of Willie Hor-
ton, a black man imprisoned for murder who had raped a woman and
tortured her boyfriend after failing to return from a weekend furlough
granted under a special Massachusetts program overseen by Dukakis.

Observing a racially polarized voting pattern comparable to 1984, *New York Times* writer Tom Wicker explained that the new GOP strategy was "not racism in a sheet and a hood; it is a race consciousness in a white as well as a blue-collar....Republicans who deny that they exploit it are disingenuous; Democrats who pretend they can win anyway are whistling past the graveyard."[28]

As president, Bush continued to play to white voters' "race consciousness" by vetoing the first attempt in 1990 to extend the Civil Rights Act on the grounds that the legislation sought to establish racial "quotas." Unfortunately for Bush, however, cumulative Republican attempts to exacerbate and then capitalize on racial polarization had helped to summon from the political netherworld one David Duke, a former Klansman turned openly white supremacist Louisiana Republican politico who won a seat in the Louisiana legislature and mounted distressingly strong campaigns for the U.S. Senate in 1990 and the governorship in 1991. Under pressure from embarrassed Republican moderates, Bush finally agreed in 1991 to sign an extension of the Civil Rights Act in a form not substantially different from the one he had vetoed the year before.[29]

The Republican right did not take kindly to Bush's decision to pull the apparently winning issue of racial quotas off the campaign strategy table for 1992, and he had already infuriated a great many conservatives by reneging on his 1988 "Read my lips, no new taxes" pledge when he agreed to a budget compromise arrangement in 1990. With the nation sliding into an economic recession and his support crumbling badly, Bush's team made a desperate attempt to reach out to the far right by giving them a prominent role in writing the 1992 platform, which included a proposed ban on all abortions, even in cases of rape and incest. At the convention itself, prime-time speeches by Pat Buchanan and Rev. Pat Robertson conveyed the image of a party dominated by right-wing ideologues.[30]

Meanwhile, for the Democrats, former Arkansas governor Bill Clinton hammered the hapless Bush relentlessly on the economy while portraying himself as a "New Democrat," more centrist than liberal, committed to welfare reform (a traditional hot-button Republican issue) and to a new national health care plan geared to help the middle class as well as the poor. Many pundits questioned Clinton's political wisdom in choosing a fellow southerner, Tennessee senator Al Gore, as his running mate, but en route to victory the "Bubba Squad" succeeded in carrying their home states as well as Georgia and Louisiana, all of which had gone to Bush by more than 60 percent of the vote in 1988.

Ultimately these states were not crucial to Clinton's win, for his was a truly national triumph, albeit one facilitated by third-party candidate Ross Perot's appeal to disaffected Republicans. There was also widespread dissatisfaction with Bush's failure to address the nation's economic problems, as well as concern among centrist swing voters that in catering to evangelicals and anti-abortion activists the Republicans themselves had swung too far to the right. This trend was readily observable in the South when Bush, who had polled 59 percent of the moderate white vote in 1988, managed only 41 percent from the same group in 1992. Bush barely bested Clinton in this category, but among southern whites overall the Democratic victor received only an estimated 35 percent of the vote, scarcely three points better than either Mondale or Dukakis had done in 1984 and 1988, respectively.[31]

Clinton again carried four southern states when he won reelection in 1996, losing Georgia (where he actually polled a higher percentage of the vote than when he won in 1992 but got less help from Perot's presence on the ballot this time around) but picking up Florida. Once again, although they were not critical to his victory, the key to Clinton's success in these states was his appeal to white moderates, whom he courted with a somewhat more conservative stance than he had taken four years earlier, including his support for a tough crime bill and for tighter restrictions on welfare eligibility. The air strikes he ordered against the Serbs in Bosnia in 1995 had given the impression of a more confident foreign policy leader, and although an off-year election trouncing in 1994 had seen Republicans seize control of both houses of Congress, the incumbent president ultimately benefited from a rebounding economy, declining interest rates, and a shrinking federal deficit.

Stepping up to claim the Democratic presidential nomination in 2000, Vice President Al Gore could invoke a strong economy as he did battle with Texas governor George W. Bush. On the other hand, the second Clinton term had brought revelations of an extraordinarily reckless extramarital dalliance in the White House that then led to a highly partisan impeachment trial, both of which seemed ultimately to damage Gore more than Clinton. White voters in the South and elsewhere tended to vote for or against Gore on the basis of their feelings about Clinton, many of them refusing to credit Gore for Clinton's economic accomplishments while nonetheless associating him with the president's sexual indiscretions.

Although some observers doubted that the stiff and wonkish Gore would do as well with black voters, who had all but idolized Clinton, in capturing 91 percent of southern black votes, the vice president actually posted a stronger showing with blacks than his boss did. Yet Gore garnered less than 39 percent of the white vote in his home state of Tennessee, compared to the 43 percent that went to Clinton in 1996. Gore suffered another, even more dramatic falloff in white support in ultimately decisive Florida, the only southern state where the third-party candidacy of consumer advocate Ralph Nader actually affected what would be at best a questionable outcome. Nader's candidacy would not have mattered in 2000, however, had Bush not picked off 16 percent of the Florida whites who had voted for Clinton in 1996. Wooden and unspontaneous in comparison to his gregarious and relaxed opponent, Gore bore the burden of association with Clinton, and his encyclopedic grasp of facts and ideas actually seemed to hurt him with some white voters who saw him as much more of the aloof, technocratic Democratic liberal than the folksy but informed Clinton had been. Across the South, Bush bested Gore by two to one among whites, capturing all of its 160 electoral votes, which amounted to 60 percent of his winning total. Thus, ironically, he became both the first Republican presidential candidate since 1972 to sweep the South and the only one since 1968 whose victory depended on the support of a single southern state.[32]

George W. Bush's decision to invade Iraq in 2003 had begun to cost him in national polls by 2004. However, he remained in good standing with typically pro-military, religiously conservative southern whites who also approved of his stances against abortion and gay marriage. Running against Democratic Senator John Kerry of Massachusetts in 2004, Bush again swept the South, improving significantly on his 2000 showing with southern white voters by capturing 85 percent of their support in Mississippi and 80 percent in Alabama and claiming from 64 to 78 percent in all the remaining southern states except Florida (57 percent). Kerry came close to equaling Gore's performance with southern black voters, but despite having the military record that his opponent lacked, his eventual opposition to the Vietnam War and his image as a traditional "tax-and-spend" northern liberal who often seemed Brahminesque and ill-at-ease with the common folk proved his undoing with southern whites.[33]

The ideological divide between the parties was less pronounced farther down the ticket, but even during the Clinton presidential inter-regnum of the 1990s the Republicans had continued to claim a pro-gressively greater share of congressional- and state-level offices. Some of these gains came from party-switching; fifteen of the twenty-five congressmen who changed their partisan affiliations between 1980 and 2005 were from the South. Beyond that, after picking up nine southern seats in the 1994 election surge that brought them control of Congress for the first time since 1952, the Republicans had improved their stand-ing in the House of Representatives with each election over the next decade. By virtue of rapid population growth, the South had gained a net of thirteen seats, courtesy of the 1990 and 2000 censuses, and the Republicans had gone from holding 40 percent of the region's House seats and 35 percent of its Senate seats in 1992 to controlling 57 percent of its House seats and 92 percent of its Senate seats by 2004.[34]

With the national outcry over the war in Iraq growing louder and Bush's popularity faltering nationwide, the GOP lost six southern seats in the House and one in the Senate in 2006. Two of the House losses were virtually unwinnable situations for the Republicans after a lobbying scandal toppled the former House majority leader Tom Delay of Texas and a sex scandal involving a House page forced Florida's Congress-man Tom Foley from office. The new Democratic Senate seat came in Virginia, where former Republican Jim Webb bested incumbent George Allen after Allen's campaign stumbled in the wake of his reference to an Indian-American supporter of his opponent as "macaca," a term some-times used to refer to a genus of monkey. Overall, however, with the old Confederacy giving Democrats only 15 percent of their congressional, gubernatorial, and legislative gains, the South was most notable for its relative resistance to national trends in 2006.

The relative conservatism of most of the surviving white Democratic politicians in the South sometimes made it difficult to differentiate between them and their Republican rivals, but the importance of black support to many Democratic office seekers generally dictated a substan-tially more moderate position on racially sensitive issues. As a result, Republicans persisted in encouraging whites to see the Democrats pri-marily as the party of blacks. Mississippi GOP chairman Jim Herring even warned his fellow whites in 2007 that the state's Democratic law-makers "will say they're like you. They'll say 'I go to church with you,' 'My kids go to school with yours.'...But when they go to the Legislature, they'll vote with the black caucus and support Hillary Clinton." Mississippi's Democratic governor Ronnie Musgrove had tried unsuccessfully to have the Confederate battle flag removed from the state flag only to lose his 2003 reelection bid to powerful lobbyist and former GOP national chairman Haley Barbour. On the way to gaining an estimated 80 percent of the white vote, Barbour ran ads urging voters to "keep the flag" but "change the governor." During the campaign he also declined to renounce the support of the Council of Conservative Citizens, the heir to the old segregationist Citizens Councils of the massive resistance era, and the group even ran his picture on their website.[35]

The politics of racial symbolism also helped to make former Democrat Sonny Perdue Georgia's first Republican governor since Reconstruction in 2002. Democratic incumbent Roy Barnes had angered many rural and working-class whites with a carefully choreographed and swiftly implemented move to get the legislature to remove the Confederate battle flag insignia from Georgia's state flag in 2001. During the campaign Perdue promised a referendum to allow Georgians to vote on restoring the old flag, which had been adopted at the defiant peak of massive resistance sentiment. Taking advantage of voter disenchantment with Barnes on other issues as well, he shocked pollsters (and Democrats) with a stunning 52 to 45 percent upset victory, as Barnes's share of the white vote dropped precipitously from 1998, when he won handily in the state's rural white counties.[36]

Tennessee Democratic congressman Harold Ford Jr. fell less than three points shy in 2006 of becoming the first black U.S. senator from a southern state since Reconstruction, but it was difficult to determine whether the outcome of the election meant that race consciousness was on the wane or still a potent political force in Tennessee. After overcoming a twelve-point deficit in favor of his Republican opponent, former Chattanooga mayor Bob Corker, Ford managed to take as much as a five-point lead in the polls by early October. At that point, however, the Republican National Committee released a campaign spot featuring a suggestively attired blond white woman claiming she had met Ford at a "Playboy party" and purring seductively, "Harold, call me." Numerous critics attacked the ad as an egregious attempt to play on white hostility to interracial dating, and even Corker disavowed it as "over the top." Observers disagreed about whether the controversial spot would actually hurt or help Corker, but before the end of October he had pulled back ahead of Ford in the polls.[37]

Despite his narrow loss Ford had claimed 40 percent of the white vote in a state where blacks made up only 16 percent of the population. This showing among whites was surely noteworthy because, as the twenty-first century unfolded, the key to reversing dwindling Democratic fortunes in the South clearly lay in finding a way to win back a significant share of the white voters who had defected to the GOP. White hostility to Democratic civil rights initiatives had obviously fueled the initial Republican "breakthrough" in 1964, when Barry Goldwater grabbed an amazing 87.1 percent of the vote in Mississippi at a time when most blacks could not yet vote and most whites apparently meant to keep it that way. More than forty years later, however, it appeared to some that the GOP's message to southern whites emphasized class more than race.[38]

As we have seen, although it was not so evident at the outset, the Reagan era was critical to Americanizing the southern strategy by distancing it from its roots in the racial polarization of the 1960s and repackaging it as something more pleasing to the ear and less troubling to the conscience of upwardly mobile whites, not simply in the South but throughout the nation. Under the popular and politically adroit Reagan, the new Republican mantra had stressed individual economic success over shared social responsibility and neighborhood autonomy over equality of opportunity or access. In the process it also cast the minorities in the central cities and the liberal proponents of an expanded federal, state, and local social welfare agenda as the principal threats to the well-being of honest, God-fearing suburban whites hoping simply to enjoy the social and economic fruits of their achievements. Without abandoning appeals to race consciousness so much as merely making them implicit to a new message couched in the more respectable and reassuring language of class, the Republicans had managed, for the most part, to jettison the clumsily coded rhetoric of "law and order" and opposition to "senseless busing" crafted forty years earlier to dissuade southern whites from "wasting" their votes on George Wallace.

In the Reagan years, the old rough-around-the-edges southern strategy had simply been subsumed by a sleeker, more racially modulated "suburban strategy" that might work equally well in white neighborhoods outside not just Atlanta or Birmingham but any number of cities elsewhere in the country. Still gloating from his party's triumph in the 1994 congressional races, Representative Newt Gingrich explained that the staunchly Republican inhabitants of his suburban

Atlanta district "don't object to upper-middle-class neighbors who keep their grass cut and move to the area to avoid crime." Rather, his supporters simply worried about "the bus line destroying one apartment complex after another, bringing people out for public housing who have no middle-class values [and] whose kids as they become teenagers are often centers of robbery and where the schools collapse because the people who live in the apartment complexes don't care that the kids don't do well in school."[39]

Even though their rhetoric had changed, when suburban whites rallied to protect the homogeneity of their neighborhoods, race was hardly the furthest thing from their minds. Since the 1970s, efforts to expand the Metropolitan Atlanta Rapid Transit Authority bus and train lines into the suburbs had met strong opposition in some counties from whites fearing an influx of inner-city blacks, so much so that critics redubbed MARTA "Moving Africans Rapidly Through Atlanta." Out in Gwinnett County voters had rejected a MARTA extension bid in 1990 by more than two to one. When the issue came up again in a nonbinding straw poll in 2008, opposition seemed no less intense as citizens weighed in with comments such as "GOD I HOPE NOT!!!!!!!!!!!! Too many criminals from Atlanta will have a basically free way to ply their trades of rape, robbery and murder!" and "I moved to Gwinnett to get away from MARTA. NO, NO, NO, NO, NO!!!!! And I certainly don't want another penny of my hard earned money to go to this!!!!!!" In the end 53 percent of Gwinnett voters rejected the 2008 proposal, with Republicans opposing it by two to one and Democrats supporting it by a slightly larger margin.[40]

GOP campaign strategist Ken Mehlman explained that in targeting voters in 2004 the party "did what VISA did" by analyzing a mass of consumer data that led him and his associates to conclude, "If you drive a Volvo and you do Yoga, you are pretty much a Democrat. If you drive a Lincoln or a BMW and you own a gun, you're voting for George Bush." Such a broad-brush approach may have paid off for the GOP in terms of big numbers in the suburbs, but the party's most loyal and dependable support in the South came from voters who probably owned several guns but were more likely to be struggling to make the payments on a Ford or Chevrolet pickup than cruising around in a Lincoln or a BMW.[41]

In 2000 George W. Bush captured more than 60 percent of the vote in only four of the thirteen Alabama counties in the top quintile for white household income but in seven of the fourteen in the lowest quintile. Across the South in 2004 he averaged 55 percent of the vote in metro counties and 60 percent in rural counties; his poorest showings were in urban core or central city counties and rural counties with relatively large black population percentages. Support for Bush along the I-85 corridor between Atlanta and Charlotte fit a national pattern where voters in counties just outside metropolitan areas went for him in higher percentages than those actually within the areas themselves. His most ardent supporters in this part of the South, however, were whites in rural counties even farther from metro areas, where he collected 63 percent of the vote.[42]

When Sonny Perdue succeeded in breaking the Democrats, 130-year gubernatorial grip on Georgia in 2002, his effort to capitalize on the hard feelings of many whites about a state flag that had been stripped of its Confederate symbolism virtually guaranteed that the campaign would have racial overtones. Thus it was not surprising that the strength of Perdue's support at the county level showed a strong positive correlation (.8097) with the relative size of the county's white population. What was striking about the election that brought the state's first Republican governor since Reconstruction was the negligible association (.1103) between household income and Perdue's strength across all the state's 159 counties. Four years later, running as an incumbent against Democratic lieutenant governor Mark Taylor, Perdue showed up a bit better in metro Atlanta, but again the correlation between his support and median white household income was minimal, even in counties with higher concentrations of white household incomes above $50,000.[43]

The Republicans had developed a more subtle and sophisticated appeal that played well among more affluent white residents of bedroom communities, but in 2004, no less than 1984, there was still ample reason to suspect that many rural southern whites were able to look past the class implications of the party's message to see its color implications as well. On the face of it, working-class white support for the GOP seemed to make little sense. Yet as Earl and Merle Black observed in 1987, the political philosophy of the "new southern middle class…retain[ed] important continuities with the [old agrarian] traditionalistic culture," differing primarily in its readiness to use "governmental resources" in ways that would stimulate economic growth, but certainly not in its opposition to using those resources to assist the South's "have-nots and have-littles." Although they may have fallen into this category economically, a great many lower-income southern whites saw such programs targeting someone else, namely blacks. Republican opposition to a higher minimum wage or a more progressive tax structure obviously did nothing to benefit blue-collar whites. By the same token, however, the GOP was at least no threat to launch new government initiatives that would elevate blacks at their expense. In fact, for all the Democratic rhetoric about helping the "working people," many working-class whites in the South clearly believed that the party had done little or nothing for them since the civil rights era began.[44]

Responsibility for the failure of organized labor to establish a foothold in the region could be spread among a variety of culprits, not the least of them being blatantly illegal and extralegal employer harassment and intimidation that too often went unchecked, regardless of which party controlled Congress or the White House. Whatever its causes, however, the exceedingly feeble union presence in the South resulted in a critical disconnect between the national Democratic Party, with its close relationship and fairly proscribed working arrangements with organized labor, and the South's unorganized and economically voiceless white workers. Rightly or not, a number of these white workers simply saw the national Democratic Party largely ignoring them while supporting educational and training programs that would make blacks more competitive for their jobs "The government will help the niggers," complained a white factory worker in North Carolina, "but they won't give us nothing." In the long run it proved difficult to separate race from class when explaining the Republican preferences of either rural or suburban southern whites. Yet, judging from George Wallace's strong showing in northern presidential primaries in the 1960s and the GOP's success in tapping into nationwide hostility to busing and affirmative action thereafter, the same might surely be said of white voters outside the South as well.[45]

In what seemed to many a most improbable development, in the 1990s the national Republican Party and black Democrats had actually become the strangest of political bedfellows, at least in their joint push to increase the number of black-majority congressional districts in the South. In this, black Democrats sought to bring more black faces and voices to Congress by simply outflanking whites' reluctance to support black candidates. Republican supporters of redistricting also claimed they were simply trying to address the lingering political legacy of white prejudice. Yet party strategists understood full well that concentrating black voters in a limited number of districts would leave the remaining districts noticeably whiter. This, in turn, would give the GOP a far better chance of capturing seats once held by white Democrats who had depended on a loyal base of black support. Up through the 1980s more than three-fifths of the South's congressional districts had been 15 percent black or more. By 1992, however, nearly half of those districts had black populations smaller than 15 percent.[46]

As Earl and Merle Black have shown, redistricting did indeed enhance the prospects for black Democrats, who had held but five southern congressional seats prior to 1992 but captured twelve new black-majority districts in that year's voting. In absolute terms, however, the biggest winners were the Republicans, who represented thirty-nine southern congressional districts in 1991 and seventy-one ten years later. The big losers, of course, were white southern Democrats, whose numbers in Congress fell from seventy-two in 1991 to thirty-seven ten years later. Before redistricting, 46 percent of southern House districts had been carried by Bush with more than 60 percent of the vote in 1988. Afterward this figure stood at 52 percent.[47]

Overall, by 2000 Mississippi and Alabama alone accounted for more blacks in elective office than could be found in the entire country in 1970. Georgia, Louisiana, and South Carolina also registered impressive numbers, each boasting more than five hundred elected black officeholders at that point. Statewide elected offices were more difficult for any minority to attain, and there were still only forty-three blacks in such posts throughout the United States in 2007. Eight of those, however, were in Georgia, which led the nation in this category by a wide margin, and along with six other southern states accounted for 42 percent of all blacks in statewide office.[48]

In addition to increasing influence on social policymaking, success in electing black public officials clearly paid some significant economic dividends. After he took office as Atlanta's first black mayor in 1974, Maynard Jackson set a goal of awarding at least 30 percent of all city contracts to minority bidders. Jackson's successor, Andrew Young, raised the target figure to 35 percent, and under Jackson and Young, between 1973 and 1988, the city gave nearly sixteen hundred city contracts to 612 minority-owned firms. Both Jackson and Young encouraged white employers to consider the merits of hiring more blacks. In the mid-1970s fewer than one in twenty black workers in Atlanta had held executive, managerial, or administrative jobs, but by 1990 that figure topped one in five. Black employment in professional and technical areas increased dramatically as well. In 1990 some 37 percent of black workers in southern metropolitan areas held white-collar jobs, an increase of 25 percent since 1980. Although white-collar employees sometimes earned less than they might have on the assembly line, it was still worthy of note that by 1990 64 percent of working black women in the metropolitan South held white-collar jobs, compared to 56 percent in 1980.[49]

Such figures were striking, although the farther one moved from the metropolis, the more exceptional they became. In rural counties fewer than one in six black men and only one in three black women in the workforce were in white-collar occupations in 1990. In fact, while the blue-collar/white-collar employment disparity between black and white workers in metropolitan areas narrowed by 11 percent among men and 20 percent among women in the 1980s, the same gap between metro and rural blacks actually widened by 24 and 16 percent, respectively.[50]

Beyond the metro areas companies tended to shy away from sites where blacks accounted for more than one-third of the population, perhaps because executives believed black workers might be more receptive to union organizers or feared that in counties where blacks were a significant political force officials might be more inclined to raise taxes in order to fund expanded public programs for the poor. When manufacturing employment was available, rural black workers were concentrated heavily in the low-wage, low-skill jobs. These were generally the first to go when global competition from even cheaper labor markets forced mass plant closings in the textile and apparel industries during the 1980s and beyond. Some, but by no means all blacks who lost their jobs to deindustrialization found new employment in the service sector, but often at even lower wages than they had earned in manufacturing. Such trends helped to explain why in nearly half of Georgia's 159 counties at least 40 percent of the black families were trying to survive on incomes below $10,000 in 1989 and why racial disparities in household incomes in Louisiana, Mississippi, Alabama, Arkansas, and South Carolina were actually wider in 1990 than they had been ten years earlier.[51]

The generally gloomy circumstances and prospects of so many rural black southerners notwithstanding, during the 1990s the South's larger and more dynamic metropolitan areas seemed to take on an almost irresistible allure for many blacks living outside the region. Between 1910 and 1960 nearly 10 million blacks had left the South, but in the mid-1970s the region began to show net gains through black in-migration. This trend continued throughout the 1980s and accelerated dramatically in the 1990s, when the South's black population grew by nearly 3.6 million overall, nearly twice the rate of increase for the previous decade. With nearly nine in ten black in-migrants settling in metropolitan areas, the fact that one out of ten blacks in the region in 2000 was a newcomer clearly reflected the economic momentum of a metropolitan South that led the nation in job creation in the 1990s. Beyond that, approximately 20 percent of the South's new black residents were college graduates, a figure well above the average for the black population at large. Dr. Terry Reynolds, a dentist, explained that he settled on Atlanta because "blacks are in businesses here that you could not conceive of them being in anywhere else." The rapid expansion of the region's black middle class clearly became a self-sustaining force for continued growth. Said one new resident of metropolitan Atlanta, "There are so many African Americans here who have made it or succeeded or gotten to that middle-class line. It's nice to see."[52]

Metro Atlanta actually added 459,000 African Americans and was home to seven of the nation's ten fastest growing counties for blacks in the 1990s. South of the city, in Henry County, where the black population increased by 158 percent between 2000 and 2005 alone, the proportion of black households with incomes above $50,000 stood at 50 percent in 1999, well over three times higher than it had been in 1989. In Gwinnett County, to the north, roughly half of black households registered earnings in this range in 1999. In Fayette County the portion of black families earning $50,000 or more a year had risen from 42 percent in 1989 to 74 percent ten years later, when nearly a third of all black families actually had an annual income in excess of $100,000.[53]

The Dallas–Fort Worth metropolitan area was also a magnet for more affluent black families. In the 1990s the number of black households earning at least $100,000 more than tripled, from 5,300 to 16,000. The growth of black wealth in the area was more widely dispersed than in metro Atlanta. In Lancaster, to the south of Dallas, upper-income black families increased more than eightfold in the 1990s. To the north, nearly 25 percent of black families reported incomes above $100,000, and in Forest Hill, near Fort Worth, blacks accounted for nearly 60 percent of the households and 84 percent of those in the higher income category. As a veteran mortgage banker explained, "Before, when I saw an application for an attorney, a doctor, or someone making $100,000 plus, I assumed they were white. That's not the case anymore." Like most suburbanites, black home seekers were looking for the best houses and neighborhoods and the shortest commute they could afford. Financial analyst Malcolm Mayo explained that although it was clearly an attractive area for a number of upscale black professionals, he had chosen Lancaster because it also offered "more bang for the buck."[54]

The primary attraction of metropolitan Dallas–Fort Worth was a booming economy, but decisions about specific communities typically turned on issues related to schools, churches, and overall quality of life. Even so, such choices were not always easy, for they generally took black families into areas where the black population, though growing, was still decidedly in the minority. This choice, admitted Kevin Davis, who moved to the Dallas–Fort Worth area from Indiana in 1996, sometimes made it "hard to find ways to connect to the community."[55]

Overall, with a 205 percent increase in upper-income black families during the 1990s, Dallas–Fort Worth ranked fifth nationally among metropolitan areas with a population of more than one million where 10 percent of households were black. The leader by a wide margin, with a 303 percent increase, was Orlando, followed by Atlanta (229 percent), Raleigh-Durham (222 percent), and Memphis (209 percent). It is surely noteworthy that all these areas were in the South and that even smaller, less dynamic metro areas like Jackson, Mississippi, posted comparable increases.[56]

Although they were well aware of the opportunities that the South now afforded, for many black returnees the region's pull seemed to go beyond simple economics. Harold Jackson, a Savannah native who left the South and eventually returned to Atlanta, insisted, "It's not just that the opportunities are here. It's that the opportunities to solve the problems that exist are here, too." Again and again black returnees registered their surprise at the changes that had come in their absence. After forty-six years in San Francisco, Etta Willis came back to Mount Olive, Mississippi, in 1994 and quickly discovered, "You don't have the racism here that you used to have." In fact, she admitted, "I have experienced less racism here than I did in San Francisco." With the South's opportunities drawing younger, college-educated blacks, their parents often followed them. Eager to boost her salary as a teacher, Ruth Colvin had left North Carolina for Connecticut in 1968, but she was thinking of returning by 2003. Not only could you "do so much more with your money down there when you retire," but beyond that, she added, "It's home....You never forget the place you grew up in."[57]

Meanwhile, with the overwhelming majority of black in-migrants settling in the suburbs, the suburbanization of the black middle class helped to explain why segregation declined 10 percent faster in the metropolitan South than elsewhere in the United States during the 1990s, leaving the region with eight of the nation's ten least segregated metropolitan areas by 2000. Nationwide the 2000 census showed that the twenty metropolitan areas with the highest percentage of the population living on blocks with both black and white residents were in the South. More than 40 percent of Virginia Beach's population fell into this category, as did nearly a third of Charlotte's; Nashville, Jacksonville, and Memphis fell in the 25 to 30 percent range. These compared rather favorably with 14 percent in Philadelphia and 13 percent in Boston, not to speak of New York City at 4 percent. Not all southern cities came out so well; two-thirds of white Atlantans lived on blocks that were more than 80 percent white, but then so did 93 percent of whites in Pittsburgh and 87 percent in Providence, Rhode Island.[58]

By 2000 seventeen of the twenty largest racial population disparities between city and suburb were in metro areas outside the South. Places like Gary, Indiana, Detroit, Buffalo, and Milwaukee registered black-white racial dissimilarity indices ranging from 66 to 76, while those for southern metro areas such as Atlanta, Houston, and Norfolk fell between 14 and 19. In public schools the average index of racial dissimilarity in southern metropolitan districts was 84 in 1968, compared to a nonsouthern average of 76. By 2000 the southern average stood at 44, while the nonsouthern figure was 56. In the same year a national comparison of segregation levels in metropolitan elementary schools showed only Birmingham, Chattanooga, and Gadsden among the thirty most segregated, while the South accounted for thirteen of the thirty metro areas with the lowest levels of school segregation. Needless to say, white southerners could not always resist the temptation to point out that school segregation was much more pronounced in such supposed bastions of northern enlightenment as New Haven and Boston than in former citadels of Jim Crow like Little Rock and Greenville.[59]

Questions about the relative overall quality of education available to black students in southern public schools began to recede a bit as well. A 2009 Department of Education Study showed that black students in all but two southern states now posted higher scores on standardized math and reading tests than black students in either Wisconsin or California. The gap between black and white students' scores was smaller in

Alabama and Mississippi than in Connecticut or Illinois and well below the national average across the region.[60]

Much of the South's progress in putting aside its most burdensome racial encumbrances could clearly be traced to its economic advancement. Likewise, as we saw earlier, no more than a decade after World II the onset of a newfound prosperity was already contributing to some marked changes in the way some southerners, in urban and metropolitan areas especially, were interpreting and practicing their legendary religious faith. Whether this trend constituted progress in its entirety was a matter of some contention, but it not only persisted but accelerated, even as the region retained its long-standing designation as America's Bible Belt.

Even with all of the distractions introduced or facilitated by economic modernization, eight of the ten states with the highest church attendance were still in the South in 2006. In fact, one of the foremost of those distractions, television, had made it possible for southerners who found that attending church did not necessarily satisfy all their spiritual needs to fill that void without leaving their homes.[61]

Rev. Billy Graham's well-publicized televised crusades in major cities across the nation and throughout the world had made him the most influential evangelist in America by the 1960s. Television was critical as well to the meteoric career of Rev. Oral Roberts, a one-time tent revivalist and faith-healer, whose dramatic, emotional broadcasts had reached millions by the mid-1950s. By the end of the decade Roberts had built a massive radio and television ministry, headquartered in a new seven-story building in Tulsa, Oklahoma. As the 1960s unfolded, however, the laying on of hands and other healing rituals began to seem a bit out of place in a South grown metropolitan and prosperous, where worshippers, Roberts conceded, "had become used to cushioned chairs and air conditioning and to watching television." Accordingly, he began to de-emphasize healing in his broadcasts and eventually left the Pentecostal Holiness Church altogether to join a fashionable Methodist congregation in Tulsa, where he had founded Oral Roberts University in 1965. At that point Roberts already presided over a financial empire worth nearly $1 billion. He was hardly alone. Electronic evangelism quickly made many a minister into a millionaire many times over. Television boasted thirty-eight syndicated religious programs in 1970 and sixty-six scarcely five years later. Over this brief span the viewing audience for these shows had more than doubled, from ten million to more than twenty million.[62]

The explosion of televangelical programming in the last quarter of the twentieth century brought celebrity status to a number of ambitious and controversial southern ministers. In 1960 Rev. Pat Robertson founded the Christian Broadcasting Network, which was headquartered in Virginia Beach, Virginia, but would eventually reach some 180 countries. Robertson later fashioned the CBN Cable Network into a financial empire that also provided him with an outlet for his conservative and frequently controversial political opinions. The son of a former U.S. senator, Robertson sought the 1988 Republican presidential nomination, and despite charges that he had misrepresented his military service in Korea, he placed second in the Iowa caucuses before faltering in the New Hampshire primary and eventually dropping out of the race.[63]

Capitalizing on his campaign organization, however, as the founder of the 1.7-million-member Christian Coalition, Robertson continued

Rev. Billy Graham, 1966. *U.S. News and World Report* Magazine Photograph Collection, Library of Congress, Prints and Photographs Division, Washington, D.C. (LC-U9-15743-7C [P8P]).

World's largest "Praying Hands" monument at the entrance to Oral Roberts University, Tulsa, Oklahoma. Courtesy of Dustin M. Ramsey.

to wield considerable political influence, preaching a mixture of fiery fundamentalism and right-wing politics on *The 700 Club,* his widely followed television show. Despite his protestations to the contrary, Robertson clearly used the Christian Coalition and his television ministry to support conservative Republican politicians, although his propensity for audacious charges and claims sometimes made even his colleagues in the religious right cringe. Attacking an initiative to add a version of the Equal Rights Amendment to the constitution of Iowa, Robertson charged that the real "feminist agenda" was "not about equal rights for women," but "a socialist, anti-family political movement that encourages women to leave their husbands, kill their children, practice witchcraft, destroy capitalism, and become lesbians." Ordained as a Southern Baptist, Reverend Robertson not only disparaged Muslims and Hindus openly, but he once compared being nice to "the Episcopalians and the Presbyterians and the Methodists" to being "nice to the spirit of the Antichrist." He was also fond of warning communities whose leaders evinced sympathy for gay rights or the theory of evolution that they were likely targets of natural disasters, and his frequent reports on his direct conversations with God conveyed the definite impression that he had a "hotline" to the Almighty.[64]

Robertson might not have accumulated more wealth than the Almighty, but he obviously had taken no vows of poverty; by 2000 estimates of his worth ranged from $200 million to $1 billion. In 1994 he had used his television show to raise several million dollars for a tax-free charitable trust, created ostensibly to purchase planes to fly in medical supplies to Rwandan refugees in Zaire. An investigative reporter claimed that, according to one of the pilots, over a six-month period, except for "one or two" of some forty flights, the planes were used to haul equipment for African Development Corporation, a diamond-mining operation owned by Robertson. An active investor in Africa, Robertson also shared an interest in a gold-mining venture with the Liberian strongman Charles Taylor and leapt to his defense when Taylor was criticized for numerous human rights violations. To say the least, there was a substantial disconnect between the lifestyles of the rich and famous televangelists and the great mass of their faithful viewers. Devoted followers often scrimped and saved to sustain or increase their, financial contributions to spiritual role models like Robertson, whose prize possessions included "Mr. Pat," a thoroughbred race horse that cost him a reported $520,000. Meanwhile, Rev. Kenneth Copeland, known for his widely televised healing services and talking in tongues, sped about in his $20 million private jet when he was not enjoying his 18,000-square-foot home near Fort Worth.[65]

Amassing such wealth was no impediment to salvation but rather a sign of God's grace in the minds of many ministers and worshippers who flocked to the hundreds of megachurches that sprang up in the South and elsewhere at the end of the twentieth century. Rev. Jerry Falwell had founded the Thomas Road Baptist Church in Lynchburg, Virginia, in 1956. Fifty years later the original congregation of thirty-five had grown to more than twenty-four thousand, and the church offered four services a week in a six-thousand-seat auditorium as well as other activities spread out over a million square feet of educational space. Thomas Road Baptist also helped to underwrite Lynchburg Bible College, which later became Liberty University. Falwell gained fame as the host of *The Old Time Gospel Hour*, a syndicated television show, and like his fellow televangelist Pat Robertson, he did not shy away from political involvement or controversial social commentary. Falwell reportedly insisted that God was a Republican, characterized AIDS as "the wrath of God against homosexuals," urged labor unions to "study and read the Bible instead of asking for more money," and longed for the day when, "as in the early days of our country, we don't have public schools because [t]he churches will have taken over again." Robertson's and Falwell's success in gaining a national following with a mixture of Bible-thumping evangelism and far-right politics seemed to bear out the dire prophesies of Kirkpatrick Sale and others who had bemoaned the conservatizing impact of a rising Southern Rim.[66]

Televised weekly services translated into celebrity status for a number of other ministers leading large, high-profile churches, but many of them seemed less like fiery evangelists intent on making their congregants squirm about their prospects in the hereafter than inspirational CEOs intent on motivating them to pursue material advancement in the here and now. These "pastorpreneurs" presided over elaborate and complex corporate campuses where formal worship services were but one of the diversions or opportunities available. With an income of $55 million in 2004, Lakewood Church moved into Houston's Compaq Center in 2005, the same year it became the first megachurch to break the thirty-thousand-a-week attendance barrier. In the cavernous auditoriums of such churches, worshippers had no real need to open hymnals when they could read computer-projected lyrics on huge screens suspended from the ceiling. In 2005 the Fellowship Church in Grapevine, Texas (near Dallas), spent approximately $4.5 million of its $30 million budget on technology alone. Such churches not only had computer- and information-technology experts on staff, but hundreds of other employees with various managerial, administrative, and financial responsibilities. In some cases parishioners could also bank, fill prescriptions, or even receive professional counseling where they worshipped. Many who felt providing such amenities detracted from a church's spiritual mission also found the messages emanating from many megachurch pulpits a bit too comforting as well. Megachurch ministers, they complained, often preached "Christianity Lite," a bland and inoffensive doctrine of individual achievement and success laced with soothing assurances that it is perfectly fine to aspire to be "rich, healthy, and trouble free" because God "wants you to achieve your personal best."[67]

Not unlike some of the nation's most famous televangelists, when it came to amassing wealth megachurch ministers frequently practiced precisely what they preached. In Houston, Lakewood pastor Joel Osteen conceded that the royalties alone from his phenomenally popular spiritual self-help book, *Your Best Life Now*, had made him "fabulously wealthy," but he made no apologies because "God wants us to be prosperous." In Georgia the aptly named Rev. Creflo Dollar owned two Rolls Royces and flew across the country in a Gulfstream jet. Dollar's ministry was particularly interesting because the overwhelming majority of those drawn to his "prosperity gospel" were, like Dollar, upwardly mobile African Americans who embraced his message that "as a Christian, you have the right to prosper or succeed in every area of life—financially, emotionally, socially, mentally, and physically." As for his own lifestyle, Dollar argued, "Just because it's excessive doesn't mean it's wrong." Located on an eighty-one-acre campus near Atlanta, with a satellite operation in New York, Dollar's World Changers Church boasted an estimated thirty thousand members, with the Atlanta church alone taking in $69 million in 2006.[68]

Dollar was hardly the only black megachurch minister to preach the gospel of prosperity. The thirty thousand members of the Potter's House Church in Dallas regularly heard Bishop T. D. Jakes lauding the pursuit of wealth, even as he enjoyed a luxurious lifestyle of his own, complete with designer suits, fancy cars, and a multimillion-dollar mansion. The move away from the socially committed liberation theology of Dr. Martin Luther King Jr. toward the gospel of personal prosperity clearly resonated with thousands of African Americans who had reaped some of the fruits of King's labors and were now intent on reconciling their strivings for material wealth with their quest for spiritual salvation.

This shift in attitudes came through rather forcefully in 2006, when Coretta Scott King's children opted to hold her funeral not at the historic Ebenezer Baptist Church in Atlanta, which had been the base for her husband's civil rights ministry, but at the sprawling suburban New Birth Missionary Baptist Church, which boasted a seating capacity of ten thousand. The pastor of this affluent twenty-five-thousand-member church was Bishop Eddie Long, a controversial figure who, over a three-year period, had reportedly received more than $3 million and numerous benefits, including the use of a $350,000 Bentley, from a charity he had organized. Although Long's pointed insistence that "Jesus wasn't poor" indicated a vast difference in spiritual outlook (and interpretation) from Dr. King, King's daughter Rev. Bernice King was an associate pastor at Long's church, and in her eulogy of her mother she seemed to suggest a symbolic passing of the torch to leaders like Bishop Long when she told the assembled mourners, "God is not looking for another Martin Luther King, or Coretta Scott King. The old has passed away. There is a new order that is emerging."[69]

Many who had supported and participated in the civil rights movement were troubled by the notion that the likes of Bishop Long, T. D. Jakes, or Creflo Dollar could somehow be seen as worthy spiritual successors to Dr. King, who had repeatedly foresworn material ambitions of any sort. Long also drew fire as one of the beneficiaries of the George W. Bush administration's Faith-Based and Community Initiatives program, which funneled money to a number of conservative black ministers and churches, ostensibly for social outreach programs. Democrats charged the Republican White House with subsidizing pro-GOP black spokesmen as part of an effort to win more African American support, and it did not seem terribly cynical to suggest that Long's praise for Bush's "very deep religious connections" had not hurt his chances for the $1 million grant his ministry received from the Department of Health and Human Services in 2003. Likewise, in South Florida $1.7 million in federal funds reportedly went to an organization headed by Bishop Harold Ray, who, not coincidentally perhaps, had given the invocation at a West Palm Beach rally for Vice President Dick Cheney.[70]

Bishop Long made little secret of his Republican sympathies or his conservatism on social issues, declaring that there had been no "unified voice out of our [black] community since Dr. King" and insisting that many blacks thought it was time "to go back to basic, fundamental, moral beliefs." Despite her mother's expressed support for gay rights, Rev. Bernice King joined Long on a December 2004 march against same-sex marriage that began at the Dr. Martin Luther King Jr. Center for Nonviolent Social Change in Atlanta. In reality, this march seemed to bother some whites more than many blacks. A 1999 poll showed that 58 percent of black respondents in the South opposed gay marriage, as compared to slightly less than 50 percent of African Americans outside the region. Birmingham civil rights pioneer Rev. Fred Shuttlesworth made it clear that he had consistently spoken out against gay marriage from the pulpit and elsewhere because "the Bible says it is an abomination before God." In 2004, when voters in five southern states voted overwhelmingly to write a ban on gay marriage into their constitutions, blacks supported these measures at least as strongly as whites did.[71]

Exit polls from the 2004 presidential election found 27 percent of black voters in northern Florida saying they voted for George W. Bush, many of them apparently for religious reasons. In Jacksonville, Laverne Davis explained, "All the days of my life, I've been a Democrat…But I voted for Bush because I believe he is a Christian. I admire him because he's not for gay marriage, and he's pro-life. He's strong in his morals." The GOP's conservative stance on certain moral issues was solidly in accord with the sentiments of many black southerners, who figured heavily in Bush's improved showing nationally among blacks in 2004, when he captured 11 percent of the black vote, as compared to his 8 percent showing four years earlier. Bush's "family values" emphasis clearly resonated in his own state of Texas, where he more than tripled his 2000 share of the black vote in 2004, as well as in Florida, where he all but doubled it, and in both North Carolina and Georgia, where his black support increased by 50 percent.[72]

Buoyed by this progress GOP leaders proclaimed 2006 "The Year of the Black Republican," but the combination of the Iraq war and the Bush administration's seemingly indifferent response to black suffering after Hurricane Katrina held black support for Republican congressional candidates at 11 percent, where it had been for Bush two years before. A 2007 poll of black South Carolinians showed that 60 percent considered themselves "very conservative" to "moderate" in their political views, but more than 66 percent identified themselves as Democrats, while only 3 percent claimed to be Republicans. Political observers agreed that a great many black voters found it hard to get past the Republican Party's race-based appeals to southern whites. Despite their preference for the Republican position on certain moral issues, blacks were also decidedly more likely than whites to oppose capital punishment and to embrace government welfare and uplift programs that were anathema to most Republicans. If the white residents of the Southern Rim had generally proven every bit as conservative politically and culturally as Kirkpatrick Sale had foreseen thirty years earlier, their black neighbors clearly inclined more toward the other end of the spectrum, although less predictably so on some issues than others.[73]

8

"A Favorable Business Climate"

The Price of Progress in the Sunbelt South

While the national Republican Party's hostility to "big government" social uplift efforts proved to be a significant impediment to broadening its exceedingly narrow base with southern blacks, this antipathy further endeared the GOP to the conservative white policymakers who remained committed to minimizing state and local revenue contributions to any sort of welfare program. A 1985 survey had shown that across the United States food stamps and AFDC assistance added up to 68 percent of the designated poverty-line income, whereas in the South these two sources amounted to barely 50 percent of the poverty-level figure. Although welfare support improved a bit over the next twenty years, at $164 Alabama's monthly stipends for a family of three were the lowest in the nation in 2006. Not only were welfare payments in most southern states decidedly meager by national standards, but stringent qualification requirements made them harder to come by. Alabama joined Florida, Georgia, North Carolina, South Carolina, Texas, and Virginia as seven of the eight states with the lowest proportion (all less than 2 percent) of families receiving welfare even though all of these except Florida and Virginia showed family poverty rates well above the national average.[1]

In keeping with what had long been standard practice, such welfare payments as were available were also still heavily subsidized by Washington. One study estimated that between 1977 and 2000 as much as 83 percent of all welfare allocations in South Carolina, Alabama, and Mississippi may have originated as federal funding. In the 2005–6 school year 20 percent of the Magnolia State's elementary and secondary school funds still came from Washington, a figure more than twice the national average and nearly five times the federal contribution to K–12 funding in New Jersey and four times that for Massachusetts. Louisiana came in at more than twice the national figure in this category, and no southern state except Virginia fell below it.[2]

Complaints that the South was feasting more sumptuously at the federal trough than other regions had flown thick and furious since the 1970s, but clearly to little avail. In comparisons of federal spending per capita, the South trailed both the Northeast and Mid-Atlantic regions in 2004, but when federal spending per capita was considered as a percentage of state per capita income, the picture looked a bit different. In what some described as the federally "occupied" state of Virginia, federal expenditures amounted to 34 percent of per capita income; less predictably perhaps, in Alabama and Mississippi the ratio was 31 percent. This figure was more than 40 percent higher than the national average, and in six other southern states the ratio of per capita federal spending to per capita income was also 18 to 24 percent above the national norm.[3]

The enormity of their constituency's fiscal dependence on Washington served as no deterrent whatsoever to the incessant fed-baiting of southern politicians like Newt Gingrich and Jesse Helms, who warned repeatedly that "big government cannot and will not solve the multitude of problems confronting our nation...because big government is the problem." When they unloosed their antigovernment tirades, Helms and Gingrich found it convenient to ignore just how much the hand they were perpetually biting was actually feeding into their states or districts and how eagerly their supporters lapped it up. In this sense, the South's Republican politicians were much like the Delta planters, who, as Walker Percy explained, "were going broke on ten-cent cotton, voted for Roosevelt, took federal money, got rich, lived to hate Kennedy and Johnson and vote for Goldwater—while still taking federal money."[4]

As Table 8.1 illustrates, the southern states that benefited most from federal largesse and thus enjoyed the highest return on their federal tax dollar were also generally those with the lowest state and local tax burdens on their citizens. Mississippi, which stood at or near the top in all three categories, received $2.02 for every federal tax dollar paid in fiscal 2005, more than triple the return for New Jersey and more than twice that for seventeen additional nonsouthern states. In the South only residents of Florida and Tennessee got back less from Washington than they paid in.

Table 8.1 National Rankings, Fiscal 2005

Lowest Per Capita Tax Burden	Federal Aid as Percentage of State and Local Government Revenue	Highest Return on Federal Tax Dollar
1 Mississippi	2 Mississippi	1 Mississippi ($2.02)
2 Louisiana	10 Arkansas	3 Louisiana ($1.85)
4 Arkansas	12 Alabama	7 Alabama ($1.66)
7 Kentucky	13 Louisiana	8 Virginia ($1.51)
8 South Carolina	14 Kentucky	9 Kentucky ($1.51)
10 Alabama	16 South Carolina	4 Arkansas ($1.41)
11 Oklahoma	17 Oklahoma	15 Oklahoma ($1.35)
13 Tennessee	18 Tennessee	16 South Carolina ($1.35)
17 North Carolina	20 North Carolina	17 Tennessee ($1.29)
21 Georgia	28 Texas	29 North Carolina ($1.08)

"Per Capita Tax Burden and Rate of Return on the Federal Tax Dollar, Fiscal 2005," www.nemw.org/taxburden.html.northeast.midwestinstitute; Congressional Quarterly, Inc., *Governing, State, and Local Sourcebook*, http://sourcebook.governing.com/index.jsp.

When southern governments did look to raise revenue themselves, the most likely resort was some form of regressive taxation. In 2005 sales tax rates were at or above the national average in all but four southern states, some of which even levied them on groceries. In Tennessee the rate was 39 percent above the national norm; in Louisiana 36 percent; and in Florida, Arkansas, and Texas 34 percent. Tennessee, Florida, and Texas relied so heavily on the sales tax because they had no income tax, but in most states with income taxes the sales tax was a buffer against higher property taxes that would affect large individual and corporate landowners. Alabamans paid sales taxes on groceries, but their per capita property tax rate was only $394 in 2005, as compared to a national average of $1,132. Alabama was but one of five southern states where the per capita property tax burden was less than half the national figure. In many cases sales tax proponents had initially sold whites on the idea by arguing that because many blacks owned little or no taxable property the sales tax was the only means of assuring that they contributed their "fair share" of public revenues. Blacks and low-income southerners in general were hit hard by sales taxes, which captured about 3.5 percent of per capita income nationally in 2005 but 5.5 percent in Louisiana and Arkansas and nearly 5 percent in Florida and Tennessee. From the fiscal standpoint heavy reliance on sales taxes might work well enough

The South and America since World War II

in good economic times, but when a downturn came, falling revenues could and did trigger some serious budget crises, forcing states to curtail or even cancel some social programs and make serious cuts in educational funding at all levels.[5]

Although heavy reliance on sales taxes could lead to disruption of vital state services, keeping income and property taxes low had long been synonymous with maintaining the "favorable business climate" that made southern locations so appealing to new industry. Although state development agencies expanded the scope of their activities in the early 1970s by opening offices in foreign cities such as Brussels and Tokyo, their sales pitch, emphasizing cheap labor, low taxes, and a variety of subsidies, remained fundamentally unchanged. This bottom-line approach appeared to pay off nicely, as the South was soon claiming roughly half the annual foreign direct investment in the United States. The acknowledged pioneer in this international recruiting effort was South Carolina, which by the end of the decade was drawing some 40 percent of its annual increase in investment capital from outside the country. In addition to Japan, the Palmetto State attracted investors from six European countries, and only West Germany could claim more West German industrial capital than South Carolina.[6]

Most of the firms choosing South Carolina sites had specialized in textile-production equipment until 1975, when the French tire giant Michelin selected Greenville for its first American plant. Known for its staunchly antiunion posture, Michelin was right at home in the South Carolina upstate (where only 2 percent of the workforce was organized), and though it paid workers more than the average local wage, its pay scales were not on par with those in northern tire plants whose workers were unionized. Michelin practiced a kind of employer paternalism long familiar in the southern textile belt, offering workers discounted merchandise and other fringe benefits intended to keep them happy without paying them as much as their northern counterparts received.[7]

Establishing factories in the United States got a lot less expensive after the Nixon administration moved in 1971 to devalue the dollar in the interest of a more favorable balance of trade. Leftist political sentiment was also on the rise in Europe in the early 1970s, with workers steadily demanding better wages and more benefits. Not surprisingly, many foreign employers soon followed Michelin's lead by opening plants in a region where officials and established employers made no secret of their hostility to organized labor. More than one potentially unionized plant had been turned away by Carolina Piedmont leaders concerned about preserving the area's reputation for cheap, docile workers. Development leaders in Spartanburg explained that they spurned a proposed Mazda assembly facility in 1984 because a "plant employing over 3,000 card-carrying, hymn-singing members of the UAW would, in our opinion, bring to an abrupt halt future desirable industrial prospects." (A few years later local business leaders a little farther north on I-85 rose up in opposition to United Airlines's plan to locate a $580 million maintenance facility in Greensboro, North Carolina, after they learned it might employ six thousand unionized workers at roughly $40,000 a year.) If their workers began even to hint at an interest in unions, local employers stood ready to coerce or simply fire them if need be. One personnel manager at a plant near Spartanburg made it clear that "if someone starts talking union, I take him out into the parking lot and explain that I know every personnel manager in this county. If he keeps talking union, I'll fire his ass and make sure that neither he, nor any member of his family, ever works in this county again."[8]

Obviously, in the South's blatantly antiunion political climate, management and supervisory personnel felt no particular need to conceal their illegal efforts to intimidate their workers. This went a long way toward explaining why union members accounted for roughly 3 to 5 percent of the workforce in the Carolinas, Georgia, Texas, and Virginia in 2008. Industrial outmigration and employer resistance continued to whittle away at union participation, which was down from just over 20 percent nationwide in 1983 to just over 12.4 percent in 2008. Even so, in the South only Kentucky (9.1 percent) and Alabama (9.5 percent) approached 75 percent of the national average for union membership.[9]

Industrial recruiters were not the least bit shy about reminding foreign executives of the anemic to virtually nonexistent union presence in their states. The South Carolina Department of Commerce assured Japanese manufacturers in March 2006 that "South Carolina offers Japanese companies a cost-effective workforce [because] ... like Japan, South Carolina emphasizes a strong work ethic and pride in workmanship." The state was the fifth cheapest operating environment in the United States because it had one of "*the lowest unionization rates in the nation*," and manufacturing wages that were "*among the lowest in the country*."[10]

If the global pursuit of industrial investment did little to discourage reliance on cheap labor as an enticement, the same was true of the

The South and America since World War II

region's reputation for generous, few-strings-attached subsidies and incentives for new employers, especially as recruitment of foreign capital grew even more competitive. Amid mounting pressure throughout the United States to create new jobs to replace those lost to industrial relocation, Tennessee officials offered Nissan a $33 million package to open its first American plant at Smyrna in 1980, and five years later Kentucky upped the ante in a big way by promising $149 million in subsidies to bring a Toyota plant to Georgetown. The price tag was comparable when BMW agreed to locate an assembly plant near Spartanburg in 1993. This commitment included a $1-per-year lease on a $36 million parcel of land, as well as highway and airport improvements, extensive worker training at state expense, and fifty-five free apartments for BMW executives. Architects of the BMW deal pointed to a multibillion-dollar investment by the company as well as the economic impact of spending by its forty-five hundred permanent employees and the thirteen thousand others who worked for its suppliers in South Carolina. Yet although the company reaped net profits worldwide of approximately $4.9 billion in 2007, under the terms of its incentive agreement BMW reportedly had yet to pay any corporate profits tax in South Carolina.[11]

Critics of such tax breaks pointed to the resultant strain on other taxpayers to support the public schools (which in South Carolina regularly ranked at or near dead last nationally in average SAT scores and high school graduation rates) as well as provide for the additional roads, sewers, and police and fire protection necessitated by BMW's arrival and subsequent expansion. Residents cited exorbitant increases in their property taxes and the proliferation of a number of other service and use taxes. Meanwhile, established local employers complained of having to pay property taxes at double the rate of favored new arrivals while having to compete head-to-head with them for workers.[12]

Alabama's successful courtship of Mercedes produced an even more striking story of huge subsidies, rapid growth, and strained services. When Alabama forked over what was at least a $325 million subsidy package, the cost for each of the fifteen hundred jobs initially available was $167,000. Some sixty-three thousand applicants sought those positions, which paid well above the state average for manufacturing but represented an estimated 30 percent savings over the going rate in Germany. Alabama also showed considerable generosity to Honda and Hyundai, and by 2002 its total estimated subsidy contributions to foreign automakers alone stood at $874 million.[13]

Mercedes plant, Vance, Alabama. Courtesy of Mercedes-Benz U.S. International, Inc.

In a state with the nation's fifth highest poverty rate, some found it a bit incongruous that part of Alabama's subsidy commitment to Mercedes in 1993 was an agreement to purchase some $75 million worth of Mercedes vehicles for use by state employees. Two years later, despite the state's consistent last- or near-last-place standing in national educational rankings, only a threatened lawsuit by an Alabama teachers group prevented Governor Fob James from raiding the state's school fund to pay off a $43 million obligation to Mercedes. Over in Mississippi, when the state promised $80 million to train four thousand workers for a new Nissan production facility, the cost per worker was more than four times its annual per pupil expenditures in grades K–12.[14]

In 2006 Alabama and Mississippi stood forty-fifth and forty-eighth, respectively, in a well-known annual ranking of public school quality. The following year a ranking of states according to their capacity to participate in the new "knowledge-based" economy showed Connecticut and South Carolina effectively sharing the distinction of having the nation's highest percentage of workers employed by foreign companies, with North Carolina, Kentucky, and Tennessee also placing in the *top thirteen* in this category. These four, however, were also among the ten southern states clustered in the *bottom fourteen* in rankings of the educational level of their workforces. Not surprisingly, eight of the fifteen states with the lowest employment in "knowledge" jobs were also in the South.[15]

Education was not the only area shortchanged when states promised special concessions to industries while passing up on their tax revenue. In May 2007 Alabama offered a package of incentives deemed ultimately to be worth in excess of $800 million in exchange for the

German steel giant ThyssenKrupp's promise to open a huge facility near Mobile that would employ some twenty-seven hundred people. At a shade over $300,000 per job, ThyssenKrupp's subsidy windfall made the $167,000 per job initially handed over to Mercedes seem almost paltry. Part of the package was a commitment to $55 million in road construction. When the cost of making good on the promises to ThyssenKrupp was combined with the $15 million in road funds pledged to another large manufacturing plant, the two projects alone represented 11 percent of the previous year's total road expenditures of $655.6 million. With skyrocketing gas prices forcing Alabamans to cut back on consumption, gasoline tax collections, the major source of road construction and maintenance funds, were down noticeably, but the legislature rejected any hike in gas taxes, leaving highway officials with the prospect of allowing planned construction or much needed maintenance work elsewhere in the state to go begging in the interest of keeping Thyssen-Krupp executives happy.[16]

If some southern communities seemed to benefit handsomely from the national and global mobility of industrial capital, others just as clearly did not. The region's low-wage, labor-intensive industries were the first to respond to the lure of even cheaper labor markets beyond the nation's borders. When sewing machine operators in Bangladesh earned roughly $0.22 per hour while working sixty hours or more a week, a similar worker in North Carolina making $9.92 per hour became an outright extravagance, especially in the intensely competitive apparel industry. As the case of the North Carolina workers illustrates, the South's labor costs may have been low by American standards, but in the global economy they were anything but.[17]

Implemented in 1994, the North American Free Trade Agreement removed trade barriers with Mexico and opened its pool of cheap labor to American garment and textile operations hitherto concentrated in the South. As the pace of industrial outmigration quickened in response, North Carolina lost 35 percent, Mississippi 28 percent, and South Carolina 25 percent of their manufacturing jobs between 1996 and 2006, while eight other southern states suffered losses in the range of 19 to 24 percent. Because of the peculiarly dispersed pattern of manufacturing activity in the region, seven of the ten states with the nation's highest concentrations of nonmetropolitan manufacturing-dependent counties were in the South in 1979. As a result, some of the worst suffering inflicted by the industrial exodus came in rural areas with little economic resiliency. Some towns hit by plant closings managed to attract new employers, but rarely were they even as generous with their wages as their tight-fisted predecessors. In many cases having kept taxes low in order to appease their now-departed industrial guests, southern communities simply lacked the educated workforce and physical infrastructure to compete for more dynamic, better-paying industries. Regardless of their actual physical proximity, the gleaming Research Triangle Park may as well have been on the moon so far as many North Carolinians were concerned. Rural North Carolina counties traditionally registered both the highest rates of dependence on manufacturing and the state's lowest levels of educational attainment, showing 28 percent of the adult population with no high school diploma in 2006 as opposed to 17 percent in metropolitan counties, and 14 percent with college degrees as compared to 30 percent in metro areas. In such places the only work available as the twenty-first century began often involved demolishing old sewing plants and cotton mills.[18]

The labor-intensive nature of North Carolina's industrial mix largely explained why foreign competition would cost the state more jobs than anywhere in the nation. Yet in cases where North Carolina officials sought to prepare laid-off manufacturing workers to compete for new and better jobs, the results were less than impressive. Its biotechnology retraining program had benefited unemployed textile workers hardly at all, according to one self-described "displaced worker in his mid-forties" who had managed "after much effort" to land only "two temp jobs" before he finally "gave up looking in biotech." Three years after the collapse of the textile manufacturer Pillowtext put 4,800 people out of work in and around Kannapolis, North Carolina, a follow-up study suggested that only 60 percent of them had managed to earn wages of any kind, and of those, half had earned less than $5,000. Although the reports on the Federal Trade Adjustment Assistance Program showed that 75 percent of retrained workers found jobs, scarcely half of those earned as much as 80 percent of their former salaries. Commenting on the plight of unemployed workers in Hickory, North Carolina, whose jobs in the furniture industry had effectively been shipped to China, a state employment official noted that although "the people in the think tanks say we are going to become...an information and service economy...that doesn't seem to be working out too good."[19]

Such jobs as remained represented a paycheck, but frequently not much of one. Some of the laid-off workers were forced to take service jobs, but where a typical sewing machine operator in North Carolina might earn $22,000 in 2006, a motel clerk might expect no more than $19,000, and the maids in the motel might be lucky to make $17,000. Meanwhile, 38 percent of the jobs in Mississippi were in occupations paying annual wages that fell below the poverty-level income for a family of four. Overall, the South accounted for six of the ten states with the nation's heaviest concentrations of such jobs and eight of the thirteen states with the highest percentages of working families living on earnings amounting to less than 200 percent of the poverty level for a family of four. A great many such families occupied the near-ubiquitous mobile homes strewn liberally across the southern landscape, especially in South Carolina, which led the nation with nearly one in five of its housing units equipped with axles in 2007, and in Mississippi, where the ratio was one in six.[20]

Conditions were hard enough in rural areas whose economies had been racked by plant closings, but they were even harder in more isolated "hard-core" poverty areas where jobs had always been scarce and were now all but nonexistent. In 2008 eastern Kentucky teenager Machlyn Blair probably spoke for a great many rural southerners when he explained that he had grown up seeing "people working hard every day and then going home with nothing": "When I was 17, I learned the phrase 'the working poor,' and I'm not sure that anything else has made me feel as small as those three words did, because then I started to realize that struggling with poverty wasn't a personal thing, that the whole problem was a lot bigger than me or where I live. . . . I can't figure out how to change things, can't go to college. For the past three years, I haven't felt like I was moving forward in life. I'm thinking about getting a job in the mines. The coal industry pays miners decent wages to do dangerous work, but the industry also tears down our mountains and pollutes our water. I guess that's a part of living in a poor place: feeling like you have to do things that are not the best choices for you or your community. You do it because it seems like the only way you'll survive."[21]

More than a few of the wage earners in the South's working poor families were employed by Walmart. In 2009 nearly half of the roughly 1.4 million Americans on its payroll were southerners. Despite its small-town Arkansas beginnings and its management's efforts to maintain a folksy, family-friendly image, Walmart was resolutely antiunion, and it drew heavy fire for its low wages and generally worker-unfriendly hours and benefits policies. In 2008 the *Wall Street Journal* reported that the company was actually mobilizing its store managers and department heads to warn other employees that layoffs might be in their future if Democratic presidential nominee Barack Obama was elected because Obama supported legislation that would make it easier for workers to form unions.[22]

Researchers put the typical starting wage for a Walmart "associate" in 2007 in the range of $7 to $8 per hour, and critics claimed that in reality a great many of the "full-time" employees company officials claimed were averaging $10.86 per hour were seldom allowed to work anything approaching a forty-hour week. Moreover, despite the company's $12.7 billion profits in 2007 and its perch atop the Fortune 500 list, not to mention the substantial subsidies it had received from many state and local governments, Walmart's workers consistently dominated the ranks of employed persons receiving Medicaid or other publicly funded, low-income family medical assistance in their states. One in four Walmart employees were getting these benefits in Tennessee in 2005, and roughly the same percentage in Georgia had a child eligible for PeachCare, the state's health insurance plan for children whose parents either could not afford or had no access to employer-sponsored health care. In Florida researchers found that Walmart, which had reportedly received more than $1 billion in state and local incentives since 1981, employed more Medicaid-eligible workers than any corporation in the state in 2005, and annual cost estimates for state and federal health care assistance to Florida Walmart workers and their dependents alone exceeded $80 million. Employees complained that the company's health plan either was not affordable on their salaries or was affordable only with deductibles requiring them to pay at least the first $1,000 of their health expenses each year.[23]

Industrial developers persisted in trying to justify the lower wages and skimpier benefits provided southern workers by citing the region's lower living costs, but in reality, the cost-of-living gap between many northern and southern locations was far narrower than the wage gap, even when comparisons involved northern cities with relatively depressed economies. The basic no-frills annual budget estimate for a family of four was some $9,000 higher in Flint, Michigan, in 2007 than in Jonesboro, Arkansas, but a sheet metal worker earned nearly $28,000 more in Flint than in Jonesboro that year. Likewise, living costs for a family of four were nearly $6,000 higher in Gary, Indiana, than in Dothan, Alabama, but a production-line supervisor in Gary bested his counterpart in Dothan by more than $15,000. Using lower living costs to rationalize lower wages was also misleading because these reduced living costs were themselves typically a reflection of generally lower local wages, especially in the service sector. Child care costs were nearly $1,300 lower in Dothan than in Gary, in some measure perhaps because child care workers in Dothan were paid $6.77 per hour as opposed to $8.57 per hour in Gary. Similarly, living costs were 26 percent lower in Hattiesburg, Mississippi, in 2007 than in Allentown, Pennsylvania, where automobile mechanics earned nearly 60 percent more each year than they would have in Hattiesburg.[24]

In keeping with a historic pattern of developing the industry-mad South's economy by exploiting its human resources, its natural and environmental resources often got short shrift as well. Nowhere was this more obvious than in Appalachia, where, as singer John Prine put it so well, the coal companies had "tortured the timber and stripped all the land." After technological breakthroughs during World War II led to the production of massive earth-moving equipment capable ultimately of tearing out several tons of earth at a single bite, large-scale surface or strip mining became increasingly common in the coal-rich areas of Appalachia. Though safer for the miners themselves than working below ground, surface mining, as Ronald Eller observed, "left the mountains disfigured and the environment altered in ways previously unimagined in the region.... Mountaintop removal leveled thousands of acres, filling the hollows between the hills and creating vast inaccessible stretches of barren land. In a region once known for the purity of its water, surface mining altered water tables, polluted nearby creeks and streams, and contaminated local wells. When it rained, sulfur in the exposed coal produced sulfuric acid that filtered into the creeks, killing the fish and most plant life." Mining companies were eventually obligated by law to replace soil and replant slopes, but enforcement was lax, and compliance even more so. A government study found soil loss in strip-mined areas to be ten times greater than elsewhere. With thousands of tons of dirt and rocks washing into streams each year, choked and silted creeks and rivers frequently escaped their banks in rainy periods, devastating nearby farms and towns.[25]

Instead of solving the problem some government agencies actually exacerbated it. After World War II the Tennessee Valley Authority shifted its emphasis from conservation and planning to providing abundant and cheap power. Thus TVA built seven of the world's largest coal-fired power plants between 1949 and 1953, spurring the demand for cheaper, surface-mined coal that was soon ravaging the Appalachian environment. Nature struck back savagely at this abuse in January 1957, when heavy rains led to the massive flooding that struck the silt-clogged streams in the coal mining areas of central Appalachia, destroying homes and churches and claiming the lives of fourteen people. With little vegetation to slow its cascade down the hillsides, twenty feet of water covered Pound, Virginia, and only rooftops were left showing in Pikesville and Hazard, Kentucky. Rural roads were washed out or away all together, and farmers found their bottomlands buried under sediment, rocks, and uprooted trees. Noting that the consequences of strip-mining "were clearly evident during and after the storm," the U.S. Forest Service warned that "the condition of the area will continue to get worse." Yet it would be another twenty-five years and several more disastrous floods later before Congress would take steps to impose anything approaching an effective set of environmental constraints on surface mining in the area.[26]

Elsewhere, since the South Carolina legislature had gone into special session in 1956 to accommodate England's Bowater Paper Company by amending the state's alien property ownership statute, it was all but a foregone conclusion that an exemption from the most burdensome of South Carolina's pollution-control regulations would be forthcoming as well. In the depths of the Great Depression, the desperate city fathers of Savannah, Georgia, had not only promised the Union Camp Paper Company both a building at nominal rent and protection from labor competition, but they vowed as well "to secure the necessary action and if possible legislate" to keep the company "harmless from any claims, demands or suits for the pollution of air or water caused by the plant." In the event litigation should arise over pollution by Union Camp, the Industrial Committee of Savannah pledged to pay all the company's legal fees up to $5,000.[27]

Three decades later the legacy of this engraved invitation to pollute was on graphic display in findings that Union Camp accounted for 80 percent of the industrial pollution in Savannah, most notably in the Savannah River, where the company's discharges of wood sugars, adhesives, and effluents dissipated the river's oxygen content as they decomposed, thus decimating the fish population. In addition to all the city's raw sewage, the Savannah absorbed the discharges from a Continental Can plant and nearly 700,000 pounds of sulfuric acid released daily by a Coal American Cyanamid facility. As a result, the river was sometimes engulfed in a thick fog of sulfur dioxide that could overcome those who worked or traveled on the stream. In addition to its heavy, offensive stench, the water's high acid content was a threat not only to human skin but even to the rubberized coatings on canoes and kayaks. If this was not enough, 160 miles upstream at Augusta the Savannah also absorbed the mercury wastes leaking from an Olin Corporation plant.[28]

The story was much the same across the South. Alabama development officials may not have moved heaven, but they certainly shifted around a lot of earth in order to provide the customized transportation access needed to get Hammermill Paper Company to locate a plant in racially torn Selma in 1965. A few years later Hammermill was repaying this hospitality with such high levels of smoky, acidic emissions that flight instructors at nearby Craig Air Force Base found it difficult to find days clear enough to allow their students to get the flying time they needed for their certification.[29]

Efforts to stiffen state environmental laws frequently fell prey to fears of lost jobs. When state authorities finally got around to pressuring Gilman Paper Company to stop polluting the North River in coastal Georgia, the plant manager opted immediately to play hardball, contending that Gilman supported at least 75 percent of local economic activity and asking why an employer responsible for 1,625 jobs should be forced to make "a very major expenditure" to clean up the river when doing so would contribute "virtually nothing to any segment" of the local population. North Carolina lawmakers moved forward with legislation to make environmental pollution a public health and welfare priority in 1967, but industrial representatives quickly persuaded them to qualify their commitment to a healthy environment with an acknowledgment of the overriding need to maintain the "maximum employment and full industrial development of the state." Soon prevention of damage to plant and animal life was limited to "the greatest degree practicable," and industries releasing pollutants into the air were to be exempted from some of the more stringent provisions in cases where the cost of cutting down on contamination seemed "unduly burdensome in comparison with the pollution abatement results which can be achieved."[30]

Needless to say, the southern states quickly developed a well-deserved reputation for coddling big-time employers who were also big-time polluters. Yet questions of environmental regulation—or the absence thereof—involved more than a simple choice between clean

Gilman Paper Company, Camden County, St. Marys, Georgia, 1952. Courtesy of Georgia Archives, Vanishing Georgia Collection (Cam 045), Atlanta, Georgia.

air and water and more jobs and tax revenue in areas where a variety of agricultural and industrial activities were part of the economic mix. In central Florida the rapid postwar expansion of phosphate mining and processing (into fertilizer) meant that the state was supplying 86 percent of the nation's total and nearly 30 percent of the world's total by 1965. The Florida phosphate industry was concentrated in Polk and Hillsborough counties, employing more than seven thousand workers by 1960 and providing 22 percent of the tax income in Polk County alone. Many of those who did not work in phosphate mines and plants, however, depended on citrus orchards or cattle raising or truck farming for their livelihoods, and it quickly became apparent that those livelihoods were threatened by airborne pollutants in the form of sulfuric acid and the various fluorides released by the phosphate companies.

By the 1950s scientists had already established a link between phosphate plant emissions and declining citrus yields, burns on leafy vegetables, and stunted cattle with stiff joints, knobby bones, and prematurely rotting teeth. Yet devoutly pro-business Florida officials steadfastly rejected claims that the phosphate industry was a threat to plant, animal, or human life in the area and lashed out at anyone who claimed otherwise, be they federal regulators or representatives of local cattle or fruit producers, even after one investigator warned in 1959, "We don't know what effects the fluorides will have on children in their formative years." Not until the 1970s did legislators, now mindful of both potential damage to the state's tourism windfall and the new Clean Air Act's threat of a federal crackdown, finally begin to step back from their almost blindly pro-industry stance and impose some meaningful restrictions and regulatory policies and procedures.[31]

Such advances were generally slow in coming, however. Texas, South Carolina, Louisiana, Alabama, Florida, and Georgia still led the nation in the release of air- and water-borne carcinogens in 2004. These states were home to more than three hundred chemical plants, forty pulp and paper plants, and ninety petroleum refineries. The concentration of 150 petrochemical plants along the Mississippi River between New Orleans and Baton Rouge doubtless contributed generously to a local cancer rate twice the national average and, hence, to the area's unofficial designation as "Cancer Alley." The British Petroleum facility at Texas City, Texas, and the 3V chemical plant at Georgetown, South Carolina, were tagged as the nation's two worst sources of carcinogens. The southern states were also at the top of the list for emissions of reproductive and neurological toxicants. EPA data for 2006 showed Texas second only to Ohio in the total volume of all toxic releases per state, with Tennessee, North Carolina, Florida, Georgia, and Louisiana also ranked among the ten states with the highest release rates.[32]

The proponents of growth and more growth frequently ran roughshod over anyone who pointed to such statistics. University of Georgia researchers announced in 2007 that each day in metro Atlanta concrete, asphalt, and rooftops were covering an additional fifty-five acres, roughly twice the area devoured daily by development as recently as 2001. Correspondingly, a roughly equivalent acreage in trees disappeared each day as well. Experts estimated that local streams began to deteriorate when approximately 9 percent of their drainage acres were hard surface. At that point fully 25 percent of Clayton County, which was home to Atlanta's massive Hartsfield-Jackson Airport, had been paved over, and the metro area's most populous counties, Cobb, DeKalb, Gwinnett, and Fulton, were at least 18 percent covered. It was small wonder that metropolitan Atlanta's two largest lakes, Lanier and Allatoona, suffered from pollution with the dirt and grease picked up by runoff water from rainstorms. Meanwhile, the voracious appetite for electricity that comes with runaway growth had moved some areas of the South well past the saturation point with coal-fired power plants that pushed the airborne particulate count up to six times higher than that observed in the western states. This heavy concentration of coal-fired power plants also contributed significantly to the carbon dioxide emissions linked directly to global warming. Home to fourteen such plants, North Carolina alone ranked ahead of Venezuela, Belgium, and the Czech Republic as a source of pollutants conducive to global warming.[33]

Not all the South's problems with pollution stemmed from its over-eager pursuit of industrial growth, of course. The agricultural insecticide DDT and the herbicide 2,4-D had been developed during the war, and both were marketed to the public, beginning in 1945. As a consequence poisons and fertilizers were arguably the region's main source of unregulated pollution throughout the postwar years. In their seemingly ceaseless struggle with the boll weevil, southern cotton producers laid on DDT and other chlorinated hydrocarbons so heavily that the insects eventually developed a resistance to such poisons, whereupon farmers turned to the truly remarkable killing power of synthetic organophosphates, which the Germans had developed during World War II in the form of nerve gases. Overspraying these poisons (concentrated in compounds such as parathion or malathion) almost indiscriminately, cotton growers killed not only their target population of boll weevils but thousands of other varieties of insects, some of them key predators needed to control the spread of other problematic species that proved resistant to the new toxins. By the 1990s growing insect resistance forced farmers to use two to five times as much poison as they had twenty years earlier.[34]

When the Texas Boll Weevil Eradication Foundation unloosed a massive application of malathion in 1995, they succeeded in killing not only boll weevils but also the natural predators of the beet army worm, which then proceeded to make farmers nostalgic for the boll weevil by ruining about $140 million worth of cotton plants. Similarly, a disastrously overdone Department of Agriculture fire ant eradication spraying campaign succeeded only in making these bothersome, sometimes menacing little creatures both more resistant to poisons and more aggressively procreative. Farther up the food chain the man-made toxins interrupted the reproductive processes or simply killed outright a variety of wild birds, from eagles to pelicans. Southern farmers were also extravagant in their use of herbicides such as 2,4-D, which killed broadleaf weeds and plants and was also applied liberally in lawn-obsessed southern suburbia. Airborne herbicides could damage broadleaf plants like cotton (which, just prior to harvesting, was frequently treated with a powerful defoliant akin to the deadly toxic Agent Orange used in Vietnam) and sicken the cattle that ate the grass where it came to earth.[35]

In 2006 researchers with the Environmental Working Group blamed fertilizer runoff, much of it from the Upper Midwest, for the appearance each summer in the Gulf of Mexico of a "dead zone" roughly the size of New Jersey where marine life had been choked out by massive algae blooms that robbed the water of oxygen as they decomposed. Experts estimated that during the spring runoff as much as 7.8 million pounds of fertilizer nitrate passed from the Mississippi River into the Gulf of Mexico each day, threatening the nation's greatest natural fishery and representing an annual waste of more than $391 million worth of fertilizer.[36]

In addition to the threats posed by commercial fertilizers, the more than a million tons of manure generated annually in Georgia's chicken houses contained both lots of nitrogen and more phosphorous than the sewage that might normally be produced by 40 million people in a year. Environmentalists warned that when chicken manure was spread on pastures and fields, the nutrient-overrich runoff could stimulate excessive algae growth in streams and lakes, leading ultimately to oxygen deprivation sufficient to kill fish. Some scientists also linked the excess nutrients and algae resulting from poultry litter runoff to the toxic microbe *pfiesteria piscicida*, which was capable of triggering not only massive fish kills but confusion, memory loss, acute skin irritation, and other forms of distress in humans. Such conditions helped to explain why Alabama and Florida were home to well over a hundred of the wildlife on the endangered species list, and Texas and Tennessee were not far behind.[37]

In his masterful but sobering assessment of the contemporary "ecological landscape" of the South in 2006, historian Jack Temple Kirby sketched a striking portrait of a region whose physical face had been altered dramatically by those seeking to profit at nature's expense. A thousand miles of Appalachian streams, Kirby noted, had been destroyed by "leveling," the process of blasting away the tops of mountains in search of coal and filling in surrounding valleys with the displaced earth, rocks, and trees. Along the Atlantic and Gulf coasts, wetlands, tidal marshes, and swamps had been drained and covered over with fill from countless drainage projects farther inland, resulting in "massive losses of wildlife habitat, natural fish hatcheries and estuarial function." Acre upon acre of scientifically engineered, chemically sustained commercial pine plantations stretched for miles, their precisely spaced rows of genetically altered conifers yielding an occasional shadowy glimpse of an old terrace where cotton or corn or oats once grew. The poisonous fruits of an unholy union of private greed and government complicity, Kirby noted, were on unblushing display in overbuilt, sprawling Florida. From Jacksonville to Daytona, "good well-drained farmland was under warp-speed conversion [to] gated golf course community developments." Farther south, in addition to residential and commercial expansion, orange and sugar plantations had encroached severely on the rapidly shrinking Everglades. Critically polluted in some areas, the state's water supply was already inadequate for its 2000 population of 15 million, much less the 20 million expected to call Florida home by 2010.[38]

It was hard to determine just how much of a health hazard such environmental disregard might have posed in the South, but in 2006 a respected annual survey placed eight southern states among the bottom ten in overall health rankings. A comparison of state rankings for 1990 and 2006 revealed that only Florida, which rose from forty-eighth to forty-first, had improved by more than one position in the overall rankings, while eight southern states had either simply held their own or declined, rather precipitately in the cases of Oklahoma, South Carolina, and Tennessee, which fell by thirteen, twelve, and ten spots, respectively. Both Oklahoma and Tennessee had seen their obesity rates more than double over the period, although statistics released in 2008 showed Mississippi, with 33 percent of its population obese, leading the nation in this category and six other southern states among the top eight. High rates of diabetes were also common in counties where obesity was a major problem. While southerners were following a national trend in giving up smoking, in general they were doing so at a notably slower rate than other Americans. Perhaps this helped to explain why the death rate from cardiovascular disease in Oklahoma was 28 percent higher than the national average. Elsewhere, beset by the long-term effects of smoking as well as hypertension and obesity, women living in low-income rural areas like Appalachia and the lower Mississippi Valley seemed particularly at risk. Overall, the South was home to an inordinate share of the 963 counties where women's life expectancy either did not improve or actually declined between 1983 and 1999.[39]

Not only did southerners seem particularly susceptible to death brought on by certain diseases or generally poor health habits, but they were also more likely to die of decidedly "unnatural causes" at the hands of their fellow southerners. Violent crime in both Oklahoma and Tennessee rose by more than 22 percent between 1990 and 2006, suggesting that residents of those states were menaced not only by disease but by each other as well. The persistence of extraordinarily high homicide rates throughout the South had intrigued several generations of researchers, including one who quipped that the South should actually be demarcated not by the Mason-Dixon line, but by the "Smith and Wesson" line. In keeping with a national trend, murder rates declined in the South

Obesity and Diabetes Map

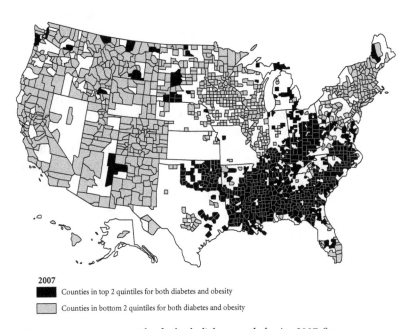

2007
■ Counties in top 2 quintiles for both diabetes and obesity
☐ Counties in bottom 2 quintiles for both diabetes and obesity

U.S. counties in top 2 quintiles for both diabetes and obesity, 2007. Source: Centers for Disease Control and Prevention, "Estimated County-Level Prevalence of Diabetes and Obesity—United States, 2007," www.cdc.gov/mmwr/preview /mmwrhtml/mm5845a2.htm#fig.

between 1996 and 2007. Long the nation's most murderous state, Louisiana saw its homicides per 100,000 people drop by nearly 20 percent over this period, but their frequency was still more than 150 percent higher than the national average in 2007. At that point the South accounted for eight of the fifteen most homicidal states.[40]

Researchers had noticed that, more so than elsewhere, homicides in the South tended to involve people who knew each other and thus were more likely than elsewhere to be crimes of passion. White southerners certainly were thought to be more hot-tempered than other Americans and known to be, on average, better armed; hence the greater likelihood of spontaneous as opposed to premeditated killings. Not only did strong traditional notions of masculinity and patriarchy linger in some parts of the South, but on top of that gang activity had also become strikingly commonplace in southern cities and even in some smaller towns. It was no surprise then to find the southern states registering seven of the nation's ten highest incidences of male-on-female killings in 2006. When the statistics were broken down, over 90 percent of southern female victims had known their killer, and a solid majority of these had been wives, former wives, or girlfriends of the men who killed them.[41]

Regardless of the form it took, the South's homicide rate said little for the deterrent effect of capital punishment in a region that accounted for 905 executions, 86 percent of the nation's total, between 1976 and 2006. If the distressing frequency with which southerners persisted in killing each other raised questions about the efficacy of capital punishment, it also cast some doubt on the day-to-day influence of their heavy participation in organized religious activities. Northeastern "blue state" liberals also took great pleasure in pointing out that among states where statistics were available, seven of the nation's ten highest divorce rates in 2004 were posted by states in the very heart of the holier-than-thou southern Bible Belt.[42]

9

"I'm Not a Feminist, But..."

Women, Work, and the Problem of Change

In addition to concerns about their health and personal safety and the stability of their marriages, southern women sometimes faced strong resistance to their efforts to gain equality in the workplace. World War II had drawn thousands of women into southern defense factories and other plants serving the war effort; at one point Marietta, Georgia's sprawling Bell Bomber plant alone had employed ten thousand women. Although they were generally the first to be laid off as the war machine cranked down, roughly one-third of the adult women in Georgia, Florida, and the Carolinas were employed outside the home in 1950, and women's participation in the labor force grew steadily throughout the region in the ensuing decades. White women soon held a substantial majority of clerical and counter sales jobs, although they effectively constituted what some have described as a "white-collar proletariat" that actually earned less than most relatively low-skilled white male factory workers.[1]

Despite an influx of female workers the better jobs, in southern factories were clearly reserved for men. In the mid-1960s less than 10 percent of white women working in industry held managerial, professional, or technical positions. On the factory floor itself, only one in twenty white women were employed as foremen or craftsmen, as compared to one in four white men. Kathy Kahn knew from personal experience that "being a working class woman means being stepped on, pushed around, degraded, overworked, and underpaid." Middle-class white women might find personal satisfaction in working outside the home in white-collar jobs, but as Kahn noted ruefully, it was hardly "gratifying"

Women working alongside men, Bell Bomber Plant, Marietta, Georgia, ca. 1943. Permission of Kennesaw University, Department of Archives and Record Management, Kennesaw, Georgia.

to grind out "the graveyard shift in a carpet mill like Burlington's Pine Tree plant in Dahlonega, Georgia." Nor was there any sense of "great reward" for those who spent "ten or twelve hours a day weaving cotton gauze for Kimberley-Clark's tampons or Kotex."[2]

Kahn would have gotten no argument from a Gastonia textile worker who spent her entire eight-hour shift in constant motion, walking, bending, and lifting as she removed and replaced bobbins from 160 spindles. She complained in 1981, "It takes a lifetime to get what you got, and you still don't have anything working in a mill. You're just surviving." At that point, nearly two-thirds of southern textile and apparel workers were female, while fewer than one-third of the jobs in the region's newer, better-paying industries such as electrical equipment and machinery or chemicals were held by women. The economic consequences of this gender disparity were starkly apparent in paycheck comparisons. The average chemical worker earned $10.59 per hour, while the average apparel worker made barely half that.[3]

Their heavy concentration in textiles and apparel made women especially vulnerable to the layoffs and plant closings in these industries that began sweeping across the South in the 1970s and 1980s. In hardhit Chester County in the South Carolina Piedmont, the unemployment rate for white women in 1982 was 13.6 percent, roughly one-third higher than for white men, though barely half the rate among black women. Because the majority of the women in these industries lived in rural areas, opportunities for retraining or reemployment were particularly scarce. If they were single mothers, whose numbers had risen dramatically after 1960, unemployed rural women faced stringent eligibility requirements for what were strikingly meager welfare payments, and if they were fortunate enough to land a new job, they frequently found adequate child care in short supply.[4]

Before the civil rights era black women without a college degree had little hope of doing more than cleaning white people's houses or, at best, cleaning offices and hotels. In fact, prior to the 1960s the primary occupations for women of either race who were intent on a professional career lay either in teaching or in nursing. When Title VII of the Civil Rights Act of 1964 forbade discrimination by sex as well as race, however, it opened the door for black women to claim many of the textile and apparel jobs once reserved almost exclusively for whites. It would take a while, but Title VII eventually proved beneficial to both black and white women seeking to enter the managerial and executive ranks as well.

Although wages in the South were generally lower for both men and women, the ratio between their earnings neared or exceeded the national average (68 percent) in most southern states by 1999. In fact, although they earned on average about $10,000 less than women in California, women in Alabama fared slightly better relative to men in their state than did their counterparts in California. When women's earnings were broken down by race, however, the story was somewhat different. Nationally, black women's earnings stood at roughly 89 percent of white women's. Although three southern states met or exceeded the national figure, in Louisiana and Mississippi the ratio stood at only 73 and 77 percent, respectively, and at only 80 percent in South Carolina and Virginia. State-by-state comparisons showed ten of thirteen southern states surpassing 90 percent of the national average for the percentage of the entire white female workforce employed in managerial or professional occupations by 1999. Only six southern states surpassed this threshold for black women, however, and with less than 25 percent of employed black women in these positions, Mississippi and South Carolina stood at the bottom in this category.[5]

Some argued that southern women might have held better jobs if more of them had a college degree, and women in the South were, in fact, less likely to have a college education than women elsewhere in the nation. Yet the same was also true for the men who competed with southern women for more desirable jobs. In 2006 not one in five men or women in Arkansas, Kentucky, Louisiana, or Mississippi was a college graduate. Women who did finish college faced a glass ceiling on their earnings, which averaged only 74 percent of those of their male counterparts nationwide. Although women graduates in a few southern states managed to match or approach this none too impressive figure, the South accounted for half of the ten states with the lowest salaries for women with a college degree and half of the ten states with the largest gender gaps in earnings between college graduates.[6]

For women, as for minorities, the best places to get ahead in the South were those with the most dynamic economies. The Raleigh-Cary, North Carolina, area was rated as the nation's best large (population of 500,000 or more) metropolitan area for women entrepreneurs in 2006, while metro Atlanta placed ninth. Texas and Florida alone accounted for roughly 44 percent of the southern businesses owned by women in 2002, and with Georgia and North Carolina thrown in, the figure rose to 62 percent. On the other hand, taken together, Alabama, Arkansas, and Mississippi were home to only about 9 percent of the region's firms owned by women.[7]

Not coincidentally perhaps, these states also registered the South's highest overall poverty rates for women. Nationally and regionally, southern women were noticeably more likely than men to be among the working poor. Two-thirds of the working poor families with children in South Carolina were headed by women in 2002. As perhaps the South's largest corporate employer of both women and the working poor, Walmart faced repeated charges of workplace discrimination against women. Critics cited multiple examples of disparities of 20 percent or more in the paychecks of male and female hourly and administrative employees, even in cases where the woman had substantially more experience and a more impressive proficiency rating. Laverne Jones began working as a sales clerk at a Walmart store in Pontotoc, Mississippi, in 1977 and was promoted to department manager in less than a year. Despite her consistently excellent evaluations and her repeated efforts to pursue higher-level managerial opportunities, twenty-five years later her first promotion was still her only promotion. Jones claimed that over the course of her quarter-century at Walmart, she had seen a great many less experienced men chosen for the management training program. When she and some female colleagues took advantage of the company's vaunted "open door" policy to lodge a complaint about sexual and racial discrimination, a female personnel executive from corporate headquarters came to Pontotoc to warn them personally, "I can fire you, without taking any steps, for using the open door."[8]

Kathleen Macdonald recalled that when she pointed out that she was making less than a number of men in comparable positions at an Aiken, South Carolina, Walmart, her male supervisor had explained quite matter-of-factly, "Women will never make as much money as men [because] God made Adam first, and so women would always be second to men." In a region where the Scriptures were so often accepted as literal truth, the Bible was a convenient and effective resource tool for anyone looking to rationalize gender inequities. As recently as 1998 delegates to the Southern Baptist Convention (SBC), the nation's largest Protestant church body, had voted to amend the official statement of Baptist Faith and Message in order to stipulate that a wife must "submit herself graciously to the servant leadership of her husband...and to serve as his helper in managing the household and nurturing the next generation."[9]

St. Paul's biblical injunction to the women of Corinth to remain silent and submissive in church got a real workout in debates among Southern Baptists about the ordination of women as ministers and deacons. In 1984, for example, the SBC approved a resolution declaring straightforwardly, "While Paul commends women and men alike in other roles of ministry and service (Titus 2:1–10), he excludes women from pastoral leadership (1 Tim. 2:12) to preserve a submission God requires because the man was first in creation and the woman was first in the Edenic fall (1 Tim. 2:13ff.)." Two years after pinning the blame on women for mankind's original sin, the convention approved a resolution declaring, "The office of pastor is limited to men as qualified by the scriptures." The statement was ostensibly nonbinding, but as of 2008 women filled the pulpits in only thirty of roughly forty thousand SBC churches.[10]

Meanwhile, responding to a lawsuit by a woman faculty member who was denied tenure at Southwestern Baptist Seminary in Ft. Worth, seminary president (and former SBC president) Dr. Paige Patterson defended the institution's policy against women teaching theology to men: "This is not a question of occupation. It is a question of an assignment from God, in this case that a woman not be involved in a teaching or ruling capacity over men." Even as they embraced such a position, Southern Baptist leaders saw no apparent contradiction when they endorsed conservative female political candidates; in 2008 SBC executive Richard Land pronounced himself "ecstatic" over John McCain's choice of Alaska's evangelical governor Sarah Palin to run beside him as a candidate for vice president of the United States even though, under SBC rules, Palin would not have been allowed to serve as the minister of Land's own church.[11]

Not all Southern Baptist women suffered their consignment to subservience in silence. Fay White of Huntsville, Alabama, mocked the men who wanted women to content themselves with "being held down and taking a back seat" while men with "their boasted egos continue to lead and work in the ministry." The loudest women's voices heard on such issues, however, came from those who defended a rigid religious, social, and political gender hierarchy. Paige Patterson's wife, Dorothy, insisted that with its "emphasis on experience and personal happiness and individual rights," feminism ran completely counter to the selfless example of Jesus Christ. She complained as well that "feminism's consciousness raising, revisionism of history and reinterpretation of Scripture...have made it very difficult for women to have a clear understanding of God's plan for their lives."[12]

Not surprisingly, strong conservative religious opposition had helped to undermine support for the Equal Rights Amendment in the South. Texas Democratic leader Frances "Sissy" Farenthold recalled that when she went to Birmingham to participate in a debate on the ERA, "someone stood up and asked me if I was a Christian. And the inference was that anyone who espoused such things as I was couldn't be." When it was approved by Congress and sent to the states in 1972, the ERA had appeared to be on its way to speedy ratification. Legislators in Texas and Tennessee approved the amendment resoundingly in 1972, and it also passed by a close vote in Kentucky. Not only would these be the only southern states to ratify the amendment, however, but Tennessee actually rescinded its ratification in 1974, and four years later only a gubernatorial veto kept Kentucky legislators from doing the same.[13]

Embracing "You can't fool Mother Nature" as its slogan, Phyllis Schlafly's Stop ERA movement won strong support in the South by citing patriarchal injunctions from the Bible and playing up gender stereotypes still widely held not only by men but also by many women in the region. ERA stood for "Exceedingly Radical Amendment," an Alabama Baptist woman warned, and its opponents seemed to score points by portraying the amendment's backers as fire-breathing, man-hating feminists. Southern women who expressed their support for the ERA frequently spoke strictly in terms of "equal pay for equal work" and, more often than not, seemed to feel constrained to preface their remarks with "I'm not a feminist, but...." Professional women and suburban housewives were the ERA's most likely supporters, but in the South even their ardor seemed cooler than elsewhere.[14]

Their general lack of enthusiasm for the ERA suggested that a great many middle- and upper-class southern white women might still believe that, for all its constraints, their symbolic place on a long-established cultural pedestal actually enhanced, rather than diminished their standing. Although working-class white women harbored no such illusions, more urgent and fundamental needs and concerns made it difficult to relate to what some scorned as "country club feminism." Some black women, meanwhile, found the ERA crusade a distraction from efforts to keep the civil rights movement alive and dismissed it as "a bunch of bored white women with nothing to do." ERA's supporters in the South refused to give up, but when the extended congressional deadline for ratification finally expired three states short of the necessary three-fourths in 1982, ten of the fifteen states that had withheld their approval were in the South.[15]

As voters, white women had accounted for more than three-fifths of the South's Democrats in the 1950s, and they were generally slower than men to join the white exodus from the party that began in the 1960s. Throughout the 1970s the majority of southern white women continued to identify themselves as Democrats. Ronald Reagan got 58 percent of their votes in 1980, however, and four years later Reagan political director Ed Rollins chortled that by choosing New York congresswoman Geraldine Ferraro as their vice-presidential candidate, the Democrats had "made the South ours." Rollins was not referring simply to opposition to Ferraro from men; the reactions of women like Florence Robinson of Memphis, a self-described "liberated woman" who nonetheless did not want to see "a woman running things in Washington," seemed to affirm Rollins's observation that Ferraro's presence on the ticket would not be warmly received among white voters of either sex in the South. Much as it had among white men, Democratic identification fell to 40 percent among white women in the South during the 1980s, and by 2002 less than 30 percent of these women saw themselves as Democrats.[16]

Even as they moved increasingly into the regular Republican ranks, white women in the region remained a bit more open than white men to voting for Democratic presidential candidates. In 2004, however, they appeared to favor George W. Bush over John Kerry even more strongly than white male voters. Southern whites were generally more supportive of the Iraq war than other Americans, but it was striking nonetheless that, compared to women in other parts of the country, southern white women were nearly 20 points more likely in 2004 to approve of Bush's handling of the war and believe the conflict had been worth the economic and human cost. White southern women showed even greater differences with women elsewhere in their preference for Bush over Kerry as the candidate who most "cares about people like you." Their faith in the Iraq war and in Bush's genuine concern for them translated into 98 percent support for him among white female Republicans, while Kerry captured only 75 percent of white Democratic women's votes in the South, as compared to the 91 percent he won among white Democratic women elsewhere.[17]

Two years later, surveys prior to the 2006 congressional elections showed some southern white women reacting to the mounting death tolls in Iraq by questioning their allegiance to the GOP. "As a mother you worry, 'Am I going to lose my baby boy?'" admitted Lynn Hamilton, who added, "A mother's view about war is often going to be a lot different than dad's is." Suffering no such doubts, however, Hamilton's fellow Georgian Clydeen Tomanio made her position clear: "There are some people, and I'm one of them, that believe George Bush was placed where he is by the Lord. I don't care how he governs, I will support him. I'm a Republican through and through." Though all of them might not have been quite so resolute as Tomanio, 61 percent of southern white women remained loyal to GOP congressional candidates in 2006, as compared to roughly 50 percent of the white women in the nation at large.[18]

In the region where the ERA had been effectively stonewalled, women pursuing political office themselves generally found it a slow go. Only two women could be found in either the Louisiana or Mississippi legislatures in 1977, and only three in Alabama's and Arkansas's. Overall, women held but 5 percent of southern legislative seats at that point, and they would make only marginal gains until the 1990s. By 1997 women's representation in southern legislatures was still less than two-thirds of the national average. Slightly more than a decade later, with legislative gains for women slowing down across the country, the southern average had at least inched close to three-fourths of the national figure, although South Carolina, Alabama, Mississippi, Kentucky, and Oklahoma still stood at the bottom in state rankings in this category. The Republican Party had clearly made steady inroads in state and local politics in recent years, but the Democrats accounted for nearly two-thirds of the southern legislative seats gained by women after 1987, and, as Table 9.1 indicates, for two-thirds of the seats they actually held in 2009 as well.[19]

Even more than their counterparts elsewhere, women seeking office in the South had reason to think the public was more interested in their hairstyles, hemlines, and maternal instincts than in their policy positions. Julian McPhillips, Alabama Senate candidate Susan Parker's opponent in the 2002 Democratic primary, actually questioned her capacity to understand family issues because she had no children of her own.

Table 9.1 Women in State Legislatures, 2009

	Total Number of Women Legislators	Dem/Rep Ratio	Total Seats	Women as Percentage of Legislature
Alabama	18	14/4	140	12.9
Arkansas	32	20/12	135	23.7
Florida	38	20/18	160	23.8
Georgia	45	34/11	236	19.1
Kentucky	21	14/7	138	15.2
Louisiana	22	16/6	144	15.3
Mississippi	25	20/5	174	14.4
North Carolina	44	30/14	170	25.9
Oklahoma	17	8/9	149	11.4
South Carolina	17	9/8	170	10.0
Tennessee	24	15/9	132	18.2
Texas	43	27/16	181	23.8
Virginia	23	18/5	140	16.4
South	3 69	66.4	2,069	17.8
U.S.	1,790	70.7	7,382	24.2

Center for American Women and Politics, "Women in State Legislatures, 2009," www.cawp.rutgers.edu/fast_facts/levels_of_office/documents/stleg.pdf.

A miscarriage had left Parker unable to bear children, but McPhillips reportedly suggested she should have used some of her campaign funds to adopt one. Getting elected was only part of the challenge for women entering southern legislatures. Male colleagues sending valentines and rising en masse whenever they entered a room frequently came across less as acts of chivalry than the dismissive gestures they often were. There were also major challenges in dealing with the ubiquitous "good ol' boy" networks. When she entered the Texas legislature in 1960, Myra Banfield discovered that "new male legislators could expect lobbyists to provide them with a case of liquor, a carton of cigarettes, and gorgeous call girls." Banfield's support for segregation and her opposition to an Equal Rights Amendment to the state constitution should have stood her in good stead with her male colleagues, but on the rare occasion when she broke with them by speaking out against legalized gambling, she was repeatedly admonished to "be quiet." When she refused to remain silent, the bill's sponsor swore to see her defeated if she ran again, and when she did, she was.[20]

By the 1990s a surprising number of the Democratic women holding legislative seats in the South were black. In fact, in proportion to their share of their state's general population, the percentage of black women in the legislatures of Mississippi, Louisiana, South Carolina, Georgia, Alabama, North Carolina, Virginia, and Tennessee was substantially higher than for white women. In Alabama, where black women held 50 percent of the seats they should have according to their population share, white women held only 11 percent of their projected target figure. Relative to their share of the population, black women's representation in these states was roughly 31 percent greater than in the nation at large, while for white women the ratio of legislative presence to population presence reached 50 percent of the national average only in Tennessee and Virginia. At least part of the explanation for this lay in the substantially greater likelihood that black legislators in states with sizable black populations were representing districts that were majority black.[21]

In 2002 when Shirley Franklin took office as the first black female mayor of Atlanta, she was faced with the daunting task of restoring the public trust by cleaning up what one investigator termed "the cesspool of corruption" left by her predecessor, Bill Campbell. Franklin also inherited a budget deficit that, at $82 million, was much larger than most had expected. Crime and homelessness were a constant concern, and the sharp recession that struck in the middle of her second term did little to help matters. The tough-minded Franklin implemented four rounds of layoffs, however, and then furloughed city employees in order to save Atlanta from bankruptcy. Calling for an increase in property taxes was clearly not a popular move, but Franklin simply shrugged off the criticism, saying, "I have a bull's-eye on my chest.... I knew that when I ran." Franklin showed a keen sense of Atlanta's identity and history, and her typically frugal approach did not stop her from securing a $32 million loan to purchase Dr. Martin Luther King Jr.'s papers from his family and announcing that she would raise that sum plus enough to build a civil rights museum from private donations.[22]

Franklin also presided over a major upgrade to the city's primitive sewer system and a new Beltline project featuring new parks and trails. When her firm stand on retrenchment forced the city council to raise both sales and property taxes and thereby put Atlanta on a more stable financial footing, even her critics had to admit that she had been both courageous and correct. "I would hope," Franklin observed as the end of her time in office drew nigh, "my legacy would be that a woman was up to the job."[23]

Higher up the political ladder, the South accounted for four of the seventeen women in the U.S. Senate and thirteen of the seventy-four women in the House of Representatives in 2009. Three of these seventeen women were black, all of them Democrats. In fact, despite the significant GOP advantage among their male counterparts, only eight southern women in the 111th Congress were Republicans. Although they were likely to show more sensitivity to women's concerns, the South's Republican women senators and congresswomen generally followed their party's conservative line. After serving as Charlotte's first woman mayor from 1987 to 1991, Sue Myrick was elected to the House of Representatives in 1994. Quickly establishing herself as a staunch political conservative, Myrick worked closely with religious conservatives, including the National Council on Bible Curriculum in the Schools. She also supported a proposed constitutional amendment in 2005 to ban burning of the American flag and won 100 percent approval ratings from the anti-abortion National Right to Life Committee. With Hispanics flooding into North Carolina, Myrick also took a strong stance against illegal immigration and even introduced a bill mandating immediate deportation for any illegal alien convicted of drunk driving.[24]

A former state legislator and Texas state treasurer, Kay Bailey Hutchison was elected to the U.S. Senate in a 1993 special election. The following year she won a resounding 61 percent of the vote when she sought a full term in the Senate, and she was twice reelected by similarly comfortable margins. Hutchison proved to be more moderate than many of her Republican colleagues on abortion issues but consistently opposed any environmental restrictions on oil and gas companies, and in 2006 she reportedly received more money from "Big Oil" than any other member of Congress. Hutchison's name was tossed about prominently as a potential running mate for GOP presidential candidate John McCain before he settled on Governor Sarah Palin. When Hutchison sought the Republican nomination for governor of Texas in 2010, however, her moderate stance on abortion hurt her among more conservative voters, and she ran a distant second to right-wing incumbent Rick Perry.[25]

Although they were noticeably more moderate than their counterparts among Republican congresswomen, southern Democratic women in Congress generally adopted more conservative policy stances than their female Democratic colleagues from other parts of the country. After Democratic Congressman Hale Boggs, who had represented the district encompassing New Orleans since 1947, died in a plane crash in 1972, his wife, Corrine Claiborne "Lindy" Boggs, easily captured his seat and held it just as easily for the next eighteen years. Congresswoman Boggs had been heavily involved in managing her husband's campaigns and his offices, and she entered the House of Representatives with a wealth of political experience and connections. Even after her district was redrawn to create a black-voter majority, Boggs had little difficulty turning back a black challenger to become the first white member of Congress to represent a majority-black constituency.[26]

Boggs was especially attuned to minority and women's issues, although she made it clear that she was less interested in crusading for the ERA than in securing better jobs and educational opportunities and "equal rights for women in business, banking, and home ownership." She took pains to assure that the Equal Credit Opportunity Act of 1974 protected unmarried women by adding "or sex or marital status" to language barring discrimination based on race or age or against veterans. Although she was a cofounder of the Congressional Women's Caucus in 1977, as a devout Roman Catholic, she also opposed Medicaid funding for abortions, a stance that may have kept her from being

Senator Walter F. Mondale's running mate in the 1984 presidential election. Boggs left Congress in 1991; six years later, at age eighty-one, she began four years of service as U.S. ambassador to the Vatican.[27]

In the years since World War II, southern women had actually been more prominently involved in disputes about race than those about gender, and a great many of them had dedicated themselves to maintaining the status quo in both areas. Florence Sillers Ogden was a Delta planter in her own right as well as the sister of ardent white supremacist Walter Sillers Jr., longtime speaker of the Mississippi House of Representatives and powerful fixture in state politics. Ogden was instrumental in creating Women for Constitutional Government (WCG), which, in the bitter aftermath of the Ole Miss violence in 1962, vigorously condemned the businessmen who had belatedly called for peaceful compliance with court-ordered desegregation. In October 1962 the group drew support from well beyond the region as it assembled fifteen hundred angry women from eight states to adopt a "bill of grievances" that deplored efforts to compel integration through the "ruthless show of federal might." The WCG did not confine itself to defending segregation, however; its reading list was also heavy on items such as the *Dan Smoot Report* and other fervently right-wing, anticommunist literature. Warning that "our constitutional rights have been swept away by armed might," Ogden attacked the New Deal (despite the generous AAA acreage-reduction subsidies she and her family had once received), the Committee on Foreign Relations, and any initiative even remotely associated with the United Nations. WCG co-founder Mary Cain, the fiery editor of the *Summit (Mississippi) Sun*, became the first woman to run for governor of Mississippi in 1951. Cain was even more rabid than Ogden in her hostility to federal programs, down to the point of refusing to pay social security taxes. When IRS agents finally padlocked her newspaper, Cain earned the nickname "Hacksaw Mary" by simply cutting off the lock.[28]

White women who spoke out in defense of the South's racial practices quickly gained the approval of their male contemporaries, but though fewer in number, those who crusaded for change proved more likely to secure a meaningful place in their region's history. No white southerner of the postwar era spoke out against the southern racial system earlier, more often, or more forcefully than Lillian Smith. In fact, Smith's strident, uncompromising attacks on the South's racial system and her calls for its immediate and total destruction soon drew criticism not only from Jim Crow's defenders but from its more moderate male

Mary Cain, campaigning for governor of Mississippi, 1951. Courtesy of Robert C. Waller Collection, McCain Library and Archives, University of Southern Mississippi, Hattiesburg, Mississippi.

critics, such as journalists Ralph McGill and Hodding Carter. Smith's 1944 novel, *Strange Fruit*, captured the essential brutality and hypocrisy of life under Jim Crow, and her unflinchingly candid 1949 treatise, *Killers of the Dream*, shocked many readers by boldly exposing the critical connections between the South's racial and gender hierarchies. Likening the constraints placed on women to those imposed on blacks, Smith also challenged southern white women to break free of those patriarchal bonds that "long ago made Mom and her sex 'inferior' and stripped her of her economic and political and sexual rights." White women, Smith believed, must make a real attempt "to change this way of life which they dimly realized had injured themselves and their children as much as it had injured Negroes."[29]

Much like her friend Lillian Smith, Pauli Murray sometimes tried to move faster than some of her fellow African American civil rights strategists thought prudent. Murray and a companion were on their

The South and America since World War II

way to visit Murray's family in Durham, North Carolina, when they were arrested in Petersburg, Virginia, in 1940 after refusing to sit in a broken seat in the Jim Crow section of a Greyhound bus. When the NAACP failed to offer full support for her appeals, Murray, a disciple of Gandhi, became convinced that the NAACP's legal gradualism must be supplemented with more direct action and public criticism of Jim Crow. She had been refused admission for graduate work at the University of North Carolina in 1938 because of her race and at Harvard in 1944 because of her gender. When she opted for graduate study at Berkeley instead, she was summarily evicted from her flat as soon as her landlord discovered that she was black. Not daunted in the least, she vowed that from then on she would never "submit to segregation…as long as my physical strength endures," even if it meant going to prison or abandoning the United States altogether. Sounding a bit like Gandhi and certainly anticipating her fellow Gandhian Martin Luther King Jr., Murray promised, "When my brothers try to draw a circle to exclude me, I shall draw a larger circle to include them."[30]

Trained in the law and a prolific and effective writer, Murray compiled a state-by-state list of laws relating to race shortly before the NAACP's suit in *Brown* was filed, and having encountered more than her share of sexism as well as racism, she was equally uncompromising in her crusade against "Jane Crow," eventually becoming a founding member of the National Organization for Women in 1966. In 1977, at age sixty-six, Murray became one of the first women to be ordained as an Episcopal priest, and true to form, when she celebrated her first Eucharist in the church in Chapel Hill where both her slave and white ancestors had once worshipped, she used her sermon to urge the congregation to press the state legislature to ratify the Equal Rights Amendment.[31]

Surely no southern woman proved a more vital and genuinely passionate voice for racial justice in the post–World War II South than former sharecropper Fannie Lou Hamer. A woman of little education but abundant courage and fierce conviction, Hamer was impossible to intimidate either politically or physically. When she was accused of being a communist agitator, she had simply snorted dismissively that she knew about as much about communism as "a horse do about Christmas." Having faced physical assault and numerous threats on her life, she remained undaunted: "Sometimes it seem like to tell the truth today is to run the risk of being killed. But if I fall, I'll fall five feet four inches forward in the fight for freedom. I'm not backing off that, and no one will have to cover the ground I walk as far as freedom is concerned."[32]

Hamer was reportedly living only on disability payments supplemented by the generosity of friends and admirers when she lost her battle with the combined forces of cancer, diabetes, and hypertension just short of her sixtieth birthday in 1977. She was buried in a scraggly field that had been part of the land where she once tried to establish a cooperative farm. Yet not only was Hamer eulogized in the *New York Times* and a host of other influential publications in the United States and elsewhere, but in a move that probably attested even more powerfully to the enormity of what she had accomplished, even that former citadel of white supremacy, the Mississippi House of Representatives, voted unanimously to commend her for dedicating her life "to equality and justice for all" and becoming "a symbol to people across the nation in their struggle for human dignity."[33]

The year after Hamer's death her fellow Sunflower Countian (and still unapologetic segregationist) James O. Eastland retired from the U.S.

Fannie Lou Hamer at the Democratic National Convention, 1964. *U.S. News and World Report* Magazine Photograph Collection, Library of Congress, Prints and Photographs Division, Washington, D.C. (LC-U9-12470B-17 [P8P]).

Senate. At one point a great many southern whites had cheered Eastland for doing his bullying, obstructionist best to block the changes that Hamer had fought so passionately to secure. Shortly after his retirement, however, efforts by the University of Mississippi Foundation to raise $13,000 for a portrait of Eastland to be hung in the U.S. Capitol fell some $10,000 short, and after his death in 1986, even in Mississippi, the name of a man who once used his enormous power to defend and perpetuate racial injustice seemed to come up primarily when discussions turned to those who had stood steadfastly on the wrong side of history. On the other hand, as Chris Myers Asch pointed out in 2008, tiny Ruleville was proudly advertising itself as "the home of Fannie Lou Hamer," and throughout Sunflower County it was her name rather than Eastland's that adorned public buildings and facilities. More broadly, as the person who perhaps best epitomized those who refused to be intimidated by Eastland's abuse of his power, Hamer's historical stock has soared. Although she was born a sharecropper and died in poverty, she now stands widely recognized as one of the most critical figures in shaping both the outcome and the enduring perception of twentieth-century America's greatest moral struggle.[34]

If Fannie Lou Hamer distinguished herself as a warrior for change, when Barbara Jordan lent her elegantly powerful and erudite voice to the cause of justice and law, she made it clear that the suffering and sacrifices of Hamer and other civil rights crusaders had not been in vain. The daughter of a minister, Jordan grew up in Houston's predominantly black Fifth Ward, and after graduating from all-black Texas Southern, she earned a law degree from Boston University in 1959 and became only the third black woman to be licensed to practice law in Texas. Jordan made her name in politics in 1966, when on her third try she became the first black woman to win a seat in the Texas State Senate. She registered another breakthrough in 1972 as the first black woman from a former Confederate state to serve in Congress.

Jordan was already known as a constitutional expert, and with a little help from her fellow Texan, former president Lyndon Johnson, she secured a place on the House Judiciary Committee. Serving on that committee during the Watergate hearings in 1974, she explained to a national television audience that her faith in the Constitution was "whole," "complete," and "total" and that she was "not going to sit [there] and be an idle spectator to the diminution, the subversion, the destruction of the Constitution." Her real time in the sun, however, came with

Barbara Jordan, addressing the
Democratic National Convention,
1976. *U.S. News and World Report*
Magazine Photograph Collection,
Library of Congress, Prints and
Photographs Division, Washington, D.C.
(USN8WRCOLL-Job No. 32937, frame
32A133 [P8P]).

her keynote address at the 1976 Democratic National Convention, in
which she cited her selection as the first black woman to deliver such a
speech as "one additional bit of evidence that the American Dream need
not forever be deferred." In the wake of the disillusionment and division
of Watergate and in the midst of the celebration of the nation's bicen-
tennial, Jordan made national unity and harmony her primary focus.
"We must address and master the future," she insisted. "It can be done
if we restore the belief that we share a sense of national community,
that we share a common national endeavor. It can be done." Urging her
fellow Democrats to take the lead in forming "a national community
in which every last one of us participates," Jordan left her audience to
ponder Abraham Lincoln's definition of democracy. "As I would not be
a slave, so I would not be a master. This expresses my idea of Democracy. Whatever differs from this, to the extent of the difference, is no
Democracy."[35]

Coupled with her stellar performance during the Watergate hearings, Jordan's convention oratory catapulted her onto lists of "influen-
tials" in Congress and spurred talk of her as a potential presidential or
vice presidential choice. Her battle with multiple sclerosis forced her to

retire from political life, however, and in 1979 she accepted a position at the Lyndon B. Johnson School of Public Affairs at the University of Texas. Eventually compelled to rely on a cane and then a wheelchair, Jordan received the Presidential Medal of Freedom in 1994. Two years later, she was dead at age fifty-nine. Recalling her eloquence during the Watergate proceedings, the *Washington Post* reporter Bob Woodward observed, "It was like if God were a woman, that would be the voice."[36]

10

"First and Last a Southerner"

Whites, Blacks, and Southern Identity after Jim Crow

It seems doubtful that Barbara Jordan could have offered such heartfelt expressions of faith in her country's institutions without the changes that had swept across her state and region in the first generation after World War II. The South's white politicians had traditionally made it a point never to be outdone in the florid, rhetorical patriotism they dispensed from the stump, but their words rang fairly hollow to anyone familiar with their blatant disregard for the constitutional rights of black citizens. Yet when black southerners who had once borne the brunt of these injustices were moved to express their love for their country and faith in its institutions with the kind of passion that Jordan displayed, it was easier to believe that the South might truly and finally have become one with America.

Among white southerners this apparent reunion was cause for celebration primarily for those who had long sought a South that was both reformed and reconciled. Yet even for them certain ramifications of their region's newfound acceptance by their fellow Americans were a bit too emotionally complicated for comfort. For 150 years or so southern whites had not only considered the rest of the country to be "the North," but from the earliest days of nationhood they had also read and listened with mounting resentment as the supposed prosperity, intellectual dynamism, and moral enlightenment of the northern states became synonymous with the very idea of America itself. Meanwhile, the impoverished, backward-looking, bigoted, and intolerant South had quickly come to represent, at best, a stubborn and embarrassing smudge on an otherwise pristine national countenance.

Needless to say, military defeat and occupation by the Yankees had further intensified this antagonism toward the North, to the point that it actually became a defining trait for most white southerners. Indeed, even as the sesquicentennial of the "unpleasantness" of 1861–65 drew nigh, some of the region's whites still found it difficult to celebrate the South's oft-hailed return to the Union wholeheartedly without first suppressing a vision of Appomattox redux and the feeling that the social and cultural struggle that had literally defined them and their ancestors for well over a century had once again ended in a surrender to forces northern in origin.

Even as a boy, Charles Mallison, the young protagonist of William Faulkner's 1948 novel, *Intruder in the Dust*, had already internalized the white southerner's obligatory but urgent predisposition to resist the North, which he saw not as "a geographical place" so much as "an emotional idea, a condition of which he had fed from his mother's milk to be ever and constant on the alert not at all to fear and not actually anymore to hate but just—a little wearily sometimes and sometimes even with tongue in cheek—to defy." Though lacking precise coordinates, to Charles the North was nonetheless an "outland and circumscribing" presence representing not simply another region but the rest of a "rich, teeming, never-ravaged" America intent on robbing him of his birthright by forcing him and his to bend to its will. Like Charles, as their increasingly embattled region emerged from World War II, many flesh-and-blood white southerners thought they could remain who they were only by defending themselves and their way of life from northern criticism and intrusion.[1]

A number of anthropologists have contended that the fundamental identity of any culture depends on its capacity to isolate and articulate the differences between it and the other cultures it encounters. With the South specifically in mind, James L. Peacock has pointed out that regional identity can become "*actively oppositional to national identity*—not just different from but opposed to and, at least in the region's own perception, oppressed by the rest of the nation [which in the minds of many white southerners also meant 'the North'] and the central government [which white southerners often saw as simply an instrument of 'the North']." Writing in 1972, John Shelton Reed cited traits such as a proclivity for violence and a hostility to change in general as the cultural residue, by and large, of the white South's long and bitter defense of Jim Crow against northern criticism and attack. Reed believed, "If their culture serves [white] southerners for better or worse, in dealing with a hostile 'outside,' it will probably continue to serve as long as the outside seems hostile." However, he added prophetically, "the traditional outside has been the North, and the occasion for sectional animosity has usually been the South's racial institutions.... If the South's race relations improve or the North's deteriorate, white Southerners may yet realize their ancient wish to be 'let alone.'"[2]

With northern self-righteousness on race receding rapidly and the once economically dynamic northern Manufacturing Belt's jobs and people steadily flowing southward as the 1970s unfolded, the process of regional convergence quickly became not just a story of the South catching up but of the North slipping back. By 1972 a *New York Times* reporter covering a conference on the South's future concluded, "[If this gathering] was any indication, Southern intellectuals have almost abandoned the North as a fit model for imitation in any field, from human rights to the building of cities."[3]

Culminating in the election of Jimmy Carter in 1976, this dramatic reversal of regional fortunes was cause for celebration and even some self-satisfaction among those who had long since grown weary of defending their region. James McBride Dabbs knew whereof he spoke, however, when he observed, "What a [white] southerner is and what he is supposed to do besides resist, nobody knows." Sure enough, for members of a new Sunbelt-era generation of white southerners no longer obliged to defend their racial system, the heady prospect of finally being "let alone" by their old northern critics also stirred anxieties about the future of their regional identity. Moreover, two decades after Harry Ashmore had penned its "epitaph," Dixie seemed to have outlived its familiar and supposedly healthier counterpoint, the old superior, condescending, and critical North. If, as Sheldon Hackney explained, white southerners were merely "Americans who have taken on an additional identity through conflict with the North," how long could that "additional identity" survive once the North was no longer there to oppose? "No North. No South. So one might predict," wrote Richard N. Current in 1983, and in fact, the task of reestablishing an identity grounded in something other than their historic defense of their region's racial traditions proved to be quite a challenge even for some highly imaginative white southerners.[4]

Traditional wisdom had long held that lower-income, less-educated southern whites were more likely than their upwardly mobile white counterparts to cling both to their identity as southerners and to the racism, provincialism, and religious intolerance and other pernicious traits that had marked that identity at its worst. When he tested this hypothesis, however, John Reed found that those most likely to insist on identifying themselves as southerners and to want others to see them that way as well were generally the well-educated, well-read white urbanites who were also least likely to hold (or at least express openly) the pathological values that seemed to define whites farther down the socioeconomic scale. A similar pattern had been observed among immigrant groups in the United States who, when their economic and educational advances propelled them to the very threshold of assimilation into the social mainstream, often appeared to pull back and reassert their native ethnic or cultural traits and ties. Certainly this pattern held among white southerners throughout the 1990s, as polls showed that a resident of the South who made more than $60,000 per year was nearly nine times more likely to express a strong personal identification with the region than one who made less than $20,000.[5]

In the natural course of distinguishing themselves, identity groups are likely to exaggerate their actual differences with other groups, and the smaller the real distinctions between South and North became, the more white southerners seemed inclined to play them up by indulging in what Freud called "the narcissism of small differences." Seeking tangible affirmation of their continuing distinctiveness, many of the Sunbelt era South's more upwardly mobile whites reached for regionally oriented publications such as *Southern Living*, which had risen quickly from its humble beginnings in 1966 to win *Forbes*'s designation in 1977 as not just the nation's most profitable magazine but the "down home equivalent of the U.S. mint." *Southern Living* became such a moneymaker in fact that in the ultimate ironic twist, its parent company, the Southern Progress Corporation, was gobbled up in 1985 by New York–based Time, Inc.

Four decades after it was launched, *Southern Living* adorned the coffee tables of more than 2.5 million subscribers. Offering not even a hint that a great many southerners still had little hope of achieving anything approaching the stylish and comfortable existence celebrated on its pages, the magazine served as what Diane Roberts called "the Lifestyle Bible of the genuine and aspiring upper middle class." Meanwhile, established in 1977 (and later also acquired by Time, Inc.) *Southern Accents* offered a somewhat more sophisticated option for even more status-conscious readers, as did the more recent arrival *Garden and Gun*, whose editor, Syd Evans, drew a rather disdainful distinction between his magazine and *Southern Living* when he sniffed, "We don't have pictures of cakes on the cover."[6]

Meanwhile, those who spurned such pretensions of class could always congregate online at Bubba-L, where patrons could swap barbecue sauce recipes and complain about the growing influx of Yankees. Other white southerners who sought a more rambunctious and perhaps slightly rebellious outlet for their identity passions even began to describe themselves eagerly and unrepentantly as "rednecks." For more than a century, this opprobrious term had been the nation's most acceptable ethnic slur, suggesting the kind of white males who lynched blacks, married their cousins, and, in their utter disdain for self-improvement or social advancement, generally served as millstones around the necks of those working for the betterment of their region. By the 1990s, however, "redneck" had become something approaching a term of endearment, suggesting an admirably fierce independence in the face of the suffocating conformity that American mass society could impose. "To call oneself a redneck is not so much to *be* a redneck by birth or occupational fate, but rather to identify with an anti-bourgeois attitude and life style," explained sociologist Richard Petersen. So it was with former IBM employee Jeff Foxworthy, who turned a long list of one-liners, such as "You may be a redneck if . . . you've ever been too drunk to fish . . . or your family tree doesn't have any branches," into a series of successful comedy albums and television shows on several networks.[7]

In the realm of products and paraphernalia, there was also Redneck beer, "Proud to Be a Redneck" sweatshirts and bumper stickers, and the "redneck briefcase" (a pair of underwear with handles attached). For all their efforts to project a militantly antibourgeois image, however, it seemed that many of those who were most enthusiastically buying (both figuratively and literally) into the redneck craze were also solidly middle-class folks who manicured the lawns and mussed up the fairways of southern suburbia and possibly even sneaked a peek at *Southern Living* now and again. Having at last acquired the resources for full-scale participation in the national consumer culture, prospering but identity-challenged whites in the Sunbelt South stood not just ready but eager to consume their own regional culture as rapidly as commercial marketers could commodify it.

Members of the South's academic community also stood ready to cash in on the growing fascination with southern identity. Amid mounting statistical evidence of the white South's assimilation into the American mainstream in the 1980s and 1990s, interest in southern cultural identity soared, leading one journalist to observe, "Institutes, centers and programs for the study of the South are becoming as ubiquitous on Southern campuses as Wal-Marts are in Southern suburbia." As the twentieth century drew to a close, the University of North Carolina at Chapel Hill sported the Center for the Study of the American South and its ambitious interdisciplinary journal, *Southern Cultures*. At the University of Alabama, there was the Center for Southern History and Culture, while the University of South Carolina boasted the Institute for Southern Studies. Fittingly enough, however, no southern university came closer to perfecting the art of regional navel gazing than the University of Mississippi. By the 1990s Ole Miss's Center for the Study of Southern Culture offered both undergraduate and graduate degrees in southern studies and hosted conferences and symposia where speakers touched on everything and everyone southern, from Elvis Presley to Eudora Welty and a great deal in between. Scholars at the Ole Miss center also compiled the massive *Encyclopedia of Southern Culture*. A five-pound treasure trove of information dedicated, according to Alex Haley, "to distilling and preserving our southern distinctiveness," the *Encyclopedia* quickly sold more than 100,000 copies, functioning, so one historian aptly noted, as "the intellectual equivalent of *Southern Living*" for southerners intent on documenting their cultural uniqueness.[8]

Although nonsoutherners seemed to find the regional persona that emerged from the 1,600 pages of the *Encyclopedia of Southern Culture* much more inviting than hostile, they would probably have reacted differently had they run across the website operated by the League of the South, an organization sworn to defend to the last "the unique social, cultural and religious traditions of the Southern people." Decrying what they saw as a deliberate campaign of northern cultural imperialism, League spokesmen even floated the notion of giving secession another whirl, churning out elaborate position papers on the subject and sporting a bumper sticker that urged, "If at first you don't secede, try, try again." Reflecting a mind-set that made no distinction between "Americanization" and "Northernization," League propagandists did their best to rekindle old sectional antagonisms by condemning "Yankee-defined archetypes" of southerners and in some cases even shunning postal zip codes, which they dismissed as "the Yankee occupation code."[9]

Promising to save future generations of white southerners from "cultural genocide," the League of the South even offered its own recommended reading list for home-schooled children and held a summer institute for high schoolers and collegians in order to inculcate a sense of regional pride and to "rectify among Southerners and others the one-sidedness of the Northern public-school view of Southern history." With the traditional regional antagonisms decidedly on the wane, the League's strategists apparently believed that their best hope of rallying whites to what was essentially the traditional whites-only version of southern identity lay in convincing them that the old oppositional North was not only still alive but as intent as ever on stripping them of their regional heritage.[10]

In reality, League of the South propagandists were simply attempting to resurrect and inflame white southerners' age-old impulse to, as in Charles Mallison's case, "defy" the North. Charles's "idea" of the North, after all, was an omnipresent gallery of gawkers "looking down at him and his in fading amazement and outrage," eager to believe practically "anything about the South not even provided it be derogatory but merely bizarre enough and strange enough." Prior to the civil rights movement keen awareness of northern scrutiny had given a sense of purpose and urgency to efforts by writers like Faulkner to explore southern identity. What Fred Hobson called a literary "rage to explain" had been stoked by "an enemy across the line issuing an indictment that had to "be answered." By the 1970s, however, with their region on the verge of achieving economic as well as moral parity with the North, southern writers were suddenly compelled "neither to defend nor to attack the South with passion and intensity."[11]

Walker Percy showed passion as well as intensity in 1965 when, describing his state as a "fallen paradise," he contrasted the valor of white Mississippians who fought to the death at Gettysburg with the cowardice of a contemporary generation "mainly renowned for murder, church burning, dynamiting, assassinations, night-riding, not to mention the lesser forms of terrorism." Percy's tone and perspective had changed dramatically by 1979, however, when he declared that "now…[the] virtues and faults of the South are the virtues and faults of the nation, no more and no less." As he saw it, this meant that "the peculiar isolation and disabilities under which the South labored for so long and which served some southern writers so well...are now things of the past." Ironically Percy, who would soon be anointed by critics as the new standard-bearer of the southern literary tradition, had insisted as early as 1971 that "the day of regional Southern writing is all gone. I think that people who try to write in that style are usually repeating a phased-out genre—or doing Faulkner badly." Instead, Percy insisted, "what increasingly engages the southern novelist as much as his Connecticut counterpart are no longer Faulkner's Snopeses or O'Connor's Crackers or Wright's black underclass but their successful grandchildren who are going nuts in Atlanta condominiums."[12]

While generations of southern liberals had made dragging their stubbornly benighted homeland into the American mainstream the key to regional salvation, to many southern writers of the Sunbelt generation and after, the people who inhabited the spruced-up, assimilated South looked not saved but, on the contrary, almost completely and perhaps even irretrievably lost. Contributors to *I'll Take My Stand* had gloomily prophesied such an outcome back in 1930, but the grinding poverty that seemed to be choking the life out of the rural South during the Great Depression had made both the Nashville Agrarians' attacks on industrialism and their often fanciful tributes to the virtues of life on the land fairly difficult to swallow at that point. Only with the economic surge triggered by World War II did a number of other southern writers begin to worry that their region might be changing not only too fast but not entirely for the better. In his 1951 novel, *Requiem for a Nun,* Faulkner described the mindlessly modernizing fictional post–World War II town of Jefferson, "awakened from its communal slumber into a rash of Rotary and Lions Clubs and Chambers of Commerce and City Beautifuls: a furious beating of hollow drums toward nowhere."[13]

Flannery O'Connor captured rural southerners' apprehensions about the post–World War II invasion of alien ideas and values in her 1954 story, "The Displaced Person." Mr. Guizac, a Polish refugee, brings what, by community standards, is an uncommonly high level of energy and organizational focus to the task of revitalizing a languishing Georgia farm. His employer, Mrs. McIntyre, likes the idea of turning a profit on her place again, but she senses that, for all of her new worker's efficiency, he also poses a threat to the only way of life she knows. Her fears are confirmed when Guizac tries to get a female cousin into the United States by arranging her betrothal to a young black man, and at the story's conclusion Mrs. McIntyre and her shiftless old hired man simply stand mute, offering no warning as poor Guizac is flattened by a runaway tractor.[14]

Readers and critics alike were taken aback by O'Connor's dispassionate treatment of this tragic event, but she explained in 1957, "The anguish that most of us have observed for some time now is not that the South is alienated from the rest of the country but...that it is not alienated enough, that every day we are getting more like the rest of the country, that we are being forced out not only of our many sins but our few virtues." Over the next few years, the South's sins would clearly overshadow its virtues, but as the region finally emerged from the civil rights struggle and began at last to attract more desirable investments, jobs, and the people who came with them, the cultural costs of the region's long-awaited entry into the American mainstream would become a primary concern for a new generation of southern writers.[15]

Though still something of a literary fledgling in 1960, Walker Percy was already observing rather glumly, "The sections are homogenized. Everyone watches the same television programs. In another hundred years, everybody will talk like Art Linkletter." Two years later, in his first novel, *The Moviegoer*, Percy introduced readers to a prosperous, materialistic, bored, and altogether bland southern white middle class of "well-fed and kindhearted people" awash in attractive neighborhoods, stylish country cubs, and luxury cars but beset by a "malaise" that has settled on them like fallout from an atomic blast. In *The Moviegoer* the alienated young stockbroker Binx Bolling explains this feeling as the sense that "the world is lost to you, the world and the people in it, and there remains only you and the world and you no more able to be in the world than Banquo's ghost."[16]

With retail sales growing nearly 25 percent faster in cities like Charlotte than in the nation as a whole between 1970 and 1989 and employment rising at nearly twice the national average in the region's larger metropolitan areas, it was, as one planning expert put it in 1989, "hard to find a southern city that's not doing well." Such observations explained why Percy's novels presented not the familiar impoverished, history-burdened, and race-bedeviled South but a place suddenly grown "happy, victorious, Christian, rich, patriotic, and Republican." This was a South where Yankees could assimilate simply by pulling on boots and adopting a drawl, while, as one literary critic put it, the descendants of Civil War generals "move to the suburbs and make fortunes converting slave quarters to $400,000 condos." The downside of the region's economic ascent was what Percy himself decried as the "Los Angelization" of the South, which now seemed destined to become nothing more than "an agribusiness-sports-vacation-retirement-show-biz culture with its spiritual center perhaps at Oral Roberts University." "What I am trying to do," Percy explained in 1981, "is figure out how a man can come to himself, living in a place like that."[17]

The people who inhabited "a place like that" were also of particular concern to Bobbie Ann Mason. In fact, Mason's fiction might well have been set anywhere, for her characters struggled consistently, as one critic put it, to come to terms "with America and not the South." Traditional southern signifiers such as history, religion, and family have generally faded into the background in Mason's stories of blue-collar or lower-middle-class white southerners who are reduced to seeking escape rather than meaning in lives dominated by contemporary popular and commercial culture. Her characters sometimes schedule their lives according to what is playing on television; in the wake of her breakup with a boyfriend one even explains her refusal to move in with her father by pointing out, "We don't like the same TV shows anymore."[18]

In Mason's world families seem more likely to be sources of pain rather than comfort, and when they do attempt to communicate, parents and children or spouses or lovers are seldom on the same wavelength. In "The Retreat" Georgianne is the unhappy and disillusioned wife of a struggling minister. Realizing that she cannot embrace her husband's spiritual commitment or the traditionally subordinate role of a southern woman, much less that of a southern minister's wife, Georgianne abandons the workshops at a religious retreat in favor of the video games in the basement of the lodge where the retreat is being held. She is captivated by the excitement of blinking lights and constant competition as she imagines herself in control of her own destiny. On the way home from the retreat, when her husband asks what he can do to make her happy, she replies somewhat absently, "I was happy when I was playing that game."[19]

Cut off from history and struggling to adapt to a radically altered physical environment, the characters crafted by Mason and her contemporaries have formed new emotional attachments to the very fast-food restaurants, strip malls, supermarkets, and other manifestations of contemporary Sunbelt consumer culture that have disrupted if not simply destroyed their old connections with past and place. One of Josephine Humphreys's characters even asks, "Who can be sad in a supermarket, with all its proof of human omnipotence?...When you see such achievement, you must be hopeful; every box of quick grits, every can of cling peaches."[20]

Humphreys, Mason, Percy, and others who explored the cultural consequences of rapid, unchecked development in their fiction were by no means alone. Shocked by the depressingly generic real-life "Santa Barbara gallery of pizza cottages and fish 'n chips parlors" that he encountered south of Atlanta in 1975, journalist Marshall Frady complained, "The downtowns of Charlotte and Columbia and Jackson have become perfect reflections of Every City, and out beyond their perimeter expressways, barbecue patios and automatic lawn sprinklers are pushing out the possums and moonshine shanties in a combustion of suburbs indistinguishable from those of Pasadena or Minneapolis." What had once been America's most strikingly distinctive region was now, Frady lamented, on the verge of becoming "pastless, meaningless, and vague of identity." By 1990 his fellow journalist Hodding Carter III was prepared to declare that Frady's gloomy forecast had been largely borne out. The South he had known and experienced as "a living, ever regenerating mythic land of distinctive personality," Carter observed glumly, "is no more....What is lurching into existence in the South is purely and contemporaneously mainstream American, for better or worse."[21]

A few years later Tony Scherman sounded like both Frady and Carter, not to mention Walker Percy and his literary disciples, when he observed that although country music sales had almost quadrupled between 1985 and 1993, the price of country's rise from "ridiculed step-child to full legitimacy in the family of American music" had been its "pungency—more, its very identity." Country music was born of the mass migration of several generations of white southerners from farm to metropolis and their struggle to make the adjustment to their new lives and surroundings. With the overwhelming majority of the descendants of these migrants now residing comfortably in suburbia, Scherman argued, a music that had once focused so consistently on matters such as "a hated job, cheating on your spouse, or the urge to go out and get roaring drunk" no longer seemed relevant. Efforts to make country music appealing to this more sophisticated metropolitan bourgeoisie had robbed it of most of the unflinching candor and raw emotion that had made it such a vital window into white working-class life. Garth Brooks and other phenomenally successful performers of the 1990s had broadened their fan base all right, but only by forsaking country's dogged realism and grit for what Scherman decried as "an almost insufferable blandness. Along with K-Mart and McDonald's," for Scherman, the new "Contemporary Country" sound simply symbolized "the end of regionalism in American life."[22]

In reality though, an overwhelming majority of new country songs were still set in the South, and mainstream country music's nationwide popularity in suburbia certainly made it no less southern; that was where the majority of southerners now lived, after all. By the end of the 1990s, with more than 40 percent of Americans listening to country music each week—roughly double the number from a decade earlier—and 36 percent of these listeners even holding postgraduate degrees, the country audience was both better educated and more affluent than those who preferred adult contemporary or rock. In short, Bruce Feiler concluded in 1999, country had become "the voice of the new American majority [of] middle class suburbanites." While Scherman was certainly correct in suggesting that in the course of its commercial ascent the music had lost some of its working-class flavor, fans still eagerly embraced Hank Williams Jr.'s aggressively blue-collar and defiantly southern anthems, such as "A Country Boy Can Survive," not to mention the ever-popular Alan Jackson's assurances that it was "OK to be little bitty" and his nostalgic tribute to the small-town "little man" who lost his old filling station because "he couldn't sell Slurpees and he wouldn't sell beer."[23]

Never a dominant component in mainstream country music, overt, class-conscious treatments of blue-collar resentment and pride had been more the stock-in-trade of southern or country rockers such as the Charlie Daniels Band and the ill-fated Lynyrd Skynyrd, whose partly ironic 1974 hit, "Sweet Home Alabama," was immediately embraced by many white southerners as a classic expression of regional pride and spoiling-for-a-fight defiance. Although Lynyrd Skynyrd had been torn asunder when lead singer Ronnie Van Zant and two other band members died in a 1977 plane crash, thirty years later the Drive-By Truckers seemed to have taken up the cause of setting the world straight on what made the still often ridiculed and belittled southern white working class tick. The aggressively blue-collar tone of the Truckers' music struck one reviewer as akin to "setting a trailer house in the rich part of town," and one of their popular offerings declared that "to the fucking rich man all poor people look the same."[24]

As the group's leader, Patterson Hood, explained, it had always been much easier for critics in the South and elsewhere to blame all the difficulties facing lower-income whites in the South on their racism rather than "accept the fact that there were other factors holding people down." The Truckers made no effort in their music to deny or defend this racism, however. White southerners who were "proud of the glory" still had to "stare down the shame." Hence, "the duality of 'The Southern Thing.'"[25]

The Drive-By Truckers were at their best simply singing about the struggles of southerners whose stories were nowhere to be found in the grand narrative of Sunbelt-era success and prosperity. In these stories tragedy and loss were so commonplace as to be an almost unremarkable part of everyday life. Thus some "plastic flowers in the highway" were the only monument to the life and death of a young man killed in a car crash as he headed out for "the city" and "the big world waiting there."[26]

It did not fall entirely to groups like the Drive-By Truckers or others in the second generation of southern rockers to tell the stories of the region's down-and-out whites. With so many talented new literary figures focusing on the relatively affluent but alienated and rootless resi-

Drive-By Truckers. Courtesy of Jason Thrasher.

dents of contemporary southern suburbia, it was fortunate that a small but equally gifted group of writers also turned their attention to the lives of those who were hunkered down in the shacks, trailer parks, and beer joints at the socioeconomic margins of the Sunbelt South.

Rick Bragg wrote evocatively about his own poor-white Alabama childhood, which was marked by long stretches of tragedy and trauma so unrelenting that anything else seemed strange, even disconcerting. In a particularly revealing account, Bragg told of his long-suffering mother's heartbreaking reaction to an apparent turnaround in the family fortunes. In 1963, after years of abuse and neglect by his drunken, irresponsible father, Rick's spirits had soared when his dad found a steady job in Dallas at a body shop and took the family out of Calhoun County, Alabama, and away from the hand-to-mouth existence that was all Rick had ever known. Suddenly there was plenty of food, money for decent clothes, and some of the "extras" that had been forever beyond their reach in Alabama. "I thought I had stepped in through some magic window," Rick recalled. "One day she was dragging me on a cotton sack, pulling all day for a dollar and change, and the next day, we were sitting on a porch step eating ice cream."[27]

Rick's dad, Charles, had his drinking under control and had given his wife no indication that he would slip back into his old self- and family-destructive ways, but his previous behavior gave her reason to remain apprehensive that he might revert to form. Then, after a couple of months that seemed like a dream to Rick and his brothers, word came from back home that the $54 monthly welfare check his mother had been receiving for her and her two boys was about to be cut off. At that point, wracked by doubt about Charles's staying power and conditioned by life to see all good fortune as fleeting at best, Margaret Bragg told her devastated husband that she was taking the boys and going home. Finding his insistent, emotional pleadings to no avail, Charles Bragg remained in Texas for a while before slipping back into his old ways and resolutely drinking himself to death while making what was an already tenuous existence for his wife and children even more difficult and painful.

Though too young at the time to process what had happened, as an adult Rick Bragg would experience the same knee-jerk suspicion of good fortune when he received word in 1999 that he had won a Pulitzer Prize for his feature writing at the *New York Times*. Fearful that there might have been a mistake, Bragg waited an hour before calling his mother because, he explained, "it is a common condition of being poor white trash: you are always afraid that the good things in your life are temporary, that someone can take them away, because you have no power beyond your brute strength to stop them."[28]

In the fiction of "white-trash" writers like Dorothy Allison, Larry Brown, Harry Crews, and Tim McLaurin, people like the Braggs face not only severe economic misfortune, but emotional trauma and physical and sexual abuse at the hands of both family and strangers. Violence and fear are virtual constants in an often brutal and desperate existence in which survival is a day-to-day rather than a long-term concern. As Harry Crews explained, "The world that circumscribed the people I come from had so little margin for error that when something went wrong, it almost always brought something else down with it. It was a world in which survival depended on raw courage, a courage born out of desperation and sustained by a lack of alternatives."[29]

Scrambling simply to get by while more fortunate whites view them through a veil of condescension and contempt, the characters created by the white-trash writers seethe with class resentment while clinging tenaciously to a fierce sense of independence and pride that is often their undoing. Allison's Ruth Anne "Bone" Boatwright knows that, for her mother, the "Illegitimate" stamped on Ruth Anne's birth certificate might as well read "trash." Her mother "hated to be called 'trash,'" and "the stamp on that birth certificate burned her like the stamp she knew they'd tried to put on her." Meanwhile, the title character in Larry Brown's novel *Fay* has walked away from her abusive and neglectful family, but she cannot escape her identity. When a spoiled young rich woman calls her a "white trash piece of shit," Fay observes rather philosophically that "she never had been called a white trash piece of shit before, but she'd been called white trash."[30]

Fay's father had prostituted her younger sister and made advances toward Fay herself, and despite her own lack of guile, wherever she goes she, too, leaves a trail of pain in her wake. Elsewhere, one of Allison's characters can point in a single photo to eight cousins whom she lost in a single year: "One went insane—got her little brother with a tire iron; the three of them slit their arms, not their wrists but the bigger veins up near the elbow; she, now she strangled the boy she was sleeping with and got sent away; that one drank lye and died laughing soundlessly."[31]

In such a world where, as the Drive-By Truckers sang, human tragedy left no more lasting imprint than "a greasy spot on the asphalt for

Larry Brown, Yocona, Mississippi, 1995. Courtesy of Tom Rankin.

a while," compassion could easily be mistaken for weakness, and those who displayed it were sometimes rewarded with contempt rather than gratitude. In Larry Brown's "Samaritans" Frank encounters a woman in a beer joint who is traveling with her mother and four children in "a junky-ass old Rambler, wrecked on the right front end, with the paint almost faded off, and slick tires, and a rag hanging out of the grill." Frank wants to avoid her but winds up taking her into the bar and buying her several beers and a pack of cigarettes. When the beer starts to hit her she complains, "People don't give a shit if you ain't got a place to sleep ner nothin' to eat. They don't care." She tells Frank that she is heading to "Morgan City, Loozeanner," where her husband has supposedly found work. Yet when he gives her thirty dollars, she simply gets her mother out of the car and the two of them head back to the bar, whereupon her young son solemnly informs her benefactor that he is "a dumb sumbitch."[32]

Things went badly indeed when four Atlanta suburbanites set out in James Dickey's 1970 novel, *Deliverance,* to test themselves by canoeing a wild northern Georgia river about to be harnessed forever by the construction of a reservoir. At the end of their horrific excursion, not only have they been humbled by the uncontrolled fury of the river, but they have been forced to kill an equally savage local backwoodsman. With one of their number dead, another sexually assaulted, and another seriously injured, the survivors hasten back to suburbia, all forever shaken by their encounter with the raw, unforgiving force of nature unrestrained and the uncivilized, grotesque, and vicious people who live closest to it. The poor whites portrayed in most white-trash fiction are treated a bit more empathetically, but like the mountain people in *Deliverance*, they are far more in tune with the region's natural environment than the white-collar denizens of the Sunbelt South's cookie-cutter suburbs and office parks. The livelihoods of lower-class white southerners frequently depended on working where there was neither air-conditioning nor escape from the blazing sun or torrential rains, but unlike their sheltered suburban contemporaries, they were also no strangers to the smells of honeysuckle and pine or the seductive baying of hounds who have struck the scent of a rabbit or coon.[33]

In his memoir, *Keepers of the Moon*, white-trash writer Tim McLaurin revealed that for seven years he had carried around a small bag of dirt from his family's homeplace, "a talisman that whispers to me the song of mourning doves, wind in longleaf pines, the low rumble of thunder from a summer storm that has recently passed and soaked the dry fields. I hope to waltz slowly to that tune the day I lift above this bright land." McLaurin expressed similar sentiments through one of his characters, Nadean Tucker, a black former prostitute who also collects a pocketful of the rubble from her rundown homeplace because "home stays in just two places—on the land where you were raised, and always, always in the back of your mind."[34]

Nadean's observations are more than fitting, for in the wake of the civil rights movement, black southerners, and black writers especially, began to step forward with surprising enthusiasm to publicly embrace the South as both their physical and emotional home. This development was particularly noteworthy because so long as the entire black population of the South was struggling to survive under the crushing weight of Jim Crow, black writers had faced enormous pressure to use their talents to dramatize the plight of their people and rally readers to their cause. "I do not care a damn for any art that is not used for propaganda," W. E. B. Du Bois once insisted, and novelist Richard Wright had attacked black authors like Zora Neale Hurston, who, to his mind, had not "taken advantage of their unique minority position" to develop "the highest possible pitch of social consciousness."[35]

Wright had certainly done his best in his own work to force many northern whites to contemplate the brutal realities of black life in the

South for the very first time. In May 1945, with white Americans still celebrating their triumph over Nazism, Wright's *Black Boy* had pointedly reminded them of the Jim Crow South's continuing mockery of the very principles for which they had supposedly gone to war in the first place. A loosely autobiographical account of Wright's childhood and adolescence in Mississippi, *Black Boy* was an even more powerful indictment of southern white racism than Lillian Smith's *Strange Fruit* because its author had suffered the injuries and injustices of the southern racial system personally and directly. In a photographic essay illustrating some of the most powerful scenes in the book, *Life* magazine described *Black Boy* as "a bitter, true story of a Negro boy's struggles against the life imposed on his race in the South" and "a powerful indictment of a caste system which is one of America's biggest problems."[36]

Young Richard's life had amounted to little more than an unbroken succession of brutal and degrading confrontations, not just with whites who saw him as "uppity" but with frustrated members of his own family who were trying to condition him simply to survive. In a society where white racism and racial stereotyping were dominant and thoroughly pervasive, Richard could not suppress the telltale signs of his intelligence and sense of individuality, neither of which enhanced a young black man's life expectancy in the South. By refusing to steal or to join his young peers in childish, light-hearted banter and by failing to conceal his interest in literature and ideas as well, Richard contradicted most of the fundamental behavioral stereotypes and expectations that whites imposed on blacks in order to justify keeping them "in their place." Unable to adapt to the delicately precise etiquette of Jim Crow or to relate to those blacks who did, Richard lived in a state of near total emotional and intellectual isolation, his environment akin to a pressure chamber that could explode at even the slightest misstep on his part. Such a world as the South afforded him was simply "too small to nourish human beings, especially Negro human beings," Wright had finally concluded, and in 1927, while still a teenager, he made his escape to Chicago, noting bitterly that the southern whites who insisted they "knew niggers had never known me—never known what I had thought, what I felt."[37]

Even as Wright headed north, however, he also realized "deep down" that he "could never really leave the South" because "my feelings had already been formed by the South, for there had been slowly instilled into my personality and consciousness, black though I was, the culture of the South." Ralph Ellison had developed the same understanding of his relationship with the South, and that relationship figured more prominently in his work. Ellison, whom Wright had befriended and encouraged when the two met in New York in the 1930s, had grown up middle class on the geographic edge of the South in Oklahoma City. Yet when he attended Tuskegee Institute in Alabama, he had been forced, like Wright, "to evaluate my own self-worth and the narrow freedom in which it existed, against those who would destroy me." Like Wright as well, though he had left the South, Ellison knew, "It has never left me, and the interests which I discovered there became my life." While working for the Federal Writers Project, Ellison met poet and essayist Sterling Brown, who became his mentor of sorts. Brown had once condemned segregation as "the denial of belonging" to black people, and Ellison's *Invisible Man* examined how it felt to have one's individual "belonging" denied by both whites and blacks. The novel's narrator is an eager and ambitious young black man who ultimately finds that he is effectively "invisible" as anything other than simply another unremarkable member of his race to whites who are unwilling to acknowledge the special talents and qualities that constitute his true identity as an individual.[38]

The young man is expelled from a Tuskegee-like black college after traumatizing one of the school's white trustees simply by acceding to the man's request to see what life was really like for poor, uneducated blacks in the South. The narrator's sense of self-worth fares no better, however, when he heads north, where he tries initially to conceal his southern roots, only to discover through a succession of emotionally painful encounters that as an individual he is just as invisible in many ways to the would-be saviors and champions of his own race as he is to whites. The person who seems to care most about him is the down-to-earth, decidedly southern, blues-singing Mary Rambo, who nurses him back to health after an explosion in the paint factory where he has found a job. Though he does not realize it at the time, Mary's statement, "I'm in New York, but New York ain't in me....Don't get corrupted," proves to be sound advice. When he finally contemplates emerging from the underground sanctuary where he has taken refuge, the narrator realizes, "I am nobody but myself." No longer ashamed of his roots as a southerner or as a descendant of slaves, he even contemplates returning to the South where he has suffered so much pain because he sometimes feels the need to "reaffirm all of it, the whole unhappy territory and all things loved and unlovable in it, for it is all a part of me."[39]

Invisible Man not only won the National Book Award for fiction in 1953 but was cited in 1965 by a group of two hundred writers, editors, and critics as the most distinguished American novel of the past twenty years. Because it appeared during the final countdown to the civil rights movement, many who read it at the time saw it primarily as a condemnation of the racism that blinded whites to the merits and distinctions of blacks as individuals. In recent decades it has become clearer that when Ellison's narrator observes, "Who knows but that on the lower frequencies, I speak for you," he is actually addressing whites as well as blacks and anyone else who confronts the increasingly potent homogenizing, identity-stripping forces of modern life.[40]

In this sense *Invisible Man* foreshadowed the work of Walker Percy and the post-Faulknerian, post–civil rights era generation of white writers, who instead of trying to explain a South that seemed impervious to racial change suddenly found themselves confronting a South rendered all but unrecognizable by economic and demographic change. In hindsight, when the protagonist of *Invisible Man* realizes that "perhaps to lose a sense of where you are implies the danger of losing a sense of who you are," he seems to anticipate Percy's Binx Bolling, who finds himself yearning to feel that he is "Somewhere and not Anywhere."[41]

Likewise, when Ellison's young man recognizes that his experience in the South is "all a part of me," he suggests what would happen when, freed from pressures to use their fiction as a form of protest, a new generation of black writers began to emphasize the strength and cultural vitality of black southerners who had resisted the potentially debilitating effects of slavery and Jim Crow to forge their own sense of identity, purpose, and belonging A hint of this development surfaced in survey data collected in the period 1964–76 that revealed significant changes in the attitudes of both southern and nonsouthern blacks toward identification with the region. In 1964 only 55 percent of southern black respondents had expressed "warm" feelings toward southerners, as opposed to nearly 90 percent of the southern whites polled. Yet by 1976 the proportion of southern blacks who expressed this warmth stood just at under 80 percent, only slightly below the percentage of white southerners who also felt this way. Analyzing this data, John Shelton Reed and Merle Black concluded that in 1964 "many Southern blacks may have been unclear about whether the category [southerners] was meant to include them and their black friends and neighbors. . . . By the 1970s, it appears, many Southern blacks did understand themselves to be southerners, and they were not unhappy about it." Throughout the 1980s and 1990s, similar polls produced similar results, and by 2001 surveys were even suggesting that the percentage of blacks in the South who identified themselves as southerners was actually slightly higher than that for whites.[42]

As we have seen, blacks who returned to the region pointed to its economic attractions, but for many of them the South was purely and simply "home." Asked why he had forsaken Manhattan to come back to Charleston, in the edge of the Mississippi Delta, actor Morgan Freeman explained, "Whatever I am I was nurtured there." When Anthony Walton reflected on his childhood experiences in a Chicago area neighborhood full of fellow migrants from Mississippi, he remembered "the same church sermons and suppers, the same food as our families had in the South," all of them "quite different from that of the mainstream north." For Walton, Chicago had simply been "the northernmost county of Mississippi." After college he had lived in Rhode Island and New York City and "tried to *be* a northerner because this was what I thought it would take to make it." In the end, however, his experience in the North taught him that regardless of where he lived, he was "first and last a southerner, as I was raised to be." Though fully aware of the sacrifice and suffering that Mississippi had exacted from his forebears, after visiting the state and acquainting himself with the "ghosts and bones" of its historical landscape, Walton understood that rather than forget them, he must "embrace the ghosts and cradle the bones and call them my own."[43]

Championing efforts to remove the Confederate insignia from the Georgia state flag, Atlanta journalist John Head declared in 1993, "The South is my home....I am a Southerner." Still, this did not obligate him, Head insisted, to accept either "the Confederacy as the South at its best" or "the Confederate battle flag as an emblem in which all Georgians can take pride." Some fifteen years later, Pulitzer Prize–winning poet Natasha Trethewey, who was born to a black mother and a white father and also raised in the South, sounded much like Head when she explained "There are other Souths beyond the white Confederate South....My South didn't lose the war. We won." Determined that her "belonging" would not be denied, Trethewey wanted to know, "Who can lay claim to the South? I don't want to take it away from anyone. I just want them to recognize that it's mine, too."[44]

For black writers no less than white, the South was clearly a constant source of vivid memories, and contrary to what some might have

Natasha Trethewey. Courtesy of Natasha Trethewey.

supposed, not all of them were unpleasant. Alex Haley's *Roots* unloosed a remarkable surge of interest in black ties to Africa, but Haley himself never left any doubt of his strong primary identification with the South, especially as he waxed nostalgic about his childhood Saturdays in Henning, Tennessee, which would be crammed with the "wagons, buggies, T-models, A-models" of people who had come to buy and sell farm produce. By noon, Haley recalled, "the town square was one big, mingled aroma....You'd smell watermelons cut open down the middle....You'd smell fried fish and then you'd smell fresh fish...celestial barbecue....It was our circus, our Carnival every Saturday." Haley was mainly reiterating the obvious when he explained, "I don't know anything I treasure more as a writer than being a southerner."[45]

Like Haley, black writers frequently stressed their ties to the South as a physical and sensory place. Tina McElroy Ansa discovered "how southern I am" while living outside the South and dreaming of "taking long car trips down red dirt roads that smelled rich and musty when a sudden cloudburst pounded them." Likewise, Alice Walker actually expressed sympathy for her "northern brothers" because "in the cities it cannot be so clear to one that he is a creature of the earth, feeling the soil between the toes, smelling the dust thrown up by the rain, loving the earth so much that one longs to taste it and sometimes does."[46]

When William Faulkner cited his attachment to Mississippi as proof that "you don't love because: you love despite," he was explaining that human connections to societies and cultures could be forged from painful as well as pleasurable experiences and recollections. Black southerners like Alice Walker might have understood this even better than Faulkner. Walker's fiction presented not only characters who are destroyed by white racism and oppression or allow it to destroy them, but those who transcend it to find fulfillment and meaning in their lives. The title character from Walker's *The Third Life of Grange Copeland* abandons his wife and son to flee to the North only to replicate in some measure the experience of Ellison's protagonist in *Invisible Man*. In the South, Grange may have been viewed with contempt by whites, but at least, he thinks, they "*knew he was there.*" On the other hand, "to people he met and passed daily" in the North, "he was not even in existence." Grange ultimately returns to the South because "though he hated it as much as anyplace else, where he was born would always be home for him…and every other place foreign."[47]

Upon his return, Grange Copeland discovers that his son Brownfield's life has become "a cesspool…an approximation of nothingness." Stripped of his manhood by the demands of living under Jim Crow, Brownfield tries to regain it by degrading and ultimately killing his wife. With his son in prison, Grange vows to protect his granddaughter, Ruth, from the forces that overwhelmed her father, and he undertakes to educate her "in the realities of life" as well as black history and the blues, which makes her feel "kin to something very old." Tragically Grange is finally forced to kill Brownfield in order to keep Ruth out of his clutches, and thus he ultimately surrenders his own life in order to save hers. Yet by fortifying her sense of identity and worth, Grange has given Ruth the self-confidence and knowledge to take on the wider, freer world beyond the South.[48]

In the wake of the civil rights movement, rather than continuing to stress the damaging effects of white persecution, black writers clearly enjoyed more freedom to explore all sorts of divisions and tensions among blacks themselves. Alice Walker stirred controversy with her critical treatment of black men in *Grange Copeland*, for the story is not simply one of blacks struggling against white oppression but of black women struggling against black male oppression as well. Walker later won the Pulitzer Prize for her moving story of a black woman's triumph over male abuse and exploitation in *The Color Purple*.[49]

Randall Kenan made no secret of his affection for the small town of Chinquapin, North Carolina, where he grew up. Yet Chinquapin was also the prototype for "Tim's Creek" whose suffocating social and moral conventions Kenan laid bare in his fiction. In *A Visitation of Spirits* a teenager struggles to come to terms with his homosexuality in a setting where exposure could mean only ostracism and community contempt. In the short story "Foundations of the Earth," a black grandmother's struggle to learn more about her dead grandson by getting to know his white former lover exposes the hypocrisy and narrow-mindedness that seems all too frequently to make southern communities inhospitable to those who are "different" either racially, religiously, or sexually.[50]

Unlike their white counterparts, most black writers who emerged in the wake of the civil rights movement did not object to being called "southern" writers, although some, like Kenan, wondered if they should be seen as both "black" and "southern." In reality, however, amid growing concern with what constituted the soul and essence of an "authentic" black identity, more and more black writers seemed to sense that their feelings of blackness might have come from the same experiences that also made them feel "southern." Northern-born writer Eddy Harris had once been ashamed that his slave ancestors had not rebelled against their white masters, but after going to the South and searching out the details of their lives and what they had managed to overcome, he was almost exultant, for he realized that his journey "to touch the soul of the South" had also led to the discovery of "my own black soul." As satellite TV and the Internet increasingly pulled tiny Chinquapin into the mass global culture, Randall Kenan realized that the religious traditions and family and community ties that had shaped both his southernness and his blackness might be living on borrowed time. "What's true of African-American identity is true for southern identity," he mused. "A lot of it is fragile and in danger, and a lot of it is so much a part of it that we don't even see it."[51]

11

"I Wouldn't Have It Any Other Way"

Division and Diversity in the Contemporary South

A common claim to southern identity and a shared concern about preserving it seemed to offer a promising foundation for interracial cooperation on a variety of regional issues. Yet as white and black southerners worked to forge the bonds of trust and understanding, they needed to address the present and the future; they faced no bigger challenge than learning to share a common but divisive past that each had experienced so differently. Stunned by the array of Confederate battle flags that seemed to confront him at every turn on his first visit to the South, Eddy Harris asked whites how they would "expect a black person to feel... in a society that so blatantly reminds him how emotionally tied his government still is to a system that fought to keep his ancestors in slavery." Flying the Confederate flag, Columbia attorney Carl B. Grant explained, "perpetuates the ideology of white supremacy": "That flag tells me that because of the color of my skin, I am considered a second-class citizen." When he heard whites defend the Confederate flag as part of their "heritage," Mississippian Rip Daniels served notice: "If it is your heritage, then it is my heritage to resist it with every fiber of my being." Black southerners objected to the Confederate flag as a public symbol not only because of its ties to white supremacy, but because they knew, as Natasha Trethewey put it, that "there are other Souths beyond the white Confederate South." As they worked to establish alternative visual representations of the South's past, African Americans were not denying their identity as southerners, but rather emphasizing its importance to them by refusing, as John Head explained, "to allow others to say what that means."[1]

The Confederate battle flag flew atop the state capitol in South Carolina until 2000, when the legislature bowed to the combined pressure of an NAACP tourism boycott of the state and the lobbying efforts of South Carolina business leaders and agreed to move the flag to a spot on the statehouse grounds. At that time the Confederate battle flag was also part of the state flags of both Georgia and Mississippi. In Georgia, Governor Zell Miller had failed in a well-publicized attempt to remove the Confederate insignia in 1992, but acting quickly and quietly, Governor Roy Barnes managed to push a new state flag through the state legislature in 2001 before defenders of the old flag had time to gather their forces. By election time the following year, however, they had rallied angrily to the support of Barnes's Republican challenger, Sonny Perdue, who promised, if elected, to hold a statewide referendum on restoring the old flag. Strong backing from the "flaggers" doubtless contributed to Perdue's victory, but once in office and under heavy pressure from Atlanta business leaders, he ultimately offered only another alternative to the Barnes flag, this one based not on the battle flag but on the Stars and Bars, the first official flag of the Confederacy, which had relatively little direct popular association with slavery or the defense of segregation. In 2004 voters approved this flag compromise decisively, making it Georgia's third in three years.[2]

In Mississippi, after a series of bitter, racially tense hearings and rallies, two-thirds of the voters opposed any effort to strip the state banner of the Confederate insignia that it had borne for 110 years. Enthusiasm or distaste for the Confederate flag generally followed racial lines, and especially so in Mississippi. In both Georgia and South Carolina, however, business leaders played a crucial and aggressive role in selling the idea of a change. The Mississippi business community, on the other hand, was less united and energized on this issue. A spokesman for the Nissan Corporation, which had recently announced plans to open an assembly plant in Mississippi, declined to take a position on what he saw as a "state issue." Meanwhile, a local industrial recruiter offered a glimpse into the real motivation for the business community's involvement in such issues when he predicted that the vote to keep the Confederate emblem would cause no problem in attracting new industry to Mississippi "unless Jesse Jackson says he's going to put pickets in every Nissan dealership."[3]

If business leaders saw the flag question as simply what one economic developer called a "pocketbook issue," it was nonetheless a major and divisive political distraction that could, as it did in Georgia in 2003, prevent lawmakers from addressing more substantive and urgent issues such as education and health care. Former Atlanta mayor Andrew Young, a prominent veteran of the civil rights movement, announced in 2001 that he simply didn't "give a damn" about the state flag and urged the legislature to concentrate on more fundamental concerns. Later, as Mississippians prepared to vote in their flag referendum, a young black man admitted, "It don't bother me either way it goes.... Money's my problem. As far as the flag and that kind of shit, I don't care. I can't live off a flag."[4]

Throughout the South blacks and whites also clashed over monuments, streets, schools, and parks named for prominent Confederates like Jefferson Davis and Nathan Bedford Forrest, whose troops were charged with the massacre of black Union soldiers at Fort Pillow in 1864. In New Orleans the school board adopted a policy against having schools named for slaveholders and had already changed the names of twenty-one other schools before deciding in 1998 to make George Washington Elementary into Dr. Charles Richard Drew Elementary in order to honor a black surgeon lauded for his research in preserving plasma.[5]

In addition to objecting to public monuments to the practitioners and defenders of slavery, a number of black leaders set out to establish memorials to those who had led the crusade to overturn the oppressive racial system that white southerners had erected in the wake of Reconstruction. By 2003 Alabama, Florida, Georgia, Louisiana, Mississippi, and Texas accounted for more than 75 percent of the cities with streets named for Rev. Martin Luther King Jr. Civil rights museums and memorials had sprung up throughout the South, from Memphis to Montgomery and Birmingham, with its renovated Kelly Ingram Park, where demonstrators had so memorably thrown themselves against Bull Connor's police dogs and fire hoses in 1963. The new civil rights park was a fitting tribute, thought one supporter, to the deeds that had made this place "the Iwo Jima of the Civil Rights movement." Regardless of where their personal feelings lay, white elected officials found it difficult to openly resist calls for such memorials, which they sometimes justified, albeit quietly, to their white constituents as relatively meaningless gestures that would undercut black demands for more substantive concessions and perhaps even boost the local tourist economy.[6]

In what was largely a symbolic process, Byron De La Beckwith was tried and finally convicted in 1994 of the murder of Medgar Evers some

The South and America since World War II

thirty years earlier, and the first decade of the twenty-first century saw a number of other belated "atonement" trials of longtime suspects in some of the civil rights era's worst atrocities. In 2001 Thomas E. Blanton was found guilty and sentenced to four life sentences in the 1963 bombing that had killed four black girls in Birmingham's Sixteenth Street Baptist Church. Four years later Edgar Ray Killen received three twenty-year sentences for his role in the slaying of civil rights workers Andrew Goodman, Michael Schwerner, and James Chaney at Philadelphia, Mississippi, in 1964. Although the FBI reopened the investigation of the Emmett Till murder in 2004, a Mississippi grand jury ultimately declined to indict Carolyn Bryant, the widow of Roy Bryant, one of the men who had killed the young Till, ostensibly for his flirtatious behavior toward her in 1955.

A resolution formally apologizing to the Till family died in committee in the state legislature in 2007, but after several months of wrangling, a special Tallahatchie County commission managed to draft a resolution declaring that members of the community were "profoundly sorry for what was done in this community to your loved one." The commission also unveiled a historical marker commemorating the event and laid out plans for a tour of key sites in the case. This event went hand-in-hand with plans to raise money to refurbish the courthouse at Sumner, where the trial was held. As one journalist observed, this was a case where "conscience and commerce" were wholly compatible, for beyond whatever sincere desire there may have been to make amends, some in the impoverished county were obviously counting on the effort to document the Till tragedy to generate some tourism dollars as well.[7]

Motives might also have been subject to some question in 2007 when, under pressure from the NAACP, the legislatures of Virginia, Maryland, North Carolina, and Alabama passed resolutions expressing "profound regret" for their state's role in promoting and sustaining slavery. State Senator Henry L. Marsh III of Virginia, a black Democrat who played a key role in getting the apology resolution through a majority Republican legislature, explained that he foresaw no "true progress in this country until we get a reconciliation and an honest dialogue about race and slavery." As Georgia lawmakers debated a similar statute, the *Atlanta Journal-Constitution* editorialized that although an apology would "not change Georgia's past," it would "confirm that Georgia is committed to a better future for all its citizens."[8]

In reality, however, it was not so clear what such expressions of regret, carefully worded so as to avoid any suggestion of a legal obligation to provide reparations for slavery, really meant or could be expected to achieve. In Virginia, one of the Republican state senators who later voted for the official apology apparently had first asked sarcastically whether Jews should be forced to apologize "for killing Christ" and suggested that black Virginians should simply "get over" slavery. Notably, in 2010 Virginia's Republican governor Bob McDonnell would declare April "Confederate History Month," with no initial reference to slavery at all. In Georgia, State Senate President Pro-tem Eric Johnson, a white Republican, initially found the NAACP's demand for an apology "rather silly" but agreed to go along with the proposal so long as the word "apology" itself was not used. "An apology is from someone who did wrong to someone who was wronged," Johnson explained. "That's not going to happen." Johnson eventually agreed to support the resolution because, more than anything, he admitted, he just wanted to "get it over with." His Republican colleague, State Senator Jeff Mullis, went a step further in demonstrating just how meaningless the whole business was to him when he reportedly offered to attach the slavery apology resolution to his oft-submitted bill calling for April to be designated "Confederate History and Heritage Month."[9]

Some of the South's most racially conservative white lawmakers refused to support such resolutions unless language such as "the vestiges of slavery are ever before African American citizens" were removed. Shorn of such sentiments, these statements might be seen not as a stepping stone toward further discussion of the obligations of the present to the past, but as just the opposite, a quick and relatively painless means of achieving closure on a debate whose end might not otherwise be anywhere in sight.[10]

By the same token, as in conflicts over state flags and monuments, it was not always clear that black leaders who indulged in the politics of symbolic gestures were addressing the most urgent concerns of their constituents. When an Annapolis councilman called for the former slave port to apologize for the "perpetual pain, distrust and bitterness" caused to black people, a writer to the *Baltimore Sun* allowed that she would "prefer that the aldermen have a resolution to atone for the lack of a decent middle school curriculum in Anne Arundel County."[11]

Although continued hammering away on symbolic issues risked a return to greater racial polarization on other matters of greater immediate import to the poor and disadvantaged, it was both easier and more politically expedient for some black leaders to focus on attacking the symbols of past white oppression than to confront pressing contemporary concerns about drug use, teenage pregnancy, and family stability among African Americans. In 1986 slightly fewer than half of the black Americans surveyed thought the NAACP was an effective leadership organization. By 2007 the figure was just under a third. As columnist Leonard Pitts put it, the NAACP's insistence on pursuing largely symbolic initiatives such as apologies for slavery suggested to some that the organization had become "stagnant, static and marginal to today's struggle."[12]

As the twenty-first century unfolded, there was reason to think that the old politics of racial grievance was losing its appeal with some black voters, especially those who had achieved a measure of economic security. From her political beginnings in the Georgia legislature, Representative Cynthia McKinney had never hesitated to play the "race card." McKinney lost her Georgia congressional seat in 2004 to Denise Majette, a decidedly more conservative black challenger with little political experience. Majette had benefited from Republican crossover voting in the Democratic primary but also claimed a surprising one-third of the black vote in a district long thought safe for McKinney. Although the fiery McKinney regained her post when Majette sought a Senate seat in 2004, her controversial statements and a highly publicized run-in with a congressional security officer reinforced her reputation for erratic, confrontational behavior. Promising more dignified and responsible representation, another black challenger, DeKalb County Commissioner Hank Johnson, bested McKinney for the Democratic nomination in 2006, winning an overwhelming percentage of the white vote and capturing an estimated 50 percent of the black vote as well. Meanwhile, as she steered her city through the economic downturn that struck the nation during the latter months of her administration, Mayor Shirley Franklin of Atlanta clearly put the city's fiscal health above the demands of some of her black supporters on more than one occasion. Finally, in April 2010 voters in Columbia, South Carolina, elected former State Department of Probation, Pardon, and Parole Director Steve Benjamin as the city's first black mayor after Benjamin promised to increase funding for law enforcement while cutting back on spending overall.[13]

Southern blacks were certainly in tune with national trends as worries grew that the widening economic gap between upwardly mobile middle- and lower-class blacks was creating a similar divide in values and priorities. One-third (slightly more than the national average) of the southern black participants in a national survey released in November 2007 believed that middle-class and poor blacks held few if any common values. The poll also revealed that whereas 57 percent of the black Americans questioned in 1986 had believed that life would be better for blacks in the future, twenty years later only 44 percent felt this way. Surprisingly to some, however, 69 percent of the southern blacks who participated in the survey claimed to be "very satisfied" with their own current circumstances, as opposed to only 55 percent in the Northeast, 57 percent in the West, and 58 percent in the Midwest. In fact, the South was the only part of the country where the level of satisfaction for blacks was comparable to that for whites (72 percent).[14]

It seems fair to assume that relatively few of the black respondents who expressed satisfaction with their circumstances at that point were residents of New Orleans, for when Hurricane Katrina hit that city on August 29, 2005, it drew back the curtain on a tragedy that was both long in the making and at once local, regional, and national in its implications. Although spared the worst of Katrina's winds, the city did not escape its brutal watery assault, as levee breaks and overflows quickly put 80 percent of New Orleans under water. Katrina's assault destroyed as many as 200,000 homes, and though estimates vary considerably, the storm likely killed five hundred to seven hundred residents outright and contributed to the subsequent deaths of many others.[15]

Reports of widespread deaths from drowning and exposure, particularly among the elderly, were sobering reminders of the devastating power of nature, but some alarming stories also centered on the fate and behavior of the storm's survivors. With some twenty thousand people reportedly crammed into the city's Superdome arena for several days, network reporters on the scene described trash piled several feet deep throughout the facility and backed-up toilets forcing inhabitants to relieve themselves wherever they could. On the outside, some reports of massive, citywide looting were clearly exaggerated, but video journalists nonetheless captured several disturbing scenes on tape. Some who emerged from stores with armloads of groceries insisted that they had been forced to take whatever food they could find in order to survive. Others, however, openly and almost gleefully pillaged, wading through waist-deep water pushing floating garbage cans filled with clothing, jewelry, and other goods, while other, less enterprising looters simply contented themselves with filling their arms with as much merchandise as they could carry. In some parts of the otherwise almost abandoned city, emergency personnel reported being fired upon as they tried to rescue people stranded on their porches and rooftops.[16]

The specter of race loomed ominous and heavy throughout the entire Katrina ordeal. Although some whites obviously engaged in various forms of criminal activity in the immediate aftermath of Katrina, photos and video of looting by blacks evoked images of the urban riots of the 1960s and set conservative commentators to blaming federal antipoverty programs for creating a permanent criminal element among urban blacks. Black leaders complained bitterly about the contrasting captions of two wire service photos, one showing a black man walking through "chest deep flood water after *looting* a grocery store," the other showing two whites wading through "chest deep water after *finding* bread and soda from a local grocery store" (all emphasis mine).[17]

Still, even discounting bias and exaggeration, there was enough visual and eyewitness evidence to make stunned onlookers wonder how what they were seeing and hearing could actually be happening in an American city in 2005. A thorough search for explanations would span the nearly three hundred years of New Orleans's history, but events and trends since World War II can certainly provide some helpful context. As historian Kent B. Germany described it, in the mid-1950s New Orleans had been "one of the most impoverished, most unequal, most violent, and least educated places in the United States." Half the black residents lived below the poverty line, and the top fifth of the city's population collected 50 percent of its total income, while the bottom fifth accounted for only 4 percent. Slightly fewer than one-third of black men age twenty-five to forty-four had made it beyond middle school.[18]

If there were a city anywhere that stood in need of President Lyndon B. Johnson's War on Poverty, it was surely New Orleans, and the impact of federal programs of that era on the Crescent City was nothing short of profound. By the end of the decade, the Model Cities Program, urban renewal, and a number of other federal initiatives had combined to bring more than $20 million into New Orleans's black neighborhoods. Meanwhile, with their emphasis on local participation, the antipoverty programs had created operational bases for black community-based organizations and leaders looking to carve out spheres of influence within the city's political network. The Voting Rights Act of 1965 had effectively doubled the black electorate in a very short time, and it appeared that the city's African American population had found its collective voice in a group of powerful black spokesmen backed by a host of well-organized and politically savvy community groups. In the 1970s, with the oil industry booming, the poverty rate had gone down and the futuristic Superdome had gone up, along with a number of shiny high-rise monuments to the unprecedented prosperity that now seemed well within the city's grasp.[19]

The 1980s would not be nearly so kind to New Orleans, however. When the oil bubble burst, it took with it a number of the port city's better jobs and plunged New Orleans into a depression, which, in a sense, has gripped it ever since. As the loss of jobs in oil underscored that industry's importance to the city's economy, the once sizable flow of funds through the federal pipeline was suddenly reduced to a comparative trickle. Between 1981 and 1985 the Reagan administration managed to cut federal support for cities by 50 percent and some other complementary programs by as much as 80 percent. In addition to destroying the operating bases of black political advocates, such moves threatened, as Mayor Ernest Morial warned, to create two societies, "one rich and one poor." As whites fled to the suburbs, their share of the city's population had already dropped from 62 percent in 1960 to 40 percent in 1980, and it would plummet to 28 percent over the next twenty years. If conditions on the eve of Katrina's onslaught did not seem as severe as they had been fifty years earlier, the racial disparities in poverty, wealth, education, and overall quality of life were not only still there but apparently widening. In short, New Orleans was just the sort of a place where a natural disaster would in many ways only illuminate and exacerbate the human disaster that bigotry, greed, and indifference had already inflicted.[20]

The changing demographic profile of New Orleans's ill-fated Lower Ninth Ward seemed to tell much of the city's story in microcosm. The Lower Ninth's nonwhite population had risen from less than one-third in 1940 to almost three-fourths by 1970. By 2000 its residents were 90 percent African American, and 33 percent of them lived in poverty. In a city known for its nearly astronomical homicide rate, the area had also become "the murder capital of the murder capital," according to one criminologist, as drug dealers and junkies moved into its vacant, decaying buildings, making it unsafe for children to play outside at any hour. As an "extreme poverty" neighborhood where at least 40 percent of the residents lived in families with incomes below the poverty line, the Lower Ninth Ward was actually little different in many respects from

25 percent of the neighborhoods in New Orleans, which ranked second in the nation in the percentage of its poor population living in such concentrated poverty areas in 2000.[21]

The city's flooded areas contained 80 percent of its minority population, a fact not lost on those effectively trapped in these neighborhoods—an estimated 54 percent of poor households in New Orleans had no vehicle in 2000—some of whom even believed that the levee failures that brought them such misery were no random act of nature but a willful, deliberate move to divert the high water from white residential areas. "I don't believe that levee broke like that," declared one Lower Ninth Ward resident. "I believe they broke that levee to save where high-class people stay." Some ten thousand people had been displaced when levees were dynamited during the historic 1927 flood, and blacks in New Orleans had long harbored suspicions that breaches had been deliberately blown in the levees during Hurricane Betsy back in 1965. Overall, the degree of mistrust and suspicion of whites in the aftermath of Katrina was truly striking. In the Lower Ninth, survivors huddled silently in darkened, watery, molding dwellings rather than answer the knocks and calls of white would-be rescuers, who they feared might haul them off against their will to suffer the real and rumored horrors of the Superdome. Outside, the faint, sickening smell of decaying bodies left residents worried about neighbors unseen since the onset of the storm. In the end, after struggling to survive without power and running water for as long as they could, the people of the Lower Ninth Ward were forced to yield to the inevitable, and two years after Katrina struck, a neighborhood that was once home to nineteen thousand people could claim fewer than one thousand residents.[22]

By that point, the city's overall population had recovered to two-thirds of its former size, but its composition was noticeably different. Before Katrina roughly 76 percent of New Orleans's residents were black, but now blacks accounted for only an estimated 58 percent of the population. This sparked accusations that Katrina had provided the city's white elites with the perfect opportunity to rid New Orleans of much of its poor, often dependent black population. Public housing had long been cited as the main breeding ground for the city's well-publicized problems with drugs and violent crime, and in the wake of the storm Republican Congressman Richard H. Baker had even chortled, "We finally cleaned up public housing in New Orleans," although he admitted, "We couldn't do it, God did it." Five thousand families had lived in the city's public housing before Katrina, but a year after the storm only eleven hundred units were occupied. Acting with federal approval and with the blessing of U.S. Housing and Urban Development executives, local officials announced plans to demolish more than forty-five hundred government apartments, many of which, outraged black leaders charged, were perfectly livable or certainly salvageable at an average cost of roughly $10,000 per apartment. HUD spokesmen announced later that after spending $762 million to tear down the existing units, the agency would build only 744 new "mixed-income" dwellings that would attract somewhat higher income families to the neighborhood.[23]

More than one commentator implied that the Bush administration's reaction to the situation in New Orleans would have been much swifter and more effective had the storm's ravages been concentrated in affluent white neighborhoods. Such allegations were almost impossible to substantiate, but at the very least the White House's belated, almost indifferent response to the suffering that Katrina inflicted on the people of New Orleans gave off the distinct odor of partisan politics. Louisiana governor Kathleen Blanco was a Democrat, as were the state's senior senator and New Orleans native, Mary Landrieu, and the city's African American mayor, Ray Nagin. On the other hand, Mississippi's governor was powerful lobbyist and former Republican national chairman Haley Barbour, and its senators were GOP stalwarts Thad Cochran and Trent Lott. President George W. Bush had carried both states in 2000 and 2004, but his numbers in New Orleans itself had barely cleared 20 percent in either election. It was difficult to separate these political realities from the fact that although 75 percent of the housing damage from Katrina had come in Louisiana, 70 percent of the Federal Emergency Management Administration's funding for alternative housing wound up in Mississippi. Likewise, although Katrina cost Louisiana an estimated twenty-six hundred hospital beds and Mississippi only seventy-nine, the latter received 38 percent of federal hospital-recovery funding. Mississippi was also the only state where the Bush administration waived the requirement that 50 percent of Community Block Grant funds must be spent on lower-income assistance programs. (Two years after Katrina such programs had received only 10 percent of the federal relief funds allocated to the state.) Reflecting on the partisan climate surrounding the federal recovery effort, former FEMA director Michael Brown conceded, "There was a feeling around the White House that Louisiana had a white, female Democratic governor, and we have a chance to rub her nose in it."[24]

Blanco's nose suffered mightily in the wake of the disaster. The *New Orleans Times-Picayune* described her as "at once paralyzed and desperate" during the crisis, and she had indeed seemed a bit panicked when she authorized the National Guard to "shoot to kill" the looters in New Orleans. She also came under fire herself for having fewer than half of the state's available guardsmen on alert when the storm hit and for rejecting the Bush administration's offer to federalize the Louisiana guard in the interest of efficiency, even though some administration insiders admitted that the offer itself had been an attempt to upstage the governor. The mortal blow to Blanco's political fortunes, however, came with the failure of her own "Road Home" program, designed to use federal funds to assist Louisiana's hurricane victims in repairing or selling their damaged residences. The program began in the summer of 2006, but as of March 2007 no more than 3,000 out of an estimated 115,000 applicants had received any payments. Two months later, complaining of Republican harassment, Blanco announced that she would not seek a second gubernatorial tern in the upcoming November election.[25]

Ray Nagin also drew widespread criticism for failing to use the 804 municipal and school buses at his disposal to evacuate some of the city's 134,000 residents who had no access to cars. Though still embattled, the mayor managed to win reelection in 2006, playing on black racial anxieties without hesitation; with many black New Orleanians still displaced and the city's African American population reduced dramatically, he suggested a white conspiracy to prevent blacks from returning and declared that it was God's will that New Orleans remain "a chocolate city."[26]

Yet although it had come at a terribly high price, there was evidence that the displacement of the city's poorest blacks had reduced racial polarization in New Orleans. A 2009 poll showed surprising agreement across racial lines on the most critical priorities for the next mayor. Black respondents actually put slightly more emphasis on both crime and education than did whites, and both groups showed overwhelming concern with the city's reputation for government corruption. Such sentiments came through a year later in the words of Mitch Landrieu, who, after becoming the city's first white mayor since his father left office in 1978, declared in his inaugural address, "Change starts here. Change starts now.... This world and we deserve a better New Orleans." As is often the case, the city's 2010 mayoral race had been a complicated affair, one in which Landrieu doubtless benefited from sharing the ballot with ten other candidates. Yet there was no denying that he collected 63 percent of the black vote, campaigning under the banner of "One team. One fight. One voice. One city."[27]

Former mayor Nagin had shown no such interest in unity when he complained shortly after Katrina that New Orleans was being "overrun with Mexican workers" who were taking jobs in the rebuilding effort that should have gone to displaced black residents. In reality, Nagin was raising what had become a sensitive issue for many African Americans across a South where racial differences were no longer mere matters of black and white. Blue-collar workers in the South may have found little to like in southern wage scales, but they looked very good indeed to a flood of Hispanic immigrants who poured into the region in the 1990s and after. A 2005 study by the Pew Hispanic Center showed the Hispanic population growing much more rapidly in the South than elsewhere in the nation. Of the ten states with the greatest change in Hispanic population between 1990 and 2000, seven were in the South. Six of these—North Carolina (394 percent), Arkansas (337 percent), Georgia (300 percent), Tennessee (278 percent), South Carolina (211 percent), and Alabama (208 percent)—had seen their Hispanic populations increase by more than 200 percent over the decade. Examining the counties in these states with the most dramatic Hispanic population growth, researchers found that a typical Hispanic immigrant to the South was a young male around twenty-seven years old without either a high school diploma or any significant facility with English. More than half of those studied had arrived since 1995, and well over half were also in the country illegally. In North Carolina, the state with the fastest growing Hispanic population, estimates put the number of illegals at around 300,000, or roughly 65 percent of the Hispanic population.[28]

When North Carolina congresswoman Sue Myrick introduced legislation to make a single DUI conviction a deportable offense for illegals and to fine employers $10,000 for every illegal alien found on the payroll, opponents argued that the measure might damage many sectors of the state's economy that were dependent on immigrant workers. Without them, one observer argued, "there wouldn't be an agriculture industry in North Carolina...because picking tobacco is hot and hard and harvesting Christmas trees is cold and hard. Farmers can't hire enough local people to do the work anymore." In 2006 a raid by federal immigration officials cost Crider, Inc., roughly 75 percent of the workforce at its Still-more, Georgia, chicken processing plant. In response executives boosted pay rates by more than a dollar an hour and hired about two hundred new workers from the southeast Georgia region, most of them black. This seemed to suggest that Hispanics had been claiming jobs that, had they paid just a bit better, would have been snapped up by locals. Yet it was not long before disputes over wages and working conditions began to surface. Plant managers complained of declining productivity and rising absenteeism, which the remaining Hispanic employees blamed on their new black coworkers. By January 2007 Crider executives had begun to recruit new employees among Laotian Hmong immigrants living in Minnesota. When this effort failed to ameliorate their labor shortage, Crider's management even fashioned an agreement with the Georgia Department of Corrections to employ probationers who could use their wages to pay off their fines.[29]

Despite the hue and cry to the contrary, the Pew researchers found that a county's increases in Hispanic employment generally came in tandem with expanded job opportunities for whites and blacks as well. Certainly, with Hispanic workers earning only about $16,000 per year in 2008, it was hard to believe that they could be taking the region's better jobs away from anyone. This concentration in low-wage employment, coupled with the steadily swelling influx of immigrants, caused the poverty rate for Hispanics in the six southern states with the most rapidly expanding Hispanic population to shoot up by 30 percent during the 1990s, in contrast to a 4 percent decline in Hispanic poverty nationwide. In a region where welfare benefits were not exactly generous, statistics showing the average Hispanic family was significantly larger than the average black or white family made the escalating poverty rate seem even more critical.[30]

This tendency toward larger families among Hispanics could also put a significant strain on often cash-strapped rural school systems struggling to absorb students from homes where English was often an all but unknown tongue. According to the Pew study's estimate that 65 percent of North Carolina's Hispanic population was undocumented, by 2005 the state was spending an estimated $487,000 educating children whose parents were in the United States illegally. On this front there seemed to be no relief in sight, for Hispanic students, who had made up 4 percent of the school-age population in these states in 2001, were estimated to account for 10 percent by 2007.[31]

Some southern parents were quick to complain that the growing Hispanic presence was impeding their children's education. "I don't have a problem with the Mexicans or the whites or nobody," said a black mother in Siler City, North Carolina, "but I do have a problem when my daughter comes home from school and says the teacher didn't have time to teach me or show me how to do my homework because she had to take up all her time to teach those Mexicans because they don't understand." Such complaints had some validity, of course, but the overriding source of black antagonism toward Hispanics was the firm conviction among many black southerners that, regardless of what the experts said, Hispanic workers were taking jobs that should have been theirs. The jobless rate for black men in Georgia was nearly triple that for Hispanic men in 2006, and despite the meager earnings of Hispanic workers, across the old Confederacy the median household income for foreign-born Hispanics was still nearly 10 percent higher than for blacks. "If you have ten factory openings, I would say Hispanics would get the majority of the jobs now," said Joyce Taylor, the black county clerk in Atkinson County, Georgia, near the Florida line. The tension between blacks and Hispanics in the South Georgia area seemed to erupt in incidents such as the robbery-murder of six Mexican farm workers in nearby Tifton and the subsequent arrest of four black men for the crime.[32]

Black workers worried not only about losing their jobs to Hispanics but about losing traction in their efforts to make their jobs better. In the 1980s a resolute group of black women had succeeded in organizing the predominantly female workforce at the Delta Pride catfish processing plant near Indianola, Mississippi. More than twenty years later, some workers could still remember all too well the thirteen-hour days standing in ankle-deep water skinning as many as twenty-eight catfish a minute, with their restroom visits timed and occasionally observed by white male supervisors. These women feared that the gains of the ensuing decades might be swept away when the area began to attract large numbers of Hispanic immigrants willing to accept whatever wages and working conditions they were offered. The union representative in the original organizing campaign, Sarah Claree White, admitted, "We struggle to hold onto what we have....Now with the Hispanic workers, it's getting harder and harder as far as concessions go." When White tried to explain the importance of union safeguards to new, frequently undocumented Hispanic workers at the Delta's catfish plants, she found, "Mostly they're afraid and desperate and will do whatever to keep food on their table. Just like us." At the same time, efforts to preach unity with Hispanics often fell on deaf ears among blacks who showed little interest in "banding together" when "the baby needs diapers or you can't afford the rent."[33]

After complaints about unreasonable policies, such as the denial of bathroom breaks and requirements that workers cut up forty-two chickens a minute over an eight-hour shift, the predominantly Hispanic workforce at the Koch Foods plant in Morristown, Tennessee, voted to affiliate with the United Food and Commercial Workers in 2005. Still, such union victories were rare among Hispanics, whose tenuous legal and economic status made it difficult for them to take a stand against management or form a united front with their black coworkers, who, understandably perhaps, frequently welcomed INS raids or employer purges of illegals. Commenting in 2000 on tensions between black and white workers at the mammoth Smithfield Packing Company plant in Tar Heel, North Carolina, one black worker predicted, "There's a day coming soon where the Mexicans are going to catch hell from the blacks, the way the blacks caught it from the whites."[34]

Blacks had accounted for just one in five of the Smithfield plant's workforce in November 2006 when an INS raid led to the arrest of twenty-one workers and triggered a two-year exodus of more than a thousand Hispanic employees. Two organizing campaigns had failed at the plant in the 1990s, and union leaders charged that the raid had actually been instigated by company executives after several Hispanics began to speak out in favor of unionization. In the aftermath of the incident, with the number of Hispanic workers dropping steadily, their less vulnerable black counterparts stepped forward to take the lead in drumming up union support. Some of the Hispanics who remained doubtless cooperated with this effort, but when 52 percent of the plant's workers voted in December 2008 to affiliate with the United Food and Commercial Workers, the most critical factor might have been that blacks now made up close to 60 percent of a workforce that had been more than 50 percent Hispanic only two years earlier.[35]

Tension and uncertainty also marked political interaction between blacks and Hispanics in the South, especially after the Census Bureau announced in 2003 that Hispanics had surpassed blacks to become the nation's largest minority group. Many liberal observers had presumed that Hispanic immigrants would join blacks in a long-anticipated coalition of have-nots that low-income whites had largely spurned, but the two groups sometimes found themselves pitted against each other politically when it came to some of the programs designed to assist minorities and the disadvantaged. For example, black legislators in Georgia opposed a measure in 2001 that made Hispanic businesses eligible for a program designed to support and strengthen minority business in the state. In Dallas, where Hispanic immigration was hardly a new development, the two groups clashed repeatedly over control of the public schools. Black leaders, one observer noted, tended to portray Hispanics as "Juanito-come-latelies" who were "trying to ride on black civil rights victories" when they had done none of the dirty and dangerous work of organizing and protesting. "The problem we have with them," a Dallas NAACP leader explained, "is that they think that because they have the majority in the school district or the city that somehow entitles them to a leg up on other minorities." In retort, a Hispanic lawyer complained, "Whatever blacks want, they get....They lead by intimidation. They threaten to riot or boycott. People don't feel threatened by us because we haven't threatened to burn the city down."[36]

Although some political observers persisted in expecting Hispanics to vote with the same solidarity they had observed among African Americans, in their political allegiances they were neither as unified nor as predictable as blacks. Hispanic voters also generally turned out at a much lower rate than blacks and, except in Texas and Florida, represented a much smaller portion of the population. Despite the recent heavy influx of Hispanics in both North Carolina and Georgia, Texas and Florida were the only southern states where Hispanics typically accounted for more than a negligible share of voters. As of 2007 forty of Texas's forty-one Hispanic legislators were Democrats, but in Florida, with its concentration of conservative anti-Castro Cubans, seventeen of nineteen Hispanic lawmakers were Republicans. There was but one Democrat among the seven Hispanics serving in the legislatures of Georgia, the Carolinas, and Tennessee in 2007.[37]

In addition to the very real potential to change the political mix, the cultural impact of the Hispanic influx was substantial. Mexican cuisine had begun to influence southwestern foodways well before World War II, and elsewhere in the South, especially in the cities, it had gained a foothold even before the immigration surge of the 1990s brought dramatic changes to the region's dining habits. Atlanta, which had only 18 Mexican restaurants in 1977, boasted 162 in 2005. With immigrants flocking to jobs in local poultry plants, even Laurel, Mississippi, a town of eighteen thousand, sported not only four Mexican restaurants but three Mexican food markets in 2008. From Arkansas to Alabama to the Carolinas the story was much the same, even in smaller towns where the Hispanic population had become more visible only in recent years.[38]

In Texas and South Florida especially, Hispanic musical influences had been apparent for a long time. After World War II Tex-Mex or Tejano music had fused south-of-the-border instrumental and vocal stylings, blues, rhythm and blues, honky-tonk, and rockabilly into a truly distinctive style. As the Texas-born son of migrant workers, Tex-Mex star Freddie Fender was best known for his rockabilly-styled "Wasted Days and Wasted Nights" and the more traditional country though definitely Hispanic-inspired "Before the Next Teardrop Falls." Though she came along a bit later, Fender's fellow Texan Rosie Flores was equally comfortable living up to her moniker as a "Rockabilly Filly" or belting out a honky-tonk classic like "God May Forgive You, But I Don't." In 1994 Selena Quintanilla Perez, known popularly simply as Selena, became the first Tejano artist to win a Grammy. Though Selena's contemporary Tish Hinojosa was known more as an alternative artist, she offered a *fronteriza* or "border" sound that was a seamless blend of folk, Tex-Mex, and country and won her a broad following well beyond her native Southwest.[39]

In South Florida, meanwhile, Hispanic immigration from the Caribbean (sometimes via New York City) brought in the more dance-oriented rhythms of salsa. In salsa a mixture of percussion instruments, horns, and strings blended with jazz, rhythm and blues, and the big-band sound to produce a broad array of combinations, all with a decidedly Latin tempo and feel. These Caribbean stylings made their first significant inroads with non-Hispanic audiences in the music of Cuban-born Gloria Estefan, whose family had fled to Miami after Fidel Castro's takeover in 1959. Riding the crest of the disco craze, Estefan and her group had been well known in Central and South America before releasing their first English-only album in 1984. The following year the single "Conga" became the first song to make *Billboard*'s Pop, Latin, Soul, and Dance charts simultaneously. Estefan's career took off, and in 1989, when the group released "Let It Loose," a triple-platinum album that contained four top-ten singles, they were billed as Gloria Estefan and the Miami Sound Machine. Estefan went on to win seven Grammys and sell 90 million albums, her astonishing success paving the way for a new generation of popular purveyors of the Miami sound, such as the Puerto Rican transplant Ricky Martin.[40]

As the twenty-first century unfolded, the broad popularity of Hispanic music in the South and elsewhere reflected an increased interest in ethnic and subregional differences at a time when many feared globalization was about to obliterate such cultural distinctions. Cajun music also enjoyed a revival of interest, as did its more syncopated cousin, Zydeco, which had originated among the French-speaking black Creoles of southwestern Louisiana. Zydeco typically featured some form of accordion or "button box" and a washboard or "rubboard" in combination with other instruments, ranging from fiddles to drums to keyboards. Like so many strains of southern music, Zydeco proved a veritable sponge for other influences, from blues to country to rhythm and blues, soul, and rock 'n' roll. Some listeners even detected a little Tex-Mex in the sound of the flamboyant Buckwheat Zydeco, who delighted 3 billion television viewers worldwide with his rendition of Hank Williams's Cajun classic "Jambalaya" during the closing ceremonies of the 1996 Olympics in Atlanta. Buckwheat's fan base had expanded dramatically after his appearance in the 1987 film *The Big Easy*. Likewise, in 2000, even as critics continued to bemoan contemporary country music's loss of authenticity, the box-office smash *O Brother, Where Art Thou?* helped to reignite interest in the old-time hillbilly and string-band music of the pre–World War II era. The movie's soundtrack had sold nearly 7.5 million copies by 2008, as audiences rediscovered the mournful, lonesome sound of artists like Ralph Stanley and classic songs such as the Carter Family's "Keep on the Sunny Side" and Albert Brumley's "I'll Fly Away."[41]

Meanwhile, although older African Americans expressed concerns that younger blacks showed relatively little interest in their blues heritage, the hip-hop generation nonetheless gave rise to a new, assertively southern style. The "Dirty South" movement had emerged, so pioneers and promoters claimed, after recording executives and fellow performers in New York and Los Angeles openly mocked southern rappers and their music as too rustic or country. Already known as the home of rap groups like Outkast and Goodie Mob, Atlanta blossomed in the mid-1990s as the capital of the Dirty South sound. Much like Lynyrd Skynyrd and its defiant southern rocker descendants, instead of apologizing for where they came from performers like Outkast celebrated their regional roots and insisted, "The South got somethin' to say!" Killer Mike and other Dirty South artists sang the praises of soul food and even asked, "If we cotton pickers, what better thing to be?" This defiant assertion of a regionally distinctive black identity reflected an already pronounced trend among black southerners in general, but calling to mind Redneck beer and other such merchandise, gimmicks such as a line of Dirty South Klothing suggested that the new sound was also part of a campaign to cash in on that identity as well.[42]

Anyone who had trouble seeing that the South had become much more diverse in its cultural tastes and expressions obviously needed only to listen to its music. As it moved toward and into a new century, however, the region's tolerance for diversity faced a new challenge in the form of a larger and decidedly more visible gay and lesbian presence. As with blacks and women, regardless of whether they were natives or newcomers to the region, the most attractive locations for gays in the South were generally its larger, more dynamic, and cosmopolitan cities. Even there, however, there were tensions and conflicts, some generated by the more politically conservative evangelical populations of the suburbs and hinterlands. While the city of Atlanta itself had long enjoyed a gay-friendly reputation, gays had come under direct assault in ultraconservative suburban Cobb County in the summer of 1993. When Marietta's Theatre in the Square offered a production of *Lips Together, Teeth Apart*, a play that contained references to AIDS and gay neighbors, Cobb County commissioners passed a resolution declaring the gay lifestyle "incompatible with the standards to which this community subscribes." They also voted to withhold all public funding for the arts, lest some of the money be spent to promote the homosexual lifestyle.[43]

Gay activists quickly launched a counteroffensive, staging a Queer Family Picnic in Marietta and spearheading an effort to divert new businesses from Cobb County, which had just constructed a $43 million convention center. The brouhaha soon spilled over into preparations for the 1996 Olympic games, and protests by Atlanta gay rights groups ultimately led Olympic organizers to withdraw the volleyball competition from Cobb County. Meanwhile, Atlanta's reputation for gay friendliness continued to soar as tourism gurus touted it as "the ideal gay travel destination" because of its ever-expanding variety of clubs, restaurants, and special events aimed at attracting a gay clientele. In 2006 an estimated 300,000 people attended Pride Atlanta, an annual gay pride festival that since its beginnings in 1970 had grown to the point of generating an estimated $20 million for the local economy each year.[44]

As one of the South's fastest-growing cities, Charlotte also boasted an active gay population, but there, too, a strong local evangelical presence in the outlying areas made conflict all but inevitable. As in Marietta, public funds had been used to support at least two dramatic productions depicting gays and lesbians, and at a stormy six-hour meeting in 1997, Mecklenburg County commissioners voted to withhold county funding from arts groups that "promote, advocate or endorse behaviors, lifestyles and values that seek to undermine and deviate from the value and social role of the traditional American family." The crowd of seven hundred who showed up for the meeting presented an intriguing mixture, which one writer described as "a cross-section of Charlotte" that included "artists in jeans and corporate executives in business suits" and "young people with nose rings and retirees with Bibles." One of the latter, a former dietitian, explained, "[I am] totally against funding things I'm opposed to.... I believe in the Bible, and the Bible is against homosexuality." Image-conscious businessmen and professionals had helped to steer Charlotte onto the more moderate path during the civil rights era, and one of the strongest statements opposing the resolution came from an executive of the powerful Nations Bank, who likened the proceedings to a cross burning. A local lawyer agreed that the commission's action was certain to give Charlotte a "bad name."[45]

Nearly a decade later the city of Charlotte itself had clearly grown more tolerant, but the area was still home to a strong conservative Christian population. Rev. Flip Benham, president of the Dallas-based Operation Save America, regularly came to town to rally local and imported followers in singing hymns and witnessing individually to participants in Charlotte's annual gay pride celebration. An exuberant Reverend Benham claimed credit after the event was scaled back in 2006, exulting, "When Christianity comes to the streets, the enemies have to return to the closet. It's like when you turn the lights on and the roaches run."[46]

Gay pride celebrations were a touchy issue in a number of other southern cities. On the one hand, they boosted the community's economy and its reputation as open-minded and tolerant, but in the minds of critics these events simply demonstrated the fundamental incompatibility of family-friendly and gay-friendly environments. Gays in Birmingham sued African American mayor Larry Langford in 2008 when he declined to allow Gay Pride Week banners to be hung in the city. Langford had also refused to sign a gay pride proclamation and threatened to deny a permit for the event. "The bottom line," Langford explained, "is I don't condone their lifestyle, and what they were asking me to do in my official capacity as mayor was to issue a proclamation which in essence endorsed the gay lifestyle." Although he would soon be indicted (and subsequently convicted) on multiple corruption charges dating from his days as Jefferson County Commission chair, Langford explained, "[By issuing a gay pride proclamation] I would in essence be saying that God's position is wrong, and I wouldn't dare take a position against God."[47]

Some liberal observers had assumed that regardless of their religious or cultural differences, members of one historically oppressed group would feel a natural empathy for members of another such group, but Langford's stance represented yet another example of a high-profile black southerner objecting to the gay lifestyle. Suggestions of cultural tensions between blacks and gays had also surfaced during the 2008 presidential race. In September 2007 a poll of black South Carolinians showed that 74 percent of respondents felt "sex between two adults of the same sex" was "unacceptable." The following month, trailing Hillary Clinton significantly among potential black voters in South Carolina's Democratic primary, Barack Obama's campaign raised eyebrows nationally by sponsoring a three-stop "tour" of the state featuring popular black gospel singer and "ex-gay" minister Donnie McClurkin, who claimed to have struggled with the "curse" of homosexuality before he was "cured" through faith. Obama's camp disavowed McClurkin's statements, but the candidate himself made no secret of his personal belief that "marriage is between a man and a woman."[48]

Before the U.S. Supreme Court ruled in 2003 that states could not make "private sexual conduct a crime," every southern state had laws not only criminalizing sodomy but in some cases making it a felony punishable by imprisonment for terms ranging from one to twenty years. Although every state in the region already had laws prohibiting same-sex marriage, by 2008 the South accounted for eleven of the twenty-seven states with this provision embedded in their constitutions as well.[49]

If injecting their apprehensions about homosexuality and the gay lifestyle into their constitution and statute books did not make their attitudes about homosexuality clear enough, the reaction of some South Carolina officials to an international gay tourism promotional campaign surely did. When he learned that "the Tube," London's famous subway, was adorned with posters proclaiming "South Carolina Is So Gay," Republican State Senator David Thomas of Greenville predicted that his fellow

South Carolinians would be irate when they realized their "hard-earned tax dollars are being spent to advertise our state as 'so gay.'" The general popular reaction to the ads was difficult to discern, but a spokesman for Republican Governor Mark Sanford quickly disavowed the advertising campaign as inappropriate, and a state tourism official was forced to resign after admitting "a serious error in judgment regarding the political sensibilities of an effort to make South Carolina seem attractive to gays." Ironically, in a striking parallel to events in Birmingham, Governor Sanford himself would soon be found guilty of "a serious error in judgment" of his own when his torrid extramarital affair with an Argentinian woman hit the headlines. Regardless of whether Sanford's behavior offended the "political sensibilities" of South Carolinians more egregiously than the gay tourism flap, it was fair to say that few outside the state's gay population seemed ready to agree publicly with the travel agency executive who declared, "We think it is just great to be so gay."[50]

Embittered by the ostracism they sometimes faced from fellow southerners, gays and lesbians in the South could sound on occasion much like African Americans who refused to let whites dictate how their regional identity would be represented. A young Alabaman who made no effort to conceal her sexual orientation insisted, "I'm southern and I grew up here, and I feel really strongly that the South is my home, the

"South Carolina Is So Gay." Courtesy of Andrew Roberts, Amro Worldwide, London, UK.

The South and America since World War II

South is my culture, and I have as much right to claim it as anyone else, and I refuse to let people's stereotypes or people's attitudes somehow take away my home." As it had for many blacks, the experience struggling with their feelings of alienation had given some gay southerners a greater sense of their collective and personal identities. "It is that outsider status that I cherish so dearly," North Carolinian Trevor Hoppe explained. "It grants a certain ability to see what those on the inside cannot. 'American by birth, Southern by the grace of God.' Despite all of my trials and tribulations, I wouldn't have it any other way."[51]

In an another interesting parallel, just as economic concerns had ultimately encouraged southern white leaders to acquiesce to desegregation, so did growing recognition of gay economic clout seem to spur greater tolerance for gay and lesbian lifestyles. Southern development leaders could hardly have ignored a 2001 Brookings Institution study that described gays as "canaries of the knowledge economy." After comparing economic and demographic data (from the 1990 census) for fifty large metropolitan areas, the Brookings researchers concluded, "A leading indicator of a metropolitan area's high-technology success is a large gay population.... The presence of gays in a metro area signals a diverse and progressive environment and provides a barometer for a broad spectrum of amenities attractive to adults, especially those without children. To some extent, the gay and lesbian population represents what might be called the 'last frontier' of diversity in our society." Not surprisingly, the four southern metro areas that ranked within the top fifteen nationally in concentrations of high-tech industry—Atlanta, Austin, Dallas, and Houston—also ranked in the top twenty-one in gay representation in the population.[52]

Gay or straight, a great many of the people drawn to the metropolitan South during the 1990s and later were in the high-tech, telecommunications, professional and business services, or information-transfer sectors. Texas took a backseat only to California in high-tech employment by 2009, with dynamic Austin leading the way. From Austin to South Florida to northern Virginia, salaries for high-tech professionals could range from 50 to 80 percent above the private employment average. Meanwhile, North Carolina's seven-thousand-acre Research Triangle Park was still the largest research park in the country and home to 160 companies (including such giants as GlaxoSmithKline, IBM, and Nortel) employing forty thousand people, with a combined payroll of $2.7 billion.[53]

Fueled by this high-tech explosion, Raleigh-Cary in North Carolina and Austin in Texas were the nation's fastest growing metro areas between 2007 and 2008. Over the same period fifteen of the top thirty metropolitan-growth centers were in the South. By 2008 the population of heavily high-tech Houston alone had climbed to 2.2 million, and its metropolitan area, the nation's sixth largest, sprawled over more square miles than New Jersey.[54]

The obvious importance of research facilities to a successful courtship of high-tech industries had intensified the postwar trend toward greater public investment in higher education. With the success of the Research Triangle's corporate-academic partnership spurring them on, more progressive lawmakers and governors championed bigger budgets and better facilities, geared toward claiming more public and private research dollars and recruiting top-flight faculty. At the same time, publicly and privately funded scholarship programs began to keep more of the best high school students in state and attract others from elsewhere. By 2009 not only were Duke, Rice, Vanderbilt, and Emory well-ensconced among the country's elite private institutions, but with nine of the top twenty-five public universities, according to *U.S. News*

Research Triangle Park, North Carolina. Courtesy of Research Triangle Foundation of North Carolina.

The South and America since World War II

and World Report's eagerly awaited national survey, the South was better represented in this category than any other region.[55]

Ironically, in addition to their enviable academic status, save for William and Mary, the remaining highly ranked southern schools—Georgia Tech, Texas A&M, Clemson, and the Universities of Florida, Georgia, Virginia, and North Carolina—also shared a common commitment to a powerful, nationally competitive athletic program. The fierce pride of many southerners in their local sports teams, whether scholastic or collegiate or professional, reflected a history of strong, localized attachments typical of a rural region. Yet big-time collegiate sports had emerged in the South in tandem with the urban and business boosterism of the 1920s, when college officials at universities such as Alabama, Tennessee, and Georgia began to see football as a means of promoting their academically undistinguished schools to a wider population within their states and beyond.

When Georgia hosted Yale in an intersectional matchup to christen its new stadium in 1929, the game drew tremendous national attention, and it would not be long before southern teams taking on northern powerhouses like Michigan, Notre Dame, and UCLA were seen as Confederate soldiers reincarnate, doing battle for the honor and pride of the entire region. No team filled this role more frequently by the strife-torn 1960s than the University of Alabama's Crimson Tide, coached by the legendary Paul "Bear" Bryant, which won national championships in 1961, 1964, and 1965. Alabama was but one of nine southern teams that managed to claim at least a share of the mythical national crown between 1946 and 1965. This achievement seems all the more remarkable, although not necessarily more admirable, in light of the fact that none of these schools had yet signed a single black player to a football scholarship. Until the late 1960s, promising black athletes pursuing college degrees and possible professional athletic careers had little option but to leave the region to play for schools in the Midwest, Northeast, or California. In 1971 Alabama fielded its first black player on its varsity, and Tide fans' acceptance of this move was likely enhanced by the 42–21 whipping put on their team by a thoroughly integrated and highly talented University of Southern California team the year before. An integrated Alabama team would prove dominant throughout the 1970s, and other southern schools would benefit enormously from the ability and desire of black players to perform before the home folks as well.[56]

It would not be long before the majority of the players on the South's major college football rosters were black, and white fans who had once been dead set against integration were now equally intent on canonizing black superstars like Georgia's Herschel Walker, Auburn's Bo Jackson, and Florida's Emmitt Smith. In the meantime, ironically enough, the declining gridiron fortunes of certain northern teams, particularly those in the Big Ten, reflected the new reality that southern black athletes no longer needed a northern refuge from Jim Crow.

Much to the delight of their large and rabid fan bases, southern schools would claim sixteen more national football titles between 1988 and 2008. For all that such success in football may have done for local morale and pride, however, critics within the region and beyond charged that too much of southerners' interest in their universities focused on athletics, football in particular, and too little on their academic needs or accomplishments. When he returned to his home state to assume the presidency of the University of Alabama in 1981, Joab Thomas found it no easy matter to deliver on his vow to give "the football team a university it can be proud of." Seven years later Thomas's continuing conflicts with

Herschel Walker, star running back,
University of Georgia, 1980-82.
Courtesy of Glenn A. Weber.

The South and America since World War II

football boosters who had no time for such foolish talk ultimately led him to leave Alabama for the presidency at Penn State University.

In reality, Alabama was but one of a number of southern universities that have launched major campaigns to upgrade their academic reputation in recent years. Such efforts have enjoyed a certain amount of success, but certainly not enough to dispel the impression that for all the talk about rising SAT scores and attracting more National Merit Scholars, athletics still reign supreme on many southern campuses. In 2009, with public higher education suffering mightily from funding cuts triggered by the severe economic downturn, nine of the nation's fifteen highest paid college football coaches were employed at southern schools. Alabama's Nick Saban headed the list at $3.9 million annually despite a $75 million shortfall in the University of Alabama System's funding for 2008. When the University of Tennessee fired head football coach Philip Fulmer in 2008, it not only promised him a $6 million payout over four years but wound up paying a new staff of coaches a whopping $5.3 million annually, all of this at a time when the university itself had already suffered such severe funding reductions that three academic programs were phased out altogether. Overall, a 2009 survey of the Southeastern Conference schools showed four-year percentage increases in spending on athletics outstripping increases in academic spending by a wide margin at ten of the twelve schools, most notably at Auburn, where the ratio was more than seven to one, and at Georgia, where it was more than five to one. Not surprisingly, the faculty colleagues of the nine highest paid southern coaches did not fare quite so well. In a ranking of colleges and universities based on salaries for senior professors, only Texas, at forty-seventh, made it into the top one hundred.[57]

Some argued that football madness was just as overpowering elsewhere, particularly in the Big Ten, but this was not an easy case to make even in Columbus or Ann Arbor and an impossible one to make anywhere else. Beyond that, anyone doubting the importance of football to southern cultural identity need only ask themselves if fans of the University of Michigan would be likely to support a despised conference rival like Ohio State in the national championship game. On the other hand, regional loyalties were still strong enough among backers of Southeastern Conference teams like Ole Miss, Georgia, or Tennessee to override their traditional antagonisms at least long enough for them to rally behind the hated Florida Gators or Alabama Crimson Tide in their battles for the BCS title. Of course fans and well-heeled boosters reserved their deepest affection and highest expectations for their own team. Presidents of the South's major public universities might boast simultaneously of their school's academic and athletic prowess, but doubtless few, if any, could yet envision a day when they would actually feel comfortable asking alumni and boosters to sacrifice the latter in the interest of the former.

The combination of long-overdue interest in shoring up the academic credentials of southern universities and continuing overemphasis on athletic success was but one of the many entanglements of continuity with change that marked a contemporary South, where apparent departures from the old ways in one context frequently seemed to appear almost simultaneously with signs of their resurgence somewhere else. James Young had been in elementary school in 1964 when an earthen dam outside his hometown gave up the bodies of three young civil rights workers and Philadelphia, Mississippi, became an enduring symbol of the savagery that had greeted those who were trying to bring racial justice to a still bitterly recalcitrant South. Nearly forty-five years later, on May 19, 2009, Young won the Democratic primary runoff that, in the absence of a Republican opponent, assured he would be the city's first black mayor. He described his victory as "an atomic bomb of change" for the town of seventy-three hundred that was still struggling to shed its reputation as a historic citadel of white racism at its murderous worst. Running against a white opponent on a budget too tight to allow either stickers or buttons, Young had won 51.5 percent of the vote from an electorate that was 55 percent white. The key to his win, he believed, lay in his comfort in campaigning in all of the town's neighborhoods, black and white. He insisted, "There was no real negativism in this campaign. . . . There was no door slammed in my face. . . . I even talked to my opponent's mother."[58]

Here was an event suggesting that a real breakthrough in racial attitudes had finally come to a place where hope for it had once seemed nothing short of foolish. Yet, almost predictably, the heartening news from Neshoba County was quickly tempered by a jarring reminder of how uneven and complicated the pace and course of such change can be. Five days after James Young's much-acclaimed triumph in Philadelphia, the *New York Times Magazine* brought optimistic South-watchers crashing back to earth with a story about Montgomery County High School in south central Georgia, where there had been only one school-sponsored, mixed-race prom since integration in 1971. In keeping with long-standing custom, on May 1, 2009, the "white folks' prom" had proceeded without incident and without black students, save for a small group who showed up to cheer and snap photos as their gussied-up white classmates made their way inside. The following evening the "black folks' prom," which was actually open to white students but attended by only one, also went off without a hitch. Students had planned both events, but neither were held on school property or supported by school funds.[59]

This situation was not peculiar to Montgomery County, Georgia. Although the actor Morgan Freeman had promised a decade earlier to pay for a big, gala-style affair if the local high school would hold its first-ever integrated prom in his hometown of Charleston, Mississippi, the event did not come off until 2008.[60]

As they had in Charleston, both white and black students at Montgomery County High insisted that their repeated efforts to hold an integrated prom had been stonewalled by school administrators. According to Timothy Wiggs, student council president and one of twenty-one black students (out of fifty-nine seniors) graduating in 2009, "We just never get anywhere with it." The white students protested, perhaps a little too much, that their parents were actually to blame for this awkward and anachronistic situation. Terra Fountain, a white 2008 graduate who was living with her black boyfriend, insisted, "It's the white parents who say no.... They're like, if you're going with the black people, I'm not going to pay for it." Kera Nobles, a black senior, noted that her white girlfriends would "tell you in a minute, 'Don't tell mama who I'm going out with' [because] ... they don't want to get put out of the house."[61]

Whatever fictions white parents might try to maintain, Terra Fountain's open cohabitation with a black man seemed to indicate that the once formidable taboos against sexual intimacy between blacks and whites now meant little to the teen set in Montgomery County. There was also the perhaps even more striking story of Skyla Deem, who, escorted by her black boyfriend of eighteen months, Barry Burch, was the only white student at the black prom. Burch admitted he felt "kind of sick, kind of down" the night before, when Deem attended the white prom without him. Aware of the attitudes of some white parents, Burch had decided not to go because he felt "it was a hostile environment," although Deem's selection as senior class president certainly suggested that their relationship bore no particular stigma among their classmates.[62]

Segregated proms were not going to stop interracial dating, Kera Nobles insisted: "One night is not going to change it." Perhaps not, but this "one night" was obviously sufficient to give black students reason to reflect on their relationships, romantic and otherwise, with the white classmates who were partying without them. "My best friend is white," one of the black girls insisted. "She's in there. She's real cool, but I don't understand. If they can be in there, why can't everybody else?" Another was puzzled because none of her white friends had texted her during the prom. "I'm thinking that these people love me and I love them, but I don't know. Tonight's a different story," she admitted.[63]

Though they were by no means representative, such cases tended to obscure the decidedly higher overall levels of integration in southern public schools than elsewhere and, to some extent, the degree of social integration achieved as well. In reality, it was an open question whether the most striking revelation in this story was what happened on prom night(s) in Montgomery County or what seemed to be happening every other night of the year. Yet when the South presented such individual cases that, depending on one's perspective, might be cited to illustrate either how much it had changed or how little, many outside the region were clearly inclined to opt for the latter interpretation. These segregated proms, one reader insisted, were merely emblematic of "the tradition of racism to which whites in the Deep South cling." Another simply declared matter-of-factly, "The South is a disgrace to the United States."[64]

12

"The Root of So Many Problems Facing the Country"

Why America Still Needs the South

Reports of southern communities still holding segregated proms in 2009 seemed to many to fly in the face of at least a generation's worth of data and the conclusions of a substantial cadre of scholars such as Earl and Merle Black, who had actually concluded some seventeen years earlier that "today, one looks at the South and sees America." Much of the apparent incongruity here arose from a deeply entrenched presumption, spanning the better part of two centuries, that all of the changes necessary for the South to truly "look like America" would have to come within the South itself. The prospect of actually steering a wayward, recalcitrant Dixie into the national mainstream had remained a dim one at best until it emerged from World War II with its economy shifting rapidly and decisively from agricultural to industrial and its racial practices coming under steadily sharper criticism from within and without. Intent at that point on promoting the reforms deemed necessary to bring the region in line with prevailing national racial, economic, and political standards, few liberals on either side of the Mason-Dixon line could have imagined that in scarcely more than a generation the South would begin to look more like America in no small measure because in a great many ways America had also begun to look more like the South. Indeed, this explanation for the striking resemblance between region and nation remains both troubling and difficult to accept for many, even today.[1]

As we have seen, observers had been insisting that the perceived differences between region and nation were rapidly disappearing long before John Egerton referred in 1973 to the "Americanization of Dixie" (meaning that "the South is becoming more urban, less overtly racist, less self-conscious and defensive, more affluent—and more uncritically accepting of the ways of the North"). Egerton was one of the first, however, to suggest that the South's loss of distinctiveness was also being driven by the concomitant "Southernization of America" (meaning that "the North, for its part, seems more overtly racist than it had been; shorn of its pretensions of moral innocence, it is exhibiting many of the attitudes that once were thought to be the exclusive possession of white Southerners").[2]

Three years later, with a Deep South Democrat pursuing the presidency, a host of liberal literati from Walker Percy to C. Vann Woodward put a more positive spin on southernization by suggesting, for example, that a healthy dose of the South's supposedly down-home values and less grandiose expectations might help other Americans find their way out of their post-Vietnam and Watergate funk. Yet even before the majority of white southerners had climbed aboard Ronald Reagan's conservative Republican bandwagon and helped to send Jimmy Carter packing in 1980, the *Texas Observer*'s Ronnie Dugger already had some bad news for those who had rushed to hail the risen South and its native son, Carter, as both the source and symbol of their great redemptive vision for a "New America." Noting that conservative southern Democrats were then unloosing a barrage of criticism at liberal Massachusetts senator Edward M. Kennedy for trying to deny a sitting President Carter's bid for renomination, Dugger warned, "The Democratic Party is now about to be thoroughly Southernized and corporatized. Surely the national liberals did not intend that."[3]

Such laments about the South's growing influence on national affairs would become commonplace as the Republicans quickly established an overwhelming southern white majority that helped to keep them safely in the White House for the next twelve years. Egerton's allusion to "the Southernization of America" had been offered as a figurative *description* of what seemed to be happening in the 1970s, but a host of liberal commentators soon seized on it instead as a literal *explanation* in which an altogether mystifying contagion of southern white values became almost singularly responsible for the nation's pronounced tilt to the right during the last quarter of the twentieth century. "Southernization," wrote George Packer, "was an attitude that spread north," carrying with it "suspicion of government, antielitism, racial resentment, [and] a highly personal religiosity." In general, the proponents of the southernization thesis traced the beginnings of this shift to southern white resentment of the Democratic Party's support for the black advances of the civil rights era. After working an all-white crowd in Columbia, South Carolina, into a near frenzy in 1966 with a flag-waving, law-and-order harangue that fairly "burned the paint off the walls," future president Richard Nixon told Pat Buchanan, "This is the future of this party right here in the South." In the southernization version of events, however, it was George Wallace, the presumed embodiment of the southern white mentality whose expert manipulation of the race issue in 1968 had seduced the Republican Party into its infamous racially coded "southern strategy." This strategy in turn had succeeded in forging white racial antagonism (not unlike that on shocking public display at the time in Chicago or Detroit or Boston) into such a sizable and apparently irreducible block of votes in the South that GOP success in national elections was virtually guaranteed in the 1980s. To be sure, the virtual certainty of prohibitively strong support from southern whites allowed Republican candidates to concentrate their resources elsewhere when Nixon crushed George McGovern in 1972, when Reagan trounced both Carter in 1980 and Walter Mondale in 1984, and when George H. W. Bush dispatched Michael Dukakis in 1988. The bottom line, however, was that with Nixon and Reagan claiming at least 90 percent of the remaining electoral votes nationally and Bush drawing nearly 75 percent, all of them had actually run nearly as well outside the South as within it, and thus not a single southern vote had been essential to any of their victories.[4]

By 1992, with the region's astonishing population growth only enhancing its political clout, Earle and Merle Black declared the South "vital" to the presidential fortunes of either party, even though Bill Clinton was about to show that a Democrat could also win the presidency without requiring southern support. Yet for these political scientists the larger point was that America's longtime "*except...for*" region had now become an "*especially in*" bellwether that "shapes the trends and sets the pace of national political outcomes and processes." When Republicans seized control of Congress in 1994 (for the first time since 1952), only sixteen of the fifty-six new seats they captured were in the South. Michael Lind saw it as a "southern coup" nonetheless because "all but one of the new leaders of the Republican Congress hailed from a former state of the Confederacy." Clearly troubled by the prospect that, as one reviewer put it, "the greatest industrial nation in world history" might soon be reduced to "a Mississippi stretching from coast to coast," Lind

Antibusing march, Boston, 1974.

concluded, "Resisting the Southernization of America is a political task principled Southerners and Northerners should be able to agree upon. If they fail, George Wallace's boast may yet prove to be a prophecy: 'Alabama has not joined the nation, the nation has joined Alabama!'"[5]

Observing the 1994 congressional contests from across the Atlantic, the *Economist* concurred: "This year's mid-term elections confirmed that the 'primitive' attitudes that east-coast liberals used to sneer at are now those of America." In summing up the "*southernisation* of America," the British writers could do no more than trot out what had already become a fairly well-traveled metaphor: "As the South and the rest of America converge, it is at least as much thanks to the rest of the country joining the South, as to the South rejoining the Union."[6]

At that point, of course, southerners held both the presidency and the vice presidency in addition to serving as Senate and House majority leaders, speaker of the House, House majority whip, and Republican Party chair, and Republicans were occupying the majority of southern state house and senate seats for the first time since Reconstruction. Beyond that, Peter Applebome suggested, in areas such as racial attitudes, social concerns, and tolerance of religious, ethnic, and sexual

The South and America since World War II

diversity, a "rising" Dixie was generally shaping "American values, politics and culture" in its own extremely conservative image.[7]

It did not escape notice, of course, that George W. Bush, who seemed to be the second-generation poster boy for the right-wing "cowboy culture" of Kirkpatrick Sale's "Southern Rim," swept the South in both 2000 and 2004. Frustrated by the southern sweep that fueled Bush's first victory, the senior editor of *Foreign Affairs*, Mark Strauss, complained that had Al Gore been running in 1972 (before migrating northerners began to inflate southern electoral clout), the states he won in 2000 would have given him an eighteen electoral vote margin over Bush. Noting that Bush lost the popular vote nationally by 500,000 votes while winning in the old Confederacy by 3.1 million votes, Strauss declared, "The North and South can no longer claim to be one nation." Rather, "North and South should simply follow the example of the Czech Republic and Slovakia: Shake hands, say it's been real and go their separate ways." If this meant that the North wound up seceding this time around, then so be it. "The South is a gangrenous limb that should have been lopped off decades ago," Strauss insisted, supporting his indictment (jokingly, one supposes) with a lengthy list of particulars, including "The flow of guns into America's Northern cities stems largely from Southern states" and "The tobacco grown by ol' Dixie kills nearly a half-million Americans each year."[8]

In a similar but more succinct reaction to Bush's reelection in 2004, the frustrated Yankees at www.fuckthesouth.com advised "the South" to "take your liberal-bashing, federal-tax-leaching, confederate-flag-waving, holier-than-thou, hypocritical bullshit and shove it up your ass!" Although the architects of this fusillade appeared to have their sights set on those below the Mason-Dixon line, in reality, they had simply designated all of the thirty-one states that went for Bush as southern, including three that lay on the Canadian border.[9]

Despite this and all the other ways that the southernization paradigm clearly ran counter to both logic and fact, a number of northern and western liberals (and even a few southern ones) found it difficult to resist, perhaps because it provided them with such a seductively simple and ultimately self-exonerative explanation for why things had gone so badly awry with their vision for America. So firmly fixed was this conviction that the white South was responsible for most of what liberals disliked about contemporary society that *New York Times* columnist Paul Krugman saw absolutely no reason to look elsewhere for culprits: "It's almost embarrassing. I talk a lot to political scientists, and you go through the numbers and the polls, and it all boils down—almost everything else goes away, except for five words: 'Southern whites started voting Republican.' The backlash against the Civil Rights Movement explains almost everything that's happened in this country for the past forty-five years." If anything, political scientist Thomas Schaller was even more forthright when he insisted that "the South proxies for a variety of national pathologies" and called on Democratic leaders to "point to the conservative South as the root of so many problems facing the country."[10]

Despite the now-familiar sense of its lurking omnipresence as what John Egerton called "the eight hundred pound, stogie-puffing gorilla in the smoke-filled rooms of national politics," the South's perceived stranglehold on political affairs began to show signs of slackening in 2006, when the Democrats managed to reclaim control of Congress by picking up more than 80 percent of their new seats outside the region. Sensing (and obviously hoping) that the South's days of supposedly calling the political shots for the entire nation might be numbered, Schaller exulted that "the link between the Democrats' Southern fortunes and national fortunes" had been "severed," while another pundit pointed out, "This is the first time in 54 years that the party without a southern majority now has the House majority. Power flows to [the] coasts."[11]

Democrats obviously hoped to turn their 2006 breakthrough into a trend in 2008, but their prospects for actually making inroads within Dixie itself seemed to evaporate when Senators Hillary Clinton and Barack Obama emerged as the frontrunners for the party's presidential nomination. White southerners had obviously shown little receptivity to the vice-presidential candidacy of Geraldine Ferraro or, for that matter, to the idea of any woman holding the highest office in the land. To most observers, as an African American, Obama's chances in the South seemed even slimmer than Clinton's.

Ironically, however, although the South would not prove critical to his victory in November, voters in a number of southern states actually helped to propel Obama to his party's nomination. With overwhelming support from blacks and a surprising share of the white vote as well, he bested Clinton in the North Carolina and Virginia primaries and in every Deep South Democratic contest except Florida, where he did not campaign. A number of the South's veteran black political leaders were initially inclined toward Clinton, who they believed would be more electable, but Obama's early primary successes soon brought most of them around. Although Obama's strength among blacks was hardly unexpected, white southern Democrats were generally seen as the party's most conservative voters. Yet generally Obama ran at or slightly better than his poll-based projections among white Democrats in the South, while frequently falling short of those numbers in primaries outside the region.

Some analysts seemed genuinely hard-pressed to explain resistance to Obama among white Democrats above the Mason-Dixon line, but *Newsweek* writer Michael Hirsh was clearly not among them. When exit polls from the Pennsylvania primary showed Obama winning only 37 percent of the white vote (as compared to 44 percent in Texas and 43 percent in Georgia), with one in six whites admitting that race had influenced their decision, this struck Hirsh as merely further proof that "the South…or…the South-Southwest is setting the agenda for our political, social and religious mores—in Pennsylvania and everywhere. This thought…has been recurring to me regularly over the years as I've watched the Southernization of our national politics at the hands of the GOP and its evangelical base." Thanks to a "now-dominant Southernism and frontierism," Hirsh complained, the "national dialogue" now included not only "creationism" and "anti-abortionism," but "faux jingoism."[12]

Conveniently ignoring decidedly unsouthern Ivy Leaguers like Robert McNamara and McGeorge Bundy, who had encouraged President Lyndon Johnson to escalate American involvement in Vietnam (even as his southern mentor, Senator Richard B. Russell, counseled against it), Hirsh insisted, "The realism and internationalism of the Eastern elitist tradition once kept the Southern-frontier warrior culture and Wilsonian messianism in check. Now the latter two, in toxic combination, have taken over…and the Easterners are running for the hills." In Hirsh's view, the South was even responsible somehow for Hillary Clinton's shameless pandering "to Roman Catholics, who have allied with Southern Protestant evangelicals on questions of morality, with anti-abortionism serving as the main bridge."[13]

Hirsh was hardly alone in his obvious disgust at what he saw as a southern power grab. Commenting a short time later on a somewhat shaky Obama appearance with conservative California television evangelist Rick Warren, another pundit concluded, "That Obama went into this hostile environment at all is to be commended, I suppose. That he gave thoughtful answers will not help him at all with the anti-intellec-tual, know-nothing 'Southernized'... American electorate."[14]

Sensing that the final weeks of the general election campaign might come down to a contest for the hearts and minds of blue-collar whites in the Rust Belt, sociologist John D. Skrentny fretted about the south-ernization of working-class whites nationwide, as evidenced in the gloomy, decaying factory towns of northern Indiana, where he had been dismayed to see blue-collar workers sporting the Confederate flag. "We are finding the American South all over the country," he complained, and nowhere more so than in politics, where there was both "tough talk appealing to nationalism and insecurities about American power" and "strong defenses of Christian values." So pervasive was the southerniza-tion process that it had apparently reached all the way to Alaska, ensnar-ing its governor and the GOP vice-presidential nominee, Sarah Palin, who, Skrentny explained, was, culturally at least, simply a "snow-bound Southerner."[15]

Although the principle concern among Obama's supporters in the final stages of both the primaries and the general election campaign would be whether he could overcome the doubts of white Democrats elsewhere in the nation, at the outset there was no denying that the majority of white southerners had not voted even for a white Demo-crat in a presidential election since 1960. Accordingly, when America's first black major party presidential nominee began his general election campaign against former P.O.W. and staunchly pro-military Arizona senator John McCain, few gave him much chance down in the race- and defense-conscious South. Even with an expected increase in black turn-out, it was hard to imagine that Obama could prevail against the intensi-fied white resistance that a black Democratic candidate was certain to arouse. This scenario ultimately played out in Alabama, where exit polls suggested that Obama had picked up only 10 percent of the white vote as compared to the 19 percent that went to John Kerry in 2004. In Mis-sissippi, Obama claimed only 11 percent of white votes, compared to 14 percent for Kerry, and in Louisiana, Kerry's 24 percent showing among whites dipped to 14 percent for Obama.[16]

Across the region, however, Obama not only equaled or surpassed Kerry's share of the white vote in nine of thirteen states, but utilizing hordes of volunteers and drawing on a huge campaign war chest, he was even able to break the GOP's chokehold on Dixie by winning Flor-ida, Virginia, and North Carolina. He captured these states by getting a significantly greater percentage of white votes in North Carolina and Virginia and matching Kerry's share of the white vote in Florida, while running five to ten points ahead of Kerry with black voters as well. Excluding Oklahoma, where no figures were available, if exit polls are to be believed, Obama averaged approximately 96 percent of the black vote across the southern states, and within states he typically ran strongest in places with large black populations and in fast-growing metropolitan areas like North Carolina's Research Triangle that boasted large numbers of younger, more affluent, better-educated voters, both white and black.[17]

The patterns of support for Obama also reflected the growing suburbanization of the South's black middle class. He carried three relatively close-in metropolitan Atlanta counties—Douglas, Newton, and Rockdale—that gave 60 percent or more of their votes to Bush in 2004 but had seen their black populations more than double since 2000. Blacks represented over one-third of the population in each of these counties by 2008, and although McCain carried four other nearby metropolitan counties with smaller but fast-growing black and Hispanic populations (including notoriously conservative Cobb), his share of the vote in these counties nonetheless fell short of Bush's by seven to twelve points. The limits of the Democrats' surge in metro Atlanta were sharply defined by race and geography, however. In the adjoining metropolitan counties of Walton, Forsyth, and Cherokee, which were both whiter and farther out from Atlanta, McCain claimed better than three of every four votes cast.[18]

Some observers wondered whether either charges that Hillary Clinton was the victim of sexism during her primary campaign or the mere fact of Sarah Palin's presence on the Republican ticket might affect the voting patterns of white women in 2008. In the South, of course, the historic tensions over white women's relationships and interactions with black men added yet another dimension. Nationwide, exit polls indicated that 46 percent of white women's votes had gone to Obama. Although Florida was the only southern state where he came within ten points of that figure among white women, as he had done with white men in the trio of southern states he carried, Obama equaled Kerry's 2004 performance with white women in Florida and improved on it significantly in North Carolina and Virginia. By the same token, in Alabama and Louisiana, where Obama's white support generally fell well below Kerry's, white women rejected him in roughly the same percentages as white men. Despite concerns that Hispanics would not support a black candidate, where Kerry had won 44 percent of the Hispanic vote in Florida and 50 percent in Texas, Obama bested him by 13 percentage points in both states.[19]

By bringing out record numbers of black voters, the Obama campaign obviously boosted the fortunes of a number of white Democratic candidates elsewhere on the ticket. Black votes helped former governor Mark Warner claim Virginia's second Senate seat for the Democrats. In Georgia, despite capturing less than 30 percent of the white vote, long-shot Democratic senatorial challenger Jim Martin was able to force a runoff with GOP incumbent Saxby Chambliss largely because blacks gave him 93 percent of their support. In North Carolina neither Democratic senatorial candidate Kay Hagan nor her gubernatorial counterpart, Beverly Perdue, won as much as 40 percent of the white vote, but with 96 and 95 percent of the black vote, respectively, both managed victories on election night.

Hagan's race was particularly satisfying to Democrats because she ousted GOP incumbent Elizabeth Dole, who, sensing that she was in trouble, had resorted to a last-minute television spot suggesting that her staunch Presbyterian opponent was actually in cahoots with an atheist organization and therefore keeping company with the "Godless." The ad even closed with a voice resembling Hagan's announcing, "God is dead." This scurrilous bit of deception seemed to backfire on Dole among metropolitan voters in North Carolina especially, and after GOP vice-presidential candidate Sarah Palin, who accused Obama of "palling around with terrorists," came to Guilford County in the Greensboro–High Point metro area and praised it as the "real [read: conservative Republican] America," the county went for Obama by eighteen points.[20]

It was tempting in some respects to interpret the Democratic triumphs in North Carolina, Florida, and Virginia as evidence that some parts of the South might be trending, if not "blue," at least a little "purple." However, the news that a surprising number of whites in these states apparently had not found Obama too liberal might have obscured the possibility that his victories actually owed something to other whites who found both Obama *and* his opponent too liberal or, at least in the latter case, too centrist to suit them. McCain's support for a path to citizenship for illegal immigrants and his somewhat fuzzy position on abortion rendered him fairly suspect among voters on the far right, regardless of region, and compared to 2004, GOP turnout was down

1.3 percent across the country in 2008. Despite the anticipated white backlash against the Obama camp's massive voter registration effort, the Republican total in fast-growing Virginia was essentially flat compared with 2004. Meanwhile, twenty-five thousand North Carolinians supported Libertarian Bob Barr in a state where the Obama victory margin fell short of fourteen thousand votes.[21]

If McCain's appeal seemed a bit tepid among some white voters in the South, there were also a great many who made no secret of their distaste for Obama and, in some cases at least, made little effort to conceal the racist attitudes behind it. Overall, only about 22 percent of U.S. counties voted more strongly Republican in 2008 than in 2004, and some 84 percent of them were in the South. In general, the populations of these predominantly rural, sparsely populated counties tended to be whiter, poorer, less educated, and more evangelical than their peers elsewhere in the region. The South could claim practically all (97 percent) the counties where the Republicans gained an additional 10 percent or more of the vote in 2008 than in 2004, and one-third of the residents of these counties were Southern Baptists.[22]

A *New York Times* report on the 2008 election's implications for the South's position in national politics focused on Lamar County, Alabama, which was one of twenty-nine (out of sixty-seven) of the state's counties where McCain ran ahead of Bush's 2004 percentages. Perhaps reacting to a flood of rumors that Obama was a Muslim, Don Dollar, an administrative worker in the county seat of Vernon, observed bitterly to a reporter that anyone not upset with Obama's victory owed God an explanation. "This is a community that's supposed to be filled with a bunch of Christian folks," he said. "If they're not disappointed, they need to be at the altar." Seeing things a bit differently, Vernon construction worker Joey Franks felt that local white opposition to Obama was not based on religion, but purely and simply on race. Franks believed that McCain had won 76 percent of the county's vote and bested Bush's 2004 showing by 5 points because a lot more whites went to the polls in 2008, "hoping to keep Obama out," and at least half of them, Franks estimated, were motivated by "racial reasons." The local woman who admitted she was worried about having a black man "over her" as president seemed to bear out Franks's impression, as did another's fears that Obama's election meant "there are going to be outbreaks from blacks."[23]

Such comments were both revealing and disturbing, but those who argued that the 2008 race showed once and for all that Democrats should stop wasting their time on the South in presidential elections seemed to see the entire region as simply Lamar County (total vote, 7,075) writ large. When the *New York Times*'s Adam Nossiter wrote that McCain's 90 percent showing among whites in Alabama was "comparable to other Southern states," he neglected to mention that this was actually true only for Mississippi and Louisiana and that, save for Arkansas, Obama had equaled or improved on Kerry's percentages among whites even in the remaining southern states where he lost. In fact, when Nossiter pointed out that "less than a third of southern whites voted for Obama compared to 43 percent of whites nationwide," he was actually saying nothing more than that, among white southerners, a black Democratic presidential nominee had run about as well as or better than any other white Democratic candidate since Bill Clinton. Finally, though there was no disputing Obama's stronger overall showing among whites in other parts of the country, had it been solely up to the majority of white voters in seven of the states he carried outside the South (including New Jersey, Pennsylvania, Ohio, and Indiana), his electoral margin over McCain would have plummeted from 192 to 18.[24]

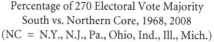

Percentage of 270 Electoral Vote Majority
South vs. Northern Core, 1968, 2008
(NC = N.Y., N.J., Pa., Ohio, Ind., Ill., Mich.)

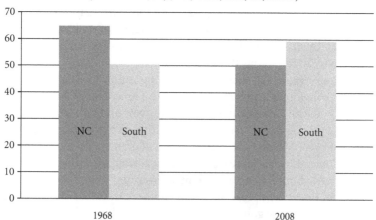

Source: "Dave Leip's Atlas of Presidential Elections," www.uselectionatlas.org.

The South and America since World War II

Among the states in the region where Obama actually won, Florida's peculiar demographic profile had long made its southernness suspect to some observers, and Nossiter believed that Virginia and North Carolina also succeeded in "breaking from their Confederate past" largely because both had also "experienced an influx of better educated and more prosperous voters in recent years." This interpretation was intriguing because by 2008 it had become something of a commonplace that the increasingly conservative climate in national politics largely reflected the rapid population growth that had boosted the South's representation in Congress by twenty-one seats between 1972 and 2008 and increased its share of the 270 electoral vote majority needed to win the presidency from 54 to 62 percent. Much of this growth, of course, had been fueled by the in-migration of nonsoutherners, in other words, Nossiter's "better educated and more prosperous voters," who, as his observation implied, had been expected to make the region's politics more liberal. This expectation might have been borne out in the Research Triangle and similar locales, but there were also fast-growing places like Cobb County, Georgia, where anti–gay rights, anti–gun control, antievolution politics were alive and well even though nearly 40 percent of the population came from outside the state. Apparently, in some areas at least, the South had been importing conservatism as well as exporting it.[25]

Noting determined efforts to effectively de-southernize any state that Obama carried, Chris Kromm complained, "Every time a Southern state starts voting for Democrats, people say, 'Oh, that's not the real South.'" Diane Roberts agreed, pointing to Florida as an example: "It's full of Yankees, Spanish speakers and refugees from the snow-shoveling states.... Never mind that in social attitudes, race relations, spending on education, etc., Florida's peer states are not New York or California, but Alabama and Louisiana. Never mind that Florida was the third state to secede from the union in 1861." Likewise, Roberts noted, "North Carolina isn't Southern because it's attracting Midwestern retirees, Latinos and tech types. Plus, there's the Research Triangle, the constellation of great universities, labs and libraries so despised by Sen. Jesse Helms. Real Southerners don't cotton to book learning." Observing that "the 'Southern' parts of the South seem to be shrinking, at least to those who define 'Southern' as white right-wingers who say 'y'all,'" Roberts warned, "At this rate, the South could soon consist only of Alabama, Mississippi, Tennessee and South Carolina—minus Huntsville (too many rocket scientists), Memphis (too many transplants), [and] Columbia (too many professors)."[26]

In the long run, efforts to write Florida, North Carolina, and Virginia out of the region seemed to suggest yet again the enduring perception that the South was defined less by its geography than by a static and monolithic mind-set thought to be peculiar to southern whites but often simply ascribed to all southerners, as if black southerners did not exist. Harold Meyerson illustrated such thinking perfectly when he assailed the Republicans in 2006 for becoming "too southern," as in "too suffused with the knee-jerk militaristic, anti-scientific, dogmatically religious, and culturally, sexually, and racially phobic attitudes of Dixie." Thomas Schaller sounded essentially the same note when he declared, "Southerners hold distinctly conservative values and have long prided themselves... [on] resisting the social transformations unfolding elsewhere across America." Therefore, Schaller concluded matter-of-factly, "the South is different because it's still full of southerners." This meant that regardless of a state's history or location, once the actions of a large number of its people could no longer be characterized as southern, neither could the state itself.[27]

Attempts to revoke the southernness of Florida, North Carolina, and Virginia notwithstanding, although they were not really necessary for an Obama victory in 2008, the fifty-five electoral votes the Democrats picked up in these three states were hardly to be sneezed at. Meanwhile, in Georgia, where McCain's final five-point margin was much slimmer than once anticipated, the Obama campaign's belated decision to run spots targeting metro Atlanta, with its large population of white newcomers and African Americans, might have indicated recognition of a lost opportunity and foretold a more formidable future effort in that state. This would appear to make sense since Georgia, North Carolina, and Florida all stood to gain electoral votes after the 2010 census. In Florida's case the possible pick up of two additional electors would actually make it as valuable a prize as New York, which was projected to lose two.[28]

On the other hand, in the short term, at least, the Democrats seemed unlikely to invest major time or resources campaigning in electorally puny states like Alabama, Mississippi, Louisiana, or South Carolina, where generally hard-line white attitudes not only on race but on religion and other social issues gave little indication of softening anytime soon. This means, much like the Democrats during most of the first two decades after World War II when they could still take a "Solid South" largely for granted, so long as their opponents leave these states uncontested in presidential elections, the Republicans have no particular incentive to pay much attention to them either.

Certainly there was still good reason for the GOP to feel secure in the South. At the state level only Alabama, Mississippi, and South Carolina had boasted Republican governors in 1992. Despite some power shifts to and fro in the interim, by 2008 they had been joined by Florida, Georgia, Kentucky, and Texas. By the same token, in southern legislatures the best the Republicans could claim in 1992 was a split with the Democrats in the Florida State Senate. Even with some Democratic resurgence, however, after the 2008 elections the GOP enjoyed a numerical advantage in both legislative chambers not only in Florida, but in Georgia, Oklahoma, South Carolina, Tennessee, Texas, and Virginia.[29]

In the wake of the 2008 election liberal blogger Jon Taplin made no effort to conceal either his partisan or regional biases when he observed rather caustically that the Republicans were simply retreating "to the deep South to fight a guerrilla war as the white people's party." Still, even a more detached assessment of the 2006 and 2008 results did seem to suggest that in the sharp and sustained tack to the right that had proved critical to Republicanizing the South, the GOP may have actually wound up southernizing itself, leaving the party with its most predictably loyal voter base in presidential and congressional elections heavily concentrated in a single region. Actually, the Republicans' fortunes in the South had begun to diverge from their performance elsewhere as far back as 1992, and since then, even as Dixie was supplying 60 to 70 percent of their electoral totals, on average, they had captured barely 20 percent of the remaining electoral votes nationally. Ten southern states supplied two-thirds of McCain's electoral votes in 2008, and although the party lost two southern seats in the Senate and four in the House, the South still accounted for nearly half of the GOP's representatives in Congress, leading Merle Black to suspect that the Republicans might have "maxed out on the South" and in the process "limited their appeal in the rest of the country."[30]

In some postelection commentaries, the real story in 2008 seemed not so much Obama's actual triumph over the Republicans as liberal America's symbolic victory over the racist and reactionary white South, which, almost overnight, it seemed, had been routed from its once commanding position and relegated yet again to the far-right fringe of

American political dialogue. Obama's win, as Nossiter put it, meant that "the Southernization of American politics—which reached its apogee in the 1990s when many Congressional leaders and President Bill Clinton were from the South—appears to have ended." With its white voters "leaving the mainstream so decisively," Nossiter predicted, "the Deep South and Appalachia will no longer be able to dictate that winning Democrats have Southern accents or adhere to conservative policies on issues like welfare and tax policy."[31]

In reality "the Deep South and Appalachia" had not been in a position to "dictate" the accent or policy stance of a Democratic presidential candidate even when Jimmy Carter won the nomination in 1976. Moreover, although Bill Clinton had carried four southern states in both 1992 and 1996, his successful appeal to moderate whites outside the region as something other than the traditional Democratic "tax and spend liberal" meant that, like the broad-based Republican triumphs of the previous decade, neither of his victories required a single southern vote. Thus when Nossiter saw the 2008 election signaling an end to "the centrality of the South to national politics," which Schaller eagerly agreed was "absolutely over," both were reveling in the death of something that existed largely in the minds of those who were reluctant to acknowledge that grassroots conservatism had enveloped much of the country for most of the past forty years. Nossiter's and Schaller's eagerness to pen yet another quite likely premature "epitaph for Dixie" was palpable. Nor were they by any means alone. More than three months after the election a writer for the *Economist* observed that the 2008 contest "had completed one of the biggest shifts in the regional balance of power in America's recent history, draining influence away from the once-mighty South and redistributing it to the coasts.... Now the South is as impotent as it has been for a century." Reacting to the jump-the-gun exuberance so evident in such assessments, the New York–based gawker.com proclaimed with tongue firmly in cheek, "Good News.... We've marginalized The South!" Based on the "totally conclusive 2008 election results," the website reported, "no longer will The South have any impact whatsoever on *National* Politics, *and we can safely ignore* them."[32]

Other observers hoped that the results of the 2008 election might foretell some slackening of the South's grip not just on the nation's politics, but on its social and cultural values as well. A few days after the election Iowa minister Matt Mardis-Lecroy asked, "Does the end of the South's dominance of our politics—if that really is what the Obama victory means—herald a similar end to southern domination of our religious life? Have we entered a time in the life of this nation in which non-Southern styles of religiosity will increasingly be seen as legitimate in their own right?...I hope so."[33]

In 2002, when Joshua Zeitz reached what he saw as the "inescapable" conclusion that "Southern culture has become American culture," he had cited "the massive influx of Southern migrants [into northern industrial cities] that began with World War II" as the key to this improbable outcome. More than 8 million whites had left the South between 1940 and 1970, and these migrants seemed the most likely carriers of the epidemic of evangelical Protestantism (not to mention racism, reactionary politics, and "redneck" tastes) that had supposedly begun to spread across the entire nation in the 1970s.[34]

One of the prime movers behind the spread of evangelical faith throughout the United States in the twentieth century was the "Texas Cyclone," Rev. J. Frank Norris, pastor of the First Baptist Church of Fort Worth. In 1935 Norris began commuting to Detroit, where he established a powerful second ministry at the Temple Baptist Church. Norris's flamboyant, fire-and-brimstone preaching style attracted many of the city's southern white in-migrants, although his church was already moving in a conservative direction before his arrival. There could be little doubt that the Southern Baptist Convention's ensuing decision to sanction SBC-affiliated churches outside the region was a response, in part at least, to the continuing southern white diaspora. Still, it was one thing for transplanted southerners to gravitate to the familiar forms of worship of their youth and quite another for their new northern and western neighbors to follow them. Beyond that, simply laying all the responsibility for the rise of the "moral majority" nationwide on southern transplants ignored the influence outside the South of conservative Roman Catholic clerics who had no more enthusiasm for legalized abortion or gay marriage or female priests than did their southern Protestant counterparts.[35]

Southern whites who had sought a better life in cities outside the region were not exactly welcomed with open arms by the locals, who frequently condemned them as "worse than the colored" and "a sore to the city and a plague to themselves." Just how such a marginalized group as these pitilessly denigrated, down-and-out "hillbillies" managed suddenly to persuade so many of those who had once mocked and scorned them to embrace their culture and values remains largely a mystery. Indeed for all their capacity for mischief, white southerners of this era would seem to be the unlikeliest of cultural imperialists. Save for the proselytizing inherent by definition in evangelical Christianity, there is precious little evidence of southern white migrants making much effort to southernize anyone. Michael O'Brien has pointed out that it is hardly as if southern whites suddenly showed up "on the doorstep of American culture" and said, "I'm here. Move over. Imitate me." "If their culture is expansive," O'Brien observed, "it is little they planned and something most of them have not noticed. This is not the stuff of which hegemony is made."[36]

Surely postwar southern transplants humming Hank Williams songs could not explain why well over half the music's fans now lived outside the South or why country music was the nation's most popular radio programming format by a wide margin. It was certainly understandable that country's emphasis on human limitations and lowered expectations would resonate throughout a nation clearly brought down a peg or two by the sobering disappointments of Vietnam and Watergate. Yet, in the long run, its success outside the South was more than anything a product of the deliberate and concerted efforts of music industry executives to maneuver it into the broader, more lucrative national pop music mainstream. Some of these executives may have cashed their checks in Nashville, but a great many of them were also nestled into corner offices in New York or Los Angeles.

The story of NASCAR, another great southern white cultural icon, was much the same. Southern transplants sporting Richard Petty's "43," Dale Earnhardt's "3," or some other driver's car number on their caps and T-shirts could not begin to account for why 60 percent of the fan base of what had once seemed the most indisputably southern sport on Earth now resided outside the South. A shrewd and relentless marketing and broadcast media effort (not unlike the one that had spread the gospel of evangelical fundamentalism so effectively) to take NASCAR upscale and make it as popular in the suburbs as it was in the mobile home parks was the primary reason why its racing circuit grew to include tracks in thirty-eight states. As executives shifted some of the bigger races from the sleepy southern towns that had hosted them for decades to major media markets like Chicago and Los Angeles, which is now the home of what was once the fabled Darlington (South Carolina) 500, a broadcasting spokesman observed rather coldly, "As NASCAR grows, it has to cut some umbilical ties with the area that gave the sport birth." Needless to say, this matter-of-factly mercenary attitude about ripping

NASCAR from its southern womb led to charges that the sport's financial czars were, as one speedway official put it, "forgetting the people that brought [them] to the dance."[37]

Clearly, there was more than a whiff here of the resentments of hard-core country music fans upset about the music industry's efforts to move it away from its southern roots. Such laments also raised the question of how long any cultural form could still be legitimately identified as southern when it had obviously been embraced by a much larger segment of American society. However, this apparent contradiction did not trouble the likes of Joshua Newman and Michael Giardina, whose examination of "NASCAR and the '*Southernization*' of America" led them to surmise in 2008 that despite its popularity across the country, with its overwhelmingly white fan base NASCAR was still more than anything a powerful signifier of the South and its traditions of "White Privilege, White supremacy, and patriarchal hegemony." From there it was but a hop and a skip for Newman and Giardina to reach the obvious conclusion that in "George W. Bush's 'southernized America'... under the auspices of a Bush-inspired, post-9/11, anti–affirmative action backlash,

Locations of NASCAR Spring and Nationwide Series Races, 2010.

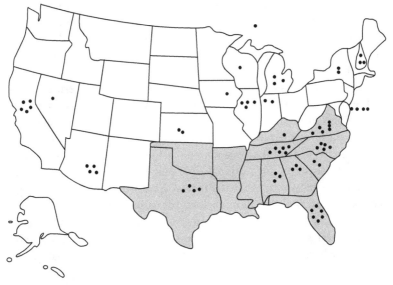

Source: www.nascar.com.

a hyper-White, neo-Confederate NASCAR gives license to the resurgent regimes of the most vigilant factions of the ethnocentric American White Right."[38]

Although they were cloaked in the jargon of the academic left (where such blatant stereotyping of any other culture would have been righteously condemned), these highly subjective assertions represented nothing more than another attempt to preserve America's claim to exceptional virtue by southernizing its vices. (Thus hate-filled Boston had quickly become "the Little Rock of the North" in the 1970s, while the attack on affirmative action in California made it the "Mississippi of the 1990s.") There was also the still predictable "This is the kind of thing you expect in Alabama or Mississippi but not here!" and similar comments that surfaced in response to a racially motivated crime or social affront in a northern or western community. For many Americans outside the region, the South would remain forever "frozen in time," wrote Jacob Levenson, who noted in 2004 that the scenes of Birmingham and Selma were still constantly "rehashed on PBS." Northerners seemed to "treasure those black-and-white memories," Levenson believed, because "they serve as symbols of what we'd like to think we're not." Literary scholars Houston A. Baker and Dana D. Nelson seemed to concur: "To have a nation of 'good,' liberal and innocent white Americans, there must be an outland where 'we' know they live: all the guilty white yahoos who just don't like people of color." This was precisely why, as sociologist Larry Griffin observed in 2000, "America still needs the South," so long, of course, as it can be seen as a static and inferior "other" wholly at odds with American character and ideals.[39]

If the South has made more progress than some Americans seem willing to concede, it is also true that nearly seventy years after Pearl Harbor and more than thirty years after the *Saturday Review* anointed it "a foretaste of the New America," the region has yet to situate itself anywhere near the pinnacle of national achievement in most categories relating to social or institutional development. On the contrary, even with all the changes for the better that we have seen, the preceding pages have surely shown well enough that, measured against a great many mathematical averages and other quantifiable national standards, the southern states still appear with distressing frequency to be down in the rankings where it's good to be up, and vice versa. Understandably, contemporary observers also find it difficult not only to comprehend all-white proms fifty-five years after the *Brown* decision but to understand the governor of Texas and other southern anti–big government zealots raising the prospect of secession nearly a century and a half after that matter seemed to have been settled for good. Witnessing such behavior some may feel as if they have truly been thrust back in time as they encounter such vestiges of the "characteristic vices" of white southerners, enumerated back in 1941 by W. J. Cash as "violence, intolerance, aversion and suspicion toward new ideas,... an incapacity for analysis,... an inclination to act from feeling rather than thought,... an exaggerated individualism,... a too narrow concept of social responsibility,... [and] above all, too great [an] attachment to racial values."[40]

Cash was hardly alone nearly seven decades ago in believing that these toxic traits were indeed peculiar to southern whites, perhaps because the very egregiousness of what he had observed in the pre–World War II South led him and his critical cohort to take too little notice of these pathologies elsewhere. With due respect for the evocative power of John Egerton's phrasing, however, for all the transformations we have witnessed since World War II, the fundamental reality of Dixie was every bit as "American" in 1941 as it is today. Finding that Massachusetts has some of the same deficiencies as Mississippi does not make Mississippi's any less regrettable, of course. Yet anyone who has not slept through the past forty years and still insists that the South's shortcomings are manifestly different in substance, and now largely even in degree, from those of the rest of the nation must be possessed of a steely determination not necessarily to see the South only at its worst but simply to see America only at its best. Obviously, for those so inclined, the South continues to serve as what Levenson called "a convenient box to contain all sorts of problems, situations, and conditions... race, white poverty, the cultural rift forming between the religious and the secular, guns, abortion, gay marriage, the gradual extinction of rural life, states' rights, the continuing debates over the size of government, the contours of American morality, and the identity of the major political parties." Levenson noted that all of these concerns were actually "national in scope," but, of course, admitting that would require addressing them as such. On the other hand, if a problem can be characterized as simply a "southern issue," as historian Laura Edwards pointed out, "there is no need to tamper with the broader political culture."[41]

C. Vann Woodward was anything but an apologist for his native region, but even as many elsewhere in the nation and the world were still trying to process the outrages of Freedom Summer and Selma, he felt constrained to point out that the South had long served the United States as "a moral lightning rod, a deflector of national guilt, a scapegoat for stricken conscience, much as the Negro has served the white supremacist—as a floor under national self-esteem." Woodward went on to suggest that northerners and southerners had frequently used each other "in the way Americans have historically used Europe—not only to define their identity and to say what they are *not*, but to escape in fantasy from what they *are*." He observed in 1972 that "anti-Southernism, performs many of the rationalizations and defenses that Anti-Americanism performs for Europeans....When something objectionable turns up in his country—super markets, student riots, traffic jams, TV commercials—the European intellectual declares that the place is becoming *Americanized*. Similarly, when the Yankee is confronted with civil rights agitators, race riots, segregated schools, school-bus burning, and central-city disintegration, he denounces the effort to southernize the North."[42]

The long-standing inclination to view the South as what Howard Zinn called "an abnormal growth on the national body" may well explain the enduring tendency to cite racial bias in Pennsylvania or hostility to gun control in Ohio as evidence that a regional malignancy has now metastasized throughout that "national body." Such a diagnosis, however, ignores a lengthy history of symptoms indicative not of a recent affliction but of a preexisting condition, perhaps because it is only as the South's distractions have grown steadily fewer and ultimately less distracting that we have become more likely to notice, although not necessarily always to acknowledge, evidence of how "southern" America has been all along.[43]

NOTES

INTRODUCTION

1. Carl Carmer, *Stars Fell on Alabama* (Tuscaloosa, Ala., 1985), xv; Clarence Cason, *90° in the Shade* (Tuscaloosa, Ala., 1983); xxvii; W. J. Cash, *The Mind of the South* (New York, 1941), vii–viii, 134.

2. Leon F. Litwack, *How Free Is Free: The Long Death of Jim Crow* (Cambridge, Mass., 2009), 85, 72; Numan V. Bartley, *The New South: 1945–1980* (Baton Rouge, 1995), 8.

3. John Gunther, *Inside U.S.A.* (New York, 1947) 657–58; V. O. Key, *Southern Politics: In State and Nation* (New York, 1949), 4; Howard Zinn, *The Southern Mystique* (New York, 1964), 218.

4. Gunnar Myrdal, *An American Dilemma: The Negro Problem and Modern Democracy* (New York, 1944), lxxi.

5. Ibid., 48, 1014.

6. Ibid., 1010, 998.

7. Gunther, *Inside U.S.A.*, 653.

8. Peter Applebome, *Dixie Rising: How the South Is Shaping American Values, Politics, and Culture* (New York, 1996); Joshua Zeitz, "Dixie's Victory," *American Heritage*, Aug./Sept., 2002, www.americanheritage.com/articles/magazine/ah/2002/4/2002_4_46.shtml.

CHAPTER 1

1. Myrdal, *An American Dilemma*, 997; Daniel J. Singal, *The War Within: From Victorian to Modernist Thought in the South* (Chapel Hill, 1982), 299.

2. Litwack, *How Free*, 54, 64, 63.

3. Ibid., 84, 79.

4. James C. Cobb, *The Most Southern Place on Earth: The Mississippi Delta and the Roots of Regional Identity* (New York, 1994), 201–2.

5. Litwack, *How Free*, 91; Bartley, *New South*, 29.

6. *Smith v. Allwright*, 321 U.S. 649 (1944); John Egerton, *Speak Now against the Day: The Generation before the Civil Rights Movement in the South* (New York, 1994), 397; Key, *Southern Politics*, 522–23 n. 13.

7. Christopher Dickey, "Southern Discomfort: A Journey through a Troubled Region," *Newsweek*, August 2, 2008, www.newsweek.com/id/150576/page/5; Neil R. McMillen, "How Mississippi's Black Veterans Remember World War II," in *Remaking Dixie: The Impact of World War II on the American South*, ed. Neil R. McMillen (Jackson, Miss., 1997), 95; Jennifer E. Brooks, *Defining the Peace: World War II Veterans, Race, and the Remaking of Southern Political Tradition* (Chapel Hill, N.C., 2004), 19.

8. Brooks, *Defining the Peace*, 42–43.

9. Cobb, *Most Southern Place*, 210.

10. Frank E. Smith, *Congressman from Mississippi* (New York, 1964), 64, 101.

11. Brooks, *Defining the Peace*, 65; Egerton, *Speak Now*, 369; McMillen, "Mississippi's Black Veterans," 103.

12. Stephen G. N. Tuck, *Beyond Atlanta: The Struggle for Racial Equality in Georgia, 1940–1980* (Athens, Ga., 2003), 42–43.

13. Ibid., 1, 44, 67.

14. Brooks, *Defining the Peace*, 71.

15. Bartley, *New South*, 80.

16. Ibid., 78, 82.

17. Harvard Sitkoff, "Harry Truman and the Election of 1948: The Coming of Age of Civil Rights in American Politics," *Journal of Southern History* 32 (November 1971): 597.

18. Bartley, *New South*, 87–93.

19. Ibid., 94–95.

20. Stetson Kennedy, "Total Equality and How to Get It," *Common Ground*, Winter 1946, 63; Stetson Kennedy, *Southern Exposure* (Garden City, N.Y., 1946), 349; Morton Sosna, *In Search of the Silent South: Southern Liberals and the Race Issue* (New York, 1977), 19.

21. Edgar Gardner Murphy, *Problems of the Present South: A Discussion of Certain of the Educational, Industrial, and Political Issues in the Southern States* (New York, 1904), 277.

22. Bartley, *New South*, 28,30; Sosna, *In Search of the Silent South*, 19, 205.

23. Kenneth Robert Janken, introduction to *What the Negro Wants*, ed. Rayford W. Logan (Notre Dame, Ind., 2001), xix, xx, xxxiii; Frederick D. Patterson, "The Negro Wants Full Participation in the American Democracy," in Logan, *What the Negro Wants*, 265, 323; James C. Cobb, *The Brown Decision, Jim Crow, and Southern Identity* (Athens, Ga., 2005), 40–41.

24. Lillian Smith, *Killers of the Dream* (New York, 1949), 158–59; Sosna, *In Search of the Silent South*, 186–89.

25. Lillian Smith, *Strange Fruit* (San Diego, 1992), 109.

26. Bartley, *New South*, 71; Sosna, *In Search of the Silent South*, 163, 166; David L. Cohn, "How the South Feels," *Atlantic Monthly* 173 (January 1944): 48–51.

27. William Faulkner, *Intruder in the Dust* (New York, 1948), 216; Joseph Blotner, *Faulkner: A Biography* (New York, 1991), 618.

28. Martha Biondi, *To Stand and Fight: The Struggle for Voting Rights in Postwar New York City* (Cambridge, Mass., 2003), 56.

29. Steven F. Lawson, *Black Ballots: Voting Rights in the South, 1944–1969* (New York, 1969), 90–93; Egerton, *Speak Now*, 397.

30. *Gaines v. Canada*, 305 U.S. 337 (1938).

31. *McLaurin v. Oklahoma State Regents*, 339 U.S. 637 (1950); *Sweatt v. Painter*, 339 U.S. 629 (1950); *Henderson v. United States*, 339 U.S. 816 (1950).

32. Richard Kluger, *Simple Justice* (New York, 1975), 268.

33. *Briggs et al. v. Elliott et al.*, 342 U.S. 350 (1952).

34. Kluger, *Simple Justice*, 4, 6.

35. Ibid., 10.

36. Ibid., 23–24.

37. Ibid., 24.

38. Ibid., 294–305.

39. Ibid., 346–66.

40. Ibid., 540.

CHAPTER 2

1. Chief Justice Earl Warren, "Opinion of the Court in *Brown v. Board of Education*, May 17, 1954," *Brown v. Board of Education: A Brief History with Documents*, by Waldo E. Martin Jr. (Boston, 1998), 173–74; Egerton, *Speak Now*, 609.

2. Kluger, *Simple Justice*, 710–11; Egerton, *Speak Now*, 609–10.

3. Kluger, *Simple Justice*, 714.

4. Ibid., 723–24; James T. Patterson, *Brown v. Board of Education: A Civil Rights Milestone and Its Troubled Legacy* (New York, 2001), 81–83.

5. J. T. Patterson, *Brown v. Board*, 113–14; William E. Leuchtenburg, *The White House Looks South: Franklin D. Roosevelt, Harry S. Truman, Lyndon B. Johnson* (Baton Rouge, La., 2000), 415–16; Bartley, *New South*, 231.

6. See Michael J. Klarman, *From Jim Crow to Civil Rights: The Supreme Court and the Struggle for Civil Rights* (New York, 2004); Cobb, *The Brown Decision*, 31–35.

7. Mark M. Smith, *How Race Is Made: Slavery, Segregation, and the Senses* (Chapel Hill, N.C., 2006), 124.

8. Ibid., 131; Winthrop D. Jordan, *The White Man's Burden: Historical Origins of Racism in the United States* (New York, 1974), 19.

9. Melton A. McLaurin, *Separate Pasts: Growing Up White in the Segregated South* (Athens, Ga., 1987), 37–38.

10. Ibid., 90.

11. Earl Black and Merle Black, *Politics and Society in the South* (Cambridge, Mass., 1987), 78; Melvin M. Tumin et al., *Desegregation: Resistance and Readiness* (Princeton, N.J., 1958), 34–46; Numan V. Bartley, *The Rise of Massive Resistance: Race and Politics in the South During the 1950s* (Baton Rouge, La., 1969), 13.

12. Robert A. Margo, *Race and Schooling in the South, 1890–1950: An Economic History* (Chicago, 1991), 91–92; Gavin Wright, "The Economics of the Civil Rights Revolution," in *Toward the Meeting of the Waters: The Civil Rights Movement in South Carolina*, ed. Winfred O. Moore Jr. and Orville Vernon Burton (Columbia, S.C., 2008), 388.

13. Mary Mebane, "Three Maxims in the Life of Mary," in *Speaking for Ourselves: Women of the South*, ed. Maxine Alexander (New York, 1984), 59.

14. James C. Cobb, ed., *The Mississippi Delta and the World: The Memoirs of David L. Cohn* (Baton Rouge, La., 1995), 76; Susan Tucker, ed., *Telling Memories among Southern Women: Domestic Workers and Their Employers in the Segregated South* (Baton Rouge, La., 1988), 39–40. Note: to preserve the anonymity of the women interviewed, pseudonyms were used.

15. Glenn T. Eskew, *But for Birmingham: The Local and National Movements in the Civil Rights Struggle* (Chapel Hill, N.C., 1997), 86; William H. Chafe, *Civilities and Civil Rights: Greensboro, North Carolina, and the Black Freedom Struggle* (New York, 1980), 107.

16. S. Tucker, *Telling Memories*, 208–210.

17. Willie Morris, *North toward Home* (Oxford, Miss., 1982), 77–78, 90; Sarah Patton Boyle, *The Desegregated Heart* (New York, 1962), 36, 89.

18. Roberta S. Maguire, "Walker Percy and Albert Murray: The Story of Two 'Part Anglo-Saxon Alabamians,'" *Southern Quarterly* 41 (Fall 2002): 20.

19. C. Vann Woodward to Howard K. Beale, July 18, 1949, Howard K. Beale Papers, B26, F7 Archives, Wisconsin Historical Society, Madison, Wis.; John Herbert Roper, *C. Vann Woodward, Southerner* (Athens, Ga., 1987), 163–70.

20. John Hope Franklin to Howard K. Beale, December 6, 1954, Beale Papers, B9, F8.

21. Boyle, *The Desegregated Heart*, 77–85; Hollinger F. Barnard, ed., *Outside the Magic Circle: The Autobiography of Virginia Durr* (Tuscaloosa, Ala., 1985), 276; Virginia Durr to C. Vann Woodward, December 5, 1955, Box 16, Folder 183, C. Vann Woodward Papers, Sterling Memorial Library, Yale University, New Haven, Conn.

22. Herbert Blumer, "The Future of the Color Line," in *The South in Continuity and Change,* ed. John C. McKinney and Edgar T. Thompson (Durham, N.C., 1965), 322–35.

23. Seth Cagin and Phillip Dray, *We Are Not Afraid: The Story of Goodman, Schwerner, and Chaney and the Civil Rights Campaign for Mississippi* (New York, 1988), 157.

24. Dan T. Carter, *Politics of Rage: George Wallace, the Origins of the New Conservatism, and the Transformation of American Politics* (Baton Rouge, La., 2000), 73; Carl Rowan, *Go South to Sorrow* (New York, 1957), 206.

25. Bartley, *New South*, 98.

26. Ibid., 54.

27. Anne Moody, *Coming of Age in Mississippi* (New York, 1968), 125–28.

28. David Halberstam, "A Country Divided against Itself," *Reporter*, December 15, 1955, 30.

29. Bartley, *Rise of Massive Resistance*, 85–86.

30. Bernard L. Stein, *This Female Crusading Scalawag: Hazel Brannon Smith, Justice, and Mississippi,* www.freedomforum.org/publications/msj/courage.summer2000/y09.html; Hazel Brannon Smith, "Bombed, Burned, and Boycotted," Alice Patterson Foundation, *APF Reporter*, www.aliciapatterson.org/APF0702/Smith/Smith.html.

31. Bartley, *Rise of Massive Resistance*, 87–107.

32. Ibid., 85; James C. Cobb, *Redefining Southern Culture: Mind and Identity in the Modern South* (Athens, Ga., 1999), 68.

33. Bartley, *New South*, 204.

34. John White, "The White Citizens Council of Orangeburg County, South Carolina," in Moore and Burton, *Meeting of the Waters*, 262.

35. Ibid., 266–67.

36. Charles S. Hynman, *The Supreme Court on Trial* (Piscataway, N.J., 2007), 21; Bartley, *New South*, 194–95.

37. Bartley, *New South*, 194–95; James C. Cobb, *Georgia Odyssey* (Athens, Ga., 2008), 110.

38. Bartley, *New South*, 197.

39. Ibid., 98; "The Southern Manifesto," *Congressional Record*, 84th Congress, Second Session, vol. 102, part 4, March 12, 1956, 4, 515–16, www.cviog.uga.edu/projects/gainfo/manifesto.htm.

40. Bartley, *New South*, 202; J. Todd Moye, *Let the People Decide: Black Freedom and White Resistance Movements in Sunflower County, Mississippi, 1945–1986* (Chapel Hill, N.C., 2004), 5.

41. "Rev. George Lee's Murderers Never Caught," *Neshoba (Miss.) News*, December 8, 2005, www.neshobanews.blogspot.com/2005/12/rev_george_lees_murders_never_caught.html.

42. For a comprehensive account of the murder and reaction to it, see Stephen J. Whitfield, *A Death in the Delta: The Story of Emmett Till* (Baltimore, 1988).

43. Ibid., 94–95.

44. Ibid., 42.

45. Ibid., 51; Arnold Hirsch, *Making the Second Ghetto: Race and Housing in Chicago, 1940–1960* (Chicago, 1998), 65.

46. Moody, *Coming of Age*, 125–26.

47. Ibid., 129.

48. Ibid., 129; "Mourners Pay Tribute to Rosa Parks: Clinton Recalls Being Inspired by Civil Rights Pioneer," CNN.com, November 3, 2005, www.cnn.com/2005/US/11/02/rosa.parks/index.html; Jo Ann Robinson and David J. Garrow, *The Montgomery Bus Boycott and the Women Who Started It: The Memoir of Jo Ann Gibson Robinson* (Knoxville, Tenn., 1987).

49. Juan Williams, *Eyes on the Prize: America's Civil Rights Years* (New York, 1987), 74; Jerrold M. Packard, *American Nightmare: The History of Jim Crow* (New York, 2003), 250.

50. E. Culpepper Clark, *The Schoolhouse Door: Segregation's Last Stand at the University of Alabama* (New York, 1993), 71–80.

51. Ibid., 80–103.

52. Clayborne Carson et al., *The Papers of Martin Luther King, Jr.*, vol. 6: *Advocate of the Social Gospel, September 1948–March 1963* (Berkeley, 2007), 257–59.

53. The following account of events in Little Rock draws heavily on Bartley, *Rise of Massive Resistance*, 251–69. For a comprehensive account of the Little Rock Crisis, see Elizabeth Jacoway, *Turn Away Thy Son: Little Rock, the Crisis That Shook the Nation* (New York, 2007).

54. Pete Daniel, *Lost Revolutions: The South in the 1950s* (Chapel Hill, 2000), 264.

55. Ibid., 261.

56. Ibid., 270.

57. Bartley, *New South*, 234–35.

58. Jacoway, *Turn Away They Son*, 297, 311, 325–27.

59. Ibid., 319–25.

60. Ibid., 350–51.

61. Tumin, *Desegregation*, 39–46.

62. Harry S. Ashmore, *An Epitaph for Dixie* (New York, 1958), 15, 22, 188; Henry Savage Jr., *Seeds of Time: The Background of Southern Thinkers* (New York, 1959), 274.

CHAPTER 3

1. Gilbert C. Fite, *Cotton Fields No More: Southern Agriculture, 1865–1980* (Lexington, Ky., 1984), 154.

2. Pete Daniel, "Going among Strangers: Southern Reactions to World War II," *Journal of American History* 77 (December 1990): 886–911.

3. Fite, *Cotton Fields No More*, 185–86.

4. Thomas D. Clark, *The Emerging South*, 2nd ed. (New York, 1968), 61; Fite, *Cotton Fields No More*, 184.

5. Bartley, *New South*, 2–3, 10–11; Ronald D. Eller, *Uneven Ground: Appalachia since 1945* (Lexington, 2008), 13, 29–30.

6. Morton Sosna, introduction to McMillen, *Remaking Dixie*, xiv; Bartley, *New South*, 123, 2–3, 9–10; George B. Tindall, *The Emergence of the New South, 1913–1945* (Baton Rouge, La., 1967), 694, 699; Eller, *Uneven Ground*, 13, 29–30.

7. Bruce J. Schulman, *From Cotton Belt to Sunbelt: Federal Policy, Economic Development, and the Transformation of the South, 1938–1980* (New York, 1991), 82; Bartley, *New South*, 124.

8. Bartley, *New South*, 124; Samuel Lubell, *The Future of American Politics* (Garden City, N.J., 1953), 119.

9. James C. Cobb, *The Selling of the South: The Southern Crusade for Industrial Development, 1936–1990* (Urbana, Ill., 1993), 54.

10. Albert Lepawsky, *State Planning and Economic Development in the South* (Kingsport, Tenn., 1949), 122–23.

11. Cobb, *Selling of the South*, 47–48.

12. Ibid., 76.

13. Ibid., 54–55, 58.

14. Ibid., 44; "Hotter Bidding for New Plants," *Business Week,* December 16, 1961, 126; Schulman, *From Cotton Belt to Sunbelt*, 200.

15. Ira Katznelson, *When Affirmative Action Was White: An Untold History of Racial Inequality in America* (New York, 2005), 70–73.

16. Ibid., 196; Bartley, *New South*, 62.

17. Cobb, *Selling of the South*, 103–104.

18. *Congressional Record,* 83rd Congress, First Session, 1953, vol. 99, part 4, 5, 320; Robert J. Newman, *Growth of the American South: Changing Regional Employment and Wage Patterns in the 1960s and 1970s* (New York, 1984), 59–62.

19. Joe A. Martin, "Some Myths of Southern Economic Growth: A Study of Comparative Growth in the Manufacturing Economy of the Eleven Southern

States," *Journal of Farm Economics* 38 (December 1956): 1363–74; Cobb, *Selling of the South*, 113–14.

20. Rosalie Tucker, "Voices from the Village," in *Textile Town: Spartanburg, South Carolina,* ed. Betsy Wakefield Teter (Spartanburg, S.C., 2002), 236.

21. Schulman, *From Cotton Belt to Sunbelt*, 118, 35.

22. Ibid., 117.

23. Ibid., 146–47.

24. Ibid., 140; Bartley, *New South*, 144.

25. Schulman, *From Cotton Belt to Sunbelt*, 158; Richard E. Lonsdale and Clyde E. Browning, "Rural-Urban Locational Preferences of Southern Manufacturers," *Annals of the American Association of Geographers* 61 (June 1971): 262–63.

26. David R. Goldfield, *Cotton Fields and Skyscrapers: Southern City and Region, 1607–1980,* (Baton Rouge, La., 1982), 142–44; Richard M. Bernard and Bradley R. Rice, eds., *The Rise of Sunbelt Cities: Politics and Growth Since World War II* (Austin, Tex., 1983), 10.

27. F. Ray Marshall and Virgil Christian Jr., "Human Resource Development in the South," in *You Can't Eat Magnolias,* ed. H. Brandt Ayers and Thomas H. Naylor (New York, 1972), 239–40; Bartley, *New South*, 263.

28. Cobb, *Georgia Odyssey*, 54–56.

29. Ralph McGill, *The South and the Southerner* (Boston, 1960), 161–62.

30. Ibid., 162; David R. Goldfield, *Promised Land: The South Since 1945* (Arlington Heights, Ill., 1987), 37.

31. Cobb, *Selling of the South*, 156; Bartley, *New South*, 70.

32. Robert J. Norrell, "Labor at the Ballot Box: Alabama Politics from the New Deal to the Dixiecrat Movement," *Journal of Southern History* 57 (May 1991): 229; Anna R. Hayes, *Without Precedent: The Life of Susie Marshall Sharp* (Chapel Hill, N.C., 2008), 110.

33. Black and Black, *Politics and Society*, 297.

34. James C. Cobb, "Politics in a New South City: Augusta, Georgia, 1946–1971," PhD dissertation, University of Georgia, 1975, 42; James C. Cobb, "Colonel Effingham Crushes the Crackers: Political Reform in Postwar Augusta," *South Atlantic Quarterly* 78 (Autumn 1979): 516–17; Hayes, *Without Precedent*, 110.

35. William H. Nicholls, *Southern Tradition and Regional Progress* (Chapel Hill, N.C., 1960), 117–18; Schulman, *From Cotton Belt to Sunbelt*, 124, 131; see Luther H. Hodges, *Businessman in the Statehouse* (Chapel Hill, N.C., 1962).

36. Erskine Caldwell, *Deep South: Memory and Observation* (Athens, Ga., 1995), 77–78.

37. Ibid., 78, 81–84.

38. Ibid., 78; Robert Emil Botsch, *We Shall Not Overcome: Populism and Southern Blue-Collar Workers* (Chapel Hill, N.C., 1980), 107.

39. Bartley, *New South*, 274–75.

40. Ibid., 137–38.

41. Christopher Silver and John V. Moeser, *The Separate City: Black Communities in the Urban South, 1940–1968* (Lexington, Ky., 1995), 110.

42. Egerton, *Speak Now*, 382; Cobb, *Selling of the South*, 127.

43. *County and City Data Book: Historic Editions* (1944–83), University of Virginia Library, http://fisher.lib.virginia.edu/collections/stats/ccdb/.

44. Nicholls, *Southern Tradition*, 181.

CHAPTER 4

1. Bartley, *New South*, 181–82.

2. Ibid., 185; Lawson, *Black Ballots*, 231–32.

3. Robert Weisbrot, *Freedom Bound: A History of America's Civil Rights Movement* (New York, 1990), 1–3.

4. Chafe, *Civilities and Civil Rights*, 97.

5. Weisbrot, *Freedom Bound*, 33.

6. Ann Waldron, *Hodding Carter: The Reconstruction of a Racist* (Chapel Hill, N.C., 1993), 247–48.

7. Harvard Sitkoff, *The Struggle for Black Equality, 1954–1992*, 2nd ed. (New York, 1993), 90–92.

8. Ibid., 93–94; Ann Bausum, class of 1979, "James Zwerg Recalls His Freedom Ride," *Beloit College Magazine*, Winter/Spring 1989, www.beloit.edu/archives/documents/archival_documents/james_zwerg_freedom_ride.php.

9. Sitkoff, *Struggle for Black Equality*, 96; Evan Thomas, *Robert Kennedy: His Life* (New York, 2000), 132.

10. Sitkoff, *Struggle for Black Equality*, 98; Dave Myers, "Young Women...Insisted on Going with Us," and Russell Jorgensen, "King Urged Us to Integrate the Airport," *Voices of Civil Rights: Ordinary People, Extraordinary Stories*, www.voicesofcivilrights.org.

11. Pat Watters and Reese Cleghorn, *Climbing Jacob's Ladder: The Arrival of Negroes in Southern Politics* (New York, 1967), 7; Bartley, *New South*, 323.

12. Bartley, *New South*, 323; Howard Zinn, *SNCC: The New Abolitionists* (Boston, 1964), 126.

13. David Levering Lewis, *King: A Critical Biography* (New York, 1970), 149.

14. Adam Fairclough, *To Redeem the Soul of America: The Southern Christian Leadership Conference and Martin Luther King, Jr.* (Athens, Ga., 2001), 101; Weisbrot, *Freedom Bound*, 65.

15. Robert J. Norrell, *The House I Live In: Race in the American Century* (New York, 2005), 207.

16. Calvin Trillin, "Reflections: Remembrance of Moderates Past," *New Yorker*, March 21, 1977, 86; Norrell, *House I Live In*, 204.

17. Carter, *Politics of Rage*, 116.

18. Ibid., 124.

19. Ibid., 124, 127.

20. President John F. Kennedy, "Radio and Television Report to the American People on Civil Rights," The White House, June 11, 1963, JFK Presidential Library and Museum, www.jfklibrary.org/Historical+Resources/Archives/Reference+Desk/Speeches/JFK/003POF03CivilRights06111963.htm; Weisbrot, *Freedom Bound*, 75.

21. Weisbrot, *Freedom Bound*, 8.

22. Carter, *Politics of Rage*, 173.

23. Ibid., 174.

24. Ibid., 177–78; Eskew, *But for Birmingham*, 321; Doris Maddox, "You Wonder How People Could Be So Bitter," *Voices of Civil Rights,* www.civilrights.org.

25. Norrell, *House I Live In*, 213; Weisbrot, *Freedom Bound,* 72; *Report of the Sibert Committee on Assassinations of the United States House of Representatives* (Washington, D.C., 1979), 271.

26. Tasha S. Philpot, *Race, Republicans, and the Return of the Party of Lincoln* (Ann Arbor, Mich., 2007), 44.

27. Chana Kai Lee, *For Freedom's Sake: The Life of Fannie Lou Hamer* (Urbana, Ill., 1999), 15, 21.

28. Ibid., 22, 26; Cobb, *Most Southern Place,* 243.

29. Lee, *For Freedom's Sake*, 40.

30. Ibid., 72.

31. Ibid., 89.

32. Cobb, *Most Southern Place,* 243, 244; Bartley, *New South*, 349, 354.

33. Weisbrot, *Freedom Bound*, 119, 122–23; Lee, *For Freedom's Sake*, 99.

34. Chris Myers Asch, *The Senator and the Sharecropper: The Freedom Struggles of James O. Eastland and Fannie Lee Hamer* (New York, 2008), 213.

35. Weisbrot, *Freedom Bound*, 128–29.

36. Ibid., 132–33.

37. Carter, *Politics of Rage*, 246.

38. Ibid., 247.

39. Ibid., 249.

40. Larry H. Anderson, *The Movement and the Sixties: Protest in America from Greensboro to Wounded Knee* (New York, 1995), 118.

41. Ibid., 119.

42. Gene Roberts and Hank Klibanoff, *The Race Beat: The Press, the Civil Rights Struggle, and the Awakening of a Nation* (New York, 2007), 119.

43. Lawson, *Black Ballots*, 330.

44. Ibid., 330–32.

45. Cobb, *Most Southern Place,* 204, 255.

46. Cobb, *Selling of the South*, 116; Gavin Wright, *Old South, New South: Revolutions in the Southern Economy since the Civil War* (New York, 1986), 244-45.

47. U.S. Bureau of the Census, *Statistical Abstract of the United States: 1966*, 87th ed. (Washington, D.C., 1966), 305; Marshall and Christian, "Human Resource Development," 255.

48. Cobb, *Most Southern Place*, 266.

49. Ibid., 257; U.S. Senate, Select Committee on Human Needs, *Poverty, Malnutrition, and Federal Food Assistance Programs: A Statistical Summary* (Washington, D.C., 1969), 33–34.

50. Cobb, *Most Southern Place*, 257; U.S. Senate, *Poverty, Malnutrition, and Federal Food Assistance Programs*, 9; Robert Coles, "The Way It Is in South Carolina," in *Farewell to the South* (Boston and Toronto, 1972), 87.

51. Norrell, *House I Live In*, 207; David J. Garrow, *Bearing the Cross: Martin Luther King, Jr., and the Southern Christian Leadership Conference* (New York, 1986), 251, 391.

52. The Anti-Defamation League of B'nai B'rith, *The High Cost of Conflict: A Roundup of Opinion from the Southern Business Community on the Economic Consequences of School Closings and Violence* (copy in possession of the author); Cobb, *Selling of the South*, 126, 129–30.

53. Edward Hass, *DeLesseps S. Morrison and the Image of Reform* (Baton Rouge, La., 1986), 267–69, 272–79, 283–88; Robert L. Crain, *The Politics of School Desegregation: Comparative Case Studies of Community Structure and Policy-Making* (Garden City, N.Y., 1969), 292–305.

54. Cobb, *Selling of the South*, 128–29.

55. Ibid., 134–35.

56. Joe David Brown, "Birmingham, Alabama: A City in Fear," *Saturday Evening Post*, March 2, 1963, 13, 17–18.

57. Cobb, *Selling of the South*, 136–38.

58. Ibid., 139.

59. Ibid., 146.

60. Ibid., 148–49; David R. Coulburn, "The Saint Augustine Business Community," in *Southern Businessmen and Civil Rights*, ed. David R. Colburn and Elizabeth Jacoway (Baton Rouge, L.a., 1982), 224.

61. U.S. Census Bureau, *County-City Data Books*, 1956, 1967, 1972, 1977, http://fisher.lib.virginia.edu/collections/stats/ccdb/php/historic5.php.

62. Chafe, *Civilities and Civil Rights*, 146–51.

63. Paul Luebke and Joseph Schneiding, "Economic and Racial Ideology in the North Carolina Elite," in *Perspectives on the American South: An Annual Review of Society, Politics, and Culture*, 4, ed. James C. Cobb and Charles R. Wilson (London, 1987), 134.

64. Harold W. Stanley, *Voter Mobilization and the Politics of Race: The South and Universal Suffrage, 1952–1984* (New York, 1987), 139, 118–19.

65. Robert Coles, *Children of Crisis: A Study of Courage and Fear* (New York, 1967), 378–80; Jason Sokol, *There Goes My Everything: White Southerners in the Age of Civil Rights, 1945–1975* (New York, 2006), 155.

66. Coles, *Children of Crisis*, 205, 377; Robert Coles, "The White Northerner: Pride and Prejudice," *Atlantic Monthly*, June 1966, www.theatlantic.com/politics/race/whitenor.htm.

67. Chafe, *Civilities and Civil Rights*, 152.

CHAPTER 5

1. *United States v. Jefferson Board of Education*, 372 F.2d 836 (5th Circuit, 1966).

2. *Green v. New Kent County School Board*, 391 U.S. 430 (1968); "The Green Decision of 1968," www.vahistorical.org/civilrights/green.htm; J. Harvie Wilkinson III, *From Brown to Bakke: The Supreme Court and School Integration: 1954–1978* (New York, 1972), 121.

3. Melany Neilson, *Even Mississippi* (Tuscaloosa, Ala., 1989), 24, 32–35.

4. *United States Census of Population, Supplementary Report, Negro Population in Selected Places and Selected Counties, 1970*, www.census.gov/prod/www/abs/decennial/1970cenpop_pcs1.htm.

5. "South's Integrationists Gloomy amid Gains," *New York Times*, March 15, 1970, 1; *Swann v. Mecklenburg Board of Education*, 402 U.S. 1 (1971).

6. Norrell, *House I Live In*, 289.

7. Wright, "Economics of the Civil Rights Revolution," 391.

8. Coles, *Children of Crisis*, 48.

9. Ibid., 51.

10. Frederick M. Wirt, *The Politics of Southern Equality: Law and Social Change in a Mississippi County* (Chicago, 1970), 166–67.

11. Stanley, *Voter Mobilization*, 143.

12. Frank R. Parker, *Black Votes Count: Political Empowerment in Mississippi after 1965* (Chapel Hill, 1990), 31–32; Cobb, *Most Southern Place*, 247.

13. Cobb, *Most Southern Place*, 247; Stanley, *Voter Mobilization*, 55.

14. Cobb, *Selling of the South*, 119.

15. Ibid., 117; Wright, "Economics of the Civil Rights Revolution," 396.

16. William W. Falk, *Rooted in Place: Family and Belonging in a Southern Black Community* (Piscataway, N.J., 2004), 35.

17. Peter A. Coclanis and Louis M. Kyriakoudes, "Selling Which South: Economic Change in Rural and Small-Town North Carolina in an Era of Globalization, 1940–2007," *Southern Cultures* 13 (Winter 2007): 93.

18. Wright, "Economics of the Civil Rights Revolution," 387.

19. Ibid., 10.

20. Ibid., 386; Gavin Wright, "The Civil Rights Revolution as Economic History," *Journal of Economic History* 59 (June 1997): 277–78.

21. Alfred Dawkins and Alaree Dawkins, "Voices from the Village," in Teter, *Textile Town,* 232–33.

22. S. Tucker, *Telling Memories,* 120.

23. Lawson, *Black Ballots,* 331; Stanley, *Voter Mobilization,* 6.

24. Joseph A. Crespino, *In Search of Another Country: Mississippi and the Conservative Counterrevolution* (Princeton, N.J., 2007), 103.

25. Cobb, "Politics in a New South City," 151.

26. Numan V. Bartley and Hugh Davis Graham, *Southern Politics and the Second Reconstruction* (Baltimore, 1975), 106–8.

27. Earl Black and Merle Black, *The Rise of Southern Republicans* (Cambridge, Mass., 2002), 139–48.

28. Bartley, *New South,* 389.

29. Bartley and Graham, *Southern Politics and the Second Reconstruction,* 114–17.

30. Bartley, *New South,* 383; Carter, *Politics of Rage,* 218–22.

31. Carter, *Politics of Rage,* 306.

32. Ibid., 303; Anderson, *Movement and the Sixties,* 157.

33. "Eisenhower Heads a List of Admired," *New York Times,* December 29, 1968, 40; Carter, *Politics of Rage,* 313; Norrell, *House I Live In,* 266.

34. Carter, *Politics of Rage,* 333.

35. Ibid.

36. Ibid., 341; "A Voter's Lexicon of 'Wallaceisms,'" *New York Times,* August 25, 1968, 61.

37. "The Racist Candidate," *New York Times,* February 9, 1968, 26; Lewis Chester, Godfrey Hodgson, and Bruce Page, *An American Melodrama: The Presidential Campaign of 1968* (New York, 1969), 293.

38. "Wallace Diagnoses the High Court as 'Sick,'" *New York Times,* July 10, 1968, 20; "Wallace Turns to Connecticut," *New York Times,* August 4, 1968, 49; "Wallace 'Phenomenon' Drive Gains Momentum," *New York Times,* August 19, 1968, 33; "A Feeling for Wallace Pervades a Peaceful Town in Michigan," *New York Times,* September 12, 1968, 36.

39. Carter, *Politics of Rage,* 346.

40. "Wallace Out-talks Milwaukee Jeerers," *New York Times,* September 3, 1968, 51.

41. Carter, *Politics of Rage,* 362.

42. "The Wallace Sickness," *New York Times,* September 22, 1968, A-19.

43. "The New Wallace Is a 'National Candidate,'" *New York Times*, September 15, 1968, E-2; "Redneck New York: Is This Wallace Country?" *New York,* October 7, 1968, 25.

44. Chester, Hodgson, and Page, *An American Melodrama*, 705, 710.

45. Ibid., 699.

46. John Robert Greene, "I'll Continue to Speak Out: Spiro T. Agnew as Vice President," in *At the President's Side: The Vice Presidency in the Twentieth Century,* ed. Timothy Walch (Columbia, Mo., 1997), 125–26.

47. "Nixon Is Found Hard to Fathom on Basis of Public Statements," *New York Times*, October 26, 1968, 21; Carter, *Politics of Rage*, 329.

48. Bartley, *New South*, 397.

49. Chester, Hodgson, and Page, *An American Melodrama*, 627; Matthew D. Lassiter, *The Silent Majority: Suburban Politics in the Sunbelt South* (Princeton, N.J., 2007), 267.

50. Kevin P. Phillips, *The Emerging Republican Majority* (New Rochelle, N.Y., 1969), 287; "Nixon's Southern Strategy: 'It's All in the Charts,'" *New York Times,* May 17, 1970, 215.

51. "The Troubled America: A Special Report on the White Majority," *Newsweek,* October 6, 1969, 28–73.

52. "Ribicoff Attacks Schools in the North," *New York Times*, February 10, 1970, 1; "Stennis Rebuffed in School Aid Vote," *New York Times*, April 2, 1970, 1; "Javits Accused by Ribicoff of 'Hypocrisy' on Schools," *New York Times*, April 21, 1971, 1; C. Vann Woodward, "Southern Styles: A Typology," unpublished manuscript, Box 73, Folder 130, C. Vann Woodward Papers, Yale University Library, New Haven, Conn.; "Green Wants Ike to Visit South," *Tri-City (Washington) Herald*, September 11, 1957, 8.

53. "Senate Rights Bloc May Founder on School Busing Issue," *New York Times*, January 23, 1972, 34; Norrell, *House I Live In*, 288.

54. Wilkinson, *Brown to Bakke*, 202.

55. Ibid., 203, 208; Weisbrot, *Freedom Bound*, 291.

56. Coles, "White Northerner."

57. Ibid.

58. Herbert S. Parnet, *Richard Nixon and His America* (Boston, 1990), 607–9; *Milliken v. Bradley*, 418 U.S. 717 (1974); Norrell, *House I Live In*, 290.

59. Carter, *Politics of Rage*, 393, 400, 409.

60. Ibid., 412–13; Bartley, *New South*, 412.

61. Lassiter, *Silent Majority*, 259, 267–68.

62. Ibid., 269–71; Bartley, *New South*, 400; Matthew J. Streb, *The New Electoral Politics of Race* (Tuscaloosa, Ala., 2002), 71; Lassiter, *Silent Majority*, 269–71.

63. Lassiter, *Silent Majority*, 261.

64. Numan V. Bartley, *The Creation of Modern Georgia* (Athens, Ga., 1990), 180–81, 206–7.

65. Bartley, *New South*, 406–407; Lassiter, *Silent Majority*, 261.

66. Earl Black and Merle Black, *The Vital South: How Presidents Are Elected* (Cambridge, Mass., 1993), 330.

67. Ibid., 331–32.

68. Black and Black, *Vital South*, 332–34; Larry King, "We Ain't Trash No More!" *Esquire* 126 (November 1976): 88; "Time for a Change," *New York Times*, November 1, 1976, 39.

CHAPTER 6

1. Robert Palmer, *Deep Blues: A Musical and Cultural History of the Mississippi Delta* (New York, 1982), 3–7, 59, 259.

2. Ibid., 222–23, 231–34.

3. Ibid., 224; Bill C. Malone, *Country Music U.S.A.: A Fifty-Year History* (Austin, Tex., 1968), 242–44.

4. Malone, *Country Music*, 184–228; Tony Scherman, "Country," *American Heritage* 45 (November 1994), www.americanheritage.com/articles/magazine/ah/1994/7/1994_7_38.shtml.

5. Malone, *Country Music*, 128–31.

6. Ibid., 305–18.

7. Jeffrey J. Lange, *Smile When You Call Me a Hillbilly: Country Music's Struggle for Respectability, 1939–1954* (Athens, Ga., 2004), 235–36.

8. Cobb, *Most Southern Place,* 302; Colin Escott, George Merritt, and William MacEwen, *Hank Williams: The Biography* (Boston, 2004), 201.

9. Lange, *Smile,* 193.

10. Daniel, *Lost Revolutions*, 121–47.

11. "Station in Home of the Blues, Forever Changed the Color of Radio," *Atlanta Journal-Constitution*, October 23, 2005, K-1, K-3.

12. Daniel, *Lost Revolutions*, 135.

13. Nick Tosches, *Country: The Twisted Roots of Rock 'n' Roll* (New York, 1996), 73, 100.

14. Bill C. Malone, *Don't Get above Your Raisin': Country Music and the Southern Working Class* (Urbana, Ill., 2002), 9–10.

15. Elvis Presley, Jerry Lee Lewis, and Carl Perkins, "The Million Dollar Quartet," copyright 1990, BMG Music. (Also see liner notes.)

16. Peter Guralnick, *Sweet Soul Music: Rhythm and Blues and the Southern Dream of Freedom* (New York, 1986), 35–36, 46.

17. Gilbert Rodman, *Elvis after Elvis: The Posthumous Career of a Living Legend* (London, 1996), 193 n. 16.

18. Malone, *Country Music*, 245–58.

19. Ibid., 262; Ronnie Pugh, *Ernest Tubb: The Texas Troubadour* (Durham, N.C., 1998), 283–84.

20. Lerone Bennett Jr., "Old Illusions and New Souths," *Ebony*, August 1971, 35.

21. *Time*, May 31, 1971, cover.

22. James C. Cobb, *Industrialization and Southern Society, 1877–1984* (Lexington, Ky., 1984), 57–60.

23. Ibid., 108.

24. Raymond Arsenault, "The End of the Long Hot Summer: The Air Conditioner and Southern Culture," in *Searching for the Sunbelt: Historical Perspectives on a Region*, ed. Raymond A. Mohl (Athens, Ga., 1993), 187, 176; "Migration Mixes a New Southern Blend," *New York Times*, February 11, 1976, 30.

25. "Migration Mixes," 30.

26. "The Good Life" and "Those Good Ole Boys," *Time*, September 27, 1976, 32–39.

27. Kirkpatrick Sale, *Power Shift: The Rise of the Southern Rim and Its Challenge to the Eastern Establishment* (New York, 1975), 180.

28. C. Vann Woodward, "The South Tomorrow," *Time*, September 27, 1976, 99; "The Southernization of America," *New York Times*, August 30, 1976, 22.

29. Richard Michael Kelly, *The Andy Griffith Show* (Winston-Salem, N.C., 1991), 10–12.

30. Jack Temple Kirby, *Media-Made Dixie: The South in the American Imagination*, 2nd ed. (Athens, Ga., 1986, 1971), 142.

31. Ibid., 156.

32. Cobb, *Redefining Southern Culture*, 86.

33. Ibid., 82.

34. Ibid., 89.

35. Kirby, *Media-Made Dixie*, 163.

36. Horace Sutton, "The South as New America," *Saturday Review* 3 (September 4, 1976), 8.

CHAPTER 7

1. Schulman, *From Cotton Belt to Sunbelt*, 181, 180; Cobb, *Most Southern Place*, 259.

2. Cobb, *Most Southern Place*, 261; U.S. Senate, Committee on Labor and Public Welfare, Subcommittee on Employment, Manpower, and Poverty, *Hunger and Federal Programs, Background Information* (Washington, D.C., 1967), 73; U.S. Senate, Committee on Appropriations, Hearings on H.R. 16913, 90th Congress, 2nd Session (Washington, D.C., 1967), 234–36, 996–97.

3. Marshall and Christian, "Human Resource Development," 256; Harry Kreisler, *Studying the Human Condition: Habits of a Militant Anthropologist. Conversation with Nancy Scheper-Hughes, Professor of Anthropology, University of California, Berkeley*, December 14, 1999, http://globetrotter.berkeley.edu/people/Scheper-Hughes/sh-con2.html.

4. Cobb, *Most Southern Place*, 265.

5. Ibid., 255–56.

6. Ibid.

7. Ibid.

8. Eller, *Uneven Ground*, 64–65, 59, 61.

9. Ibid., 154; "Kennedy Calls Antipoverty Program a Failure," *New York Times*, February 15, 1968, 26.

10. "Hunger in America: Appalachia Ill-Fed Despite a National Effort," *New York Times*, February 20, 1969, 32.

11. Eller, *Uneven Ground*, 181–85, 204.

12. Sale, *Power Shift*, 17.

13. Ibid., 7, 189–91.

14. Ibid., 94; "Southernization of America."

15. Sale, *Power Shift*, 3–53; Samuel Lubell, *The Hidden Crisis in American Politics* (New York, 1970), 105; John Egerton, *Americanization of Dixie: Southernization of America* (Ann Arbor, Mich., 1974), xix; Phillips, *Emerging Republican Majority*, 437.

16. "Aging Process Catches Up with Cities of the North," *New York Times*, February 13, 1976, 1, 14.

17. "Federal Funds Pour into Sunbelt States," *New York Times*, February 9, 1976, 24; "Federal Spending: The North's Loss Is the Sunbelt's Gain," *National Journal*, June 26, 1976, 879, 884.

18. Thomas G. Dyer, "A New Face on Southern Higher Education: Dimensions of Quality and Access at the End of the Twentieth Century," in *The American South in the Twentieth Century*, ed. Craig S. Pascoe, Karen Trahan Leathem, and Andy Ambrose (Athens, Ga., 2005), 292.

19. Cobb, *Selling of the South*, 163.

20. Schulman, *From Cotton Belt to Sunbelt*, 197.

21. "Mississippi Gropes for a Way to Get Schools 'Off Bottom,'" *Washington Post*, December 13, 1982, A-1.

22. "Mississippi Lawmakers Vote Funds to Upgrade Education," *New York Times*, December 22, 1982, A-1.

23. Stephen L. Carter, *God's Name in Vain: The Rights and Wrongs of Religion in Politics* (New York, 2000), 47.

24. Alexander P. Lamis, *A Two-Party South*, 2nd ed. (New York, 1990), 26.

25. Ibid., 238–40.

26. Ibid., 250, 249.

27. Black and Black, *Rise of Southern Republicans*, 222; Joseph A. Aistrup, *The Southern Strategy Revisited* (Lexington, Ky., 1996), 51.

28. Lamis, *Two-Party South*, 310.

29. Steven A. Shull, *American Civil Rights Policy from Truman to Clinton: The Role of Presidential Leadership* (Armonk, N.Y., 1999), 103–4.

30. Kenneth L. Karst, *Law's Promise, Law's Expression: Visions of Power in the Politics of Race, Gender, and Religion* (New Haven, Conn., 1995), 29.

31. Black and Black, *Rise of Southern Republicans*, 230, 220.

32. Harold W. Stanley, "The South in the 2000 Elections," in *The 2000 Presidential Election in the South: Partisanship and Southern Party Systems in the Twenty-first Century,* ed. Robert P. Steed and Laurence W. Moreland (Westport, Conn., 2000), 219–31.

33. "Decision 2004: Exit Polls," MSNBC.com, www.msnbc.msn.com/id1 5297118.

34. "Just How Bad Off Is the Republican Party?" part 2, *Salon,* March 18, 2009, www.salon.com/news/feature/2009/03/18/state_of_the_gop/.

35. "GOP Leader's Remarks Seen as Racist," *Jackson Clarion-Ledger,* August 18, 2007, B-1; "His Southern Strategy Made a Dent," *Huffington Post,* October 11, 2007, www.huffingtonpost.com/byron-williams/his-southern-strategy-mad_b_68123 .html.

36. Cobb, *Georgia Odyssey*, 129.

37. "Tennessee Senate: Corker (R) 51 Percent, Ford (D) 47 Percent," *Rasmussen Reports,* www.rasmussenreports.com/public_content/politics/elections/senate_races/tennessee_senate_corker_r_48_ford_d-47.

38. "State Exit Polls: Senate Hangs in the Balance," FoxNews.com, www.foxnews.com/politics/2006/11/08/state-exit polls-senate-hangs-balance/blacks; Crespino, *In Search of Another Country*, 104.

39. Black and Black, *Rise of Southern Republicans*, 6–7.

40. "Old Animosity over MARTA Alive and Well in Gwinnett," *Decatur Metro,* July 15, 2008, http://decaturmetro.com/2008/07/15/old-animosity-over-marta-alive-and-well-in-gwinnett/; "Gwinnett County Voters Defeat Plan to Extend MARTA into County," WSBTV.com, July 16, 2008, www.wsbtv.com/news/16896419/detail.htm.

41. "Bush Campaign Manager Views the Electoral Divide," *New York Times,* November 19, 2004, 23.

42. Calculations from data gathered by the Center for Business and Economic Research at the University of Alabama, Tuscaloosa, http://cber.cba.ua.edu/edata/maps/alabamamaps/.html/; Lawrence Hamilton, "Rural Voting in the 2004 Election, Fact Sheet No. 2, Fall 2006," www.carseyinstitute.unh.edu/publications/FS_ruralvote_06.pdf; Stephen L. Sperry, "Are Republicans Sprawlers and Democrats

Near Urbanists? Understanding the Spatial Analysis of the 2004 Presidential Vote," 2005 ESRI International User Conference Proceedings, http://proceedings.esri.com/library/userconf/proc05/papers/pap2184.pdf.

43. Figures available from "County Guide," 2003, 2007, Georgia Statistics System, www.geogiastats.uga.edu/.

44. Black and Black, *Politics and Society*, 297.

45. Botsch, *We Shall Not Overcome*, 159.

46. Black and Black, *Rise of Southern Republicans*, 334–35.

47. Ibid., 331–32, 357.

48. "Black Officials Holding Elected Statewide Offices," 2007, Table 2f, Joint Center for Political and Economic Studies, www.jointcenter.org/index .php/current_research_and_policy_activities/political_participation/black_ elected_officials_roster_introduction_and_overview/table_2f_black_officials_ holding_elected_statewide_offices_2007.

49. Adrienne S. Harris, "The Southern Magnet—Atlanta, Georgia," *Black Enterprise*, June 1992, http://findarticles.com/p/articles/mi_m1365/is_n11_v22/ ai_12249139/.

50. Robert M. Gibbs, "Trends in Occupational Status among Rural Southern Blacks," Economic Research Service, U.S. Department of Agriculture, www.ers.usda .gov/publications/aer731/aer731f.pdf.

51. "County Guide," 2000, Georgia Statistics System; "White-Black Disparity in Income Narrowed in 1980s, Census Shows," *New York Times*, July 24, 1991, A-1.

52. "Reversing a Long Pattern, Blacks Are Heading South, *Washington Post*, May 5, 2001, A-1; "A Sweetness Tempers South's Bitter Past," *New York Times*, July 31, 1994, www.nytimes.com/1994/07/31/us/a-sweetness-tempers-south-s-bitter-past .html; William H. Frey, "Migration to the South Brings Blacks Full Circle," *Population Today*, May/June 2001, www.prb.org/Content/NavigationMenu/PT_articles/ April-June_2001/Migration_to_the_South_Brings_U_S__Blacks_Full_Circle.htm; Gavin Wright, "The Persistence of the South as an Economic Region," *Journal of Atlanta History* 44 (Winter 2001): 78; Sandra Yin, "Southern Comfort," *Forecast*, July 16, 2001, 1.

53. "County Guide," 2008, Georgia Statistics System.

54. "Black Wealth Blossoms in the Suburbs: D-FW Ranks among Top U.S. Areas for Well-off Professionals," *Dallas Morning News*, June 25, 2005, www.dallas-news.com/sharedcontent/dws/news/longterm/stories/062605dnmetbpcoview.4638 4de4.html.

55. Ibid.

56. William H. Frey, "Revival," *American Demographics*, October 2003, 27, 31; "Southern Migration Fuels Gains for Blacks," *Jackson (Miss.) Free Press*, www .jacksonfreepress.com/forums/threads.php?id=6382_0_25_0_C.

57. Cobb, *Georgia Odyssey*, 149; "Reversing a Long Pattern"; Yin, "Southern Comfort," 1–3, 332; Edward L. Glaeser and Jacob L. Vigdor, "Racial Segregation in 2000 Census: Promising News," Brookings Institution Survey Series, April 15, 2001, www.brookings.edu/es/urban/census/glaeser.pdf; "Blacks Find Affluent Suburban Niche," *Hartford Courant*, September 7, 2003, www.s4.brown.edu/cen2000/othersay/090703Hartford.pdf.

58. Lois M. Quinn and John Pawasarat, "Racial Integration in Urban America: A Block-Level Analysis of African American and White Housing Patterns," Employment and Training Institute, University of Wisconsin-Milwaukee, December 2002, revised January 2003, www.uwm.edu/dept/ETI/integration/integration.htm; Glaeser and Vigdor, "Racial Segregation in 2000 Census."

59. William H. Frey, "Melting Pot Suburbs: A Census 2000 Survey of Diversity," Brookings Institution, Center on Urban and Metropolitan Policy, June 12, 2001, www.frey-demographer.org/reports/R-2001-3_MeltingPotSuburbs.pdf; "Segregation of Elementary Students in Metropolitan Regions, 1999–2000," (Index of Dissimilarity), Initiative in Spatial Structures in the Social Sciences, Brown University, www.s4.brown.edu/cen2000/SchoolPop/SPsort/sort_d1.html.

60. "Racial Gap in Testing Sees Shift by Region," *New York Times*, July 14, 2009, www.nytimes.com/2009/07/15/education/15educ.html?_r=1&ref=us.

61. Gallup News Service, "Church Attendance Lowest in New England, Highest in South," April 27, 2006, www.gallup.com/poll/22579/church-attendance-lowest-new-england-highest-south.aspx.

62. Bartley, *New South*, 276, 284.

63. Much of the following discussion of Robertson is based on Bill Sizemore, "The Christian with Four Aces," *Virginia Quarterly Review* 84 (Spring 2008): 52–79.

64. "Equal Rights Initiative in Iowa Attacked," *Washington Post*, August 23, 1992, A-15, www.highbeam.com/doc/1P2–1021641.html; Gregory Palast, "Pat Robertson: 'I Don't Have to Be Nice to the Spirit of the Antichrist,'" August 23, 2005, originally published in *The Guardian* (UK), May 1999, www.gregpalast.com/pat-robertson-i-dont-have-to-be-nice-to-the-spirit-of-the-antichrist/.

65. Palast, "I Don't Have to Be Nice"; "Pat Robertson's Gold," *Washington Post*, September 22, 2001, A-29; "Jet Flight Records Spur Copeland Ministry Questions," WFAA.com, www.wfaa.com/sharedcontent/dws/wfaa/latestnews/stories/wfaa070228_mo_churchjet.87be631.html.

66. Robert McElvaine, *Grand Theft Jesus: The Hijacking of Religion in America* (New York, 2008), 35; Glen Feldman, *Politics and Religion in the White South* (Lexington, Ky., 2005), 298; Eugene F. Provenzo, *Religious Fundamentalism and American Education: The Battle for the Public Schools* (Albany, N.Y., 1990), xvii; "Outspoken Evangelist Whose Moral Majority Coalition Hastened a Rightward Shift in U.S. Politics," *Independent (U.K.)*, May 17, 2007; Jerry Falwell, "Lest We Forget," May 15, 2007, www.independent.co.uk/news/obituaries/the-rev-jerry-falwell-449109.html.

67. "A Church That Packs Them In, 16,000 at a Time," *New York Times*, July 18, 2005, A-1; "Mega-Churches Spread the Word via High-Tech Digital Aids," *Boston Globe*, July 3, 2005, A-1; "Jesus, CEO," *Economist*, December 20, 2005, http://teachingamericanhistory.org/library/index.asp?document=1443.

68. "Faith's Real Riches," *Washington Post*, August. 6, 2008, A-17; "Figures Released by Megachurch," *Atlanta Journal-Constitution*, November 11, 2007, E-1; "Church of the Almighty Dollar," *Business Week*, May 23, 2005, www.businessweek.com/magazine/content105_211b3934016_mz001.htm.

69. "Not All at Seminary Welcome Bishop," *Atlanta Journal-Constitution*, May 11, 2006, A-1; "At Mrs. King's Funeral, a Mix of Elegy and Politics," *New York Times*, February 8, 2006, 1; "The Seeds of Coretta Scott King," *All Sewn Up*, February 7, 2006, www.allsewnup.com/2006/02/07/the-seeds-of-coretta-scott-king/.

70. William Reed, "Thee of Little Faith: An African American Guide to Faith-Based Funding," *East Texas Review*, May 11, 2006, www.religionandsocialpolicy.org/news/article.cfm?id=4244.

71. "March Divides King Followers," *Atlanta Journal-Constitution*, December 11, 2004, A-1; Southern Focus Poll Reports, "Southern Cross Tabulations," Fall 1999, "Non-Southern Cross Tabulations," Fall 1999, Odum Institute for Research in Social Science, University of North Carolina, www.irss.unc.edu/odum/jsp/content_node.jsp?nodeid=242.

72. "Gay Marriage Gained Bush Black Votes," *Newsday*, November 14, 2004, www.edisonresearch.com/home/archives/Newsday11–14–2004.pdf.

73. "Will Conservative Black Voters Remain Cemented to Democratic Party?" *State (Columbia, S.C.)*, September 21, 2007, www.accessmylibrary.com/article-1G1–168915424/opinion-conservative-black-voters.html.

CHAPTER 8

1. Schulman, *From Cotton Belt to Sunbelt*, 199; "Florida's Welfare Rate Is Lowest in the Nation," *Tampa Tribune*, September 17, 2007, www.accessmylibrary.com/article-1G1–168745896/florida-welfare-rate-lowest.html.

2. Schulman, *From Cotton Belt to Sunbelt*, 196–99; U.S. Bureau of the Census, *Federal, State, and Local Governments, 2006, Public Education Finance Data*, www.census.gov/govs/www/school06.html.

3. Curtis S. Dubay, "Federal Tax Burdens and Expenditures by State," Special Report No. 139, www.taxfoundation.org/research/show/62.html; Northeast-Midwest Institute, Center for Policy Initiatives, www.Nemw.org/fundsrank.htm.

4. "Senator Jesse Helms Dead at Eighty-Six: Polarizing North Carolina Lawmaker Was Known as 'Senator No,'" ABC News Services, July 4, 2008, http://abcnews.go.com/US/story?id=5309543&page=1; Walker Percy, "Mississippi: The Fallen Paradise," *Harper's* 230 (April 1965): 169–70.

5. Congressional Quarterly, Inc., *Governing, State, and Local Sourcebook,* http://sourcebook.governing.com/index.jsp; Institute on Taxation and Economic Policy, *Who Pays? A Distributional Analysis of the Tax System in All Fifty States,* 2nd ed., www.itepnet.org/whopays.htm.

6. Cobb, *Selling of the South,* 189.

7. Ibid., 191–92.

8. Dean Foust and Maria Mallory, "The Boom Belt," *Business Week,* September 27, 1993, www.businessweek.com/archives/1993/b333848.arc.htm; Karsten Hülsemann, "Green Fields in the Heart of Dixie: How the American Auto Industry Discovered the South," in *Second Wave: Southern Industrialization from the 1940s to the 1970s,* ed. Phillip R. Scranton (Athens, Ga., 2001), 225; Charles M. Kelly, *The Great Limbaugh Con, and Other Right-Wing Assaults on Common Sense* (Santa Barbara, Calif., 1994), 152.

9. Bureau of Labor Statistics, "Union Members Summary," news release, January 28, 2009, www.bls.gov/news.release/union2.nr0.htm.

10. "Opportunities for Japanese Manufacturers in South Carolina," South Carolina Department of Commerce, March 2006, www.sccommerce.com/teamscpdfs/japanmanufacturing.pdf; italics in original. This item has been removed from the website, but it is documented in "U.S.-Japan Economic Partnership for Growth," United States–Japan Investment Initiative, 2006 Report, www.mac.gov.

11. "BMW Announces 9 Percent Rise in Net Profit for 2007, Same-Day Analysis," *IHS Global Insight,* March 14, 2008, www.globalinsight.com/SDA/SDADetail11863.htm.

12. Jay Hancock, "S.C. Pays Dearly for Added Jobs: South Carolina's Economy Was Supposed to Improve, but Taxes Exploded While Services Crumbled," *Sunspot, Maryland's Online Community,* October 12, 1999, www.strom.clemson.edu/teams/ced/tax_news/sc-tax-news.html.

13. James C. Cobb, "Beyond the Y'all Wall: The American South Goes Global," in *Globalization and the American South,* ed. James C. Cobb and William W. Stueck (Athens, Ga., 2005), 1–2.

14. Ibid., 3.

15. "Which State Is Smartest?" Morgan Quitno Press, www.morganquitno.com/edri06.htm; Information Technology and Innovation Foundation, *The 2008 State New Economy Index: Benchmarking Economic Transformation in the States,* Washington, D.C., 2008, www.itif.org/files/2008_State_New_Economy_Index.pdf.

16. "Southern States Ply the Art of the Deal," *EconSouth* 10 (first quarter, 2008), www.frbatlanta.org/pubs/econsouth/econsouth_vol_10_no_1_southern_states_plyart_ofdeal.cfm?redirected=true; "Industry Siphons Roadwork Funding," *Tuscaloosa News,* June 16, 2007, www.tuscaloosanews.com/article/20070616/news/706160323; Rick Weddle, "The Research Triangle Park: A Legacy of Economic Transformation...Lessons for Regional Economies," Research Triangle Founda-

tion of North Carolina, November 15, 2007, www.doi.wayne.edu/pdf/rick_weddle_presentationleaders_without_bordersnov_2007.pdf.

17. "Bangladeshi Garment Workers Get Low Wages: Study," *Thaindian News*, June 1, 2008, www.thaindian.com/newsportal/world-news/bangladeshi-garment-workers-get-low-wages-study_10055256.html.

18. "Annual Manufacturing Employment, 1996–2006," NEMW, www.nemw.org/mfgemp96–06.htm; Coclanis and Kyriakoudes, "Selling Which South?" 97.

19. Coclanis and Kyriakoudes, "Selling Which South?" 97; "In North Carolina, Damage Not Easily Mended," *Washington Post*, November 10, 1999, www.washingtonpost.com/wp-dyn/content/article/2009/11/09/AR2009110903705.html.

20. Working Poor Families Project, "Still Working Hard, Still Falling Short," www.workingpoorfamiiesorg/pdfs/NatReport08.pdf.; U.S. Census Bureau, *Mobile Homes, Percent of Total Housing Units,* 2007, www.census.gov/compendia/statab/ranks/rank38.html.

21. Machlyn Blair, "Poverty Is about Real People, Not Politics," www.npr.org/templates/story/story.php?storyId=90327703.

22. "Wal-Mart Warns of Democratic Win," *Wall Street Journal*, August 1, 2008, A-1; "Wal-Mart's Health Crisis Costs You Money: Tax Payer Cost by State," Wakeup-Walmart.com, http://wakeupwalmart.com/feature/healthcrisis/map.html.

23. "Lured Employers Now Tax Medicaid: Employees of Companies Given Incentives to Create Jobs Are Relying Heavily on Health Care for the Poor. The Biggest: Wal-Mart," *St. Petersburg Times,* March 25, 2005, www.sptimes.com/2005/03/25/State/Lured_employers_now_t.shtml; "Wal-Mart's Health Crisis Costs You Money."

24. Economic Policy Institute, *Basic Budget Calculator,* www.epi.org/budget-calc.cfm; Bureau of Labor Statistics, "Metropolitan and Nonmetropolitan Area Occupational Employment and Wage Estimates," May 2007, www.bls.gov/oes/current/oessrcma.htm#5.

25. Eller, *Uneven Ground*, 37; John Prine, "Paradise," www.mp3lyrics.org.

26. Eller, *Uneven Ground*, 40.

27. Cobb, *Selling of the South*, 230; James Fallows, Ralph Nader, and Harrison Wellford, *Water Lords: Ralph Nader's Study Group Report on Industry and Environmental Crisis in Savannah, Georgia* (New York, 1971), 159.

28. Cobb, *Selling of the South*, 229–30, 232.

29. Ibid., 234.

30. Ibid., 230–33; Fallows, Nader, and Wellford, *Water Lords*, 105–6.

31. Scott H. Dewey, "The Fickle Finger of Phosphate: Central Florida Air Pollution and the Failure of Environmental Policy, 1957–1970," *Journal of Southern History* 65 (August 1999): 565–603.

32. Cobb, *Selling of the South*, 235; New Jersey Public Interest Research Group, Law and Policy Center, *Toxic Pollution and Health: An Analysis of Toxic Chemicals*

Released in Communities across the United States, 2007, 4–14, http://njpirg.org/ reports/ToxicPollutionandHealth2007NJ.pdf (rankings exclude Alaska); Environmental Protection Agency, "2005 National Fact Sheet," www.epa.gov/cgi-bin/ broker?view=STCO&trilib=TRIQ0&state=All+states&SFS=YES&year=2005&_ service=oiaa&_program=xp_tri.sasmacr.tristart.macro.

33. "When Growth Isn't Green: Dozens of Acres of Trees Disappear Daily as Metro Atlanta Booms," *Atlanta Journal-Constitution*, May 2, 2007, A-1; Southern Alliance for Clean Energy, "North Carolina Global Warming Fact Sheet," www .cleanenergy.org/resources/factsheets/NC_GW_pollution.pdf.

34. Albert E. Cowdrey, *This Land, the South* (Lexington, Ky., 1995), 172–73; Pete Daniel, "Not Predestination: The Rural South and Twentieth Century Transformation," in Pascoe, Leathem, and Ambrose, *The American South*, 9–102; Pete Daniel, *Toxic Drift: Pesticides and Health in the Post-World War II South* (Baton Rouge, La., 2005), 2–6, 50.

35. Daniel, *Toxic Drift*, 2–3, 99, 167, 169; "In South Texas a Swat at an Old Pest Stirs a Revolt," *New York Times*, January 24, 1996, A-10.

36. Environmental Working Group, "Dead in the Water: Farm Subsidy Reform Key to Restoring Gulf of Mexico 'Dead Zone,'" April 10, 2006, www.ewg.org/node/ 21049.

37. U.S. Fish and Wildlife Service, "Species Reports," http://ecos.fws.gov/tess_ public/StateListing.do?state=all.

38. Jack Temple Kirby, *Mocking Bird Song: Ecological Landscapes of the South* (Chapel Hill, N.C., 2006), 314–16.

39. United Health Foundation, "America's Health Rankings: A Call to Action for People and Their Communities," 206, 20, 92, 20, 105, www.unitedhealthfoundation .org/ahr2006/media2006/shrmediakit/2006ahr.pdf. The study defined health rather broadly to include not only the extent of certain traditional medical problems, but also the incidence of violent crime and child poverty and some other social factors.

40. "The Short End of the Longer Life," *New York Times*, April 27, 2008, 1; Death Penalty Information Center, "Murder Rates, 1996–2007," www.deathpenaltyinfo. org/murder-rates-1996–2007.

41. Violence Policy Center, "Where Men Murder Women: An Analysis of 2006 Homicide Data," www.vpc.org/studies/wmmw2008.pdf.

42. "Walking the Walk on Family Values," *Boston Globe*, October 31, 2004, www. boston.com/news/globe/editorial_opinion/oped/articles/2004/10/31/walking_the_ walk_on_family_values/; "Lifestyle Statistics, Divorce Rate (Most Recent) by State," Statemaster.com, www.statemaster.com/graph/lif_div_rat-lifestyle-divorce-rate; "Regional Murder Rates, 2001–2007, Murder and Non-Negligent Homicide (Most Recent) by State," Statemaster.com, www.statemaster.com/graph/cri_mur_and_ non_man-crime-murder-and-nonnegligent-manslaughter; Death Penalty Information Center, www.deathpenaltyinfo.org/article.php?did=169&scid=12#MRreg.

CHAPTER 9

1. Bartley, *New South*, 264.

2. Kathy Kahn, *Hillbilly Women* (Garden City, N.Y., 1973), 18, 20–21.

3. Jan K. Bryant, "Southern Women and Textile Work: Job Satisfaction," in *Southern Women*, ed. Caroline Matheny Dillman (New York, 1988), 177–81.

4. Barbara Ellen Smith, *Women of the Rural South: Economic Status and Prospects* (Lexington, Ky., 1986), 42.

5. Amy Caiazza et al., *Women's Economic Status in the States: Wide Disparities by Race, Ethnicity, and Region*, Institute for Women's Policy Research, Washington, D.C., www.iwpr.org/pdf/R260.pdf.

6. American Association of University Women Educational Foundation, "State-by-State Data on Women's and Men's Educational Attainment and Earnings, 2004–2006," www.pay-equity.org/PDFs/AAUWpayequity-bystate.pdf.

7. AllBusiness.com, Inc., "Best Metros for Women Entrepreneurs, October 2006," www.allbusiness.com/asset/document/news_&_special_reports/3776375 .pdf; U.S. Economic Census, "Women-Owned Firms: 2002, 2006," www.census.gov/ econ/sbo/#women.

8. Working Poor Families Project, "Still Working Hard, Still Falling Short"; "Declaration of the Plaintiff Laverne Jones in Support of Plaintiff's Motion for Class Certification," http://74.125.47.132/search?q=cache:WoDaSnCfbuIJ:www .walmartclass.com/staticdata/walmartclass/declarations/Jones_Laverne .doc+Laverne+Jones+v.+Wal-Mart+Pontotoc,+Mississippi&cd=1&hl=en&ct=clnk &gl=us&client=firefox-a.

9. Jeffrey Goldberg, "Selling Wal-Mart: Can the Company Co-opt Liberals?" *New Yorker*, April 2, 2007, www.newyorker.com/reporting/2007/04/02/070402fa_ fact_goldberg; "Love, Honor, and Obey?" and "The NewsHour with Jim Lehrer," *Online Focus*, June 10, 1998, PBS, www.pbs.org/newshour/bb/religion/jan-june98/ baptist_6-10.html.

10. "Blaming Men Is Not Good Theology," *Washington Post*, July 21, 2009, http:// newsweek.washingtonpost.com/onfaith/panelists/robert_parham/2009/07/is_blam- ing_men_for_inequitable_treatment_of_women_good_theology.html; Adelle M. Banks, "A Woman Vice-President? Sure. A Woman Pastor? Not Likely," *Religion News Service*, September 11, 2008, http://pewforum.org/news/display.php?NewsID=16464; Staff of the Executive Committee of the Southern Baptist Convention, "Southern Baptists and Women Pastors," www.baptist2baptist.net/printfriendly.asp?ID=58.

11. Gregory Tomlin, "Patterson: Women Are Treasured by God, Have High Calling," *Baptist Press*, October 25, 2004, www.bpnews.net/printerfriendly .asp?ID=19402; Sarah Pulliam, "Richard Land Glows over Palin Pick," *Christianity Today*, September 1, 2008, http://blog.christianitytoday.com/ctpolitics/2008/09/ richard_land_gl.html.

12. Wayne Flynt, *Alabama Baptists: Southern Baptists in the Heart of Dixie* (Tuscaloosa, Ala., 1998), 586; Kevin L. Howard, "Dorothy Patterson: Speaker, Author, Professor," Need Not Fret, www.neednotfret.com/content/view/171/106//.

13. Jack Bass and Walter Devries, "Oral History Interview with Frances Farenthold," December 14, 1974, Southern Oral History Program Collection, Interview A-0186 (#4007), *Documenting the American South,* http://docsouth.unc.edu/sohp/A-0186/menu.html; Bartley, *New South,* 425–26.

14. Ibid.; Flynt, *Alabama Baptists,* 439.

15. Bartley, *New South,* 425–26.

16. Robert P. Steed, Lawrence W. Morehead, and Tod A. Baker, *The 1984 Presidential Election in the South: Patterns of Southern Politics* (Westport, Conn., 1985), 307; Evan Thomas, Joseph N. Boyce, and John E. Yang, "Election '84: Every Region, Every Age Group, Almost Every Voting Bloc," *Time,* November 19, 1984, www.time.com/time/magazine/article/0,9171,950187,00.html; Black and Black, *Rise of Southern Republicans,* 251.

17. Karen Kaufman, "The Gender Gap," American Political Science Association online, *Journal of Political Science and Politics,* July 2006, www.apsanet.org/imgtest/PSJuly06Kaufmann.pdf.

18. "Southern Women Turning from the GOP," MSNBC.com, September 7, 2006, www.msnbc.msn.com/id/14714800/from/RS.5/; "America Votes, 2006," CNN.com, www.cnn.com/ELECTION/2006/.

19. Center for American Women and Politics, "Women in State Legislatures, 2009," www.cawp.rutgers.edu/fast_facts/levels_of_office/documents/stleg.pdf.

20. Asjylyn Loder, "Southern Women Racing for Congress Face Tough Odds," *Women's News,* October 25, 2002, www.womensenews.org/article.cfm/dyn/aid/1083/context/archive; Nancy Baker Jones and Ruthe Winegarten, *Capitol Women: Texas Female Legislators, 1923–1999* (Austin, Tex., 2000), 139–42.

21. Elizabeth M. Esterchild and Jen L. King, "The Race, Ethnic and Gender Composition of State Legislatures: How Does It Happen and Why Does It Matter?" paper presented at Eighth International Women's Policy Research Conference, June 2005, www.iwpr.org/pdf105_proceedings/esterchild-elizabeth.pdf; American Political Science Association, "New Study Explores Impact of Voting Rights Act on Election of Non-white Officials," press release, July 23, 2007, www.apsanet.org/content_44448.cfm; "Minnesota Legislature Ranks Near Bottom in Proportional Representation of African-Americans," http://blog.lib.umn.edu/cspg/smartpolitics/2009/03/minnesota_legislature_ranks_ne.php. Black men were also overrepresented relative to white men in southern legislatures. In fact, Virginia, Arkansas, and Louisiana were the only states where the overall ratio of black percentage of the legislature to black percentage of the population fell below the national average in 2009.

22. Lev Grossman, "Restorer of Faith," *Time,* April 18, 2005, www.time.com/time/magazine/article/0,9171,1050283,00.html.

23. "Seldom-Heard Compliment for Atlanta's Mayor: You Were Right," *New York Times,* September 8, 2009, A-11.

24. U.S. Representative Sue W. Myrick, "'Real' Immigration Legislation," February 2005, www.house.gov/list/speech/nc09_myrick/REALIDACT0205.html; "Project Vote Smart, Representative Sue W. Myrick (NC)," www.votesmart.org/voting_category.php?can_id=21789.

25. Jim Jubak, "Big Oil's Ten Favorite Members of Congress," *MSN.money,* October 24, 2006, http://articles.moneycentral.msn.com/Investing/JubaksJournal/BigOils10FavoriteMembersOfCongress.aspx; "Primary Results for Texas Governor," http://www.texasgopvote.com/blog/primary-results-texas-governor-030214.

26. Black and Black, *Rise of Southern Republicans,* 199.

27. Thomas H. Ferrell and Judith Haydel, "Hale and Lindy Boggs: Louisiana's National Democrats," *Louisiana History* 35 (Fall 1984): 389–402; "Boggs, Marie Corrine Morrison Claiborne (Lindy)," in *From Suffrage to the Senate: An Encyclopedia of Women in Politics,* ed. Suzanne O'Dea Schenken (Santa Barbara, Calif., 1999), 2:79.

28. Crespino, *In Search of Another Country,* 77–78.

29. L. Smith, *Killers of the Dream,* 151, 143.

30. Glenda Elizabeth Gilmore, *Defying Dixie: The Radical Roots of Civil Rights, 1919–1950* (New York, 2008), 315–29, 401–2.

31. Ibid., 399, 417, 442–43.

32. Cobb, *Most Southern Place,* 243.

33. Ibid., 244.

34. Asch, *Senator and the Sharecropper,* 290–91.

35. Bill Moyers, *Moyers on Democracy* (New York, 2009), 169–70; Max Sherman, ed., *Barbara Jordan: Speaking the Truth with Eloquent Thunder* (Austin, Tex., 2003), 40.

36. "Rediscovering Barbara Jordan: Transcript," KUT 90.5 FM, Austin, Tex., www.kut.org/items/show/5525; Edith L. Payne, "Jordan, Barbara," in *The Encyclopedia of Southern Culture,* ed. Charles Reagan Wilson and William R. Ferris (Chapel Hill, N.C., 1989), 1580–81.

CHAPTER 10

1. Faulkner, *Intruder in the Dust,* 152–53.

2. James L. Peacock, *Grounded Globalism: How the U.S. South Embraces the World* (Athens, Ga., 2007), 4; Reed, *Enduring South,* 90.

3. "Southern Intellectuals' Parley Scorns North as Guide," *New York Times,* January 16, 1972, 45.

4. James McBride Dabbs, *Who Speaks for the South?* (New York, 1964), 320; Sheldon Hackney, "The South as Counterculture," *American Scholar* 42, no. 2 (1973): 21; Richard N. Current, *Northernizing the South* (Athens, Ga., 1983), 83.

5. John Shelton Reed, *Southerners: The Social Psychology of Sectionalism* (Chapel Hill, N.C., 1983), 109, 111, 114; Larry J. Griffin and Ashley B. Thompson, "Enough about the Disappearing South: What about the Disappearing Southerner?" *Southern Cultures* 9 (Fall 2003): 56.

6. James C. Cobb, *Away Down South: A History of Southern Identity* (New York, 2005), 233; Diane Roberts, "Living Southern in *Southern Living*," in *Dixie Debates: Perspectives on Southern Cultures*, ed. Richard H. King and Helen Taylor (London, 1996), 86; Kathleen L. Endres and Theresa L. Lueck, *Women's Periodicals in the United States: Consumer Magazines* (Westport, Conn., 1955), 348; "The South, Sportingly: Garden and Gun Magazine Hunts for Well-heeled: Lock, Stock and Barrel, Magazine Devoted to Southern Way of Life," *Atlanta Journal-Constitution*, August 26, 2008, www.ajc.com/news/content/living/stories/2008/08/26/gun_garden_magazine.html.

7. Cobb, *Away Down South*, 223, 227.

8. Ibid., 229–30.

9. Ibid., 233.

10. Ibid., 234.

11. Faulkner, *Intruder in the Dust*, 150; Fred C. Hobson, *Tell about the South: The Southern Rage to Explain* (Baton Rouge, La., 1983), 15; Walker Percy, "Southern Comfort," *Harper's* 258 (January 1979): 80, 83.

12. Percy, "Mississippi: The Fallen Paradise," 166; Percy, "Southern Comfort," 83–90.

13. William Faulkner, *Requiem for a Nun* (New York, 1975), 4.

14. Flannery O'Connor, "The Displaced Person," in *The Complete Stories of Flannery O'Connor* (New York, 1978), 234.

15. Cobb, *Away Down South*, 246.

16. Walker Percy and Patrick Samway, *Signposts in a Strange Land: Essays* (New York, 2000), 81; Walker Percy, *The Moviegoer* (New York, 1998), 166, 120.

17. "The Nation: Challenging Atlanta; The South Has Its Second Cities, and They Thrive," *New York Times*, April 23, 1989, www.nytimes.com/1989/04/23/weekinreview/the-nation-challenging-atlanta-the-south-has-its-second-cities-and-they-thrive.html; Walker Percy, *The Last Gentleman* (New York, 1968), 150; Malcolm Jones, "Moralist of the South," in *More Conversations with Walker Percy*, ed. Lewis A. Lawson and Victor A. Krammer (Jackson, Miss., 1993), 170; "Walker Percy, Interview with Jan Nordby Gretlund, January 2, 1981," *South Carolina Review* 13 (Spring 1981): 12.

18. Robert H. Brinkmeyer Jr., "Finding One's History: Bobbie Ann Mason and Contemporary Southern Literature," *Southern Literary Journal* 19 (1987): 32.

19. Laura Fine, "Going Nowhere Slow: The Post-South World of Bobbie Ann Mason," *Southern Literary Journal* 32 (Fall 1999): 87–97.

20. Josephine Humphreys, *Dreams of Sleep* (New York, 1985), 136.

21. Marshall Frady, "Gone with the Wind," *Newsweek,* July 28, 1975, 11; Hodding Carter III, "The End of the South," *Time,* August 6, 1990, 82.

22. Scherman, "Country."

23. Bruce Feiler, *Dreaming Out Loud: Garth Brooks, Wynonna Judd, Wade Hayes, and the Changing Face of Nashville* (New York, 1999), 37–38; Hank Williams Jr., "A Country Boy Can Survive," www.jp3lyrics.org; Alan Jackson, "Little Bitty," www.mp3lyrics.org.

24. S. Renee Dechert, "Setting a Trailer House in the Rich Part of Town," PopMatters, September 25, 2001, http://popmatters.com/music/reviews/d/drive-bytruckers-southern.shtml.

25. Ibid.

26. Drive-By Truckers, "Plastic Flowers on the Highway," UMG Recording, Inc., 2002.

27. Rick Bragg, *The Prince of Frogtown* (New York, 2008), 200.

28. Rick Bragg, *All Over but the Shouting* (New York, 1997), 297.

29. Harry Crews, *A Childhood: The Biography of a Place* (New York, 1978), 40.

30. Dorothy Allison, *Bastard out of Carolina* (New York, 1993), 3; Larry Brown, *Fay* (Chapel Hill, N.C., 2000), 86–87.

31. Dorothy Allison, "River of Names," in *The Vintage Book of Contemporary American Short Stories,* ed. Tobias Wolff (New York, 1994), 5.

32. Larry Brown, "Samaritans," in *Facing the Music* (New York, 1988), 87–100.

33. James Dickey, *Deliverance* (New York, 1970).

34. Janisse Ray, *Ecology of a Cracker Childhood* (Minneapolis, Minn., 1999), 13, 4; Tim McLaurin, *Keeper of the Moon: A Southern Boyhood* (New York, 1991), 316; Tim McLaurin, *Woodrow's Trumpet* (New York, 1991), 157.

35. Steve Watson, *The Harlem Renaissance* (New York, 1995), 93; Richard Wright, "Blueprint for Negro Writing," *New Challenge,* Fall 1937, 54.

36. "Black Boy: A Negro Writes a Bitter Autobiography," *Life,* June 4, 1945, 87.

37. Richard Wright, *Black Boy: A Record of Childhood and Youth* (New York, 1945), 201–83, 284.

38. Sterling A. Brown, "Count Us In," in Logan, *What the Negro Wants,* 308; Ralph Ellison, "Working Notes for *Invisible Man,*" in *The Collected Essays of Ralph Ellison,* ed. John F. Callahan (New York, 1995), 169.

39. Ralph Ellison, *Invisible Man* (New York, 1995), 255, 15, 579.

40. Ibid., 581.

41. Ibid., 577; Percy, *The Moviegoer,* 63.

42. Merle Black and John Shelton Reed, "Blacks and Southerners: A Research Note," *Journal of Politics* 44 (February 1982): 169; Griffin and Thompson, "Enough about the Disappearing South," 59.

43. Anthony Walton, *Mississippi* (New York, 1997), 258, 275; Anthony Walton, "Chicago as the Northernmost County of Mississippi," *Southern Cultures* 8 (Spring 2002): 52, 54, 55.

44. Cobb, *Georgia Odyssey*, 147; Karen Smith, "Telling Stories," *Georgia Magazine*, September 2007, 43.

45. Ann Hawthorne, "Alex Haley: At Home in the Hills of East Tennessee," *Appalachia*, Winter 1992, 37; Applebome, *Dixie Rising*, 339.

46. "Tina McElroy Ansa," in *The Prevailing South: Life and Politics in a Changing Culture*, ed. Dudley Clendenin (Atlanta, 1988), 184; Alice Walker, *In Search of Our Mothers' Gardens: Womanist Prose* (New York, 1983), 20–21.

47. Alice Walker, *Third Life of Grange Copeland* (New York, 1988), 206, 202.

48. Ibid., 199, 190.

49. Alice Walker, *The Color Purple* (New York, 1982).

50. Randall Kenan, "The Foundations of the Earth," in *Let the Dead Bury Their Dead* (New York, 1992), 49–72.

51. Eddy L. Harris, *South of Haunted Dreams: A Ride through Slavery's Back Yard* (New York, 1993), 171, 192–93; Michelle Orecklin, "Down the Mississippi: The Pulse of America: A Twist on Tradition," *Time*, www.time.com/time/reports/mississippi/literature.html.

CHAPTER 11

1. Harris, *South of Haunted Dreams*, 125–25; K. Smith, *Telling Stories*," 43; "Time to Lower Rebel Flag, a Southern Governor Says," *New York Times*, November 27, 1996, A-16; Cobb, *Georgia Odyssey*, 147; John Shelton Reed, "The Banner That Won't Stay Furled," *Southern Cultures* 8 (Spring 2002): 94.

2. Cobb, *Georgia Odyssey*, 111–16, 127–30.

3. "Keeping Flag May Cost Mississippi Jobs," *Atlanta Journal-Constitution*, April 19, 2001, 6-A.

4. "The Georgia Compromise," *Cleveland (Ohio) Plain Dealer*, February 10, 2001, B-8; "Mississippi Voters to Decide on Use of Confederate Emblem," *Washington Post*, March 25, 2001, A-3; "Mississippi to Decide Flag Issue on Tuesday," *New Orleans Times-Picayune*, April 16, 2001, 1.

5. "Blacks Strip Slaveholders' Names Off Schools," *New York Times*, November 12, 1997, A-1.

6. Derek H. Alderman, "Martin Luther King Jr. Streets in Georgia," *The New Georgia Encyclopedia*, www.georgiaencyclopedia.org/nge/Article.jsp?id=h-802; Paul Hemphill, *Leaving Birmingham: Notes of a Native Son* (New York, 1993), 10.

7. "Decades Later, an Apology," *Atlanta Journal-Constitution*, October 2, 2007, A-1.

8. "Slavery Apologies Are Bad for Blacks," *Anniston (Ala.) Star*, April 15, 2007, http://nl.newsbank.com/nl-search/we/Archives?p_product=ANSB&p_theme= ansb&p_action=search&p_maxdocs=200&p_topdoc=1&p_text_direct-0=11888088B2EB9178&p_field_direct-0=document_id&p_perpage=10&p_ sort=YMD_date:D&s_trackval=GooglePM; "Alabama Governor Signs Bill Apologizing for Slavery," MSNBC.com, May 31, 2007, www.msnbc.msn.com/ id/18961394/; "North Carolina Senate Apologizes for Slavery: Lawmakers Express Contrition; Follow Virginia's Lead," MSNBC.com, April 5, 2007, www.msnbc.msn .com/id/17967662/; "Slavery: State's Apology Justified," *Atlanta Journal-Constitution*, March 21, 2007, A-14.

9. "Like Everything Else, Slavery Statement Caught Up in the Swirl around the Budget," *Atlanta Journal-Constitution*, April 1, 2007; "Slavery Apology Measure Ignites Debate," *Charlottesville (Va.) Daily Progress*, January 16, 2007, www2.dailyprogress. com/cdp/news/local/local_govtpolitics/article/slavery_apology_measure_ignites_leg-islative_debate1/13699/; "Top Senator Calls for Slavery Apology," Georgia Public Broadcasting News, March 16, 2007, http://gpbnews.blogspot.com/2007/03/top-sen-ator-calls-for-slavery-apology.html; "GOP Standoff Stalls Non-apology on Slavery," *Atlanta Journal-Constitution*, April 1, 2007, B-4; "McDonnell's Confederate History Month Proclamation Irks Civil Rights Leaders, *Washington Post*, April 7, 2010, www .washingtonpost.com/wp-dyn/content/article/2010/04/06/AR2010040604416.html.

10. "Legislators Pass Two Resolutions on Slavery," *Birmingham News*, April 25, 2007, A-1.

11. James C. Cobb, "Truth and Consequences: Official Slavery Apologies Are Bad for Blacks," *New Republic*, April 9, 2007, www.tnr.com/article/truth-and-consequences-0.

12. Leonard Pitts, "Advancing the Definition of the NAACP," RealClearPolitics. com, www.realclearpolitics.com/articles/2007/03/advancing_the_definition_of_th .html.

13. "Barr, McKinney Lose in Georgia, August 21, 2002, Primaries," CNN .com, www.cnn.com/2002/ALLPOLITICS/08/20/primarypreview/index/html; "McKinney Beaten but Unbowed," CNN.com, August 9, 2006, www.cnn.com/2006/ POLITICS/08/09/congress.mckinney; "Steve Benjamin Elected South Carolina's First Black Mayor," *BV Black Spin*, April 22, 2010, www.bvblackspin.com/2010/04/22/ steve-benjamin-elected-south-carolinas-first-black-mayor/.

14. "Blacks See Growing Values Gap between Poor and Middle Class: Optimism about Black Progress Declines," Pew Research Center, http://pewsocialtrends .org/assets/pdf/race.pdf.

15. "NAHB Releases Study on Impact of Katrina," HGTVPro.com, September 2, 2005, www.hgtvpro.com/hpro/nws_dstr_huric_torndo/article/0,2624,HPRO_26 522_4050646,00.html.

16. "Superdome Evacuation Completed," MSNBC.com, September 3, 2005, www.msnbc.msn.com/id/9175611; "Looters Take Advantage of New Orleans Mess," MSNBC.com, August 30, 2005, www.msnbc.com/id/91314931.

17. "'Looting' or 'Finding'?" *Salon*, September 1, 2005, http://dir.salon.com/news/feature/2005/09/01/photo_controversy.

18. Kent B. Germany, "The Politics of Poverty and History: Racial Inequality and the Long Prelude to Katrina," *Journal of American History* 94 (December 2007): 744.

19. Ibid., 747–49.

20. Ibid., 749.

21. "Last of the Ninth," *Salon*, September 13, 2005, http://dir.salon.com/story/news/feature/2005/09/13/ninth/print.html; Juliette Landphair, "'The Forgotten People of New Orleans': Community, Vulnerability, and the Lower Ninth Ward," *Journal of American History* 94 (December 2007): 842.

22. "Once More, a Neighborhood Sees the Worst," *Washington Post*, September 8, 2005, A-18.

23. "New Orleans Retains Black Majority," AP report, September 22, 2007, www.assatashakur.org/forum/afrikan-world-news/24448-new-orleans-retains-black-majority.html; "First Came Katrina, Then Came HUD," *In These Times*, January 16, 2008, www.inthesetimes.com/article/3504/first_came_katrina_then_came_hud/; "Who Exiled New Orleans' Poor?" *Washington Post*, May 17, 2007, A-17; "New Orleans Council Votes for Demolition of Housing," *New York Times*, December 21, 2007, A-37.

24. "In Mississippi, Poor Lag in Hurricane Aid," *New York Times*, November 16, 2007, A-22; "A Harder Look at Haley Barbour's Post-Katrina Miracle." *Salon*, May 25, 2007, www.salon.com/news/feature/2007/05/25/mississippi/.

25. "Governor Kathleen Blanco Will Not Seek Re-election," FoxNews.com, March 20, 2007, www.foxnews.com/story/0,2933,260020,00.html.

26. "In New Orleans, Smaller May Mean Whiter," *New York Times*, January 22, 2006, 1.

27. Clancy Dubos, "More Alike Than Different," blogofneworleans.com, April 24, 2009, http://blogofneworleans.com/blog/2009/04/24/more-alike-than-different; "Landrieu Takes Office as Mayor of New Orleans," WWWL.com, May 3, 2010, www.wwl.com/Video–Landrieu-takes-office-as-Mayor-of-New-Orlea/6953696.

28. Russell McCulley, "Hurricane Blows Hispanic Workers Back to New Orleans," TerraDaily.com, June 16, 2007, www.terradaily.com/reports/Hurricane_Blows_Hispanic_Workers_Back_To_New_Orleans_999.html; "The New Latino South: The Context and Consequences of Rapid Population Growth," Pew Hispanic Center, October, 23, 2008, www.pewhispanic.org; Rick Martinez, "Immigration Hits 'Critical Mass' in N.C.," *Carolina Journal*, December 12, 2005, www.carolinajournal.com/exclusives/display_exclusive.html?id=2983.

29. Martinez, "Immigration Hits Critical Mass"; Cobb, *Georgia Odyssey*, 136–37.

30. Pew, "New Latino South."

31. Martinez, "Immigration Hits Critical Mass"; Pew, "New Latino South."

32. "When David Duke Goes Marching In," *Salon*, April 4, 2000, www.salon.com/news/feature/2000/04/04/latinos/index1.html; "Bridging a Racial Rift That Isn't Black and White," *New York Times*, October 3, 2006, 1.

33. Dawn Turner Trice, "Immigration Issues Redefine Catfish Industry in the Mississippi Delta," *Chicago Tribune*, June 15, 2006, www.encyclopedia.com/doc/1G1-147051539.html.

34. "At a Slaughterhouse, Some Things Never Die: Who Kills, Who Cuts, Who Bosses Can Depend on Race," *New York Times*, June 14, 2000, 1.

35. "Union Organizers at Poultry Plants in South Find Newly Sympathetic Ears," *New York Times*, September 6, 2005, A-16; Steven Greenhouse, "Smithfield Workers Finally Unionize: After Fifteen Years North Carolina Plant Unionizes," *Dollars and Sense: Real World Economics*, December 12, 2008, www.dollarsandsense.org/blog/2008/12/smithfield-workers-finally-unionize.html; "Immigrant Crackdown Upends a Slaughterhouse's Workforce," *New York Times*, October 12, 2007, A-1; "Workers at Pork Plant in North Carolina Vote to Unionize after a Fifteen-Year Struggle," *New York Times*, December 13, 2008, 10; "Unions Come to Smithfield," *America Prospect*, December 17, 2008, www.prospect.org/cs/articles?article=unions_come_to_smithfield.

36. Melvin Delgado, *Social Work with Latinos: A Cultural Assets Paradigm* (New York, 2006), 4.

37. "Hispanics, Blacks Find Futures Entangled," *U.S.A. Today*, September 10, 1999, A-21; National Hispanic Caucus of State Legislatures, www.nhcsl.com/his_legislators.html; "Exit Polls" (2004–8), MSNBC.com, www.msnbc.msn.com/id1529711811/23926593 and www.msnbc.msn.com/id23926593.

38. Tore Olsson, "Your DeKalb Farmers Market: Food and Identity in Atlanta," *Southern Cultures* 13 (Winter 2007): 48, 54; Russell Cobb, "The Chicken Hangers," *inthefray*, February 1, 2004, http://inthefray.org/content/view/208/39/.

39. Bill C. Malone, *Southern Music, American Music* (Lexington, Ky., 2003), 61, 156–58.

40. "Hispanic Heritage: Gloria Estefan," Gale Cengage Learning, www.gale.cengage.com/free_resources/chh/bio/estefan_g.htm.

41. Malone, *Southern Music,* 159–60.

42. Darren E. Grem, "The South Got Somethin' to Say: Atlanta's Dirty South and the Southernization of Hip-Hop America," *Southern Cultures* 12 (Winter 2006): 55–73.

43. Cobb, *Georgia Odyssey*, 138–39.

44. Ibid., 139–40.

45. "Anti-Gay Funding Cut in Charlotte, North Carolina," *Charlotte (N.C.) Observer*, April 2, 1997, www.religioustolerance.org/hom_0036.htm.

46. Eric Ervin, "Charlotte Pride Defies Death," *Southern Voice*, May 5, 2006, 22.

47. "Birmingham Gays Sue Mayor," *365Gay*, August 28, 2008, www.365gay.com/news/082808-birmingham-mayor/; "Birmingham Mayor Larry Langford Indicted," *Birmingham (Ala.) News*, December 2, 2008, http://blog.al.com/spotnews/2008/12/tuesday_eyeopeners_highlights_20.html.

48. "Winthrop ETV Poll: Social Issues," SCETV.org, www.scetv.org/television/productions/the_big_picture/winthrop_etv_polls/poll2/survey2page7.html; "The Candidates on Gay Marriage," Pew Forum on Religion and Public Life, http://pew-forum.org/religion08/compare.php?Issue=Gay_Marriage.

49. "50-State Rundown on Gay Marriage Laws," *Stateline.org*, www.stateline.org/live/ViewPage.action?siteNodeId=136&languageId=1&contentId=15576.

50. Alex Johnson, "South Carolina Is So Gay: A New Tourism Ad Creates an Uproar," *Newsweek*, July 15, 2008, http://newsweek.com/id/146279/output/; "South Carolina Governor Mark Sanford Admits Affair," politico.com, June 25, 2009, www.politico.com/news/stories/0609/24146.html.

51. Patti Duncan, "Claiming Space in the South: A Conversation among Members of Asian/Pacific Islands Lesbian, Bisexual, Transgendered Network of Atlanta" in Carlos L. Dews and Carolyn Leste Law, *Out in the South* (Philadelphia, 2001), 36; Trevor Hoppe, "The Making of a Southern Faggot," *Beyond Masculinity*, www.beyondmasculinity.com/articles/hoppe.php?page=6.

52. Richard Florida and Gary Gates, "Technology and Tolerance: The Importance of Diversity to High-Technology Growth," Brookings Institution, www.brookings.edu/es/urban/techtol.pdf.

53. Rick Weddle, "The Research Triangle Park: A Legacy of Economic Transformation...Lessons for Regional Economies," Wayne State University, November 15, 2007, http://doi.wayne.edu/pdf/rick_weddle_presentationleaders_without_bordersnov_2007.pdf.

54. "Austin's High-Tech Jobs Paying Off, Average Wage Ranked Third among U.S. Cybercities," *AeAnet*, June 23, 2008, www.aeanet.org/PressRoom/prjj_cc2008_austin.asp.

55. Bartley, *New South*, 445–46; "Best Colleges 2010," *U.S. News and World Report*, www.colleges.usnews.rankingsandreviews.com/best-colleges/national-top-public.

56. Andrew Doyle, "On the Cusp of Modernity: The Southern Sporting World in the Twentieth Century," in Pascoe, Leathem, and Ambrose, *The American South*, 193–203.

57. "Chart: 2009, College Football Coach Salaries," *Orlando Sentinel*, www.orlandosentinel.com/sports/orl-spt-coach-salary-chart-2009,0,3767955.htmlstory; "Alabama and Tennessee Institutions Announce Program and Job Cuts," *Chronicle*

of Higher Education, June 4, 2008, www.chronicle.com/article/AlabamaTennessee/41097; "Spending on Sports v. Academics" and "A Powerful League Piles Up Its Advantages," *Chronicle of Higher Education,* August 31, 2009, www.chronicle.com/article/Rise-of-the-SEC/48197; "AAUP Faculty Salary Survey, 2008–2009," *Chronicle of Higher Education,* www.chronicle.com/stats/aaup.

58. "Black Mayor of Mississippi Brings 'Atomic Bomb of Change,'" CNN.com, May 22, 2009, www.cnn.com/2009/US/05/22/mississippi.black.mayor/index.html; "First Black Mayor in City Known for Klan Killings," *New York Times,* May 21, 2009, www.nytimes.com/2009/05/22/us/22mayor.html?scp=1&sq=May%2022%20 2009%20James%20Young%20Philadelphia%20Mississippi&st=cse">Looking back</a></a>.

59. Sarah Corbett and Gillian Laub, "A Prom Divided," *New York Times Magazine,* May 21, 2009, A-12, www.nytimes.com/2009/05/24/magazine/24prom-t .html?ref=magazine.

60. "Charleston's First Integrated Prom," *The Independent (U.K.),* June 13, 2008, www.independent.co.uk/news/world/americas/charlestons-first-integrated-prom-846261.html.

61. Corbett and Laub, "A Prom Divided."

62. Ibid.

63. Ibid.

64. "Deep South Clings to Last Vestige of Segregation," CatherineMacivor .com May 25, 2009, http://catherinemacivor.com/2009/05/25/deep-south-clings-to-last-vestige-of-segregation/; "NY Times and HBO Highlight Issue of Segregated Proms Still Held in the South," Celebitchy.com, May 25, 2009, http://www.celebitchy .com/52434/ny_times_and_hbo_highlight_issue_of_segregated_proms_still_ held_in_the_us_south/.

CHAPTER 12

1. Black and Black, *The Vital South,* 366.

2. Egerton, *Americanization of Dixie,* 19.

3. Ronnie Dugger, "The Trashing of Teddy," *The Nation,* June 21, 1980, 742.

4. Kathleen Parker, "Them Dang Southerners," Townhall.com, August 5, 2009, http://townhall.com/columnists/kathleenparker/2009/08/05/them_dang_ southerners; George Packer, "The Decade Nobody Knows," *New York Times Book Review,* June 20, 2001, www.nytimes.com/books/01/06/10/reviews/010610.10 packert.html.

5. Black and Black, *The Vital South,* 366; Michael Lind, "The Southern Coup," *New Republic,* June 19, 1995, 29.

6. "The Southernisation of America," *The Economist* 333, no. 7893, special section (1994): 17–18, 2p, 2bw.

7. Applebome, *Dixie Rising*.

8. Mark Strauss, "Let's Ditch Dixie: The Case for Northern Secession," *Slate*, March 14, 2001, www.slate.com/id/102291/pagenum/al/.

9. "Fuck the South," November 3, 2004, www.fuckthesouth.com/.

10. Jeff Poor, "Krugman's 'Conscience': Economic Woes Caused When 'Southern Whites Started Voting Republican,'" Business and Media Institute, October 24, 2007, www.businessandmedia.org/articles/2007/20071024135302.aspx; Thomas F. Schaller, *Whistling Past Dixie: How Democrats Can Win without the South* (New York, 2008), 271–72.

11. John Egerton, "The Southernization of American Politics," in *Where We Stand: Voices of Southern Dissent*, ed. Anthony Dunbar (Montgomery, Ala., 2004), 217; Chris Bowers, "Just a Step Forward—But What a Step!" MyDD.com, November 8, 2006, www.mydd.com/story/2006/11/8/45817/2313; Thomas Schaller, "Dixie Is Gone with the Wind," *Salon*, August 19, 2008, www.salon.com/opinion/feature/2008/08/19/south_schaller/.

12. Michael Hirsh, "How the South Won (This) Civil War," *Newsweek.com*, Web exclusive, April 25, 2008, www.newsweek.com/id/134116.

13. Ibid.

14. John Talton, "American Theocracy," Rogue Columnist, August 18, 2008, http://roguecolumnist.typepad.com/rogue_columnist/2008/08/american-theocr.html.

15. John D. Skrentny, "The White Working Class: Just Who Are These Voters?" SignOnSanDiego.com, October 1, 2008, www.signonsandiego.com/uniontrib/20081001/news_mz1n1skrentn.html.

16. America Votes 2004, "U.S. President/National/Exit Poll," CNN.com, www.cnn.com/ELECTION/2004//pages/results/states/US/P/00/epolls.0.html; "Exit Polls," CNN Election Center 2008, CNN.com, www.cnn.com/ELECTION/2008/results/polls.main/.

17. "Exit Polls," CNN Election Center, 2008.

18. "Are Atlanta's Suburbs Turning Blue?" *Atlanta Journal-Constitution*, November 9, 2008, A-1; "General Election, Votes Cast, Percent Republican, 2008," Georgia Statistics, www.georgiastats.uga.edu/.

19. "Exit Polls," 2008, MSNBC.com, www.msnbc.com/id/26843704; "Exit Polls," 2004, MSNBC.com, www.msnbc.com/id/5297118.

20. "Palin Keeps It Positive: Economy, Energy Policies Stressed," *Greensboro (N.C.) News and Record*, October 17, 2008, 1.

21. "United States Presidential Election Returns: 2008," *Dave Leip's Atlas of U.S. Presidential Elections*, www.uselectionatlas.org/RESULTS/.

22. "For South, a Waning Hold on National Politics," *New York Times*, November 11, 2008, 1, www.nytimes.com/2008/11/11/us/politics/11south.html?pagewanted=2&ei=5070&emc=eta1; www.uselectionatlas.org.

23. Ibid.

24. Ibid.;"Exit Polls," *Decision 2008.*

25. "For South, a Waning Hold."

26. Chris Kromm, "A New South Rising," *Facing South,* www.southern studies.org/2008/11/a-new-south-rising.html; "The South Just Isn't What It Was," *St. Petersburg Times,* January 25, 2009, www.tampabay.com/news/perspective/article969751.ece.

27. Harold Meyerson, "GOP's Southern Exposure," *Washington Post,* December 7, 2006, www.washingtonpost.com/wp-dyn/content/article/2006/12/06/AR2006120601671.html; Schaller, *Whistling Past Dixie,* 4, 115.

28. Kromm, "A New South Rising."

29. U.S. Census Bureau, "Elections: Gubernatorial and State Legislatures," *The 2009 Statistical Abstract,* www.census.gov/compendia/statab/cats/elections/gubernatorial_and_state_legislatures.html.

30. "Bushwhackers," John Taplin's Blog, November 11. 2008, http://jontaplin.com/2008/11/11/bushwhackers/; Ronald Brownstein, "For GOP, a Southern Exposure," *National Journal,* May 23, 2009, www.nationaljournal.com/njmagazine/print_friendly.php?ID=cs_20090523_2195; "For South, a Waning Hold."

31. "For South, a Waning Hold."

32. Ibid.; Alex Pareene, "North Finally Wins Civil War," Gawker.com, November 11, 2008, http://gawker.com/5083106/north-finally-wins-civil-war; "For South a Waning Hold"; Lexington [pseud.], "The Californication of Government," *The Economist,* February 26, 2009, www.economist.com/world/unitedstates/displaystory.cfm?story_id=13184916.

33. http://mattmardislecroy.blogspot.com/2008/11/southernization-revisited.html (as accessed January 2010).

34. Zeitz, "Dixie's Victory."

35. James N. Gregory, *Southern Diaspora: How the Great Migration of Black and White Southerners Transformed America* (Chapel Hill, N.C., 2005), 200–203.

36. Eller, *Uneven Ground,* 25; Michael O'Brien, "The Apprehension of the South in Modern Culture," *Southern Cultures* 4 (Winter 1998): 11.

37. Matthew Benjamin, "Life in the Fast Lane," *U.S. News and World Report,* November 22, 2004, 64–66.

38. Joshua I. Newman and Michael D. Giardina, "NASCAR and the 'Southernization' of America: Spectatorship, Subjectivity, and the Confederation of Identity," *Cultural Studies, Critical Methodologies* 8, no. 4 (2008): 479, 483.

39. Matthew D. Lassiter and Joseph Crespino, *The Myth of Southern Exceptionalism* (New York, 2009), 9; Jacob Levenson, "Divining Dixie: Is It Another Country? Or a Place to Stow National Problems?" *Columbia Journalism Review,* March 1, 2004, www.allbusiness.com/information/publishing-industries/765769–1.html;

Houston A. Baker Jr. and Dana D. Nelson, "Preface: Violence, the Body and 'The South,'" *American Literature* 73 (June 2001): 235; Larry J. Griffin, "Southern Distinctiveness Yet Again or Why America Still Needs the South," *Southern Cultures* 6 (Fall 2000): 68.

40. "Governor Rick Perry: Texas Could Secede, Leave Union," *Huffington Post*, April 15, 2009, www.huffingtonpost.com/2009/04/15/gov-rick-perry-texas-coul_n_187490.html; Cash, *Mind of the South*, 439–40.

41. Levenson, "Divining Dixie"; Laura F. Edwards, "Southern History as U.S. History," *Journal of Southern History* 75 (August 2009): 564.

42. C. Vann Woodward, "From the First Reconstruction to the Second," in *The South Today: One Hundred Years after Appomattox,* ed. Willie Morris (New York, 1965), 14; Woodward, "Southern Styles."

43. Zinn, *Southern Mystique*, 218.

INDEX

Page numbers in **bold** indicate illustrations. Page numbers in *italics* indicate tables.